Cooking at Home

Brownies, Cakes and Cookies

More than 600 delicious desserts
perfect for any occasion!

Marye Audet and Sarah K. Sawyer

JG
PRESS

Published by World Publications Group, Inc.
140 Laurel Street, East Bridgewater, MA. 02333
www.wrldpub.com

ISBN 10: 1-57215-755-0
ISBN 13: 978-1-57215-755-2

Printed and bound in the United States of America.

10 9 8 7 6 5 4 3 2 1

Many of the designations used by manufacturers and sellers to distinguish their products are claimed as trademarks. Where those designations appear in this book and Adams Media was aware of a trademark claim, the designations have been printed in initial capital letters.

This publication is designed to provide accurate and authoritative information with regard to the subject matter covered. It is sold with the understanding that the publisher is not engaged in rendering legal, accounting, or other professional advice. If legal advice or other expert assistance is required, the services of a competent professional person should be sought.
—From a Declaration of Principles jointly adopted by a Committee of the American Bar Association and a Committee of Publishers and Associations

Previously published as the *Everything*® *Cake Mix Cookbook*
and the *Everything*® *Cookies and Brownies Cookbook*.

Contents

Cookies and Brownies

25 The Best Cookies for Shipping 401

32 Cookies for Special Needs. 517

33 Refrigerator Cookies 527

Introduction to Cake Making

CAKES ARE THE FOOD of celebration. People bake them for the special events in life, or just to celebrate the end of a particularly lovely meal. They can have the simple flavors you'd expect from a basic cake, or they can surprise and delight the palate with unusual additions and creative ingredients. They can be homely in appearance or elaborately decorated. They can be a flavorful showcase of the cook's artistry or a fun collaboration for the kids. The possibilities are endless, and cake mix makes them easy enough for cooks of all levels.

Baking a cake is more than ticking off an item on the big night's to-do list; it's continuing a traditional art form. It's the creation of something delicious and wholesome to share with others. Every attempt to bake a cake holds within it the possibility that it will become a favorite recipe, one to be shared with friends and family and to be anticipated whenever dear ones gather.

The first step in baking a cake is, of course, planning. This doesn't have to include huge amounts of research—that's already been done. All that's really required is calmly thinking through the details. How many people are eating? Is this event fancy or family style? Do the diners enjoying this cake have dietary restrictions or allergies you must consider? Last, and most important, what recipe, ingredient, or technique would be fun to tackle next?

With these questions answered, searching for the perfect recipe is much easier. A quick glance at this book's table of contents will point you to recipes designed for holidays and special occasions as well as for family dinners. You'll also find recipes for those with special dietary needs, or cooks ready to try new ingredients. Read interesting recipes through carefully and entirely before selecting one. It's easy to miss a step, a piece of equipment, or an ingredient by reading too quickly, so take it slow. Make a list of things you need and then gather them before you start. There's nothing worse than being halfway through a project and realizing you're missing an ingredient or tool.

The must-have list of ingredients in this book starts with one thing: cake mix. Some recipes call for a specific brand or flavor, but most allow a little wiggle room. Keep a stash of basic flavors and frostings in a cool, dry cabinet and you'll be ready to bake when the event presents itself.

Now, a quick word about this main ingredient. Some feel that baking with cake mix is "cheating" and that a cake isn't truly home-baked unless the cook spent hours in the kitchen measuring, mixing, baking, frosting, and plating the picture-perfect slice. But home is where the heart is, and home-baked is anything baked with love. Most cake mixes are nothing more than basic ingredients that are simply pre-mixed for you. Why on earth not let a trusted brand do the measuring for you? It can mean a few more minutes spent living, loving, and laughing and a few less spent measuring, sifting, and sorting. Enjoying life is so much more than the icing on the cake.

CHAPTER 1

All about Cake Mix

It's found in a box, in many flavors, and in a certain aisle of your local grocery store, but what else do you know about cake mix? Unless you remember its debut in the late 1920s, you probably consider boxed cake mix a staple that always was and always will be—but, of course, there's more to it than that. Boxed cake mix has a cultural and culinary history that's worth knowing. Happily, this chapter is here to spill the details.

History of Cake Baking and Innovation

Cakes were born almost the same time humans learned to make flour. Today folks around the world bake and enjoy cakes or cake-like treats, but cake was not originally developed as a dessert. The Greeks did develop cheesecake at a very early date, and there are some records of fruitcake-like breads being baked in early Rome. In addition, ancient sweetened biscuit-style cakes have been found in Egyptian and other archeological digs. Nevertheless, today it is generally acknowledged that the development of cake as we know it originated on the British Isles.

Most historians agree that the first records of cake were found in medieval England—but this was not cake as it is today. Early cakes were probably nothing more than sweetened breads; in fact, for centuries the terms *cake* and *bread* were all but interchangeable. Try to imagine an early cake. Think oat bread or biscuit. They were certainly smaller in size than cakes are today, and weren't topped with a glaze, icing, or frosting.

As early as the fourteenth century, the poet Chaucer mentioned cakes made of flour, butter, eggs, cream, currants, and spices. In the seventeenth century, English writers began to describe cakes and methods for baking them. They began to sound much more like the confections we encounter today. While some cakes were still formed by hand, some were baked in tin or wooden hoops much like springform pans we use today. However, baking at that time involved using a fireplace oven rather than the controllable electric and gas ovens we use today.

The first cakes were baked with no leavening at all or with yeast, but that changed in the middle of the nineteenth century. Alfred Bird's innovative baking powder made it possible to have greater leavening than ever before. This was the beginning of the spongy cake texture we enjoy today.

Around this time, the tradition of taking tea and cake in the afternoon began. Royalty started gathering for tea and small bits of layer cake with jam fillings around five o'clock in the afternoon. This was when the layer cake came into fashion.

Trends in baking came and went much as they do today. Some favorite recipes became classics and other recipes fell from favor. Flavors and fashions changed, but the process of baking remained mainly the same. Cake baking still required weights, measures, and elbow grease. It would be years before that changed.

Boxed Cake Mix

Boxed cake mix was introduced in the late 1920s and early 1930s, but it was not well received at first. Cake mix languished on the shelves for twenty years before it really took off. After World War II, sales of store-bought baked goods rose, and sales of flour sank fast. Flour companies needed to find a way to encourage people to bake more to keep demand for their product high. Their answer? Make home baking faster and easier. Sell more flour in the form of cake mix.

What started as a simple marketing ploy sparked a new age of cake baking. Slowly but surely, home bakers began to see the baking of the cake itself as a simple first step. The icing, decoration, and serving of the cake became an art form. With the basic foundation of the cake perfected by flour companies, home bakers followed a few simple steps and were free to get creative with fillings, frostings, alternative preparations, and other creative treatments.

All cake mixes used to include dried egg, but a consumer psychologist named Ernest Dichter found that women were afraid that baking with mixes threatened the value of their job—homemaking. Dichter recommended that companies replace the dried egg with an instruction to add fresh eggs. This seemed to make bakers feel more involved and more comfortable with the idea of baking from a mix.

Many studies regarding the use of cake mix were conducted in home economics classes all over the country. One study at Michigan State University found that the average cook saved thirteen minutes and two seconds by using cake mix.

But baking with cake mix will likely save you money in addition to time. Of course, this depends on the specific ingredients in the recipe and the cost of each ingredient.

In the end, the biggest saving that baking from a mix will bring you is the saving of mental energy. The average American cook leads a busy life filled with meeting the demands of work and family life. How many times have you heard someone say, "Oh, it takes more time to explain this than it would to do it myself?" You may have even said it yourself! This statement reflects the effort to weigh the cost of the mental energy it takes to explain a task against the physical energy and time it takes to get the job done. Often, the option that requires less mental energy wins. It's the same reason people bake with cake mix.

The Science of Cake Mix

Have you ever wondered what's in the box? Not too surprisingly, cake mix ingredients include many of the things you'd use to bake a cake from scratch. Most cakes are composed of a base grain (flour), a sweetener (sugar), a binder (eggs), and a fat for moistness (butter). In fact, classic pound cake requires nothing more than these basic ingredients: one pound each of flour, sugar, eggs, and butter. The trick when it comes to baking is not to upset this balance of ingredients too much.

Alterations can be made, but they still must allow the basic ingredients to do their magic and produce a basic cake. If a baker wants to create something just a little richer than a basic cake, she might add extra fats. If someone else wants a denser cake, he might opt for a batter with less egg. Bakers who want a more bread-like product might add a bit more flour. There's a variation for almost every taste.

The problem here is probably pretty clear. When baking from scratch, the baker must first see that the basic chemical balance is in order. If she wants to change the cake she produces, she must find a way to do so without upsetting this balance. Again, this assumes the balance is right to begin with.

As the saying goes, "You have to know the rules before you can break them." Today's bakers are lucky. Cake mix companies learned the rules inside and out. Unless home bakers upset the cake's chemical balance in a very extreme way, they're all but guaranteed a successful cake.

Baking Equipment

You need more than just a cake mix and the additional ingredients listed on the box to make a flawless cake. Turning out a delicious and beautiful cake takes some basic equipment. If you're sure you'll be baking, go ahead and buy the highest quality equipment you can afford. If you're relatively new to baking, you don't have to spend a lot of money on equipment. Big box and discount stores sell equipment at low prices. Also, secondhand stores and yard sales can be great places to pick up quality bakeware for spare change.

In *Dewey: The Small-Town Library Cat Who Touched the World*, author Vicki Myron describes a library with a collection of cake pans that library patrons could check out. This is highly unusual, but it's a great idea. Perhaps your local library would like to gather pieces and start a collection. Another option might be to loan and borrow equipment among friends who are bakers.

Cake Pans

For even baking, a thin aluminum, stainless steel, or tin cake pan is best. These metals reflect heat and allow batter to bake evenly. Thicker, darker metals, nonstick metals, and glass pans can absorb heat and cause outer edges of your confection to overcook quickly. For best results when using a pan like this, set the oven 25 degrees lower than the temperature listed in the recipe. It's possible to bake a beautiful cake using almost any pan—the trick is to understand the personality and function of your particular equipment. Manufacturer's instructions and websites often include helpful information.

Wonder what size pan to use? Refer to pan size and shape instructions detailed on the cake mix packaging. The manufacturers pay close attention to batch volume and loft and will steer you in the right direction every time. The only exception to this rule is if you're trying to achieve an unusual shape. Then refer to recipe instructions or instructions on the pan itself.

Cookie Sheets

Cookie sheets are often made from stainless steel, tin, or nonstick metals. They are flat. Jellyroll pans are similar but have a one-inch lip around the outer edges. Many people use them interchangeably, but the lip around the edge of the jellyroll pan can keep cookies from baking evenly.

Cookie bakers will need more than one cookie sheet. Having two will usually work; having three is a luxury.

Measuring Tools

Because many basic ingredients are already measured out in the mix, there is usually little measuring when you bake with a cake mix. But because balancing the grains, sweetener, fats, and binders is so important, it's crucial to measure all additional ingredients exactly. All it takes is the proper equipment and a little attention to detail.

Measuring Dry Ingredients

Making sure you have exact measurements of dry ingredients requires measuring cups and measuring spoons. Measuring cups for dry ingredients often come in a set of differently sized, clearly labeled cups. Simply fill the cup or spoon marked to hold the correct amount and level it off with a table knife or spatula. The only exception to this rule is if a recipe calls for "tightly packed" ingredients, in which case you press ingredients into the cup with a spoon or other rounded object to pack as much into the cup as possible. Brown sugar usually needs to be packed into the measuring cup.

Wet Ingredients

Measuring cups for wet ingredients are usually glass or plastic and are printed with levels for various measurements. Because liquids shift easily, exact measurements can be difficult to read. In order to get the best possible reading, fill the cup and then set it on a level surface. Adjust your stance so that you are at eye level with the measuring line. This assures that you're not adding too much or two little due to a slant, tilt, or another shift of the level line. Newer liquid measuring cups are often designed so that you can get a correct reading from above, eliminating the need to bend over.

About Fluid Ounces

Fluid ounces are a popular notation of measurement for wet ingredients. When this amount is listed, it is generally because the ingredient is a store-bought item with a measurement marked on the package. The marking generally exists to let you know what size package to buy in order to fill the recipe's requirement. For example, in an ingredient list, the amount of milk you need will be listed in cups, but evaporated milk will be listed in ounces. This is because you'll probably buy a gallon of milk and only use part of it for your cake, but you'll buy the exact amount of evaporated milk and use all of it to bake your cake.

You can also measure out ounces. A general rule of thumb is that 1 tablespoon is equal to ½ fluid ounce, 1 cup of liquid is equal to 8 ounces, 2 cups is equal to 16 ounces, and so on.

Measuring Butter and Shortening

Butter and shortening are often sold in sticks. Simply slice off the amount called for according to the measurement line given on the package. If you buy margarine or shortening in a tub, you can simply spoon your ingredients into a dry measuring cup. Pack ingredients in with a spoon to eliminate bubbles, holes, or other inconsistencies that could throw off your measurement. Take care to level off the top of the cup using a knife or another utensil with a sharp edge; you don't want to use too much.

Utensils

Baking requires basic utensils: wooden spoons, flat-edged knives for measuring, a rubber scraper for transferring ingredients, and spatulas for lifting baked cookies from sheet to wire rack. Most bakers have favorite utensils that serve them well in a variety of cooking projects. These utensils are usually among the standard favorites and are easy to find in almost any discount store.

Tools for Mixing

Mixing thoroughly is a crucial step in most cake recipes. It's a simple step, but it does require appropriate equipment.

Mixing Bowls

A set of mixing bowls is essential for almost any cooking project. Cake batters are fairly easy to mix and do not generally leave colors or odors behind in porous bowls, so mixing bowls made of almost any material will do. Still, a stainless steel or thick glass set of mixing bowls is a fantastic investment. Neither is porous, so they're safe from cross-contamination, and you'll be able to use them for a variety of cooking projects. They are also sturdy enough to stand up to the power of an electric beater.

Multiple mixing bowls are a good idea, even for those who wash as they go. Some recipes call for you to use bowls of different sizes.

Electric Mixers

The taste and texture of a cake rely on the beating of the batter. If you beat it too little, your batter might taste like flour or contain lumps. If you beat it too much, the resulting cake is tougher. There was a time—and it wasn't long ago—when home bakers could achieve the perfect texture with a wooden spoon and elbow grease, but the cook who does that these days is tough to find. Most home bakers use either a tabletop mixer or handheld electric beaters. For most cake batters a hand-held mixer does the job admirably. But if you do lots of baking or think you might graduate to breads and other thicker batters, a tabletop mixer is a better fit for the job.

Cooling Racks

A cooling rack is simply a wire rack that lifts cooling baked goods off a solid surface like a table or countertop so that they can cool. It can be tempting to skip this finishing step. Don't! Baked goods that remain in hot bakeware continue to cook. Skipping this last step can mean overcooked edges and baked goods that stick to the pan.

To successfully remove a cake layer onto a wire rack, remove the pan from the oven and put it directly onto the wire rack. Allow it to cool for about ten minutes. Loosen the layer from the side of the pan by running a knife or spatula around the edges. Place a clean linen towel or thick paper towel over the top of the layer. Place the wire rack on top of the towel. Flip the rack and the pan over at once so that the rack rests on the counter and the cake pan is upside down on top of the rack. This supports the cake while you flip it. Gently remove the pan. Once the cake is resting on the rack and free of the pan, let each cake layer cool completely before continuing with the recipe instructions. The process is tricky, but it can result in a perfect, tender layer of cake if it is approached with patience and care.

Three First Steps

In order to have a perfect cake every time, you need to follow three easy steps.

Read Carefully

It cannot be stressed enough that the first step in baking any cake is to read the directions thoroughly. If you are unprepared for or uncertain of any particular step, it's best to straighten it out before starting.

Nonstick pans do not usually need to be treated, but they do occasionally require that you adjust cooking time or temperature to accommodate their thicker walls or treated metals. Thoroughly read the manufacturer's instructions that come with the pan or check the manufacturer's website for hints and tips specific to your particular bakeware.

Always Preheat

Most recipes begin with preheating the oven. It is important that cake batter is exposed to an even baking temperature throughout its baking time. If the batter must sit in the oven while it heats up, it is likely the cake won't bake evenly and increases risk of burning. To prevent this, check the temperature with an oven thermometer before placing the batter in the oven. It's the surest way to protect your cake.

Cake Pan Preparation

Many recipes will instruct you to prepare the cake pan a certain way before you add the batter. In cases where there are no specific instructions, it's a good rule of thumb to grease and flour the pan. This is easily done. Simply put a small amount of shortening or butter on wax paper and use it to evenly grease the inside of the pan. Dust the inside of the pan with a small amount of flour. Shake the pan and tap it against a solid surface to make sure the flour is evenly distributed.

Cooking sprays are a quick and effective alternative to greasing and flouring the pan. Read instructions on the package to make sure a spray-on product is safe and effective for baking.

This may feel like a lot of information upfront, but it really is important to understand the basics about your ingredients and equipment before you plan your baking project. It makes following any recipe easier and a touch more foolproof.

CHAPTER 2

Classic Cakes

Bettered Box Mix

This combination of ingredients and techniques will give you bakery-quality results from store-bought boxed mix.

INGREDIENTS | SERVES 12

1 18.25-ounce box cake mix

4 eggs

⅓ cup vegetable oil

1¼ cups cold water

1 2-ounce box pudding mix in a complementary flavor

1 16-ounce tub prepared frosting

Why Not Just Follow the Instructions?

Many home bakers follow the package instructions to the letter. It's a time-tested way to bake a very predictable cake. But many home bakers seek a product that is a bit more moist and a touch more flavorful. Adding different ingredients to the basic building blocks in the package is the secret to getting a professional-quality cake from a simple boxed mix.

1. Preheat oven to 350°F. Grease and flour cake pan. Set aside.

2. Combine all ingredients in a large mixing bowl. Use an electric mixer set to medium speed to blend the batter for 6 minutes. Pour batter into the cake pan.

3. Bake according to cake mix instructions. Allow cake to cool for 10–15 minutes before inverting onto a serving plate. Cool cake completely before frosting.

Buttermilk Cake Batter

By changing one ingredient in the cake mix, you'll get a richer, creamier batter with a crumb that's moist and irresistible. If you don't have buttermilk handy, substitute the same amount of 2% milk with a scant splash of vinegar.

INGREDIENTS | SERVES 12

1 18.25-ounce box cake mix plus ingredients called for on box (except water)

Buttermilk (equal to the amount of water called for on box)

1 16-ounce tub prepared frosting

1. Preheat oven according to cake mix instructions. Grease and flour cake pan. Set aside.

2. Mix batter according to package instructions, substituting buttermilk for water. Pour batter into cake pan. Bake according to package instructions. Cool cake.

3. Frost.

Creamy White Cake

White cake is a favorite flavor and a frequent base for a fancy decorated cake. Vanilla gives this cake an aromatic deliciousness, and the sour creams adds a moist richness.

INGREDIENTS | SERVES 8

1 18.25-ounce package white cake mix plus ingredients called for on box

1 additional egg

2 teaspoons vanilla extract

1 cup sour cream

1 16-ounce tub prepared frosting

1. Preheat oven according to cake mix instructions. Grease and flour cake pan. Set aside.

2. Mix and batter according to instructions on box, but add the extra egg and the vanilla before you add the water.

3. When a smooth, creamy batter has formed, fold in sour cream. Bake according to instructions on the box. Cool completely before frosting.

Lemon Chiffonette Cake

This simple take on classic lemon chiffon cake is sure to please. The combination of lemon and vanilla creates a sweet, refreshing flavor that's perfect for summer celebrations.

INGREDIENTS | SERVES 8

1 18.25-ounce box white cake mix plus ingredients called for on box

1 3.9-ounce package instant vanilla pudding mix

1 3.9-ounce package instant lemon pudding mix

1 cup milk

1 16-ounce tub whipped topping

1 pint fresh blueberries, halved

1. Preheat oven according to cake mix instructions. Grease and flour 2 round layer cake pans. Set aside.

2. Mix cake mix and vanilla pudding mix together and then follow baking directions for layers. Allow layers to cool on wire racks as you mix filling.

3. Mix lemon pudding with milk until thickened. Fold in half the whipped topping. Spread half of the filling on one layer of cake and top with blueberries.

4. Add next cake layer and top with remaining lemon filling. Frost sides of cake with remaining whipped topping. Keep cool until ready to serve.

Nutty White Cake

If you want to make an elaborately decorated cake, a simple recipe is the perfect way to start. The two additions to the basic cake mix in this recipe will give your baking that homemade taste and moistness you're looking for without taking all day.

INGREDIENTS | SERVES 8

1 18.25-ounce box white cake mix plus ingredients called for on box

1 cup almonds, very finely ground

1 additional egg

1. Preheat oven according to cake mix instructions. Grease and flour cake pan. Set aside.

2. Add almonds to dry mix and follow mixing instructions on the package, adding the extra egg with the rest of the eggs called for. Bake according to instructions.

3. Cool completely before frosting.

Classic Chocolate Cake

Want cake from a box that really tastes like rich, dark chocolate? Adding a little cocoa makes the flavor boom! Don't skimp here—buy the best baking cocoa you can afford.

INGREDIENTS | SERVES 8

1 18.25-ounce box chocolate cake plus all ingredients called for on box (except water)

¼ cup baking cocoa

1 additional egg

1 cup milk

1 16-ounce tub prepared frosting

Extra Richness

Adding ½ cup finely ground nuts can be a lovely complement to a simple cake. Cashews would be a rich addition to this cake. Keep in mind, however, that some people have serious allergies to nuts. You'll want to make sure that everyone at your table is informed of your secret ingredient.

1. Preheat oven according to cake mix instructions. Grease and flour cake pan. Set aside.

2. Mix cake mix according to package instructions, with these changes: add cocoa to dry ingredients; add extra egg to eggs called for on the package; and substitute the 1 cup milk for water. Bake.

3. Allow to cool completely before frosting.

Classic Strawberry Cake

Opt for frozen strawberries or strawberry preserves in place of the fresh strawberries to enjoy a taste of summer on cold winter nights. For variation, try raspberries or blackberries in place of the strawberries (changing the gelatin flavor to match the berries), or lemon gelatin with berries of your choice.

INGREDIENTS | SERVES 8

1 18.25-ounce package white cake mix plus ingredients called for on box

4 cups strawberries, mashed

3-ounce package strawberry gelatin

1 additional egg

1 16-ounce tub thawed whipped topping

1. Preheat oven to 350°F. Generously grease cake pan. Set aside.

2. Combine mashed strawberries and gelatin in a small bowl and set aside.

3. Prepare batter according to instructions on package, adding the additional egg. Turn batter into cake pan. Spoon strawberry mixture onto the top of the cake batter.

4. Bake for 35 minutes or until a toothpick comes out clean. Allow cake to cool completely before frosting with whipped topping.

Italian Wedding Cake

This is a cake for the serious sweet tooth. Pineapple, coconut, almond, and cream cheese meld with sweet white cake batter to create a rich, traditional favorite. Consider adding ½ cup finely ground almonds to the batter for an extraordinarily rich cake.

INGREDIENTS | SERVES 8

1 18.25-ounce box white cake mix

½ cup salted butter, softened

1¼ cups buttermilk

3 eggs

1 tablespoon vanilla extract

½ teaspoon almond extract

½ cup sweetened flaked coconut, flaked

1 8-ounce can crushed pineapple, drained

2 cups chopped pecans

2 16-ounce tubs cream cheese frosting

1. Preheat oven to 350°F. Grease cake pan and set aside.

2. Combine cake mix, butter, buttermilk, eggs, vanilla extract, and almond extract in a large mixing bowl.

3. Using an electric mixer set to low speed, beat until completely smooth and combined. Fold in coconut, pineapple, and half the pecans. Pour into cake pan.

4. Bake for 35 minutes or until a toothpick comes out clean. Allow cake to cool completely before turning onto serving platter.

5. Meanwhile, mix remaining nuts and frosting. When cake is cool, frost and serve!

Devil's Food Cake

The decadence of devil's food cake and the sweet, rich taste and slightly chewy texture of coconut make this dessert a real treat. The whipped topping lightens things up. For a quick variation, top this cake with cherry pie filling and whipped cream instead of the whipped topping.

INGREDIENTS | SERVES 8

1 18-ounce box devil's food cake mix plus ingredients called for on box

1 additional egg

2 cups sour cream

2 cups coconut

1 16-ounce tub whipped topping

1. Preheat oven to 350°F. Grease and flour two layer cake pans. Set aside.

2. Mix according to cake mix instructions, adding the extra egg with the eggs called for in the directions. Bake according to package directions for a two-layer cake.

3. As cake cools, mix sour cream, coconut, and whipped topping in a bowl. When layers are cool, use this mixture to frost as you would a two-layer cake.

Neon Angel Cake

Don't be afraid to get crazy now and then. Slices of star fruit may give your artistic creation that star quality you're looking for.

INGREDIENTS | SERVES 8

1 18.25-ounce box angel food cake mix plus ingredients called for on box

1 3-ounce package instant gelatin in a wild, neon color/flavor

Food coloring

Whipped topping

1. Preheat oven according to cake mix instructions. Grease and flour cake pan. Set aside.

2. Mix batter according to instructions. Add gelatin to batter spoonful by spoonful until you reach desired color/flavor intensity. Bake cake according to package instructions.

3. Cool cake completely. Meanwhile, mix food coloring and whipped topping to desired color. Frost cake with whipped topping for a color-crazy surprise.

Chocolate Bundt Cake

The blend of real chocolate morsels and flavorful vanilla pudding are the power combination that enhances the flavor of this favorite cake.

INGREDIENTS | SERVES 8

1 18.25-ounce box marble cake mix
4 eggs
½ cup oil
1 cup milk
1 3.9-ounce box instant vanilla pudding mix
½ cup chocolate chips
1 16-ounce tub prepared frosting

1. Preheat oven to 350°F. Grease and flour a 12-cup bundt pan. Set aside.

2. In a large bowl, combine cake mix, eggs, oil, and milk. Mix until a smooth batter forms.

3. Reserve 1 cup of the batter. Pour the rest into the prepared bundt pan. In a small bowl, combine the reserved cup of batter with the chocolate powder.

4. Fold chocolate chips into chocolate mixture. Spoon chocolate mixture on top of batter.

5. Cut through each spoonful of chocolate mixture a few times with a knife to create a marbled batter. Bake for 35 minutes or until a toothpick comes out clean.

6. Allow cake to cool completely before turning onto serving platter to frost.

Lemon Cooler Cake

Because this cake is best when flavors are allowed to combine during chilling, this is a fantastic choice to prepare ahead of time.

INGREDIENTS | **SERVES 8**

1 18.25-ounce box lemon cake mix plus ingredients called for on box

2 14-ounce cans sweetened condensed milk

½ cup freshly squeezed lemon juice

1 16-ounce tub frozen whipped topping

1. Preheat oven according to cake mix instructions. Grease and flour two layer cake pans. Set aside.

2. Mix cake according to instructions for two-layer cake. Remove from oven and allow to cool completely. Lay cooled cake layer on a clean, flat surface. Mark the middle of the cake layer with toothpicks. With toothpicks as your guide, slice cake horizontally, using a few slow, even strokes of a serrated knife. Carefully remove top layer to a clean, flat surface. Repeat this process with the second layer to create four layers total.

3. Combine condensed milk and lemon juice. Reserve half of the mixture. Spread one-third of the remaining mixture on one layer; top with another layer and repeat. Do not spread mixture on top of fourth layer.

4. Combine remaining mixture with whipped topping to create frosting. Frost cake. Chill 24 hours before serving.

Earth Angel Food Cake

The chemistry of a well-baked cake is a delicate balancing game—especially with the light and airy angel food cake. However, adding an extra egg white gives you a richer texture and taste!

INGREDIENTS | SERVES 8

1 box angel food cake mix plus
   ingredients called for on box
1 additional egg white
Whipped topping
Fresh fruit of choice

1. Preheat oven according to cake mix instructions. Grease and flour cake pan. Set aside.

2. Mix batter according to instructions, adding extra egg white with the rest of the eggs. Bake according to instructions.

3. Allow cake to cool completely before topping with whipped topping and fresh fruit.

Chocolate Chip Cookie Cake

When comfort food is the name of the game, there's nothing better than a chocolate chip cookie. This recipe captures the flavor in a light, delicious cake.

INGREDIENTS | SERVES 8

1 18.25-ounce box yellow cake mix plus
   ingredients called for on box
1 additional egg
1 12-ounce package semisweet
   chocolate morsels
1 16-ounce tub prepared frosting

1. Preheat oven according to cake mix instructions. Grease and flour cake pan. Set aside.

2. Mix cake according to instructions, adding extra egg with the other eggs. When batter is smooth, fold in chocolate chips. Pour batter into a cake pan.

3. Bake according to instructions on the package. Cool and frost.

Peachy Yellow Cake

Baby food is the secret ingredient in this delicately flavored cake. Lower in fat than most cakes and light in flavor, this cake is great with a cold glass of milk.

INGREDIENTS | SERVES 8

1 18.25-ounce box yellow cake mix plus ingredients called for on box (except oil)
1 additional egg
1 4-ounce jar peach baby food
1 16-ounce tub prepared frosting

Peaches and More

Bakers have long substituted a fruit purée for oil when baking with prepared mixes. It often yields a more complex flavor and more homemade texture. You can use any purée you like, so feel free to experiment with mixes and fruits. You'll love testing the results.

1. Preheat oven to 350°F. Grease and flour cake pan. Set aside.

2. Mix batter according to instructions on the package, adding the extra egg with the other eggs and substituting the baby food for the oil.

3. Bake cake according to instructions on the box. Remove from oven and allow cake to cool completely before frosting.

Fluffiest Cake Ever

Recipes like this one are the darlings of cake decorators who long for a home-baked taste. Meringue powder and extra egg give this cake the same lightness and loft of a bakery cake.

INGREDIENTS | SERVES 8

1 18.25-ounce box cake mix without pudding, plus ingredients called for on box
2 tablespoons meringue powder
1 extra egg

1. Preheat oven according to cake mix instructions. Grease cake pan and set aside.

2. Add meringue powder to dry ingredients and mix according to package instructions, adding the extra egg with the other eggs.

3. Beat batter for 5 minutes using an electric mixer set to medium speed. Turn batter into the pan and bake according to package instructions.

4. Allow cake to cool completely before frosting and decorating.

Simply Better Chocolate Cake

This recipe takes just a little extra measuring, but the results are well worth it. With cocoa and sugar for extra sweet richness, this is a great foundation recipe for all your fancy cake decoration projects.

INGREDIENTS | SERVES 8

1 18.25-ounce box chocolate cake mix plus ingredients called for on box

2 tablespoons cornstarch

3 tablespoons cocoa

1 additional egg

½ cup sugar

1 16-ounce tub prepared frosting

1. Preheat oven according to cake mix instructions. Grease and flour cake pan. Set aside.

2. In a large mixing bowl, combine cake mix and ingredients called for on box. Add cornstarch, cocoa, extra egg, and sugar. Stir to combine. Add additional egg.

3. Beat batter for 5 minutes using an electric mixer set to medium speed. Pour batter into cake pan. Bake cake according to instructions on package.

4. Allow cake to cool completely before turning out onto serving platter. Frost.

Vanilla Cake

In ancient times, vanilla was known as an aphrodisiac. Today it's the smell of someone baking with love for those close to her heart.

INGREDIENTS | SERVES 12

1 18.25-ounce box white cake mix
½ cup butter, softened
½ cup sugar
4 eggs
4½ teaspoons vanilla extract
¼ teaspoon baking powder
1 cup milk
1 16-ounce tub prepared frosting

Buying Vanilla

Vanilla can be bought in natural (bean) and processed (extract) forms. If you like very strong flavor, you might prefer vanilla extract. If, however, you prefer a more subtle taste and aroma, consider vanilla beans. If you're feeling extra festive, split the bean lengthwise, remove the tiny seeds, and incorporate them into your batter.

1. Preheat oven to 350°F. Grease and flour cake pan. Set aside.

2. Cream butter and sugar using an electric mixer set to medium speed.

3. Slowly incorporate cake mix and all remaining ingredients except frosting, beating for 4 minutes. The batter should be light and smooth. Turn batter into cake pan.

4. Bake for 30 minutes or until a toothpick comes out clean. Allow cake to cool completely before frosting.

Mega-Moist Chocolate Cake

The addition of extra eggs and sour cream give this cake the same spongy spring found in a cake you'd bake from scratch. You can get creative here by adding a little extra cocoa, some chocolate morsels, or almost anything else that strikes your fancy.

INGREDIENTS | **SERVES 8**

1 18.25-ounce box chocolate cake mix
1 cup sour cream
1 cup vegetable oil
4 eggs
½ cup water
1 16-ounce tub prepared frosting

1. Preheat oven to 350°F. Grease and flour cake pan. Set aside.

2. In a large mixing bowl, combine cake mix, sour cream, oil, eggs, and water. Pour into a cake pan. Bake for 50 minutes.

3. Remove from oven and allow to cool completely before turning onto a plate. Frost when entirely cool.

Simply Better Yellow Cake

This recipe is great for a cake that requires you to pour your concentration into decoration. It's simple, reliable, and lovely. Substitute other cake mix flavors for variety.

INGREDIENTS | SERVES 8

1 18.25-ounce box yellow cake mix plus ingredients called for on box (except water)

Whole milk in the same amount as water called for on box

1 additional egg

1 16-ounce tub prepared frosting

1. Preheat oven according to cake mix instructions. Grease and flour cake pan. Set aside.

2. Mix batter according to package instructions, substituting whole milk for water and adding the extra egg with the other eggs.

3. Using an electric mixer set to medium speed, beat batter until it is smooth and entirely lump-free. Pour batter into cake pan. Bake according to instructions.

4. Allow cake to cool completely before frosting.

CHAPTER 3

Birthday Cakes

Baby's First Cake

What better way to celebrate the close of a year of feedings, late nights, and precious parenting moments than by incorporating baby's favorite food into a cake everyone will enjoy? You can use any sweet baby food in this recipe.

INGREDIENTS | SERVES 12

1 18.25-ounce box moist yellow cake mix
½ cup white sugar
1 cup vegetable oil
4 eggs
1 4-ounce jar apricot baby food
1 4-ounce jar plum baby food
1 16-ounce tub prepared frosting

Decorating Baby's Cake

It may be tempting to paint up this cake with frosting roses or other elaborate decorations, but remember, baby is going to eat this cake—and the sugar can be just too much. Consider using less frosting or even substituting whipped cream for frosting. The cake will be yummy, and little partiers will stay happier longer.

1. Preheat oven to 375°F. Grease and flour a 10" bundt pan. Set aside.

2. Combine all ingredients except frosting in a large mixing bowl. Blend with an electric mixer on medium speed until a smooth batter forms.

3. Pour cake mixture evenly into the pan. Bake for 1 hour. Remove from oven and let cool in the pan.

4. Tip pan onto serving plate and allow gravity to let cake drop. Frost with desired frosting.

Birthday Cake in a Cone

Easy to eat and fun to bake, this is the perfect way to bake up a little fun on birthdays, rainy days, or any other day you choose.

INGREDIENTS | SERVES 36

1 18.25-ounce box white cake mix plus ingredients called for on box

36 ice cream cones

Dark chocolate chips

36 scoops ice cream

Sprinkles

1. Preheat oven to temperature listed on the box in cupcake instructions. Prepare batter according to instructions on the package.

2. Place 2 tablespoons cake batter in each ice cream cone and top with chocolate chips.

3. Place cones on cookie sheet and bake according to instructions on cake mix package. Remove from oven and allow to cool completely.

4. Top each cone/cake with a scoop of ice cream. Allow guests to decorate their cones with sprinkles.

PB&J Cupcakes

PB&J is a winning flavor combination with the young and the young at heart. The combination of rich protein and sweet fruity preserves makes a perfect, wholesome treat. These cupcakes are a surprising way to enjoy an old favorite.

INGREDIENTS | SERVES 24

1 18.25-ounce package yellow cake mix plus ingredients called for on box (except oil)

1 cup creamy peanut butter

½ cup jelly

24 paper baking cups

1 16-ounce tub prepared frosting

1. Preheat oven to 350°F. Line muffin pan with 24 paper baking cups. Set aside.

2. Beat cake mix and peanut butter using an electric mixer on medium speed until crumbs form. Then continue according to the instructions on the cake mix package, omitting oil.

3. Fill each muffin cup halfway. You should have batter remaining when finished. Add 1 teaspoon jelly to each cup.

4. Cover jelly with batter so that the paper cup is ¾ full and the jelly is covered entirely. Bake cupcakes for 24 minutes, or until a toothpick comes out clean.

5. Remove pan to a wire rack and allow cupcakes to cool for 15 minutes. Remove cupcakes from pan and allow to cool completely before frosting.

Birthday Cake with Sprinkles

Colorful and festive sprinkles are a sure sign that a celebration is afoot. Dress up a weeknight dinner or create a birthday masterpiece with this playful recipe.

INGREDIENTS | SERVES 12

1 18.25-ounce box white cake mix with pudding
¾ cup water
½ cup sour cream
2 eggs
1 16-ounce tub prepared frosting
Sprinkles

1. Preheat oven to 350°F. Grease and flour cake pan. Set aside.

2. Mix all ingredients together to form a smooth batter. Turn batter into pan and bake 25 minutes.

3. Allow cake to cool completely before frosting. Frost cake evenly and top with cheerful sprinkles.

Simple Pleasures

We are often tempted to pull out the stops to create a complicated character cake or spend large amounts of money at a local bakery in order to delight a birthday celebrant—but there's something delightful about a home-baked cake. Top it with brightly colored sprinkles and you have a cake that's a feast for the eyes and the taste buds.

Princess Pink Strawberry Cake

There's just something about pink—the sweet strawberry colors and creamy add-ins make for a Southern-style cake fit for a party of extra-girly proportions.

INGREDIENTS | SERVES 12

1 18.25-ounce box white cake mix
1 cup mayonnaise
2 tablespoons flour
1 3-ounce package strawberry gelatin
4 eggs
½ cup cold water
½ 10-ounce package frozen strawberries, thawed

1. Preheat oven to 350°F. Grease and flour cake pan. Set aside.

2. Combine cake mix, mayonnaise, flour, gelatin, and eggs. Mix well to form a smooth batter. Fold in water and strawberries.

3. Turn batter into pan. Bake for 45 minutes. Allow cake to cool completely before frosting.

Strawberry Frosting

Reserve the liquid from the package of frozen strawberries for this frosting. Combine 2 tablespoons melted butter, 3 tablespoons strawberry liquid, and 1 cup confectioners' sugar to make a naturally pink frosting for this strawberry cake.

Flower Pot Trifle

You can personalize this cake by adding plastic fairies or creepy bugs. The magic ingredient here is your imagination. Serve it in the garden for a playful presentation.

INGREDIENTS | SERVES 12

1 large 18-ounce package chocolate sandwich cookies with crème filling

¼ cup butter, softened

1 8-ounce package cream cheese

¾ cup confectioners' sugar

2 3.9-ounce packages instant vanilla pudding mix

2¾ cups cold milk

1 12-ounce tub nondairy whipped topping

1 clean, 8" porcelain or terra cotta flower pot

Gummy worms

Clean plastic flowers or grasses

1. Place cookies in a plastic bag or blender and crush completely. Set aside.

2. In a large bowl, mix butter, cream cheese, and confectioners' sugar.

3. In a separate bowl, mix together the vanilla pudding and milk. Add to butter mixture, and then add nondairy whipped topping.

4. Pour batter and crushed cookies into the flower pot in alternating layers, starting and ending with a cookie layer. Refrigerate for 12 hours to set.

5. Garnish with gummy worms and plastic flowers.

Belle of the Ball Fashion Doll Cake

Whether made simply or with elaborate decoration, the doll cake is an enduring favorite. Perfect for a birthday party or for other girly gatherings.

INGREDIENTS | SERVES 12

1 18.25-ounce box white cake mix plus ingredients called for on box
1 16-ounce tub prepared frosting
Clean 12" fashion doll

Simple Piping

To create simple designs, fill a sandwich bag with icing, snip one bottom corner, and squeeze the bag to create dots, lines, and other details. Start with lines or cursive writing, and work up to dots and more complicated patterns. It might take a little practice, but the end result is worth it!

1. Preheat oven to 350°F. Grease and flour a 2-quart ovenproof Pyrex bowl.

2. Mix cake batter according to package directions and pour into the bowl. Bake for 60 minutes or until a toothpick comes out clean.

3. Remove cake from oven and allow to cool in the bowl for 15 minutes. Invert the bowl over a serving plate. Allow gravity to pull the cake out of the bowl.

4. Allow cake to set for 3½ hours before icing. Insert a clean fashion doll feet first into the cake so that the cake becomes the doll's skirt.

5. Frost the cake and a bodice onto the doll so that the icing creates a dress for the doll.

All-American Burger Cake

Sliders (mini burgers) are a trendy appetizer in many restaurants. To mimic this trend, create cupcake-sized versions of this cake.

INGREDIENTS | SERVES 12

1 18.25-ounce box white cake mix plus ingredients called for on box

1 18.25-ounce brownie mix plus ingredients called for on box

1 12-ounce can ready-to-spread vanilla frosting

1 12-ounce can ready-to-spread chocolate frosting

Red food coloring

Yellow food coloring

¼ cup granulated sugar

1. Preheat oven to 350°F. Generously grease two 8" layer pans.

2. Prepare and bake white cake mix according to package directions. Remove from oven and let cool for 20 minutes. Remove cakes from pans to wire racks and allow to cool completely.

3. While cake layers cool, prepare brownies according to package directions and bake in an 8" layer pan. Remove from oven and allow to cool for 15 minutes in the pan. Invert pan and allow layer to cool on a wire rack.

4. Reserve 1 cup vanilla frosting. Mix remaining vanilla frosting and all of chocolate frosting together with a drop each of red and yellow food colorings to create the color of a bun.

5. Place one cake layer on serving plate; cut off the top if it is too rounded to sit flat. Frost with half of the bun-colored frosting. Top with brownie layer.

6. In separate bowls, mix some vanilla frosting with yellow coloring for mustard and red for ketchup. Top brownie with frosting.

7. Add top layer of cake and frost with remaining bun-colored frosting.

Yellow Pop Cake

This recipe has that certain "mad scientist" feel to it, and it goes great with pizza.

INGREDIENTS | SERVES 12

1 18.25-ounce box lemon cake mix
½ cup oil
1 3.9-ounce box pineapple instant pudding mix
1 8-ounce can Mountain Dew
6 eggs, divided use
½ cup butter
½ cup sugar
1 cup crushed pineapple, drained.

1. Preheat oven to 350°F. Grease and flour two 9" cake layer pans. Set aside.

2. Combine cake mix, oil, pudding mix, Mountain Dew, and 4 of the eggs in a large mixing bowl. Turn batter into pans. Bake for 25 minutes.

3. Meanwhile, combine remaining 2 eggs, butter, sugar, and crushed pineapple in a small saucepan and warm over low heat until thickened.

4. Remove cake from oven and allow to cool for 10 minutes in the pan before removing to a wire rack. Frost while still warm.

Birthday Cake Ice Cream

This recipe lets you honor the tradition of having a birthday cake while skipping the baking altogether. It's a particularly big hit on hot summer birthdays.

INGREDIENTS | SERVES 5

⅔ cup granulated sugar
1 cup whole milk, chilled
2 cups heavy cream, chilled
1 teaspoon vanilla extract
⅔ cup confetti cake mix
Ice cream maker

1. Dissolve sugar into milk by whisking briskly. Add heavy cream and vanilla. Mix well. Sift in cake mix to avoid lumps.

2. Add mixture to an ice cream maker and follow instructions given for the appliance.

Think Outside the Box

Birthday cake doesn't always have to be a cake, nor does it require candles or frosting or any other traditional elements. The truly important part of the celebration is that the birthday celebrant feels special. If an ice cream cake will make her smile, then go that route.

Peanut Butter Cup Cake

Themed cakes like this one are a special treat with a personalized touch.
Peanut butter candies make a tasty addition to this recipe.

INGREDIENTS | SERVES 24

1 18.25-ounce box yellow cake and ingredients called for on package instructions.

¼ cup water

10 peanut butter cups, quartered

1 12-ounce tub cream cheese frosting

Whole peanut butter cups for garnish

1. Preheat oven to 350°F. Grease and flour cake pan. Set aside.

2. Combine cake mix and all ingredients called for on the box as instructed, and add an extra ¼ cup of water.

3. Fold in the candy chunks. Turn batter into prepared cake pan and bake for 45 minutes.

4. Remove cake from heat and allow to cool 15 minutes before turning out onto serving platter.

5. Frost cake and garnish with whole peanut butter cups. Consider using the candies as a base for birthday candles.

Swirl Cake

Can't decide between chocolate cake and confetti cake? Choose two different flavors of cake mix for this recipe. Almost anything goes. Experiment with flavors, but remember that sometimes less is more.

INGREDIENTS | SERVES 15

2 18.25-ounce boxes cake mix plus ingredients called for on boxes

2 12-ounce tubs prepared frosting

1. Preheat oven to 350°F. Grease and flour an 18" × 13" cake pan. Set aside. Mix the first box of cake mix according to instructions on the box. In a separate bowl, mix the second box of cake mix.

2. Spoon a strip of the first cake batter into pan. Then spoon in a strip of the second batter. Alternate strips until the pan is filled.

3. Using a knife, cut through the batter so that the two cake batters mix and marble. Bake according to instructions on the package.

4. Allow cake to cool completely before frosting.

Lemony Birthday Cake

This light and fruity cake—made with real juice—is perfect for a luncheon or for a springtime birthday. Its refreshing and lighter taste make it an instant favorite.

INGREDIENTS | SERVES 12

1 18.25-ounce box lemon cake mix
½ cup sugar
4 eggs
1 cup orange juice
½ cup shortening
1 cup confectioners' sugar
Juice from 1 lemon

Shopping for Lemons

Lemons that are best for juicing feel heavier than expected. Smooth-skinned lemons tend to be easier to juice and will give a better yield, which means more flavor for your cake. Consider organic lemons. They may not look as pretty as the huge, waxed, conventional ones, but their taste is often purer.

1. Preheat oven to 350°F. Grease a 12-cup bundt pan and set aside.

2. Mix first five ingredients in a large bowl with an electric mixer set to medium speed until a smooth batter forms. Turn batter into the pan.

3. Bake for 45 minutes or until a toothpick comes out clean. Remove from oven and allow to cool for 15 minutes before inverting the pan over a serving plate.

4. Using a fork, thoroughly mix confectioners' sugar and lemon juice. Drizzle over warm cake.

Cookies and Cream Birthday Cake

There's something so comforting about the taste (and crunch) of a classic sandwich cookie. Serve this cake with ice cold milk for a wholesome treat.

INGREDIENTS | SERVES 8

1 18.25-ounce box devil's food chocolate cake mix plus ingredients called for on box

4 squares semisweet baking chocolate

¼ cup butter

1 8-ounce package softened cream cheese

½ cup granulated sugar

2 cups nondairy whipped topping

12 chocolate sandwich cookies, crushed

Whole sandwich cookies for garnish

Complementing Cookies

Nothing goes better with a cookie than cold milk. But if milk's not your cup of tea—well, consider tea. (Coffee or punch also work.) The cake is often the focus of the birthday, but beverages are important too, especially for young guests. Soft drinks are often too sweet to complement cakes, but milk and lemonade do nicely.

1. Preheat oven to 350°F. Grease and flour two layer cake pans. Set aside.

2. Prepare and bake cake according to instructions on box for a two-layer cake.

3. Remove baked cakes from oven and allow to cool for 5 minutes before removing to wire racks to cool completely.

4. Meanwhile, make chocolate glaze by melting chocolate and butter in the microwave. Melt for 1 minute on medium high. Remove from microwave. Stir. Continue to microwave in 10-second intervals until the mixture is smooth and creamy. Cool for 5 minutes.

5. In a large bowl, mix cream cheese and sugar until well blended. Fold in whipped topping and crushed sandwich cookies.

6. Spread cream cheese filling between the two layers of cake. Cover top layer of cake with the chocolate glaze.

7. Tile the top of the cake with round halves of sandwich cookies (twist to separate) for an elegant effect.

Tropical Birthday Cake

This rich, sweet cake is perfect for a sultry summer birthday.
You'll need to keep it refrigerated, so serve it close to home.

INGREDIENTS | SERVES 12

1 18.25-ounce package white cake mix
  plus ingredients called for on box
1 14-ounce can cream of coconut
1 14-ounce can sweetened condensed
  milk
¾ cup pineapple juice
1 16-ounce tub whipped topping

Decorating the Tropical Birthday Cake

This moist, sweet treat may not have the look you expect for a birthday cake, but it's nonetheless great for a grown-up get-together. Garnish with coconut, pineapple rings, colored sugar, or even edible flowers like pansies to create a special feel.

1. Preheat oven to 350°F. Grease and flour 9" × 13" cake pan. Set aside.

2. Mix batter according to instructions on the package. Turn batter into cake pan; bake according to instructions. Remove from oven.

3. While the cake is still hot, poke holes in it using a long-pronged fork.

4. Combine cream of coconut, condensed milk, and pineapple juice. Mix well. Pour over the warm cake so that it fills holes poked in the cake. Let cake cool completely.

5. Frost cake with whipped topping. Refrigerate until ready to serve.

Éclair Birthday Cake

There's a creamy richness to this cake that recalls an indulgent custard-filled éclair. Serve with hot coffee for a lovely treat.

INGREDIENTS | SERVES 15

1 18.25-ounce box fudge chocolate cake mix, plus ingredients called for on box

4 cups ricotta cheese

1 cup sugar

4 eggs

1 teaspoon vanilla

1 3.9-ounce box instant chocolate pudding mix

1 cup milk

1 8-ounce tub nondairy whipped topping

1. Preheat oven to 350°F. Grease and flour 9" × 13" cake pan. Set aside.

2. Prepare cake batter according to instructions on the package and pour into pan.

3. In a mixing bowl, combine cheese, sugar, eggs, and vanilla. Blend completely and layer over cake batter. Bake according to cake mix instructions.

4. Remove cake from oven and allow to cool completely.

5. While cake cools, mix pudding, milk, and whipped topping. Spread over cake. Refrigerate until ready to serve.

Pizza Cake

Bake smaller cakes using mini quiche pans or ramekins. Allow guests to decorate their own pizzas.

INGREDIENTS | SERVES 12

1 18.25-ounce box yellow cake mix plus ingredients called for on box

1 tub 12-ounce prepared vanilla frosting

Red food coloring

1 tub 12-ounce prepared frosting (caramel color to be "crust")

Sliced fruit for toppings

Shredded coconut for "cheese"

1. Preheat oven according to cake mix instructions. Grease and flour a round cake pan. Set aside.

2. Prepare and bake cake according to package instructions. Allow cake to cool completely before inverting onto serving plate to decorate.

3. Add red food coloring drop by drop to vanilla frosting to create "sauce." Frost the top of the cake with red frosting and the sides with caramel-colored frosting.

4. Place sliced fruit on cake to resemble pizza toppings and sprinkle lightly with coconut to resemble cheese.

Crust for Ice Cream Pie

These crusts are a perfect complement to cake batter ice cream. Make two batches of ice cream for a pie your guests will flip over!

INGREDIENTS | MAKES 2 PIE CRUSTS

1 18.25-ounce package chocolate cake mix

1 16-ounce tub prepared chocolate frosting

¾ cup water

1 cup semi sweet chocolate chips

1. Preheat oven to 350°F. Grease pie pans generously with shortening.

2. In a large mixing bowl, combine cake mix, frosting, and water. Mix well. Pat half the mixture into one pie pan and repeat for the second pan.

3. Bake for 20–24 minutes or until the crusts are slightly plumped. Cool in pans.

Creating an Ice Cream Pie

You'll use 4 cups (1 quart) of ice cream for each pie. Allow the ice cream to soften before spooning it into the pie crust. Shape it using a flat spoon. Top with ice cream toppings, sprinkles, nuts, or anything else you fancy. Freeze pie until firm. Remove from freezer 20 minutes before serving. This pie is perfect for a birthday or festive occasion.

Boston Crème Cake

Creamy custard-like filling and extra sweet chocolate topping recall the flavor of Boston cream pie. This easy-to-bake cake is sure to impress.

INGREDIENTS | SERVES 12

1 18.25-ounce box vanilla cake mix plus ingredients called for on box

1 3.9-ounce package instant French vanilla pudding mix plus ingredients for making pie filling

1 12-ounce package semisweet chocolate morsels

½ cup heavy whipping cream

1. Preheat oven according to cake mix instructions. Grease and flour two layer cake pans. Set aside.

2. Prepare cake batter and bake according to package instructions for a two-layer cake. Remove from oven and allow to cool completely.

3. As cake cools, prepare pudding mix according to directions for pie filling found on pudding package.

4. Lay cooled cake layers on a clean, flat surface. Mark the middle of the cake layer with toothpicks. With toothpicks as your guide, slice layer horizontally, using a few slow, even strokes of a serrated knife. Carefully remove top layer to a clean, flat surface. Repeat this process with the second layer to create four layers total. Spread pie filling evenly between the layers.

5. In a microwave-safe bowl, combine chocolate morsels and heavy cream. Microwave for 1 minute. Remove from microwave and stir until smooth.

6. Pour chocolate over cake, spreading evenly with rubber spatula. Allow cake to cool for 2 hours in the refrigerator before serving.

Black Forest Birthday Cake

Cherries and chocolate are always a winning pair. This sweet, rich, sophisticated cake is a special treat for a chocolate lover's birthday.

INGREDIENTS | SERVES 12

1 18.25-ounce package chocolate cake mix

1 21-ounce can cherry pie filling

2 eggs

⅓ cup vegetable oil

1 teaspoon almond extract

1 cup granulated sugar

5 tablespoons butter

⅓ cup milk

1 cup chocolate chips

1. Preheat oven to 350°F. Grease and flour cake pan. Set aside.

2. In a large bowl, combine cake mix, pie filling, eggs, oil, and almond extract. Mix to form a smooth batter. Bake for 30 minutes.

3. Meanwhile, combine remaining ingredients in a saucepan, bringing gently to a boil. Stir until smooth and use to frost warm cake.

Cherry Cordial Birthday Cake

This cake has it all. Rich cake, creamy pudding, cherry flavor, chocolate morsels, and gooey candies on top. This sweet, sensual treat wins your sweet tooth right over and makes a lovely presentation.

INGREDIENTS | SERVES 12

1 18.25-ounce box chocolate cake mix

1 3.9-ounce package instant chocolate pudding mix

4 eggs

1¼ cups water

½ cup vegetable oil

1 tablespoon cherry extract or flavor

1 cup chocolate morsels

1 tub prepared chocolate frosting

Cherry cordial candies to garnish

1. Preheat oven to 350°F. Grease and flour cake pan. Set aside.

2. In a large mixing bowl, combine cake mix, pudding mix, eggs, water, oil, and extract. Blend using an electric mixer set to low speed for 2 minutes.

3. Pour batter into a cake pan. Sprinkle chocolate morsels evenly on top of wet cake batter. Bake for 55 minutes. Let cake cool completely before frosting and decorating with candies.

CHAPTER 4

Family Favorites

Chess Cake

There are times when you want a dessert with an artful presentation—and times when you want a wholesome sweet to finish a weekday meal. Chess cake is a perfect everyday treat, and leftovers will keep well enough to enjoy another night.

INGREDIENTS | SERVES 12

1 18.25-ounce box yellow cake mix
4 eggs, divided
1 cup butter, melted, divided
1 8-ounce package cream cheese
4 cups confectioners' sugar

1. Preheat oven to 350°F. Grease and flour a 9" × 13" cake pan. Set aside.

2. Mix cake mix, 2 of the eggs, and ½ cup of the melted butter in a large bowl. Turn batter into pan.

3. Mix cream cheese with the remaining ½ cup butter and two eggs in a separate bowl. Fold confectioners' sugar into cream cheese mixture.

4. Layer cream cheese mixture over batter in pan. Bake for 1 hour. Cool in the pan.

Chess Cake Squares

This recipe makes a slightly more solid "bar" than the cake recipe. Easy to cut and serve, it's a great choice for potlucks and other events as it travels very well.

INGREDIENTS | SERVES 12

1 18.25-ounce box yellow or butter cake mix
½ cup butter
4 eggs, divided use
½ cup white sugar
1 8-ounce package cream cheese, softened

1. Preheat oven to 350°F. Grease and flour a 9" × 13" pan. Set aside.

2. In a large bowl, mix cake mix, butter, and 1 egg until a shortbread-like mixture forms. Pat mixture into the bottom of the pan.

3. In a separate bowl, combine sugar, remaining eggs, and softened cream cheese. Layer on top of crust. Bake for 40 minutes or until slightly browned.

4. Allow to cool in the pan before scoring into bars.

Butter Cake

This Southern favorite offers a mild taste and creamy texture that's sure to be the belle of any dinner you attend. Every family has a recipe for butter cake—but yours is the easiest.

INGREDIENTS | SERVES 12

1 18.25-ounce package yellow cake mix
½ cup butter
3 eggs, divided
1 8-ounce package cream cheese
1 1-pound box confectioners' sugar
1 teaspoon vanilla

1. Preheat oven to 350°F.

2. Combine cake mix, butter, and 1 egg until a shortbread-like batter forms. Pat this mixture into an ungreased 9" × 13" pan.

3. Using a wooden spoon, combine cream cheese, remaining 2 eggs, confectioners' sugar, and vanilla.

4. Layer cream cheese mixture over cake mixture, covering cake batter completely. Bake for 35 minutes.

Peachy Skillet Bake

Peaches are particularly delicate fruits. Overripe peaches can become grainy—definitely not a texture you want for your baked goods. Always select ripe peaches with a firm texture for the sweetness you want for this and other desserts.

INGREDIENTS | SERVES 12

1 15-ounce can sliced peaches in syrup
1 18.25-ounce box white cake mix
½ cup butter

1. Preheat oven to 350°F.

2. Pour peaches and juice into a hot oven-safe 12" skillet. Cover the peaches with dry cake mix and dot with pats of butter. Cover and bake for 40 minutes.

Harvest Fruit Bake

Autumn is a time to enjoy the harvest—and this recipe is a wonderful excuse to do so. Canned fruits make it easy. Top with whipped cream for an irresistible autumn treat.

INGREDIENTS | **SERVES 12**

1 21-ounce can peach pie filling
1 16-ounce can whole cranberry sauce
½ teaspoon ground cinnamon
¼ teaspoon ground nutmeg
1 18.25-ounce box yellow cake mix
1 cup cold butter

1. Preheat oven to 350ºF.

2. Mix peach pie filling and cranberry sauce and turn into an ungreased 9" × 13" pan.

3. In a separate bowl, add spices to dry cake mix and cut in butter. Sprinkle over fruit mixture. Bake for 45 minutes. Allow to cool 15 minutes before serving.

Quickest Brownies

Nothing beats homemade brownies. Whip up this treat any night of the week for a sweet end to a great meal.

INGREDIENTS | **SERVES 12**

1 18.25-ounce box chocolate cake mix
½ cup butter, melted
2 eggs, divided
½ box confectioners' sugar
1 8-ounce package cream cheese, softened

1. Preheat oven to 325ºF. Grease and flour cake pan. Set aside.

2. Combine cake mix, butter, and 1 egg. Mix well. Press mixture into baking pan. Combine remaining egg with last two ingredients and spread over top of cake mixture.

3. Bake for 28 minutes. Allow to cool completely in the pan before cutting into squares.

Friendship Cake

The friendship cake is a wholesome treat that's perfect to share with people close to your heart. Similar cakes are labor intensive, but this easy recipe gives you more time to focus on friends—and other joys of living.

INGREDIENTS | SERVES 12

1 3.9-ounce box instant vanilla pudding mix

⅔ cup vegetable oil

4 eggs

1 18.25-ounce box yellow cake mix

1½ cups brandied fruit, drained

1 cup chopped pecans

1 cup raisins or golden raisins

Confectioners' sugar

Original Friendship Cakes

The original version of this cake has a sourdough base. If you're baking it from scratch, you need to factor in the time it takes the sourdough to ferment. This time-consuming step is omitted from this recipe, but the friendship is not. Double the batch and make one cake to enjoy and one to share.

1. Preheat oven to 325°F. Butter a 12-cup bundt or angel food cake pan and set aside.

2. Combine pudding, oil, eggs, and cake mix in a large mixing bowl and beat for 3 minutes with an electric beater set to medium speed.

3. Gradually add fruit, nuts, and raisins until they are well incorporated into batter. Turn batter into the pan. Bake for 55 minutes.

4. Allow to cool slightly before inverting onto a wire rack to cool. Dust with confectioners' sugar if desired.

Creamy Coconut Dessert

What is it that keeps coconut cake on the favorites list? Is it the tropical flavors? The lightness of the whipped topping? The beautiful presentation? The only way to find out is to bake and enjoy this cake—often. Note: Be sure to use pudding that calls for milk.

INGREDIENTS | SERVES 8

1 18.25-ounce box yellow cake mix

2 tablespoons water

1 cup shredded sweetened coconut

1 egg

½ cup butter

1 3.9-ounce package instant lemon pudding plus ingredients called for on box

1 12-ounce tub nondairy whipped topping

1. Preheat oven to 350°F. Grease and flour 9" × 13" cake pan. Set aside.

2. Combine all ingredients except pudding and whipped topping in a large mixing bowl and combine using a wooden spoon.

3. Press dough into pan so that it is evenly distributed and about ¼" thick. Bake for 20 minutes. Allow to cool completely in the pan.

4. Meanwhile, mix lemon pudding according to package instructions.

5. When cake is cool, layer pudding on top of crust. Dollop nondairy whipped topping on top of the pudding.

Strawberry Shortcake Bake

Lighter and quicker to bake than traditional shortcakes, this fruity favorite is an everyday dessert that's easy enough to enjoy often. You can use fresh or frozen strawberries.

INGREDIENTS | SERVES 8

1 18-ounce box yellow cake mix plus ingredients called for on box

1 5.1-ounce package instant vanilla pudding plus milk called for on box

3 cups strawberries, mashed

1 12-ounce tub nondairy whipped topping

Shortcakes

Discerning consumers of the shortcake may expect a denser cake under their berries. Adding a bit less pudding can create this effect. Experiment until you reach the texture you like. Don't forget to make notes. There's nothing worse than getting the desired result and forgetting how to re-create it.

1. Prepare and bake cake according to package instructions for two round layer pans. Allow to cool completely.

2. Lay cooled cake layers on a clean, flat surface. Mark the middle of the cake layer with toothpicks. With toothpicks as your guide, slice layer horizontally, using a few slow, even strokes of a serrated knife. Carefully remove top layer to a clean, flat surface. Repeat this process with the second layer to create four layers total.

3. Mix pudding according to instructions on the package. In a large glass bowl, alternate layers of cake, strawberries, and pudding.

4. Top with a generous helping of nondairy whipped topping.

Sundae Cake

A great way to enjoy the yummy taste of a sundae without all the dairy. This recipe is just a guideline to get you started. Experiment with your favorite combinations of toppings. Combine flavors. Add fruits. With any luck, this cake will never be the same twice!

INGREDIENTS | SERVES 12

1 18.25-ounce chocolate cake mix plus ingredients called for on box

1 15-ounce tub nondairy whipped topping

3 sliced bananas

1½ cups sliced strawberries

1 14-ounce can crushed pineapple, drained

¼ cup maraschino cherries, drained

4 tablespoons chocolate sauce

1. Prepare and bake cake according to cake mix instructions for a two-layer cake. Sandwich half the whipped topping and all of the fruit pieces between layers of cake.

2. Top with a layer of nondairy whipped topping. Drizzle chocolate sauce over top.

Chocolate Gooey Cake

Use this sticky treat to celebrate a great day. This fancy-looking cake is simple enough for an everyday dessert.

INGREDIENTS | SERVES 12

1 18.25-ounce box German chocolate cake plus ingredients called for on box

⅔ cup fudge ice cream topping

¾ cup butterscotch topping

¾ cup sweetened condensed milk

6 chocolate-covered toffee candies

1 15-ounce tub nondairy whipped topping

1. Prepare and bake cake according to cake mix instructions. While cake is still warm in the pan, use a skewer to poke holes all over the top.

2. Pour fudge topping over top of the cake, followed by butterscotch topping and sweetened condensed milk, so that the holes fill with liquid.

3. Place candies in a bag and crush with a rolling pin. Top cake with crushed candies. Frost cake with nondairy whipped topping. Refrigerate until ready to serve.

Quick Bake Carrot Cake

This bundt carrot cake is sweet and moist—and may overflow the pan. Bake with a cookie sheet under it to catch drips and dribbles, just in case.

INGREDIENTS | SERVES 12

1 18.25-ounce box carrot cake mix

4 eggs

1½ cups shredded carrots

¾ cup oil

1 cup milk

1 12-ounce tub prepared sour cream frosting

Frosting Dilemma

To frost or not to frost? That is the question. This cake is so moist and sweet you could almost forgo the frosting, but hardcore fans won't think of it. No worries—just pick up a tub of frosting and slather it on. Enjoy!

1. Preheat oven to 350°F. Grease and flour a 12-cup bundt pan. Set aside.

2. Combine all ingredients except frosting in a large bowl. Mix well until a smooth batter forms. Pour into bundt pan and bake for 55 minutes. Insert a toothpick to check for doneness.

3. Remove cake from oven and allow to cool in the pan for 15 minutes. Invert pan onto wire rack and allow cake to fall free of pan.

4. Allow cake to cool completely before frosting.

Lemon Goo Cake

Sure, baking icing into the cake is a little counterintuitive. But this moist, lemony cake is a snap to bake. This cake bakes up very moist and fluffy. Resist testing with a fork or toothpick; the cake can fall easily.

INGREDIENTS | **SERVES 12**

1 18.25-ounce box lemon cake mix
4 eggs
1 cup milk
1 12-ounce tub lemon frosting

1. Preheat oven to 350°F. Grease and flour 12-cup bundt pan. Set aside.

2. Combine all ingredients in a large mixing bowl. Mix well using an electric mixer set to medium speed to form a smooth batter.

3. Pour into pan and bake for 1 hour. Allow cake to cool slightly before inverting pan onto a wire rack to remove the cake.

Candied Pumpkin Dessert

Pumpkins are for more than carving on Halloween. Their buttery texture and sweet flavor make for wholesome desserts when the temperatures drop.

INGREDIENTS | **SERVES 12**

1 15-ounce can pumpkin (not pumpkin pie filling)
1 12-ounce can evaporated milk
3 eggs
1 cup granulated sugar
4 teaspoons pumpkin pie spice
1 18.25-ounce box white cake mix
¾ cup butter, melted

1. Preheat oven to 350°F. Grease and flour 9" × 13" pan. Set aside.

2. Mix pumpkin, evaporated milk, eggs, sugar, and pumpkin pie spice in a large bowl. Turn mixture into pan. Top with dry cake mix.

3. Pour melted butter on top. Bake 55 minutes. Remove from oven and serve warm.

Playful Sprinkles Cake

*Sprinkles are a no-effort way to add a little something special to a cake.
The playful colors in the cake mix combo make this cake a winner.*

INGREDIENTS | SERVES 12

1 18.25-ounce box confetti cake mix

1 12-ounce tub prepared icing with sprinkles

1 cup milk

4 eggs

Your Cake Pan Overfloweth?

Recipes with icing in the mix are famous for overflowing. To be on the safe side, always keep a cookie sheet (or two) on the rack below your cake. That'll keep drippings off your oven floor and cut down on cleaning time for you!

1. Preheat oven to 350°F. Grease and flour 12-cup bundt pan. Set aside.

2. Combine all ingredients in a large mixing bowl. Mix well using an electric mixer set to medium speed to form a smooth batter.

3. Pour into pan and bake for 1 hour. Allow cake to cool slightly before inverting pan onto a wire rack to remove the cake.

Peanut Butter Cup Fondue

This less-formal version of the elegant chocolate fondue sneaks a little protein into the mix. This fondue is served at a cooler temperature, and you can use your fingers to dunk the cake.

INGREDIENTS | SERVES 8

1 18.25-ounce box angel food cake plus ingredients called for on box

1 12-ounce package chocolate morsels

½ cup peanut butter

1. Prepare and bake cake according to cake mix instructions. Cut cake into cubes.

2. Melt chocolate pieces in a double boiler or fondue pot. Stir in peanut butter. Pour into a serving bowl and serve.

Cantaloupe Squares

This melon-topped tart boasts a surprising combination of flavors, a lovely texture, and a rich, cream-cheese flavor. Serve in the morning with coffee or at the end of a summer day.

INGREDIENTS | SERVES 24

1 18.25-ounce box yellow cake mix

4 eggs, divided

2 tablespoons vegetable oil

16-ounce package cream cheese, softened

⅓ cup granulated sugar

¼ teaspoon salt

1 cup puréed cantaloupe

1 teaspoon vanilla extract

½ cup milk

1 tablespoon lemon juice

1. Preheat oven to 300°F. Grease 9" × 13" pan.

2. Reserve 1 cup cake mix. Mix remaining cake mix, 1 egg, and oil to form a thick batter. Press batter into the pan to form a bottom layer. Set aside.

3. In a large mixing bowl, combine cream cheese, sugar, and salt. Beat with an electric mixer until smooth.

4. Fold in remaining 3 eggs and the 1 cup reserved cake mix. Beat until thoroughly incorporated. Slowly add remaining ingredients and beat until smooth.

5. Pour cheese mixture on top of bottom layer in pan. Bake for 45 minutes or until center is slightly firm to the touch. Remove to refrigerator and chill for 2 hours before serving.

Raspberry Chocolate Bars

Raspberry jam and real chocolate chips melt into butter and milk to create a gooey, sweet bar. Added nuts are optional, but they add a rich crunch.

INGREDIENTS | SERVES 12

1 18.25-ounce box chocolate cake mix
⅓ cup evaporated milk
1½ cups melted butter
1 cup chopped nuts (optional)
½ cup seedless raspberry jam
12-ounce chocolate chips

1. Preheat oven to 350°F. Grease and flour 9" × 13" pan. Set aside.

2. Combine cake mix, evaporated milk, butter, and nuts to form a very sticky, gooey batter. Pour half the batter into the bottom of a pan and bake for 10 minutes.

3. Meanwhile, melt the jam in the microwave.

4. Remove baked crust from oven and cover with melted jam and chocolate chips. Cover with remaining cake batter and bake for 20 minutes.

5. Cool completely before cutting.

Chocolate Cherry Bars

Enjoy these bars warm out of the oven or cover them and save them for later. They taste fantastic either way.

INGREDIENTS | SERVES 12

1 18.25-ounce box chocolate cake mix

1 15-ounce can cherry pie filling

1 teaspoon almond extract

1 teaspoon vanilla extract

2 eggs

1 cup sugar

7 tablespoons butter

⅓ cup whole milk

1 12-ounce package semisweet chocolate chips

1. Preheat oven to 350°F. Spray a 13" × 9" pan with nonstick spray. Set aside.

2. Combine cake mix, pie filling, extracts, and eggs in a large bowl and beat with an electric mixer until well blended.

3. Pour batter into pan and bake at 350°F for 25 minutes or until set all the way through. Remove from oven.

4. Mix sugar, butter, and milk in a large saucepan. Bring to a boil. Remove pan from heat and add chocolate chips, stirring as they melt.

5. Pour chocolate mixture over warm cake and spread to cover. Allow to cool and harden before cutting into bars.

Chocolate Fondue

This elegant classic is a dessert you can dip. Fondue is easy to make and fun to eat, but it does require some equipment. Small children will need to be closely supervised.

INGREDIENTS | SERVES 8

1 18.25-ounce box angel food cake mix plus ingredients called for on box

16 ounces dark chocolate

1½ cups half-and-half

1 teaspoon vanilla extract

1. Prepare and bake cake according to cake mix instructions. Cut cake into cubes.

2. Break chocolate into small pieces and place in fondue pot. Gently add half-and-half and stir until melted and smooth. Add vanilla.

3. When melted and mixed, sauce is ready for dipping.

Yellow Cake Dessert

Four favorites combine for a sweet dessert offering layers of creamy flavor. It's perfect to pass at potlucks and family dinners.

INGREDIENTS | SERVES 8

1 18.25-ounce box yellow cake mix

2 tablespoons water

1 cup coconut

1 egg

½ cup butter, melted

1 3.9-ounce package lemon pudding plus milk called for on box

1 15-ounce tub whipped topping

1. Preheat oven to 350°F. Grease and flour 9" × 13" pan. Set aside.

2. In a large bowl, mix cake mix, water, coconut, egg, and butter using a wooden spoon.

3. Spoon mixture into pan and even out with flat side of a spoon. Bake for 20 minutes. Cool completely.

4. Prepare lemon pudding as directed on box and spread on cooled cake. Top with whipped topping.

Ricotta Cake

Somewhere between lemon cake and cheesecake, this recipe finds the perfect balance of richness and sweetness. Topped with confectioners' sugar, it's hard to resist.

INGREDIENTS | **SERVES 10**

1 18.25-ounce box lemon cake mix with pudding plus ingredients called for on box

1 pound ricotta cheese

¾ cup sugar

3 eggs

Confectioners' sugar

1. Preheat oven to 350°F. Grease and flour cake pan. Set aside.

2. Prepare batter according to cake mix instructions and turn into cake pan. Mix cheese, sugar, and eggs and spoon on top of batter in cake pan. Bake for 50 minutes.

3. Sift confectioners' sugar on top of cake to finish.

Banana Bread

Freeze overripe bananas (in the peel) and save them to use in recipes like this one. The peel will turn black when frozen, but the fruit will be great for baking when thawed.

INGREDIENTS | **SERVES 8**

¼ cup sour cream

1 teaspoon baking soda

Water

1 18.25-ounce box yellow cake mix without pudding

2 eggs

1 cup mashed bananas

1 cup walnuts or walnut pieces

1. Preheat oven to 350°F. Grease and flour cake pan. Set aside.

2. Mix sour cream and baking soda in a 1 cup measuring cup. Add water to 1-cup level and pour mixture into a large mixing bowl.

3. Fold cake mix into sour cream mixture, mixing well. Slowly add eggs, bananas, and nuts.

4. Pour into a loaf pan and bake according to cake mix instructions.

Chocolate Toffee Shortbread

This delicious shortbread can be made with any flavor cake mix. If you want to use white or yellow cake mix, use 1 cup of white chocolate chips, ground, in place of the semisweet.

INGREDIENTS | YIELDS 48 COOKIES

1 18.25-ounce package chocolate cake mix

1 12-ounce package semisweet chocolate chips, divided

½ cup butter, softened

1 3-ounce package cream cheese, softened

1 egg

1 teaspoon vanilla

1 cup toffee baking bits

1 cup chopped pecans

About Shortbread

Shortbreads traditionally don't use leavening agents. But cake mixes include baking powder or baking soda, so the dough will puff up slightly. Lots of fat, in the form of butter or cream cheese, will help keep the dough from puffing too much.

1. Preheat oven to 375°F. In large bowl, place cake mix. Grind 1 cup of the chocolate chips in a food processor until fine; stir into cake mix.

2. Add butter, cream cheese, egg, and vanilla to cake mix and mix until a crumbly dough forms.

3. Press dough into 15" × 10" jelly roll pan. Sprinkle with toffee baking bits, pecans, and remaining 1 cup chocolate chips.

4. Bake for 15–20 minutes until shortbread is set. Cool on wire rack, then cut or break into squares. Store in airtight container.

Lemon Crunch Cake

This elegant cake is easy to make, and it serves a crowd.
Look for different types of nut brittle to vary the recipe.

INGREDIENTS | SERVES 16

1 18.25-ounce package lemon cake mix

½ cup buttermilk

¼ cup water

½ cup butter, melted

1 teaspoon lemon extract

3 eggs

2 tablespoons lemon juice

2 16-ounce cans ready to spread vanilla frosting

¼ cup lemon juice

1½ cups powdered sugar

1 8-ounce package peanut brittle, crushed

1. Preheat oven to 325°F. Spray a 10" tube pan with nonstick baking spray containing flour and set aside.

2. In large bowl, combine cake mix, buttermilk, water, melted butter, lemon extract, eggs, and 2 tablespoons lemon juice; beat until combined. Then beat 3 minutes at medium speed; pour into prepared pan.

3. Bake for 50–60 minutes or until cake springs back when lightly touched in center. Cool completely on wire rack.

4. In medium bowl, combine frosting with lemon juice and powdered sugar; beat until fluffy. Remove cake from pan and cut horizontally into four layers.

5. Reassemble cake, using frosting, sprinkling each layer with some of the crushed brittle. Cover and let stand for 3–4 hours before serving.

Lemon Crème Cake

Pockets of pie filling add a sweet, sensual surprise to this simple dessert. And you don't need a pastry bag or any tricky techniques to whip up this weeknight dessert.

INGREDIENTS | SERVES 12

1 18.25-ounce box white cake mix plus ingredients called for on box

1 19-ounce can lemon pie filling

1 12-ounce tub prepared sour cream icing

1 15-ounce tub nondairy whipped topping

Flavor Combinations

Feel free to switch out cake mix and pie filling flavors with this recipe. White cake and peach pie filling or chocolate cake and cherry filling are great options—but they're only the beginning. Let your imagination go!

1. Preheat oven to 350°F. Grease and flour 9" × 13" pan. Set aside.

2. Mix batter according to package instructions and pour into pan. Spoon pie filling on top of cake batter in evenly spaced dollops.

3. Bake according to package instructions. As cake bakes, mix together frosting and whipped topping. Allow cake to cool before frosting.

Sweet Potato Cake

Nutritionists will tell you that a sweet potato is one of the best things for curbing a sweet tooth. Your first thought may be to run toward the chocolate, but sweet potato is the one that truly satisfies.

INGREDIENTS | SERVES 12

1 18.25-ounce box white cake mix

1 3.9-ounce package vanilla pudding mix (not instant)

1 teaspoon cinnamon

½ teaspoon nutmeg

1⅔ cups cooked sweet potatoes, mashed

4 eggs, beaten

½ cup oil

1 12-ounce tub prepared cream cheese frosting

1. Preheat oven to 350°F. Spray a 13" × 9" pan with nonstick spray. Set aside.

2. Sift together cake mix, pudding, cinnamon, and nutmeg. In a separate bowl mix potatoes, eggs, and oil.

3. Slowly add wet ingredients to dry and mix until a smooth batter forms. Bake for 40 minutes. Cool completely before frosting.

CHAPTER 5

Savory Surprises

Sweet Tooth Cornbread Cake

This sweeter cornbread makes an old timey treat crumbled in a cold glass of milk or served alongside a spicy stew. Slightly sweet breads ease the bite of an extra-spicy dish.

INGREDIENTS | SERVES 6

5 tablespoons butter
1 cup frozen sweet corn
1 cup whole milk
2 eggs
1 egg yolk
1 teaspoon vanilla
1 8.5-ounce package corn muffin mix
1 9-ounce package yellow cake mix
¼ cup granulated sugar
Confectioners' sugar

1. Preheat oven to 350°F.

2. Slowly melt butter in a 10" cast iron skillet. Add corn and remove skillet from heat.

3. In a large mixing bowl, combine milk, 2 eggs, 1 egg yolk, and vanilla. Mix well until smooth. Fold in corn mix, cake mix, and granulated sugar.

4. Pour mixture over corn and butter in skillet. Bake for 35 minutes. Allow cake to cool for 15 minutes. Invert pan over wire rack or serving plate.

5. Dust with confectioners' sugar if desired or serve with butter.

Cornbread Croutons

These sweet and wholesome crunchy bits are fantastic in a salad, floating on a soup, or used in a favorite stuffing recipe at Thanksgiving.

INGREDIENTS | **MAKES 6 CUPS FINISHED CROUTONS**

¼ cup olive oil

Salt and pepper to taste

Herbs to taste

1 recipe Sweet Tooth Cornbread Cake (page 68)

Storing Croutons

These tiny toasts will keep for a few weeks in a sealed plastic bag. If you want to save them for a special occasion, pop them in the freezer. They'll easily thaw when you're ready to use them.

1. Preheat oven to 350°F.

2. Pour ¼ cup olive oil in a shallow dish. Mix in salt, pepper, and herbs. Cut cornbread into cubes and place on cookie sheet. Lightly brush with the seasoned oil.

3. Bake 8 minutes. Remove croutons from oven and turn with spatula. Return to the oven and bake for another 8 minutes.

4. Allow croutons to cool completely before serving.

Ham, Beans, and Cornbread

This slow cooked meal is a Southern style treat and a weeknight favorite waiting to happen.

INGREDIENTS | SERVES 6

1 pound dried great northern beans, soaked overnight according to package instructions

½ pound chopped, cooked ham

½ cup brown sugar

1 tablespoon onion powder

1 tablespoon garlic salt

½ teaspoon black pepper

¼ teaspoon cayenne pepper

1 recipe Sweet Tooth Cornbread Cake batter (page 68), unbaked

1. Combine all ingredients except Sweet Tooth Cornbread Cake batter in a slow cooker and add water to cover by 2 inches.

2. Set slow cooker to low and simmer for 10½ hours, stirring occasionally. Add Sweet Tooth Cornbread Cake batter in dollops. Cover and cook for 1½ hours. Ladle into bowls.

Fruity Brunch Pizza

Choose fresh fruit in season. Some fruits, like apples and peaches, bake well. You may choose to bake them when you bake the crust. You may choose not to bake others. Get creative with this recipe. The rewards are great!

INGREDIENTS | SERVES 4

Refrigerated pizza crust

2 tablespoons butter, melted

½ cup yellow cake mix

¼ cup brown sugar

½ cup vanilla yogurt

Fresh fruit

1. Preheat oven to temperature specified in pizza crust instructions.

2. Lay pizza crust out on a cookie sheet. Baste with butter and sprinkle with cake mix. Sprinkle with brown sugar. Bake according to pizza crust package instructions.

3. Top with a thin layer of vanilla yogurt. Playfully arrange fresh fruit on the pizza for "toppings."

Dinner Rolls

These are a perfect complement for a dinner—and a great start for some other exciting recipes. For an irresistible spread, mix honey with your favorite butter or margarine.

INGREDIENTS | **MAKES 20 ROLLS**

1 0.25-ounce envelope active dry yeast
1½ cups warm water
1 9-ounce package yellow cake mix
3¼ cups flour
¼ cup butter, melted
2 egg whites, beaten

Dinner Roll Variations

Add the following ingredients in Step 3: For an Italian flavor, add 1 tablespoon mixed Italian herbs, 2 teaspoons crushed garlic, 4 tablespoons grated Parmesan cheese, and 1 tablespoon dried herbs. If you like rosemary, add 3 tablespoons Parmesan cheese and 3 tablespoons finely chopped fresh rosemary or 1 tablespoon dried rosemary. For an autumn twist, add ½ cup dried cranberries and 1 tablespoon pumpkin pie spice mix. For sweet potato rolls, add ½ cup mashed sweet potatoes.

1. Preheat oven to 350°F.

2. In a large mixing bowl dissolve yeast in warm water. Let stand 10 minutes, or until a milky texture appears.

3. Fold in cake mix and flour, beating until a smooth dough forms.

4. Prepare another large mixing bowl with a light coating of spray oil or olive oil.

5. Place dough in oiled bowl, cover with a clean cloth, and leave in a warm place until dough doubles in volume, usually 1 hour. Punch down dough and divide into two halves.

6. Roll out each half into foot-wide circles. Cut each circle into 10 pie-shaped wedges.

7. Brush wedges with melted butter and beaten egg white. Roll each wedge into a crescent shape.

8. Place rolls on a cookie sheet, cover, and let rest for 25 minutes, or until doubled in size. Bake for 12 minutes or until slightly golden.

Pizza Rolls

This is a more wholesome take on the pizza rolls you might find in your grocer's freezer. Bake 'em for movie night, but be warned that they won't stick around long.

INGREDIENTS | **MAKES 20**

1 recipe Dinner Rolls dough (page 71), unbaked

2 tablespoons butter

1½ cups marinara sauce

2 cups shredded mozzarella cheese

40 slices pepperoni

Variations

Make this with ham and cheese for a great complement to scrambled eggs, or with herbed butter to serve alongside spaghetti or lasagna. Add onions, mushrooms, anchovies, and all of your other favorite pizza toppings to lend a personal touch to this tasty snack.

1. Prepare Dinner Rolls through Step 6. Brush rolls with butter, add a scant spoonful of sauce, some cheese, two pieces of pepperoni, and other toppings as desired.

2. Start at largest side and roll dough toward smallest point to form a crescent shape.

3. Place rolls on a cookie sheet, cover with a clean tea towel, and allow to sit for 25 minutes, or until doubled in size. Bake for 15 minutes or until golden.

4. Allow to cool slightly before serving.

Peach Pecan Pizza

Cake mix makes a spicy and delicious crust for this sweet pizza. If you like your desserts spicy, add even more cinnamon, nutmeg, or mace to the cake mix before mixing in the other ingredients.

INGREDIENTS | SERVES 8

1 cup quick cooking oatmeal, divided
1 18.25-ounce package spice cake mix
½ cup butter, softened
1 egg
1 cup chopped toasted pecans, divided
½ teaspoon cinnamon
¼ teaspoon nutmeg
1 21-ounce can peach pie filling
1 cup dried cranberries

Dessert Pizzas

Dessert pizzas like this one can be varied many ways. Use apple or cherry pie filling instead of peach, and use dried cherries or raisins. A different type of cake mix will also change the flavor. This pizza is good for a dessert or for a fancy brunch.

1. Preheat oven to 350°F. In food processor, grind half of the oatmeal into fine crumbs. Combine the ground oatmeal with cake mix in large bowl; mix well. In same processor bowl, combine cream cheese with butter; process until well blended.

2. Cut butter mixture into cake mix mixture until crumbly. Remove 1 cup of these crumbs and place in small bowl. Add egg to remaining crumbs and mix. Press mixture with egg into greased 13" × 9" cake pan. Bake for 10 minutes.

3. Add remaining ½ cup oatmeal and pecans to reserved 1 cup crumbs. Place pie filling in small bowl; stir in dried cranberries, cinnamon, and nutmeg. Spoon evenly over baked crust. Top with pecan mixture.

4. Bake for 20–25 minutes longer until crumbs are golden brown. Let cool for 30 minutes, then cut into squares to serve.

Mexican Chili Pie

Craving a little something spicy for supper? This dish combines sweet cornbread, spicy chili, and creamy cheese in one simple casserole.

INGREDIENTS | **SERVES 6**

1 1.25-ounce package McCormick Chili Seasoning Mix

1 pound lean ground beef or turkey

1 14½-ounce can diced tomatoes, undrained

1 15-ounce can kidney or pinto beans, undrained

1 9-ounce box yellow cake mix

1 9-ounce package cornbread mix

2 eggs

⅓ cup milk

½ cup water

2 cups Cheddar cheese, grated

1. Preheat oven to 350°F. Grease a 9" × 13" baking dish.

2. Combine chili seasoning mix, ground meat, tomatoes, and beans and cook according to directions on envelope. While chili simmers, mix cake mix, cornbread mix, eggs, milk, and water in a separate bowl.

3. Pour chili into a 9" × 13" baking dish. Top with cornbread mixture and sprinkle liberally with Cheddar cheese. Bake for 30 minutes or until crust is golden.

Sweet Potato Fritters

This sweet treat can be served alongside a meal or dusted with confectioners' sugar for dessert. Delicious with aioli or mayonnaise as a savory side.

INGREDIENTS | SERVES 4

1 cup sweet potato, grated

1 cup white cake mix, sifted

1 egg, beaten

½ cup milk

2 cups oil for frying

In a large bowl mix all ingredients well to form a batter. Drop by large spoonfuls into hot oil. Fry for approximately 20 seconds on each side. Lift out browned fritters and drain on a paper towel.

Spoon Bread Casserole

This easy-to-bake take on a traditional and butter-drenched Southern favorite is a great dish for potlucks and family gatherings.

INGREDIENTS | SERVES 4

1 cup butter, melted

2 cans whole kernel corn, drained

2 12-ounce cans cream style corn

2 cups sour cream

4 eggs, beaten

1 9-ounce package corn muffin mix

1 9-ounce package yellow cake mix

1. Preheat oven to 375°F.

2. Grease a 3-quart casserole dish. Pour butter and both kinds of corn into dish. Fold in sour cream. Add eggs and both mixes, stirring to combine thoroughly. Bake for 35 minutes.

Beef Pot Pie

This warm, nourishing comfort food is a true one-pot meal. Use leftover rolls, lean ground beef, and delicious veggies to make a home-baked supper.

INGREDIENTS | SERVES 4

1½ pounds ground beef

1 onion, chopped

1 15-ounce jar Alfredo sauce

2 cups frozen corn

1 cup frozen green beans

1 cup chopped tomatoes, fresh or canned

1 teaspoon dried basil

½ recipe Dinner Rolls dough (page 71), unbaked

1 tablespoon grated Parmesan cheese

¼ teaspoon oregano

1. Preheat oven to 400°F. Lightly grease a 2-quart baking dish and set aside.

2. In a large skillet, brown ground beef and onion. Add Alfredo sauce, corn, beans, tomatoes, and basil. Bring to a boil. Pour mixture into baking dish.

3. Dot beef mixture with Dinner Rolls dough. Sprinkle with Parmesan cheese and oregano. Bake for 15 minutes or until bread topping is golden brown.

Scalloped Corn Casserole

If you like corn pudding, give this savory take a try. This rich, creamy corn casserole is fantastic with ham or roast chicken.

INGREDIENTS | SERVES 3

2 eggs

1 cup sour cream

½ cup butter, melted

1 12-ounce can creamed corn

1 12-ounce can whole kernel corn, undrained

1 9-ounce package yellow cake mix

1 cup shredded Cheddar cheese

1. Preheat oven to 350°F. Lightly grease a 9" × 9" baking dish.

2. Lightly beat eggs. Fold in sour cream, butter, and both kinds of corn. Mix well. Fold in cake mix. Spoon into baking dish. Top with shredded cheese.

3. Bake for 55 minutes or until center is set.

Breakfast Bake Casserole

This sweet and savory morning treat is easy to make as long as there's a steaming cup of coffee at your side.

INGREDIENTS | SERVES 6

2 cups yellow cake mix, divided

8 slices bacon, cooked

1 4-ounce can sliced mushrooms, drained

2 green onions, thinly sliced

1½ cups shredded mild Cheddar cheese

4 eggs

2 cups whole milk

½ cup butter

1. Sprinkle 1 cup cake mix in the bottom of a well-buttered 8" square baking dish. Top with bacon, mushrooms, onions, and cheese. Sprinkle with remaining cake mix.

2. In a medium bowl, whisk together eggs and milk. Pour over layered ingredients. Refrigerate at least 1 hour, preferably overnight.

3. Dot with butter and bake, uncovered, for 1 hour or until center is set.

Sweetest Hushpuppies

Serve these round treats at your next fish fry for a sweeter savory crunch. Dip in tartar sauce or ketchup or sprinkle with malt vinegar for an extra burst of flavor.

INGREDIENTS | MAKES 24 HUSHPUPPIES

1 9-ounce package cornbread mix

1 9-ounce package yellow cake mix

2 eggs

4 teaspoons baking powder

1 teaspoon salt

1 large onion, finely chopped

¼ cup milk

Oil for frying

1. Combine all ingredients except milk and oil. Mix to form a crumbly mixture. Add milk and stir to form a batter. Drop by teaspoons into 1 inch hot oil in a 12" skillet.

2. Cook until golden on both sides. Remove from oil and let drain on paper towels. Serve warm.

Hamburger Cornbread Casserole

This wholesome and easy-to-bake savory recipe will warm you up on a chilly evening. Serve with a salad or green beans for a well-balanced meal.

INGREDIENTS | SERVES 6

2 pounds ground beef

1 yellow onion, chopped

1 14½-ounce can tomato sauce

2 12-ounce cans sweet corn, drained

2 tablespoons chili powder

1 9-ounce package cornbread mix

1 9-ounce package yellow cake mix

2 eggs

⅓ cup milk

⅓ cup water

1. Preheat oven to 350°F. Grease a 9" × 13" pan.

2. Brown ground beef and onion. Drain fat. Add tomato sauce, corn, and chili powder to skillet and sauté for 10 minutes to release the spice.

3. Mix the cornbread mix and cake mix. Add eggs, milk, and water. Beat until a smooth batter forms, adding more water if needed.

4. Spread hamburger and onion mixture in greased pan. Pour cornbread mixture over top. Bake 20–30 minutes or until crust is golden.

Sweet Potato Casserole

This dish is delicious enough for the Thanksgiving table but easy enough for an average Thursday night. This easy-to-make recipe brings wholesome goodness to the table.

INGREDIENTS | SERVES 6

3 cups mashed sweet potatoes

3 cups granulated sugar

1 cup butter

2 eggs

1 teaspoon vanilla

⅓ cup milk

1 cup sweetened shredded coconut

1 cup brown sugar

1 cup white cake mix

1 cup pecans

1. Preheat oven to 350°F.

2. Mix sweet potatoes, sugar, ½ cup melted butter, eggs, vanilla, milk, and coconut in a large mixing bowl with a wooden spoon. Pour into a buttered baking dish.

3. In a smaller mixing bowl, mix brown sugar, cake mix, and pecans. Sprinkle dry mixture over potatoes. Dot evenly with remaining butter. Bake for 25 minutes.

CHAPTER 6

Morning Glory Cakes

Rich Topped Coffee Cake

This moist, rich coffee cake makes any coffee klatch a special occasion. Serve with a side of fresh blueberries or creamy yogurt for a lovely full breakfast.

INGREDIENTS | **SERVES 6**

1 18.25-ounce box yellow cake mix
1 3.9-ounce box instant vanilla pudding
1 cup sour cream
4 whole eggs
½ cup canola oil
½ cup skim milk
3 teaspoons ground cinnamon
¼ cup sugar
1 tablespoon flour

1. Preheat oven to 350°F.

2. Mix cake mix and vanilla pudding mix in a bowl. Add sour cream, oil, and milk. Lightly beat eggs and fold into mixture. Blend using electric mixer on medium speed for 10 minutes. Pour into an angel food pan or bundt pan.

3. In a separate bowl combine cinnamon, sugar, and flour. Pour into pan on top of cake mix mixture.

4. Use a knife to cut through batter at intervals to marble topping through batter. Bake for 50 minutes or until knife comes out clean. Serve with coffee.

Citrus Muffins

The bright, sparkling taste of orange makes this fresh and sweet morning treat perfect for days at the beach house, by the pool, or with friends.

INGREDIENTS | **MAKES 24 MUFFINS**

1 18.25-ounce box white cake mix
1 cup water
2 eggs
1 16-ounce box confectioners' sugar
Zest of 1 orange
Juice and zest of 2 lemons

1. Preheat oven to 325°F. Butter and flour a muffin tin.

2. Blend cake mix, water, and eggs with an electric mixer for 4 minutes. Fill muffin cups ½ full with batter. Bake for 6 minutes.

3. Meanwhile, combine confectioners' sugar, orange zest, and lemon zest and juice to make a glaze. Set aside.

4. Remove muffins from oven. Let cool on rack. When only slightly warm to touch, dip the top of each muffin in glaze to cover. Return to rack.

Cake Mix Pancakes

This is less of a recipe and more of a trick. But it's a great one to know! With this in your toolbox you can whip up some surprising and yummy pancakes on short notice any day of the week!

INGREDIENTS | 12 PANCAKES

1 18.25-ounce box cake mix plus ingredients called for on box

½ cup butter or ¼ cup oil for frying

Get Creative

Don't be afraid to toss fruit, nuts, or even bits of candy bar into the mix on very special occasions. Make banana bread pancakes with walnuts and real maple syrup on top, white cake mix pancakes with blueberries and blueberry syrup, cherry cake mix pancakes with chocolate syrup, confetti cake mix pancakes for a birthday, and pineapple cake mix pancakes with blueberry syrup. Have fun!

1. Make cake mix batter according to package directions. Melt 1 tablespoon butter or heat ½ tablespoon oil in a skillet or griddle. Ladle ¼ cup pancake batter per pancake into skillet.

2. Flip when bubbles form on top of pancakes. Serve with fresh fruit, syrup, and/or whipped cream!

Better Buttermilk Breakfast Cake

Rich, sweet buttermilk cake for breakfast. Sounds too sweet to be true, doesn't it? Well, hold on to your sweet tooth! This morning treat is all dolled up and headed for a plate near you.

INGREDIENTS | SERVES 8

1 18.25-ounce box white cake mix

1 cup plus 1 tablespoon buttermilk, divided

½ cup plus 1 tablespoon melted butter, divided

5 eggs

3 tablespoons brown sugar

2 teaspoons ground cinnamon

1 tablespoon granulated sugar

1 cup finely chopped nuts

1 cup confectioners' sugar

1 teaspoon vanilla extract

1. Preheat oven to 350°F. Grease a 10" tube pan.

2. Combine cake mix, 1 cup buttermilk, and ½ cup melted butter. Mix using an electric mixer set to medium speed for 2 minutes. Add eggs and continue beating.

3. In a separate bowl, mix brown sugar and cinnamon.

4. Sprinkle granulated sugar and nuts into bottom of tube pan. Pour in one-third of the batter. Sprinkle batter with brown sugar mixture. Top with remaining batter. Bake for 45 minutes.

5. Remove cake from oven and cool in pan for 15 minutes. Invert pan onto serving surface and let cool an additional 30 minutes.

6. Meanwhile, mix confectioners' sugar, vanilla extract, the remaining 1 tablespoon buttermilk, and the remaining 1 tablespoon melted butter to form a glaze. When cake has cooled, drizzle with glaze.

Chocolate Cheese Muffins

*Chocolate, cream cheese, and crunchy walnuts work together
to make this home-baked muffin a sweet, rich favorite.*

INGREDIENTS | **MAKES 24 MUFFINS**

1 18.25-ounce box chocolate cake mix
plus ingredients called for on box

1 8-ounce package cream cheese,
softened

¼ cup sugar

1 egg

1 cup chocolate chips

½ cup chopped walnuts

1 16-ounce container cream cheese
frosting

1. Preheat oven to 350°F. Grease muffin tin or line with paper cups. Set aside.

2. Prepare cake batter according to package instructions. Fill muffin cups ½ full.

3. In a separate bowl, mix cream cheese, sugar, and egg until fluffy. Fold in chocolate chips and walnuts. Mix evenly.

4. Drop a heaping teaspoon of the cream cheese mixture into the center of the batter in each muffin cup. Bake muffins for 15 to 20 minutes. Remove from oven and cool completely.

5. Frost cooled muffins with cream cheese frosting.

Easy as Apple Pie Muffins

These warm delicious muffins are surprisingly easy to make. With just five ingredients, they're easy to whip up almost any day.

INGREDIENTS | MAKES 24 MUFFINS

2 large eggs
1 cup sour cream
1 21-ounce can apple pie filling
1 18.25-ounce box spice cake mix
Optional: Freshly ground cinnamon

1. Preheat oven to 350°F. Grease muffin tin or line with paper baking cups. Set aside.

2. Mix eggs, sour cream, and apple pie filling in a bowl with a wooden spoon. Gently fold in cake mix. Do not overmix. Fill muffin cups ½ full.

3. Sprinkle with cinnamon if desired. Bake for 25 minutes. Cool in pan. When cool enough to touch, remove from pan. Serve slightly warm with real butter.

Baking Apples

Fuji, Gala, Braeburn, Jonathan, McIntosh, Newton Pippin, Rome Beauty, and Winesap apples are generally considered best for baking, but you can try any apple you like. If you find one you like, make a note of when they're in season—that way you can make this cake a yearly tradition.

Lemon Poppyseed Muffins

Lemon Poppyseed Muffins are a coffeehouse favorite that are easy to make at home. Adding a few extra ingredients to lemon cake mix makes for some sweet sailing.

INGREDIENTS | MAKES 24 MUFFINS

1 18.25-ounce box lemon cake mix
2 tablespoons flour
3 eggs
⅔ cup milk
⅓ cup vegetable oil
1 teaspoon baking powder
2 tablespoons poppyseeds

1. Preheat oven to 375°F. Grease muffin tin or line with paper cups. Set aside.

2. Mix all ingredients in a large mixing bowl using an electric mixer set to medium speed. Fill muffin cups ½ full. Bake for 20 minutes or until tops are golden.

3. Serve warm.

Warm Spice Muffins

The comforting blend of spices in the batter are heightened with an extra sprinkle of cinnamon. What could be better on a cozy morning?

INGREDIENTS | MAKES 24 MUFFINS

1 18.25-ounce box spice cake mix
2 tablespoons flour
3 eggs
⅔ cup milk
⅓ cup vegetable oil
1 teaspoon baking powder
2 tablespoons each cinnamon and sugar
   to garnish

1. Preheat oven to 375°F. Grease muffin tin or line with paper cups and set aside.

2. Mix all ingredients except cinnamon and sugar in a large mixing bowl using an electric mixer set to medium speed. Fill muffin cups ½ full.

3. Sprinkle cinnamon and sugar on top of each muffin. Bake for 20 minutes or until tops are golden. Serve warm.

Raspberry Muffins

Love sweets in the morning? This recipe creates a treat that's really a cake masquerading as a muffin. Sweet berries and aromatic vanilla make for a lovely start to the morning.

INGREDIENTS | MAKES 24 MUFFINS

1 18.25-ounce box French vanilla cake mix
2 tablespoons flour
3 eggs
⅔ cup milk
⅓ cup vegetable oil
1 teaspoon baking powder
1 cup raspberries

1. Preheat oven to 375°F. Grease muffin tin or line with paper baking cups. Set aside.

2. Mix all ingredients in a large mixing bowl using an electric mixer set to medium speed. Fill muffin cups ½ full. Bake for 20 minutes or until tops are golden.

3. Serve warm.

Toasty Blueberry Loaf

This really is the best thing since sliced bread! It's great for a group or for traveling. Simply bake, wrap in foil, and you're good to go!

INGREDIENTS | SERVES 12

2 large eggs
1 cup sour cream
1 21-ounce can blueberry pie filling
1 18.25-ounce box white cake mix
Sugar for dusting

1. Preheat oven to 350°F. Grease loaf pans and set aside.

2. Mix eggs, sour cream, and blueberry pie filling in a bowl with a wooden spoon. Gently fold in cake mix. Do not overmix. Fill loaf pans halfway with batter.

3. Sprinkle with sugar to taste. Bake for 25 minutes. Cool in pan. When cool enough to touch, remove from pan. Slice and serve.

Blueberry Muffin French Toast

This day-after recipe is the perfect way to use up any leftover slices of blueberry loaf.
In fact, a night on the counter gives the flavors time to blend.

INGREDIENTS | SERVES 6

1 Toasty Blueberry Loaf (page 88), baked
2 eggs, beaten
1 cup corn flakes, crumbled
Butter for frying
Blueberry syrup
Whipped topping (optional)

1. Dredge slices of Toasty Blueberry Loaf through egg. Roll in corn flakes to coat. Fry slices in butter until golden and transfer to plate immediately.

2. Serve warm with blueberry syrup and a dollop of whipped topping.

Toasting Tips

If you're working with thicker slices of muffin loaf, allow the slices to soak for 15 seconds in the egg batter. The egg will have just a little more time to incorporate into the muffin so you'll have a slightly firmer consistency when it's cooked.

Super-Easy Fruity Muffins

This recipe is unbelievably simple. The secret to success is choosing
the right cake mix flavor and fruit combination. Be creative!

INGREDIENTS | MAKES 24 MUFFINS

1 12-ounce can unsweetened fruit, drained
1 18.25-ounce box cake mix

1. Preheat oven to 350°F. Grease muffin tin or line with paper baking cups. Set aside.

2. Gently stir fruit into mix to form a thick, lumpy batter. Fill muffin cups ½ full. Bake for 30 minutes or until a toothpick comes out clean.

3. Serve warm with sour cream or butter.

Banana-Nut Muffins

Banana-nut has been a flavor favorite for generations. There's something about the combination of smooth fruit and crunchy nuts that keeps us coming back for more!

INGREDIENTS | MAKES 24 MUFFINS

1 18.25-ounce box butter pecan cake mix

1 3.9-ounce package instant banana pudding

4 eggs

2 bananas, mashed

½ cup vegetable oil

½ cup water

1 teaspoon banana extract

¾ teaspoon ground cinnamon

1 cup finely chopped walnuts

1. Preheat oven to 350°F. Grease muffin tin or line with paper baking cups. Set aside.

2. Mix all ingredients except nuts in a large bowl until smooth. Fold in nuts with a wooden spoon. Fill muffin cups or loaf pans ¾ full.

3. Bake for 20 minutes or until toothpick comes out clean. Serve warm with butter.

Ripe Bananas

Have ripe bananas before you're ready to bake? Simply peel them, cut them into chunks, wrap them in plastic wrap, and pop them in the freezer. This way, when baking day rolls around all you'll need to do is defrost them and toss them in the batter.

Healthier Brownie Muffins

*This recipe is a secret weapon for the health-minded baker.
It's a chocolaty way to sneak some fiber into your day.*

INGREDIENTS | MAKES 24 MUFFINS

3 cups bran cereal
2¼ cups water
1 package low-fat brownie mix
1½ teaspoons baking powder

Shopping for Bran Cereal

Every box in the cereal aisle touts some sort of health benefits. Many are fortified with vitamins, dehydrated fruits, or—less healthy—tiny marshmallows. Look for whole-grain cereals that are high in fiber. Make these a part of your daily diet and you could see a more stabilized blood sugar level as well as lower cholesterol.

1. Preheat oven to 350°F. Line muffin tin with paper baking cups.

2. In a small bowl, soak cereal in the water for 5 minutes. Then, in a separate and larger bowl, mix soaked cereal, brownie mix, and baking powder till a moist batter forms.

3. Fill up each cupcake cup to the brim. Bake for 25 minutes. Serve with butter.

Sweet Bran Muffins

Orange and vanilla give this basic bran muffin a little extra something sweet!
For those with a sweet tooth, it's a lovely start to the morning.

INGREDIENTS | MAKES 24 MUFFINS

2 cups 40% bran cereal
1¼ cups hot milk
2 tablespoons oil
1 egg
1 18.25-ounce box yellow cake mix
½ teaspoon vanilla extract
¼ teaspoon orange extract
2 tablespoons butter, melted

1. Preheat oven to 400°F. Generously butter muffin pan.

2. Mix cereal and hot milk in a large mixing bowl and let mixture rest for 10 minutes. Use an electric beater set to high speed to mix oil and egg and extracts into cereal and milk.

3. Use a wooden spoon to fold in cake mix. Mix gently until batter is wet. Do not overmix. It's okay if this batter is a little lumpy.

4. Cover the bowl with a tea towel and let batter rest for 20 minutes. Spoon batter into muffin pan. Bake for 25 minutes.

5. Remove from oven and brush with butter. Let cool before serving.

Sweet Rolls

These are the perfect rolls to serve with homemade jam and butter. In autumn, serve with apple butter for a side that celebrates the season. This also makes a great side for good old bacon and eggs.

INGREDIENTS | MAKES 24 ROLLS

1 18.25-ounce box white cake mix
2 0.25-ounce packages active dry yeast
5 cups all-purpose flour
2½ cups hot water
2 tablespoons butter, softened
Ground cinnamon
Granulated sugar
½ cup margarine
¼ cup firmly packed brown sugar
¼ cup light corn syrup
1 cup chopped nuts

1. Preheat oven to 375°F.

2. Combine cake mix, yeast, and flour in a large bowl. Mix in hot water. Set aside to rise until dough doubles in size. Cut dough in half.

3. Roll half of dough into a rectangle on a floured surface. Coat with softened butter, then sprinkle with cinnamon and granulated sugar to taste. Roll jellyroll style and cut into 2" slices. Place into a greased baking pan. Repeat with the rest of the dough.

4. Let cut rolls rise in the pan until they've doubled again. Meanwhile, mix margarine, brown sugar, corn syrup, and nuts. Pour nut and syrup mixture over rolls.

5. Bake for 25 minutes. Let cool.

Cake Doughnuts

Doughnuts are a treat, but homemade doughnuts are a slice of heaven. If you've never had a homemade doughnut, make sure you change that right away. With a recipe this easy there's no excuse not to!

INGREDIENTS | **MAKES 24 DOUGHNUTS**

1 tablespoon yeast

2 cups warm water

1 18.25-ounce box white cake mix

4 cups flour

2 cups vegetable oil for frying

Doughnut Glaze

Whisk ¼ cup whole milk and 1 teaspoon vanilla extract in a saucepan over low heat. Sift in 2 cups confectioners' sugar. Remove from heat and submerge pan in a bowl of warm water to keep glaze from hardening.

1. In a large bowl, mix yeast and warm water until yeast is dissolved. Add cake mix and flour. Mix with spoon to make a soft dough. Set aside for 1 hour so dough can rise.

2. With a floured pin, roll dough out onto a flat surface. Cut with a floured biscuit cutter. Remove to flat board or cookie sheet for 30–45 minutes to rise. Meanwhile, prepare glaze.

3. Fry doughnuts in 2 inches of vegetable oil or in mini-deep fryer. If using a skillet, fry doughnuts on each side and remove with a slotted spoon. If using a deep fryer, follow manufacturer's instructions.

4. Set fried doughnuts on a paper towel to drain and cool slightly. Glaze doughnuts before they cool completely. Serve warm.

Apple Delight Brunch Cake

*Baked apples are one of the homiest smells in the world. Fill your house—
and your stomach—with some of the sweetest comfort food around.*

INGREDIENTS | SERVES 12

1 18.25-ounce box yellow or butter cake
  mix
3 eggs
½ cup butter, softened
⅔ cup water
5 apples, pared, cored, and sliced
3 tablespoons sugar
4 teaspoons ground cinnamon
Confectioners' sugar as desired for
  garnish

Pared Down

Paring apples is easy when you know how
to do it. Consider buying an apple corer.
These handheld devices allow you to cut
the core from the apple before you slice
the flesh and then peel the slices. This may
seem like an extra step, but it'll save you
prep time.

1. Preheat oven to 375°F. Butter and flour a 10" tube pan.
   Set aside.

2. Mix cake mix, eggs, butter, and water in a large bowl.
   Beat with an electric mixer for 2 full minutes. Turn ⅔
   of the batter into the tube pan.

3. In a separate bowl combine apples, sugar, and
   cinnamon. Layer apple mixture on top of batter in
   pan. Pour remaining batter over apples.

4. Bake for 45 minutes or until toothpick comes out
   clean. Invert onto cooling rack without removing pan.
   After 30 minutes, lift pan off of cake. Cool completely.

5. Garnish with powdered sugar. Slice and serve.

Mandarin Orange Muffins

Keep these two ingredients on hand in case company stops by—
or you find a little extra time some morning.

INGREDIENTS | **SERVES 15**

1 18.25-ounce box white cake mix marked "just add water"

1 12-ounce can mandarin oranges

1. Preheat oven to 350°F. Grease muffin tin or line with paper baking cups. Set aside.

2. Combine cake mix and oranges in a large mixing bowl. Mix until incorporated; do not expect a smooth batter. Fill muffin cups ⅔ full.

3. Bake for 25 minutes.

Chocolate Waffles

Who would have thought waffles could get more decadent? This extra-sweet
treat is a delight for late-night gatherings or the morning after a sleepover.

INGREDIENTS | **SERVES 24**

1 18-ounce box chocolate cake mix, plus ingredients called for on box

Whipped topping

Fresh strawberries (optional)

1. Mix cake batter according to instructions on the box. Prepare waffle iron and bake waffles according to manufacturer's instructions.

2. Top warm waffles with whipped topping and strawberries.

Piña Colada Sunrise Muffins

*This tropical sweet gets your morning started right. Serve with a wedge of pineapple
or with a tray of fruit and cheese for a morning to remember.*

INGREDIENTS | **MAKES 24 MUFFINS**

1 18.25-ounce box yellow cake mix plus
 ingredients called for on box

1 teaspoon coconut extract

1 teaspoon rum extract

1 cup flaked coconut

½ to 1 cup chopped nuts

1 8-ounce can crushed pineapple, with
 juice

1. Preheat oven to temperature listed on cake mix box
   for cupcakes. Grease muffin tins or line with paper
   liners and set aside.

2. Mix cake batter according to package instructions.
   Add remaining ingredients. Beat with an electric
   mixer for exactly 1 minute on low speed.

3. Fill muffin cups ½ full with batter. Bake for amount of
   time listed on cake mix box for cupcakes. Garnish
   with a parasol. Serve with coffee and juice.

Tropical Angel Muffins

*This light, elegant citrus recipe is great on a summer day or with
a cup of hot coffee. Add a side of sweet yogurt.*

INGREDIENTS | MAKES 24 MUFFINS

1 16-ounce box fat-free angel food cake
mix

1 14-ounce can crushed pineapple with
juice

1 10-ounce can mandarin oranges, drained

Zest of 1 orange

Buy Organic

If possible, choose organic citrus fruits for
recipes that require zest. Some conventional citrus growers use waxes or pesticides that become concentrated in the
rinds. Organic options may mean many
fewer toxins and a fresher, cleaner taste.

1. Preheat oven to 350°F. Coat muffin pans with nonstick
spray. Set aside.

2. Combine cake mix, pineapple and juice, and
mandarin oranges. Mix well. Gently mix in orange
zest. Fill each muffin cup ½ full. Bake for 15 minutes.

3. Remove muffins from pan and cool on a rack.

CHAPTER 7

Cooking for a Crowd

Summary on the Patio Cake

This fruity sheet cake is perfect for a crowd. Get creative with toppings.
Peaches, strawberries, and blueberries make beautiful choices.

INGREDIENTS | SERVES 12

1 18.25-ounce box white cake mix plus ingredients called for on box

1 8-ounce box cream cheese

1 cup confectioners' sugar

1 teaspoon vanilla

1 15-ounce tub nondairy whipped topping

Seasonal fruit

1. Prepare and bake cake according to cake mix instructions. Let cake cool completely.

2. Mix cream cheese, confectioners' sugar, vanilla, and nondairy whipped topping completely. Spread on cooled cake. Arrange fresh fruit on top of topping.

3. Cover and keep cool until ready to serve.

Freshest Fruit

Fruit looks luscious when you slice it but can wilt and become brown shortly thereafter. To keep it looking plump, fresh, and juicy, consider tossing the cut fruit with a squeeze of fresh lemon juice or a dash of a fruit-preserving product. Either of these will help. However, the best way to ensure that fruit looks fantastic is to slice it as close to serving time as possible.

Jack Horner's Chocolate Cake

This moist and generous cake is intended for a truly big crowd. Extended family gatherings, church suppers, and neighborhood picnics are all great reasons to pull this recipe off the shelf.

INGREDIENTS | **SERVES 48**

1½ pints canned, pitted plums with liquid

2 18-ounce boxes chocolate cake mix

12 egg whites

¼ cup vegetable oil

1 cup chocolate chips

2 tablespoons confectioners' sugar

1. Preheat oven to 350°F. Coat a 26" × 18" × 1" sheet cake pan with cooking spray. Set aside.

2. Reserve plum liquid and purée pitted plums to get 2¼ cups. Add ¾ cup of the reserved plum liquid.

3. In a large bowl, using an electric mixer set to medium speed, mix both boxes of cake mix with plum mixture, egg whites, and oil. Fold in chocolate chips. Pour into cake pan.

4. Bake for 20 minutes. Allow cake to cool completely. Dust with confectioners' sugar.

Brownies for a Crowd

Make a large batch of moist, rich, double chocolate brownies for a hungry crowd with a sweet tooth. Just make sure you've got a glass of cold milk for everyone.

INGREDIENTS | **SERVES 24**

2 3.9-ounce packages chocolate instant pudding mix

4 cups whole milk

2 18.25-ounce packages chocolate cake mix without pudding

4 cups chocolate chips

Confectioners' sugar for garnish

1. Preheat oven to 350°F. Grease and flour two 10" × 15" jellyroll pans. Set aside.

2. In a large bowl, whisk together both boxes of pudding mix and milk. Slowly fold in both boxes of cake mix. Fold in chocolate chips. Bake 35 minutes. Dust with confectioners' sugar.

3. Allow to cool completely before cutting into squares.

Lemon Sheet Cake

To add even more of a lemony kick, add a couple teaspoons of lemon zest to the batter before you bake it. Freeze in an airtight container; remove and thaw cake for 5 minutes before serving.

INGREDIENTS | SERVES 30

1 18-ounce box lemon cake mix
4 eggs
1 can lemon pie filling
1 3-ounce package softened cream cheese
1 cup butter, softened
2 cups confectioners' sugar
1½ teaspoons vanilla

1. Preheat oven to 350°F. Coat a 15" × 10" × 1" baking pan with cooking spray. Set aside.

2. Mix the cake mix, eggs, and pie filling to form a smooth batter. Pour batter into pan. Bake for 20 minutes. Cool on a wire rack.

3. While cake cools, mix cream cheese, butter, and confectioners' sugar until smooth. Add vanilla and mix well. Frost the cooled cake. Refrigerate until ready to serve.

Fruity Cake for a Crowd

Milk, cheese, and fruit add a wholesome touch to this nourishing, sweet cake. Beautiful to see and easy to serve, it's a go-to recipe for large parties.

INGREDIENTS | SERVES 24

1 18.25-ounce box yellow cake mix plus ingredients called for on box
1½ cups milk
1 8-ounce box cream cheese
1 3.9-ounce box banana-flavored instant pudding
1 can crushed pineapple
6 bananas
Fresh strawberries
1 15-ounce tub whipped topping

1. Preheat oven to 350°F. Grease and flour cake pan. Set aside.

2. Prepare and bake cake according to package instructions. Allow cake to cool completely while you mix the topping.

3. Combine the milk and cream cheese and pudding. Layer on top of cooled cake.

4. Add a layer of pineapple, sliced bananas, and fresh strawberries. Top with whipped topping.

Get-Together Coffee Cake

*Make sure the first and last layers are batter layers. Sugar can
burn too quickly on an unprotected top layer.*

INGREDIENTS | SERVES 24

1 18.25-ounce box yellow cake mix

1 3.9-ounce box instant vanilla pudding
   mix

¾ cup oil

¾ cup water

4 eggs

1 teaspoon vanilla extract

1 teaspoon butter flavoring or extract

1½ cups chopped nuts

1¼ cups sugar

4 teaspoons cinnamon

1. Preheat oven to 350°F. Grease and flour a tube pan.
   Set aside.

2. Mix cake mix, pudding mix, oil, water, eggs, vanilla
   extract, and butter flavoring for 5 minutes using an
   electric mixer set on low speed.

3. In a separate bowl, combine nuts, sugar, and
   cinnamon.

4. Pour ½" layer of cake mix into the pan. Sprinkle a
   layer of nuts and spices on top. Repeat as often as
   needed in order to fill the pan, ending with batter.
   Bake for 50 minutes.

5. Allow cake to cool completely before serving.

Favorite Potluck Bars

Consider these for bake sales and other community events. These bars are sweet, tasty, and completely portable. They arrive at your event in style and fly off the plate.

INGREDIENTS | **MAKES 48 BARS**

1 18.25-ounce box white cake mix
2 large eggs
⅓ cup vegetable oil
1 can sweetened condensed milk
1 cup semisweet chocolate chips
Walnuts, peanuts, or coconut to taste
¼ cup butter

1. Preheat oven to 350°F. Butter a 13" × 9" × 2" baking dish. Set aside.

2. Combine cake mix, eggs, and oil in a bowl and beat until evenly mixed. Press ⅔ of the batter in the bottom of the pan.

3. Combine condensed milk, chocolate chips, and butter in a microwave-safe bowl. Microwave for 1 minute on high power. Remove and stir with a fork until smooth.

4. Pour chocolate mixture over crust. Layer nuts or coconut on top of chocolate layer. Dot with remaining cake batter.

5. Bake for 20 minutes or until lightly browned. Let cool in baking dish. Cut into squares and serve.

Easy Black Forest Cobbler

*When feeding a large crowd, it's a good idea to fall back on familiar
and well-loved flavors like chocolate and cherries.*

INGREDIENTS | SERVES 24

1 15-ounce can cherry pie filling
½ cup butter, softened
1 18.25-ounce box chocolate cake mix
Semisweet chocolate chips to taste
Vanilla ice cream or whipped topping

1. Preheat oven to 375°F.

2. Pour cherry pie filling into a greased 9" × 9" cake pan. Set aside.

3. Cut butter into chocolate cake mix until a crumbly mixture forms. Layer cake mixture on top of cherry pie filling. Dot with chocolate chips. Bake for 30 minutes.

4. Allow to cool slightly. Top with ice cream or whipped topping. Serve warm.

Peach Cobbler

*It's hard to find a simpler recipe that yields a more lovely dish. Prepared filling and boxed batter
mean most of the work has been done for you. All that's left is to bake and enjoy.*

INGREDIENTS | SERVES 12

1 15-ounce can peach pie filling
1 18-ounce box spice cake mix
½ cup butter, softened
Vanilla ice cream or whipped topping

1. Preheat oven to 375°F. Grease a 9" × 9" cake pan.

2. Pour peach pie filling into pan. Set aside.

3. Cut butter into spice cake mix until a crumbly mixture forms. Layer cake mixture on top of pie filling. Bake for 30 minutes.

4. Allow to cool slightly. Top with ice cream or whipped topping. Serve warm.

Cherry Tunnel Cake

Cherries and cream are a crowd-pleasing combination. Team with a dark cup of coffee for a sweet treat.

INGREDIENTS | **SERVES 12**

1 18.25-ounce box white cake mix plus ingredients called for on box

1 cup boiling water

1 3-ounce package cherry flavored gelatin

1 21-ounce can cherry pie filling

1 16-ounce tub nondairy whipped topping

1. Preheat oven to 350°F. Grease and flour 9" × 13" cake pan. Set aside.

2. Prepare and bake cake mix according to package instructions for a 9" × 13" cake. After baking, while cake is still warm, use a fork to poke holes in the cake from the top down.

3. Allow cake to cool. Meanwhile, mix water and gelatin. Pour mixture over cake so that it fills in the holes.

4. Seal the top of the cake with a generous layer of cherry pie filling. Frost the cake with whipped topping. Chill cake for at least 1 hour before serving.

Fuzzy Navel Cake

Allow two days for this cake. It's not complicated, but some of the ingredients need to sit overnight.

INGREDIENTS | SERVES 12

1 16-ounce can sliced cling peaches with liquid

½ cup peach schnapps

1 cup sugar

1 18.25-ounce package yellow cake mix

1 3.9-ounce package instant vanilla pudding

4 eggs

⅔ cup oil

1 cup chopped pecans

1⅓ cups confectioners' sugar

1. Drain peaches and reserve liquid. Chop peaches. Combine peaches, schnapps, and sugar. Let sit overnight, stirring occasionally.

2. The next day, preheat oven to 350°F. Grease and flour a 12-cup bundt pan. Set aside.

3. In large bowl, combine peach mixture, cake mix, pudding, eggs, and oil. Beat for 3 minutes using an electric mixer set to high speed. Gently stir in pecans by hand.

4. Pour batter into the bundt pan and bake for 55 minutes.

5. Remove from oven and let cool completely.

6. Combine ¼ cup reserved peach liquid with 1⅓ cups confectioners' sugar to make a glaze. Drizzle glaze over cake.

Amaretto Dream Cake

This richly flavored layer cake combines the richness of cream cheese, the fruity sweetness of apricots, and the unmistakable flavor of amaretto.

INGREDIENTS | SERVES 8

1 18.25-ounce box yellow cake mix

3 eggs

1 cup buttermilk

¼ cup plus 2 tablespoons amaretto, divided

¼ cup vegetable oil

1 15-ounce can apricot halves, drained

1 16-ounce box cream cheese

4 cups confectioners' sugar

1. Preheat oven to 350°F. Butter and flour two round 9" cake pans. Set aside.

2. Combine cake mix, eggs, buttermilk, ¼ cup amaretto, and oil. Beat for 4 minutes using an electric mixer set to low speed. Turn batter into cake pans.

3. Bake for 35 minutes. Allow cakes to cool completely.

4. When cakes are completely cool to the touch, lay cake layers on a clean, flat surface. Mark the middle of the cake layer with toothpicks. With toothpicks as your guide, slice horizontally, using a few slow even strokes of a serrated knife. Carefully remove top layer to a clean, flat surface. Repeat this process with the second layer to create four layers total.

5. Combine drained apricots and ½ cup plus two tablespoons amaretto in a blender and blend until completely smooth.

6. Center bottom layer of cake on platter. Smooth one third of the apricot mixture on top of the cake layer. Repeat for next two layers.

7. Beat cream cheese and remaining 3 tablespoons amaretto until cheese is soft. Add confectioners' sugar and beat until smooth. Frost cake with cream cheese mixture.

Citrus Crush Cake

This treat is perfect for summer parties and a sweet reminder of warmer days on a winter evening.

INGREDIENTS | SERVES 24

1 18.25-ounce box yellow cake mix

3 eggs

1 can mandarin oranges

1 can crushed pineapple with juice

1 12-ounce tub nondairy whipped topping

1 3.9-ounce package instant vanilla pudding

1. Preheat oven to 350°F. Grease and flour 9" × 13" pan. Set aside.

2. Combine cake mix, eggs, and mandarin oranges using an electric mixer set to medium speed for 3 minutes. Turn batter into pan. Bake for 30 minutes. Allow to cool completely.

3. Combine crushed pineapple with juice, dessert topping, and vanilla pudding mix; stir to mix well. Top cooled cake with this mixture. Refrigerate until ready to serve.

Shortcake Trifle

Gather with friends and go to pick your own strawberries. Bring them home and enjoy each other's company while putting together this simple—and simply delicious—dessert. Or try this trifle with fruit salad instead of strawberry filling.

INGREDIENTS | SERVES 25

2 18.25-ounce boxes angel food cake mix plus ingredients called for on boxes

2 16-ounce packages strawberry glaze

1 quart fresh strawberries, sliced

1 15-ounce tub nondairy whipped topping

1. Prepare and bake angel food cakes according to cake mix instructions. Cool cakes. Cut into cubes.

2. Combine sliced strawberries and glaze.

3. Place a layer of cake cubes in the bottom of a punch bowl. Top with a layer of strawberry mixture and then a layer of whipped topping. Repeat layers until bowl is full.

4. Top with a layer of whipped topping. Keep trifle cool until ready to serve.

Cheesecake for 24

Try this recipe with raspberry, blackberry, or blueberry pie filling. For a chocolaty twist, substitute chocolate cake mix for the white cake mix and chocolate whipped topping for the whipped topping. Garnish with chocolate syrup and chocolate shavings.

INGREDIENTS | SERVES 24

1 18.25-ounce box white cake mix plus ingredients called for on box

4 cups confectioners' sugar

2 8-ounce boxes cream cheese, room temperature

1 15-ounce tub nondairy whipped topping

2 16-ounce cans cherry pie filling

1. Preheat oven to 350°F. Grease and flour two 9" × 13" cake pans. Set aside.

2. Prepare batter according to cake mix instructions. Divide batter evenly between cake pans. Bake for 20 minutes. Remove cakes from oven and allow to cool.

3. Meanwhile, use an electric mixer to beat together confectioners' sugar and cream cheese until fluffy. Fold whipped topping into cream cheese mixture.

4. Spread cream cheese mixture on cakes. Top with pie filling. Refrigerate until ready to serve.

Pajama Party Pizza Cake

To really impress your guests, serve this in a clean pizza box. (Ask your local pizzeria nicely; they'll probably give you one.) Use a pizza cutter to cut this into wedges and serve.

INGREDIENTS | **SERVES 8**

1 9-ounce box Jiffy golden brown cake mix plus ingredients called for on box

1 3-ounce package strawberry gelatin

1½ cups hot water

1 firm banana, sliced to resemble pepperoni

1 cup sliced strawberries

1 cup blueberries

Whipped topping

1. Preheat oven to 350°F. Grease and butter a pizza pan. Be sure to use a pan with a raised lip or batter will run over the edge.

2. Prepare cake batter according to package directions. Pour into pan and bake for 10 minutes.

3. Mix gelatin with water and let thicken.

4. Remove cake from oven and let cool. Arrange fruit on cake as you would pizza toppings. Pour thickened gelatin over all and chill.

5. Top with whipped topping and serve.

Grown-Up Chocolate Trifle

*This dessert is best after being allowed to "set" for a day. The rich trifle
makes a lovely presentation and is so easy to make!*

INGREDIENTS | SERVES 8–10

1 18.25-ounce box devil's food cake mix
plus ingredients called for on box

2 3.9-ounce boxes instant chocolate
pudding plus ingredients called for on
boxes

2 15-ounce tubs whipped topping

Optional: ½ cup Kahlua

Maraschino cherries, strawberries, or
raspberries for garnish

Chocolate syrup for garnish

1. Prepare and bake cake according to cake mix instructions for a 9" x 13" cake. Allow cake to cool completely.

2. Prepare both boxes of pudding according to package instructions.

3. Cut cake into quarters. Crumble one of the quarters into a large bowl. Layer 2 cups pudding on top of crumbled cake. Crumble another cake quarter and top with half a tub of whipped topping. Repeat for remaining cake quarters.

4. Douse generously with Kahlua if desired. Top with a dollop of whipped topping and garnish with cherries, strawberries, or raspberries. Drizzle with chocolate syrup.

5. Refrigerate overnight. Keep chilled until ready to serve.

Lower-Cholesterol Apple Bake

Here's a healthier take on a baked dessert. Bake this treat ahead of time and warm it up before serving. Garnish with whipped cream or ice cream for a cool, creamy contrast.

INGREDIENTS | **SERVES 16**

1 18.25-ounce box yellow cake mix

½ cup low-cholesterol margarine, softened

¼ cup packed brown sugar

1 teaspoon ground cinnamon

2 large baking apples, cored, peeled, and thinly sliced

¼ cup cholesterol-free egg product (i.e., Egg Beaters)

1 cup low-fat sour cream

1. Preheat oven to 350°F. Grease baking pan.

2. Mix cake mix, margarine, brown sugar, and cinnamon until large crumbs form.

3. Set aside ⅔ cup of the crumb mixture. Press remaining mixture into the bottom of a rectangular baking pan. Arrange apples on top of this layer.

4. Combine egg product and sour cream and pour this mixture on top of the fruit. Top with reserved crumb mixture. Bake for 30 minutes or until topping browns slightly.

5. Cool before serving.

Kahlua Cake

Drizzle liquor on the grownups' cake and chocolate syrup on the kids'.
This elegant cake is lovely for parties and easy to transport.

INGREDIENTS | SERVES 8

1 18.25-ounce box devil's food cake mix

1 3.9-ounce package instant chocolate pudding

1 pint sour cream

⅔ cup vegetable oil

4 eggs

2 cups semisweet chocolate chips

1 15-ounce tub nondairy whipped topping

1. Preheat to 350°F. Butter a 12-cup bundt pan. Set aside.

2. Thoroughly mix all ingredients except chocolate chips and whipped topping in a large bowl. Fold in chocolate chips. Pour mixture into the pan. Bake for 1 hour.

3. Cover and let cool in pan overnight. The next morning, flip pan over, cover again, and let set one more day. When ready to serve, garnish with whipped topping and drizzle with Kahlua.

Family-Friendly Punch Bowl Trifle

Easy to bake, easy to make, and lovely to see, this dish is a variation on a favorite recipe that's as delightful for the kids as it is for the adults.

INGREDIENTS | SERVES 25

2 18.25-ounce boxes chocolate cake mix plus ingredients called for on boxes

2 12-ounce tubs chocolate whipped topping

1 20-ounce can cherry pie filling

1 15-ounce tub nondairy whipped topping

1. Prepare and bake cakes according to cake mix instructions. Cool cakes. Cut into cubes.

2. Place a layer of cake cubes in the bottom of a punch bowl. Add a layer of chocolate whipped topping. Add a layer of cherry pie filling. Repeat layers until bowl is full.

3. Top with plain whipped topping. Keep trifle cool until ready to serve.

CHAPTER 8

Cooking with Kids

Toy Oven Cake

While most adults can't imagine trying to bake a cake using a light bulb as a heat source, children have met this culinary challenge for years and years. Please note that small children should not cook unsupervised.

INGREDIENTS | SERVES 1 CHILD

3 tablespoons cake mix
1 tablespoon milk
Frosting

1. Preheat toy oven as instructed by manufacturer. Grease and flour toy pan. Set aside.

2. Combine cake mix and milk. Beat with a fork until batter is smooth. Bake for about 15 minutes or until a toothpick comes out clean.

3. Allow cake to cool before frosting.

Yummiest Play Dough Ever

Finally, you don't have to stop the kids from eating the play dough. This recipe is not only fun, it's edible.

INGREDIENTS | SERVES 10 CHILDREN

1 18.25-ounce box white cake mix
½ cup margarine, softened
3 tablespoons water
Food coloring

1. Mix cake mix and margarine in a large bowl. Add water bit by bit until dough reaches the desired consistency. Divide dough into batches and color each batch.

2. Store uneaten dough in plastic bags for future use.

Little Helping Hands

Allow kids to choose food coloring and mix it into the dough themselves. You might want to do the initial mixing yourself because food coloring stains. Keep this in mind and have the kids wear old clothes or smocks. Kids will get a kick out of kneading the dough until it is mixed completely.

Kisses from Kids Cupcakes

This is a fun collaboration. Kids love the responsibility of placing the candies—even if they do eat a few.

INGREDIENTS | SERVES 12

1 18.25-ounce box cake mix plus
  ingredients called for on box
12 chocolate kiss candies
Frosting

Teachable Moments

Even young children can learn some basics
of cooking. There's no better time to teach
them than when you're doing a fun project
together. They also love having a "job," so
try to pick a step for young children to
complete themselves when you're cooking.

1. Preheat oven according to cake mix instructions. Line a muffin tin with paper baking cups.

2. Prepare batter according to cake mix instructions for cupcakes. Fill baking cups with batter.

3. Allow kids to unwrap candies and place one candy in the middle of each cup of batter. It will sink on its own with a gentle tap.

4. Bake according to instructions on package. Allow cupcakes to cool completely before frosting.

Heart-Shaped Cupcakes

Want an easy way to show you care? These cupcakes are perfect for showers, parties, and Valentine's Day. If you don't have marbles, use aluminum foil rolled into marble-sized balls.

INGREDIENTS | SERVES 24

Glass marbles
1 18.25-ounce box cake mix plus
  ingredients called for on box
1 16-ounce tub red or pink frosting

1. Preheat oven according to cake mix instructions. Line a muffin tin with paper baking cups. Place one marble on the outside of each cupcake cup so that a dent is formed, creating a heart-shaped baking cup.

2. Mix batter according to instructions. Pour batter into baking cups. As cakes rise, they will form heart-shaped tops.

3. Allow cakes to cool completely before frosting.

Cake of Many Colors

This is one of the most delicious art projects you can take on with children. Try not to go in with a preconceived notion of the looks of your product. You'll have more fun if you're in it for pure enjoyment.

INGREDIENTS | SERVES 8

1 18.25-ounce box white cake mix plus
  ingredients called for on box
Food coloring
Frosting

1. Preheat oven according to cake mix instructions. Grease cake pan and set aside.

2. Prepare batter according to instructions. Spoon batter evenly into four bowls and add a few drops of food coloring to each bowl.

3. Allow children to mix coloring into the batter and then spoon batter into cake pan in any color order they like. Bake according to instructions.

4. Allow cake to cool completely before frosting.

Fortune Cupcakes

More than a clever and sweet dessert, this is a fun game for slightly older kids. Whether they help in the baking, the eating, or both, there's plenty to entertain in this project.

INGREDIENTS | SERVES 24

1 18.25-ounce box cake mix plus
  ingredients called for on box
24 large gumdrops
2 16-ounce tubs prepared frosting

1. Preheat oven according to package instructions. Line a muffin tin with paper baking cups.

2. Prepare cake mix according to instructions. Place 1 gumdrop in each cupcake. Bake cupcakes. Allow cakes to cool completely before frosting.

3. Draw up a chart with different fortunes for each color of gumdrop. Eat the cupcakes to discover your fortune!

No Bake Candy Treats

These treats are easy to make and don't require an oven. Be warned:
You might eat a few while you make them.

INGREDIENTS	SERVES 24
1 18.25-ounce box cake mix	
1 16-ounce tub prepared frosting	

Combine cake mix and frosting in a large mixing bowl. Mix thoroughly. Pinch off small amounts and roll into balls. Keep cool until ready to snack.

No-Bake Snow People

For a wintry twist, use white cake mix and sour cream frosting to make the No Bake Candy Treats. Make snowmen out of the balls of dough and use sprinkles and other decorations to make faces. This project has very few steps but has fun sensory components. Talk your children through the steps and let them create their own snow people.

Easy Protein Cookies

Tofu is a great source of protein, and this is an easy way to sneak a little into the kids' diet.
These cookies are so easy to make that they'll quickly become a go-to favorite.

INGREDIENTS	SERVES 24
1 18.25-ounce box cake mix	
½ cup silken tofu	
¼ cup olive oil	
1 egg	

1. Preheat oven to 350°F.

2. Mix all ingredients well in a large mixing bowl. Drop by spoonfuls onto a nonstick cookie sheet. Bake for 20 minutes.

3. Allow to cool and remove to wire rack.

Campfire Cobbler

This easy recipe requires only two ingredients plus a Dutch oven and a campfire. It's a memory maker, that's for sure.

INGREDIENTS | SERVES 8

1 15-ounce can cherry or peach pie filling
1 18.25-ounce box white cake mix

Historical Baking

Bakers of yore did not bake with cake mix or canned pie filling, but they did bake in the embers of a fire. Talk to your kids about what it would be like to cook this way every day. Ask them to imagine how life might be different. Let your imagination wander— that's what campfires are for.

1. Pour pie filling into the bottom of a Dutch oven. Pour dry cake mix over pie filling. Cover Dutch oven and place in the coals of a fire.

2. Place some hot coals on the lid of the Dutch oven. Cook for 15 minutes.

Orange Campfire Cakes

The rounded shape you can achieve here is amazing. The oranges lend a delicate flavor to the cake.

INGREDIENTS | SERVES 12

1 (18.25-ounce) box white cake mix plus ingredients called for on box
12 oranges
2 16-ounce tubs sour cream frosting

1. Prepare cake batter according to instructions. Cut the tops off the oranges and hollow out the insides.

2. Fill each orange ¾ full with cake batter and surround the orange completely with tin foil.

3. Place foil-wrapped oranges in the hot part of the fire and wait for about 20 minutes, turning once.

4. Remove from fire and allow to cool. Frost if desired.

Microwave Cake

This recipe is so quick and easy that older kids can make it for themselves as a warm, nourishing after-school snack. It doesn't need icing, but it is great with ice cream.

INGREDIENTS | SERVES 8

1 18.25-ounce box cake mix

1 15-ounce can pie filling

3 eggs

Baking in a Microwave

While microwaves have become a staple in American kitchens, they are still far from the most reliable friend when it comes to baking. Intensity and heat vary, as will the time it takes to bake this cake. This recipe may take a couple of attempts to perfect, but once you get it, you'll love it.

1. Grease a microwave-safe dish. Mix all ingredients together in a large mixing bowl, taking care to combine completely. Pour batter into dish and shake until level.

2. Cook cake in the microwave for 10–12 minutes on high. Remove cake from microwave and allow to set for 3 minutes.

Cinnamon Toast Cake

This treat is lovely with coffee. When older kids decide to bring the folks breakfast in bed, this is an easy, wholesome option.

INGREDIENTS | SERVES 6

1 18.25-ounce box white cake mix plus ingredients called for on box

Cinnamon-sugar mixture

¼ cup butter

Breakfast in Bed

There's something kids like about serving the folks breakfast in bed now and then. If your kids are old enough and have the kitchen skills to safely pull this off, plant the idea in their heads. With any luck you'll get a great breakfast in bed and some fun family memories out of the deal.

1. Grease a microwavable dish. Mix batter according to cake mix instructions. Pour into dish. Sprinkle liberally with cinnamon-sugar mixture.

2. Microwave on high for 10 minutes. Remove cake from microwave. Dot warm cake with butter and sprinkle again with cinnamon-sugar mixture.

3. Let cake stand 3 minutes before serving.

Mardi Gras Cakes

Traditional king cakes baked in New Orleans have a little plastic baby doll hidden inside. Whoever finds the baby gets good luck. We've avoided choking hazards here by substituting a gumdrop for a plastic toy.

INGREDIENTS | SERVES 24

1 18.25-ounce box cake mix plus ingredients called for on box

1 16-ounce tub prepared frosting

Food coloring

Sprinkles and other decorations

1 gumdrop

1. Preheat oven according to cake mix instructions. Line a muffin tin with paper baking cups.

2. Prepare batter according to instructions for cupcakes. Pour into muffin cups. Allow your child to hide a candy in one of the cups of batter.

3. Bake according to instructions. Allow cupcakes to cool completely.

4. Separate the tub of frosting into smaller batches and color them with food coloring. Allow your child to stir the color into the frosting. Frost and decorate cupcakes.

5. Before serving, explain that the person who finds the candy in his or her cupcake can look forward to a year of good luck.

Magic Potion Cookies

Let the kids figure out what to add in. Let them try combinations and measure them out themselves. Nothing's more fun than a "magic potion" cooked up by mad scientists. Who knows? You might invent a favorite cookie.

INGREDIENTS | SERVES 24

1 18.25-ounce box yellow cake mix

3 eggs

⅓ cup oil

½ teaspoon vanilla

1 cup oatmeal

3 cups add-ins: candies, chocolate morsels, coconut, nuts, trail mix, or other favorites

1. Preheat oven to 350°F.

2. Mix cake mix, eggs, oil, vanilla, and oatmeal together in a large mixing bowl. Let children choose, measure, and add their own combination of add-ins.

3. Drop cookies by spoonfuls onto an ungreased cookie sheet. Bake for 9 minutes. Remove from oven and cool on a wire rack.

Imaginative Baking

Kids love to mix foods. While they might scream when the macaroni touches the green beans, they'll sometimes jump at the chance to brew concoctions. Let them get imaginative with the add-ins. They'll love the sense of involvement and the cookies they produce!

Berry Snacky Pizza

The surprisingly lovely flavors of sweet, fruity raspberry filling and sharp Cheddar cheese are inspiring.

INGREDIENTS | SERVES 6

1 18.25-ounce box white cake mix
1 cup quick-cooking oats
½ cup grated Colby or Cheddar cheese
½ cup butter, softened
1 egg
1 21-ounce can raspberry pie filling

1. Preheat oven to 350°F. Grease a round, solid-bottomed pizza pan.

2. In a large mixing bowl, combine cake mix, oats, grated cheese, and ½ cup butter.

3. Mix thoroughly using an electric mixer set to low speed until a crumbly mixture forms. Remove 1 cup of mixture and place in a separate, smaller bowl.

4. Add egg to the remaining mixture and mix well. Press into the pizza pan. Bake for 10 minutes.

5. Remove baked crust from oven and layer on pie filling like pizza sauce. Top with reserved crumb mixture and additional grated cheese if desired.

6. Bake an additional 15 minutes. Allow pizza to cool somewhat before serving.

Peanut Butter Cake

Play to favorite—and familiar—flavors for the young, picky eaters in your life. This nutty recipe is a winner with the small fry.

INGREDIENTS | SERVES 8

1 18.25-ounce box yellow cake mix

3 eggs, beaten

1⅓ cups water

½ cup crunchy peanut butter

Peanut Butter Icing (page 128)

1. Preheat oven to 350°F. Butter and flour a 9" × 13" cake pan.

2. In a large mixing bowl, combine cake mix, eggs, water, and peanut butter. Using an electric mixer set to medium speed, beat the mixture for 3 full minutes.

3. Turn batter into pan and bake for 35 minutes. Allow cake to cool completely before frosting.

Add Layers

To make your PB cake an extra special PBJ cake, invert it onto a serving platter. Mark the center with toothpicks all the way around. Slice the cake in half horizontally and fill with a generous layer of your favorite jelly. Try this on cupcakes as well.

Peanut Butter Icing

Slightly reminiscent of the filling of a Buckeye or peanut butter cup,
this icing is so easy the kids can make it themselves.

INGREDIENTS | **SERVES 8**

½ cup crunchy peanut butter
¼ cup butter, softened
6 tablespoons heavy cream
1 pound confectioners' sugar
Dash salt
1½ teaspoons vanilla

Use an electric mixer to cream peanut butter and butter. Slowly incorporate cream, sugar, salt, and vanilla. Use this mixture to frost cooled cake.

Four-Ingredient Apple Bake

If your kids are old enough to handle the oven, they can do this with minor supervision. If they're not
quite ready to touch the oven, you can do that part for them—but they can set the timer.

INGREDIENTS | **SERVES 12**

1 18.25-ounce box spice cake mix
3 eggs
1 15-ounce can apple pie filling
1 16-ounce tub nondairy whipped topping

1. Preheat oven to 350°F.

2. Mix together cake mix, eggs, and apple pie filling. Pour into a 9" × 13" pan. Bake for 45 minutes. Remove from oven and allow to cool until just warm. Top with whipped topping.

Choco-Cherry Cake

Similar to the apple bake, this simple recipe is an easy and rewarding project for brand new cooks.

INGREDIENTS | SERVES 12

1 18.25-ounce box chocolate cake mix
3 eggs
1 15-ounce can cherry pie filling
Vanilla ice cream
Chocolate syrup

1. Preheat oven to 350°F.

2. Combine cake mix, eggs, and pie filling in a large mixing bowl. Pour batter into a 9" × 13" baking dish. Bake for 45 minutes. Serve warm with a scoop of ice cream and a drizzle of syrup.

Slow Cooker Cobbler

A slow cooker is a great place for older kids to try cooking on their own. This easy and delicious dessert requires no lifting in and out of the oven. Adults will still want to supervise, but the kids can probably handle this all on their own.

INGREDIENTS | SERVES 8

1 16-ounce can cherry pie filling
1⅓ cups chocolate cake mix
1 egg
3 tablespoons evaporated milk
Cocoa powder for dusting

1. Grease the inside of the slow cooker or Crock Pot with butter.

2. Pour pie filling into slow cooker and cook on high for 30 minutes. Combine remaining ingredients in a small mixing bowl. Spoon mixture on top of warm pie filling. Cover and cook for 2½ hours. Dust each serving lightly with cocoa powder.

Mud Pie Cupcakes

Decorations hold up better if the icing has a few minutes to set. To make sure gummy worms—and other decorations—stay in place, let icing rest for 10 minutes before serving.

INGREDIENTS | SERVES 24

1 18.25-ounce box chocolate cake mix plus ingredients called for on box

1 16-ounce tub chocolate frosting

2 cups crumbled chocolate sandwich cookies

Chocolate syrup for garnish

1 8-ounce package gummy worms

1. Prepare and bake cupcakes according to cake mix instructions. Allow cupcakes to cool completely before frosting. Top frosting with cookie crumbles and drizzle with chocolate syrup.

2. Halve gummy worms. Place each cut edge in frosting to create the illusion of a worm slithering in mud.

Ice Cream Sandwiches with Sprinkles

Ice cream sandwiches are a summer favorite for kids of all ages. What could be better than baking up a batch of your very own? Wrap finished sandwiches in foil and store in the freezer where they'll be ready for playdates and after-school snacks.

INGREDIENTS | **MAKES 24 SANDWICHES**

⅔ cup butter

2 eggs

1 18.25-ounce box devil's food cake

1 tub ice cream

Sprinkles or jimmies to taste

1. Preheat oven to 350°F.

2. Combine butter and egg. Stir in cake mix. Blend together well. Drop by spoonfuls onto a greased cookie sheet. Bake cookies for 10–12 minutes.

3. Remove cookies to cooling rack. When cookies are cool, invite kids to sandwich 2 tablespoons of ice cream between two cookies. Roll cookies through sprinkles or jimmies so they stick to the ice cream. Wrap in foil and freeze.

CHAPTER 9

Cake Mix Cookies

Blank Canvas Cookie Recipe

This is a very basic cookie recipe that's perfect if you're just itching to experiment. Add baking chips or dried fruit to your choice of cake mix for a flavor combination that's yours and yours alone.

INGREDIENTS | 4 DOZEN COOKIES

1 18.25-ounce box cake mix (any flavor)
½ cup butter, softened
1 egg

1. Preheat oven to 350°F.

2. Combine cake mix, softened butter, egg, and any add-ins that strike your fancy. Mix using an electric mixer set to low speed.

3. Drop batter by spoonfuls onto ungreased cookie sheets, leaving two inches between cookies. Bake for 12 minutes or until golden.

4. Let cookies cool on the pan for 3 minutes. Gently remove to a serving plate.

German Chocolate Cake Cookies

This lighter-tasting chocolate cookie provides that little taste of chocolate you're looking for without the heavy sugar or high caffeine.

INGREDIENTS | 4 DOZEN COOKIES

1 18.25-ounce box German chocolate cake mix
1 cup semisweet chocolate chips
1 cup oatmeal
½ cup vegetable oil
2 eggs, slightly beaten
½ cup raisins
1 teaspoon vanilla

1. Preheat oven to 350°F.

2. Combine all ingredients. Mix well using electric mixer set to low speed. If floury crumbs develop, add a dribble of water.

3. Drop dough by spoonfuls onto an ungreased cookie sheet. Bake for 10 minutes. Cool completely before lifting cookies off sheet and onto a serving dish.

Oatmeal and Chocolate Chip Cookies

Oatmeal is a great source of vitamins, minerals, and fiber. It is also reputed to be a natural antidepressant. These cookies are a great way to sneak some oatmeal into your diet.

INGREDIENTS | **MAKES 24 COOKIES**

1 18-ounce box yellow cake mix
⅔ cup rolled oats
½ cup margarine
1 egg
½ cup chocolate chips

1. Preheat oven to 375ºF.

2. Combine cake mix, oats, margarine, and egg in a bowl and mix well. Fold in chocolate chips. Drop by spoonfuls onto an ungreased cookie sheet.

3. Bake for 10 minutes, or until lightly golden. Remove warm cookies from sheet and allow to cool on a wire rack.

Peanut Butter Cup Cookies

Peanut butter and chocolate complement each other as few other foods do. Enjoy this decadent treat with a glass of cold chocolate milk.

INGREDIENTS | **MAKES 24 COOKIES**

1 18.25-ounce box chocolate cake mix
½ cup butter, softened
2 eggs
½ cup semisweet chocolate morsels
½ cup peanut butter morsels

1. Preheat oven to 350ºF.

2. Mix cake mix, butter, and eggs together in a bowl to form a smooth batter. Fold in chocolate and peanut butter morsels. Drop by spoonfuls onto an ungreased cookie sheet.

3. Bake for 9 minutes. Remove from oven and allow cookies to set for 5 minutes before removing them to a wire rack. Allow cookies to cool completely.

Double-Devil Chocolate Crunch Cookies

The devil himself would find this recipe heavenly. The rich chocolate taste and satisfying coconut are a winning combination. Just be sure to avoid cake mixes with pudding for this recipe.

INGREDIENTS | MAKES 60 COOKIES

1 18.25-ounce box devil's food cake mix
½ cup vegetable oil
2 eggs, slightly beaten
½ cup chopped pecans
5 regular milk chocolate bars, divided into squares
½ cup sweetened flaked coconut

1. Preheat oven to 350°F.

2. Combine devil's food cake mix, vegetable oil, and eggs in a bowl and mix completely. Gently fold pecans into batter.

3. Drop batter by spoonfuls onto ungreased cookie sheets. Bake for 10 minutes. Remove when cookies are set but still a bit soft in the center.

4. Place one square of milk chocolate on each cookie. When it melts, spread to create a chocolate coating on the cookie's top.

5. Transfer cookies immediately to a wire rack and allow them to cool completely.

Chocolate Biscotti

This is an elegant treat with a good cup of coffee and friendly conversation.
You can make them far in advance; biscotti keep for weeks.

INGREDIENTS | MAKES 36 BISCOTTI

1 18-ounce box chocolate cake mix

1 cup all-purpose flour

½ cup melted butter

¼ cup chocolate syrup

2 eggs

1 teaspoon vanilla extract

1 12-ounce package miniature semisweet
chocolate chips

1. Preheat oven to 350°F.

2. Mix dry cake mix, flour, butter, chocolate syrup, eggs, and vanilla well in a large bowl. Fold in chocolate chips.

3. Divide the batter in half. Shape each half into a 12" × 2" log. Place both halves on an ungreased baking sheet. Bake for 30 minutes.

4. Remove from oven and let cool for 15 minutes. Transfer logs to a cutting board and carefully cut into ½" slices. Cutting on the diagonal is easiest.

5. Return slices to the baking sheet and bake for another 15 minutes. Remove from oven and cool biscotti on wire racks.

Coconut Kisses

Rich, sweet coconut and irresistible dark chocolate meld together beautifully in this luscious, decadent cookie.

INGREDIENTS | MAKES 24 COOKIES

1 18-ounce box white cake mix
½ cup vegetable oil
2 eggs, slightly beaten
1 cup dark chocolate chips
1 cup shredded sweetened coconut

1. Preheat oven to 350°F. Lightly grease a cookie sheet. Set aside.

2. Mix cake mix, vegetable oil, and eggs in a bowl to form a smooth batter. Fold in chocolate chips. Fold in coconut.

3. Use a tablespoon to drop balls of cookie dough onto the cookie sheet. Bake for 10 minutes or until golden.

4. Remove cookies from oven and allow to cool on a wire rack.

Butter-Pecan Cookies

These are a quick fix when you want a rich, buttery treat. Serve with pralines, caramel, and/or creamy vanilla ice cream for an interesting take on the ice cream sundae.

INGREDIENTS | MAKES 24 COOKIES

1 18.25-ounce box butter pecan cake mix
2 eggs, slightly beaten
½ cup vegetable oil
2 tablespoons water

1. Preheat oven to 350°F.

2. Combine ingredients and mix to form an even batter. Drop by spoonfuls onto an ungreased cookie sheet. Bake for 15 minutes or until golden and set.

3. Let cool on cookie sheet for 5 minutes. Remove to wire rack to cool completely.

Peanut Butter Cookies

This lunchbox classic is a favorite with the whole family, and this recipe is a cinch to whip up.

INGREDIENTS | **MAKES 24 COOKIES**

1 18-ounce box yellow cake mix
1 cup peanut butter
½ cup vegetable oil
2 tablespoons water
2 large eggs

1. Preheat oven to 350°F.

2. Combine all ingredients and mix thoroughly. Use a teaspoon to drop balls of cookie dough onto an ungreased cookie sheet.

3. Laying the tines of a fork across the top of each cookie, press down to create a crisscross pattern. Bake for 12 minutes. Allow cookies to cool for 2 minutes on the warm cookie sheet.

4. Remove cookies to a wire rack and let cool completely.

Peanut Butter Kisses

These wholesome cookies are so easy to bake you can have them quickly at the ready for any occasion.

INGREDIENTS | **MAKES 24 COOKIES**

1 18.25-ounce box yellow cake mix
2 eggs
½ cup vegetable oil
1 cup crunchy peanut butter
2 teaspoons water

1. Preheat oven to 350°F.

2. Combine all ingredients in a large mixing bowl. Use an electric mixer to blend completely.

3. Drop dough by spoonfuls onto nonstick cookie sheet, leaving 2 inches between cookies. Laying the tines of a fork across the top of each cookie, press down to create a crisscross pattern.

4. Bake cookies for 12 minutes. Remove cookies to a wire rack to cool completely.

Whipped Cream Brownie Bakers

Who can resist the sweetness of whipped topping? This cookie pairs whipped topping and rich chocolate for a taste that's sure to satisfy.

INGREDIENTS | MAKES 48 COOKIES

1 18-ounce box chocolate cake mix
1 tablespoon cocoa powder
1 egg
1 cup pecans, chopped
¼ cup confectioners' sugar
4 ounces whipped topping

1. Preheat oven to 350°F.

2. Combine cake mix, cocoa powder, and egg and mix well. Gently fold pecans into dough.

3. Sift confectioners' sugar into a separate bowl. Coat your hands with confectioners' sugar, then shape dough into small balls. Coat cookie balls with confectioners' sugar.

4. Place onto cookie sheet, leaving 2 inches between cookies. Bake 12 minutes or until set. Remove from oven and transfer to wire rack to cool. Top with whipped topping.

Double Chocolate Chip Cookies

Chocolate chip cookies are delicious, so make someone's day with a dark, decadent delight.

INGREDIENTS | MAKES 36 COOKIES

1 18-ounce box devil's food cake mix with pudding
½ cup water
2 eggs
1 cup semisweet chocolate morsels

1. Preheat oven to 375°F. Grease cookie sheet. Set aside.

2. Mix all ingredients in a bowl using electric mixer on low speed.

3. When batter is completely smooth, drop by spoonfuls onto the cookie sheet, leaving 2 inches between cookies. Bake for 9 minutes.

4. Remove from oven and allow cookies to cool for 1 minute before removing them to a wire rack to cool completely.

Harvest Cookies

This autumnal treat is lovely with a cup of hot cider. Cranberry raisins give these cookies a zippy, tangy taste that's a perfect complement to a glass of cold milk.

INGREDIENTS | MAKES 60 COOKIES

1 18-ounce box spice cake mix
1 cup cranberry raisins
½ cup vegetable oil
½ cup applesauce
1 egg

1. Preheat oven to 350ºF.

2. Combine all ingredients in a large bowl. Mix for 1 minute with an electric mixer set to medium speed.

3. Drop batter by spoonful onto an ungreased cookie sheet, leaving 2 inches between cookies. Bake for 12 minutes.

4. Let cool on cookie sheet before removing to a serving dish.

Lemon-Lover's Cookies

There's nothing so refreshing and elegant as a lemon cookie. These cookies are equally good as a summer treat or a winter refreshment.

INGREDIENTS | MAKES 36 BARS

1 18-ounce box lemon cake mix
1 egg, slightly beaten
1 cup confectioners' sugar
1 8-ounce tub whipped topping
1 tablespoon lemon juice
1 cup confectioners' sugar
Lemon zest to taste

1. Preheat oven to 350ºF. Lightly grease a cookie sheet and set aside.

2. Gently mix all ingredients except lemon zest. Drop by teaspoon into confectioners' sugar and roll to coat. Place on a cookie sheet.

3. Bake for 10 minutes, watching carefully to make sure cookies do not overbake. Remove from oven. Sprinkle with lemon zest. Let cool on cookie sheet.

Sandwich Cookies

Remember the sandwich cookies that were served during snack-time at school? The home-baked version is even better!

INGREDIENTS | MAKES 12 COOKIES

1 18.25-ounce box devil's food cake mix

2 eggs

2 tablespoons water

2 tablespoons oil

½ cup cocoa powder

1 0.25-ounce envelope unflavored gelatin

¼ cup cold water

1 cup shortening

1 teaspoon vanilla

1 pound plus 1 cup confectioners' sugar

1. Preheat oven to 400°F. Grease a cookie sheet.

2. Combine cake mix, eggs, water, oil, and cocoa powder. Mix well using electric mixer on medium speed.

3. Butter your hands, form dough into balls, and place on the cookie sheet. Flatten each ball with the palm of your hand or a fork. Bake for 9 minutes.

4. Remove cookies to a paper towel. Flatten each cookie with the bottom of a clean mug. Let cool for 20 minutes.

5. In a smaller, microwave-safe bowl, mix gelatin powder and cold water. Heat in microwave until gelatin is transparent. Set gelatin mixture aside to cool completely.

6. Meanwhile, in a separate bowl beat the shortening until fluffy. Gently fold in vanilla and confectioners' sugar. Mix cooled gelatin into shortening mixture.

7. Sandwich the filling between two cookies, rounded sides facing out. Serve with milk for dunking.

Lemon Squares

Colorful and flavorful with a creamy melt-in-your-mouth texture, this quick-bake take on a time-tested Southern favorite is sure to please.

INGREDIENTS | **MAKES 24 SQUARES**

1 18-ounce box lemon cake mix
4 eggs, divided use
¾ cup melted butter, divided use
¾ cup buttermilk
⅓ cup freshly squeezed lemon juice
⅓ cup sugar
1 tablespoon grated lemon zest
3 tablespoons confectioners' sugar
Paper-thin lemon slices to garnish

1. Preheat oven to 350°F.

2. Line a 9" × 13" Pyrex pan with aluminum foil. Leave enough foil sticking up from the pan to allow you to use it to lift out the baked bars. Grease the foil.

3. Set aside 1 cup cake mix; reserve for later use.

4. In a large mixing bowl, beat the remaining cake mix, 1 egg, and ¼ cup melted butter with an electric mixer on low speed to form a smooth batter.

5. Pat this mixture into the bottom of the pan.

6. In a separate bowl, mix remaining 3 eggs, remaining ½ cup melted butter, buttermilk, lemon juice, sugar, and lemon zest. Beat for 2 minutes with an electric mixer on medium speed.

7. Add lemon mixture over batter layer in pan. Bake for 35 minutes or until set and golden.

8. Use oven mitts to lift cookies out of pan by the aluminum foil edges. Remove to wire rack to cool completely. Sprinkle with confectioners' sugar and garnish with lemon slices.

Chocolate and Strawberry Cookies

*These pink and brown cookies make a lovely presentation. They bring
to mind the lusciousness of a chocolate-covered strawberry.*

INGREDIENTS | MAKES 24 COOKIES

1 18-ounce box strawberry cake mix
½ cup softened butter
2 eggs
1 cup dark chocolate chips

1. Preheat oven to 350°F.

2. Mix cake mix, butter, and eggs until very well blended. Fold in chocolate chips. Drop dough by spoonfuls onto an ungreased cookie sheet. Bake for 9 minutes.

3. Cool cookies on baking sheet for 3 minutes before removing to a cooling rack.

Angel Food Cookies

*Serve these light and tasty morsels with dark coffee and ripe
strawberries and you'll have a treat to remember.*

INGREDIENTS | MAKES 24 COOKIES

1 16-ounce box one-step angel food
  cake mix
½ cup diet lemon-lime soft drink
1 teaspoon vanilla extract

1. Preheat oven to 350°F. Grease cookie sheet and set aside.

2. Mix all ingredients together. Drop cookies by spoonfuls onto the cookie sheet. Bake for 5 minutes, watching closely. Remove before cookies turn brown.

3. Remove to wax paper and allow to cool completely.

Best-Ever Brownies

Don't let the lighter taste of German chocolate cake fool you. These brownies are rich and delicious by anyone's standards.

INGREDIENTS | **MAKES 20 BROWNIES**

1 18.25-ounce box German chocolate cake mix
1 cup chopped walnuts
⅓ cup plus ½ cup evaporated milk
½ cup melted butter
1 14-ounce package vanilla caramels
1 cup dark chocolate chips

1. Preheat oven to 350°F.

2. Combine cake mix, nuts, ⅓ cup evaporated milk, and butter in a large bowl and mix well. Layer half of the batter into a 13" × 9" × 2" Pyrex dish.

3. Bake for 8 minutes. Remove from oven.

4. Melt together caramels and remaining ½ cup evaporated milk in the top of a double boiler. Pour mixture over baked layer.

5. Layer chocolate chips on top of caramel/milk mixture. Press remaining batter on top of the chocolate chip layer. Return to oven and bake for 30 minutes.

6. Remove from oven and let cool completely in pan.

Lemon Mint Cookies

Lemon and mint is a refreshing flavor combination that's quite sophisticated. The ground chocolate chips and cream cheese make the cookies creamy, and the tart, minty frosting is a wonderful flavor contrast.

INGREDIENTS | **YIELDS 32 COOKIES**

1 18.25-ounce package lemon cake mix

$^2/_3$ cup white chocolate chips, ground

2 eggs

$^1/_3$ cup melted butter

1 3-ounce package cream cheese, softened

$^1/_4$ cup butter, softened

3 cups powdered sugar

$^1/_3$ cup lemon juice

$^1/_2$ teaspoon mint extract

1. Preheat oven to 325°F. Line 2 cookie sheets with parchment paper and set aside.

2. In large bowl, combine cake mix, ground white chocolate, eggs, and butter and mix well until combined. Batter is very thick; you may need to use your hands.

3. Form into 1" balls and place on prepared cookie sheets. Flatten slightly with your palm. Bake for 7–11 minutes or until the cookies are puffed and just set. Slide the parchment paper onto a cooling rack; let cool, then peel cookies off paper.

4. In medium bowl, combine cream cheese and butter; beat until smooth. Alternately beat in the powdered sugar and lemon juice until desired consistency is reached. Beat in mint extract. Frost cookies and let stand until set.

Peanut Butter Tea Cakes

Like a Russian Tea Cake, but flavored with peanut butter and made easy with a cake mix, these cookies are so good!

INGREDIENTS | YIELDS 48 COOKIES

½ cup butter, softened
¾ cup peanut butter
1 18.25-ounce package yellow cake mix
4 dozen chocolate kisses, unwrapped
Powdered sugar

Chilling Dough

Chilling dough makes a more tender cookie. The gluten in the flour has a chance to relax a bit, which makes the dough easier to handle. Chilling also makes soft doughs a bit harder, so the insides stay soft and tender while the outside becomes crisp.

1. In large bowl, combine butter and peanut butter and mix well. Add yellow cake mix; mix until a dough forms. Cover and chill for 4–6 hours.

2. When ready to bake, preheat oven to 400°F. Roll dough by tablespoons around a chocolate Kiss; form into a ball and place on parchment paper–lined cookie sheet.

3. Bake cookies for 8–12 minutes or until just set. Let cool on sheet for 3 minutes, then drop into powdered sugar and roll to coat. Let cool completely on wire racks, then coat in powdered sugar again when cool.

Richest Yellow Cake Cookies

*These surprisingly rich cookies are great with frosting but still fantastic on their own.
They're so easy to bake that you'll want to try them all kinds of ways.*

INGREDIENTS | MAKES 24 COOKIES

¼ cup butter, softened

1 8-ounce package cream cheese, softened

1 egg yolk

¼ teaspoon vanilla extract

1 18-ounce box yellow cake mix

1. Preheat oven to 375°F.

2. Cream butter and cream cheese. Mix in egg yolk and vanilla. Add dry cake mix a little at a time, mixing well as you go. Cover and refrigerate for 2 hours.

3. Drop rounded spoonfuls onto an ungreased baking sheet. Bake for 12 minutes or until lightly golden.

Granola White Chocolate Cookies

These tender and chewy cookies are perfect for the lunchbox or a coffee break.

INGREDIENTS | YIELDS 36 COOKIES

1 18.25-ounce package yellow cake mix

¾ cup butter, softened

½ cup packed brown sugar

2 eggs

1 cup granola

1 cup white chocolate chips

1 cup dried cherries

1. Preheat oven to 375°F. In large bowl, combine cake mix, butter, brown sugar, and eggs and beat until batter forms.

2. Stir in granola and white chocolate chips. Drop by teaspoonfuls about 2 inches apart on ungreased cookie sheets.

3. Bake for 10–12 minutes or until cookies are light golden brown around the edges. Cool on cookie sheets for 3 minutes, then remove to wire rack to remove completely.

Old Fashioned Sugar Cookies

Sugar cookies have a flaky texture that is achieved by cutting the butter into the cake mix.

INGREDIENTS | **YIELDS 48 COOKIES**

1 18.25-ounce white cake mix

¾ cup butter

2 egg whites

2 tablespoons light cream

Easy Variations

Use different flavors of cake mix to make different types of sugar cookies, but use the butter, egg whites, and cream for a flaky texture. These can be frosted or glazed, or sprinkle them with colored sugar before baking for a festive touch.

1. Place cake mix in large bowl. Using a pastry blender or two forks, cut in butter until particles are fine. Blend in egg whites and cream until mixed. Shape dough into a ball and cover.

2. Chill for at least two hours and as many as 8 hours in refrigerator. Then preheat oven to 375°F. Roll dough into 1" balls and place on ungreased cookie sheets. Flatten to ¼" thickness with bottom of glass.

3. Bake for 7–10 minutes or until cookie edges are light brown. Cool on cookie sheets for 2 minutes, then remove to wire racks to cool completely. Serve as is or frost as desired.

CHAPTER 10

Cupcakes

Coconut Cupcakes

Coconut cake is a favorite pick at parties and daytime events. This rich, sweet cupcake is a sophisticated treat. Garnish with jellybeans for an easy springtime treat.

INGREDIENTS | **MAKES 24 CUPCAKES**

1 18.25-ounce box white cake mix with pudding

1¼ cups buttermilk

2 eggs

¼ cup softened butter

2 teaspoons vanilla extract

½ teaspoon coconut extract

1 recipe Whipping Cream (page 166)

Semisweet chocolate chips for garnish

Sweetened flaked coconut for garnish

1. Preheat oven to 350°F. Line a muffin tin with paper baking cups. Spray lightly with cooking spray.

2. Using an electric mixer set on low speed, combine the cake mix, buttermilk, eggs, butter, and extracts until a moist batter begins to form.

3. Turn batter into cups, filling just a touch more than half full. Bake for 25 minutes. Allow cupcakes to cool completely.

4. Frost cupcakes with Whipping Cream and garnish with flaked coconut and a few chocolate chips.

Chocolate Cupcakes

The chocolate cupcake is the little black dress of the dessert world. Consider topping these cupcakes with whipped cream and chocolate shavings. You'll need to refrigerate them and serve shortly after frosting, but nothing beats the taste.

INGREDIENTS | **SERVES 36**

1 18.25-ounce box chocolate or devil's food cake mix

1 teaspoon baking powder

1½ cups water

1 egg

1. Preheat oven to 350°F. Line a muffin tin with paper baking cups.

2. Combine all ingredients in a large bowl, using an electric mixer to beat until a smooth batter forms. Turn batter into baking cups, filling each paper cup ½ full.

3. Bake according to cake mix instructions. Frost with whipped topping or prepared frosting.

Peanut Butter Cupcakes

For chocolate/peanut butter frosting, combine 1 16-ounce tub dark chocolate frosting and
⅓ cup chunky natural peanut butter. It's an easy frosting that's sure to get rave reviews.

INGREDIENTS | MAKES 24 CUPCAKES

1 18.25-ounce box yellow cake mix plus
   ingredients called for on box
½ cup natural, chunky peanut butter

1. Preheat oven to 350°F. Line a muffin tin with paper baking cups.

2. Prepare cake mix according to instructions. Add peanut butter just after you add the eggs.

3. Spoon batter into baking cups, filling each more than half full. Bake for 20 minutes. Allow cupcakes to cool on a rack.

Gooey Praline Cupcakes

The candied sweetness of the praline has been a traditional favorite for hundreds of years.
Now you can get the taste—and the crunch—with much less work.

INGREDIENTS | MAKES 24 CUPCAKES

1 18.25-ounce box yellow cake mix
1 cup buttermilk
¼ cup vegetable oil
4 eggs
Caramel ice cream topping
Chopped pecans for garnish
72 pralines

1. Preheat oven to 350°F. Line a muffin tin with paper baking cups.

2. Combine cake mix, buttermilk, oil, and eggs in a large mixing bowl and beat using an electric mixer set to low speed until a smooth batter forms. Fill baking cups halfway.

3. Bake 15 minutes or until tops are golden. Remove cupcakes from the oven and allow to cool completely before adding toppings.

4. Top cupcakes with caramel topping; sprinkle with pecans and garnish with 3 pralines per cupcake.

Piña Colada Cupcakes

This light, tropical blend of flavors is a favorite for summer parties or beach-themed affairs. To toast coconut, spread sweetened flaked coconut in a baking dish and bake at 350°F for 15 minutes, stirring frequently. You can do this while the cupcakes are cooling.

INGREDIENTS | MAKES 24 CUPCAKES

1 18.25-ounce box white cake mix

1 3.9-ounce box instant French vanilla pudding mix

¼ cup vegetable oil

½ cup water

⅔ cup light rum, divided

4 eggs

1 14-ounce can plus 1 cup crushed pineapple

1 cup sweetened, flaked coconut

1 16-ounce tub vanilla frosting

1 12-ounce tub nondairy whipped topping

Toasted coconut for garnish

Cocktail parasols

1. Preheat oven to 350°F. Butter and flour two 8" layer cake pans.

2. Mix cake mix, pudding mix, oil, water, and ⅓ cup rum using an electric mixer on medium speed. Add eggs one at a time, slowly beating the batter as you go.

3. Fold in can of pineapple and coconut. Pour into pans and bake for 25 minutes.

4. To make the frosting, mix 1 cup crushed pineapple, remaining ⅓ cup rum, and vanilla frosting until thick. Add nondairy whipped topping.

5. Frost completely cooled cupcakes and garnish with toasted coconut and a parasol.

Chocolate Truffle Cupcakes

This is a perfectly delightful treasure for the true chocolate lover.
These rich cupcakes have a surprisingly creamy, molten center.

INGREDIENTS | SERVES 24

1 cup semisweet chocolate chips
½ cup butter
3 eggs
3 egg yolks
1 16-ounce package brownie mix
2 tablespoons chocolate milk
2 tablespoons confectioners' sugar
¼ cup cocoa powder

1. Preheat oven to 400°F. Line a muffin tin with paper baking cups.

2. In a microwave-safe bowl, combine chocolate chips and butter.

3. Microwave on high for 60 seconds, stirring halfway through. Set aside to cool for at least 5 minutes.

4. In a larger mixing bowl, combine eggs and yolks; use an electric mixer to beat on high speed for 5 minutes. The eggs should look foamy and double in volume.

5. Fold dry brownie mix, chocolate milk, and microwaved chocolate mixture into the egg mixture using a wooden spoon. Pour even amounts into the baking cups.

6. Bake for 13 minutes. The centers of the cake should be soft, but the edges should be set. Sprinkle cupcakes with confectioners' sugar and cocoa powder.

Perfect Lemon Cupcakes

We associate lemon smells and flavors with light, clean, happy experiences. These cupcakes make the most of that association by offering a sunny burst of flavors.

INGREDIENTS | MAKES 24 CUPCAKES

1 18.25-ounce box lemon cake mix
1 cup buttermilk
¼ cup vegetable oil
4 eggs
1 12-ounce tub ready-to-spread frosting

1. Preheat oven to 350°F. Line a muffin tin with paper baking cups.

2. Combine all ingredients in a large mixing bowl and beat using an electric mixer set to low speed until a smooth batter forms. Turn batter into cups, filling halfway.

3. Bake 15 minutes or until tops are golden. Remove cupcakes from the oven and allow to cool completely before frosting.

Chocolate Chip Cupcakes

Warm chocolate chips are the ultimate comfort food. Match that sensual flavor with moist buttermilk cake for a home-baked sensation. Choose chocolate chips with a higher cocoa content for a richer taste.

INGREDIENTS | SERVES 24

1 18.25-ounce box white cake mix
1 cup buttermilk
4 large eggs
¼ cup vegetable oil
1 12-ounce package chocolate chips
1 12-ounce tub chocolate ready-to-spread frosting

1. Preheat oven to 350°F. Line a muffin tin with paper baking cups.

2. Combine cake mix, buttermilk, eggs, and oil, blending completely with an electric mixer. Gently and evenly fold in chocolate chips. Fill each baking cup halfway.

3. Bake 20 minutes. Allow to cool completely before frosting.

Cherry Cola Cupcakes

This reintroduced sock-hop favorite taste is reborn in a cupcake. Top with whipped cream and a cherry for a sweet ending to a meal of grilled burgers and hot dogs.

INGREDIENTS | SERVES 24

2 eggs

1 teaspoon vanilla

1 18.25-ounce box white cake mix

1¼ cups cherry-flavored cola

1 12-ounce tub ready-made frosting of your choice

1. Preheat oven to 350°F. Line a muffin tin with paper baking cups. Spray lightly with cooking spray.

2. Combine eggs, vanilla, cake mix, and cherry cola in a mixing bowl and mix well using an electric mixer. Bake for 20 minutes. Completely cool cupcakes before frosting.

Chocolate Chip Red Velvet Cupcakes

Everyone loves to guard a secret ingredient. This one is surely a treasure. No one will guess that soda pop is the magic-maker in this moist cupcake. Sprinkle just a dusting of cocoa powder on these cupcakes for a decadent extra touch.

INGREDIENTS | MAKES 24 CUPCAKES

2 egg whites

1 18.25-ounce box red velvet cake mix

1 12-ounce bag chocolate chips

1 12-ounce can lemon-lime soda pop

1 12-ounce tub ready-to-spread sour cream frosting

1. Preheat oven to 350°F. Line a muffin tin with paper baking cups.

2. Combine egg whites, cake mix, chocolate chips, and soda in a large mixing bowl. Mix well until a smooth batter forms. Pour batter into baking cups.

3. Bake for 20 minutes. Allow cupcakes to cool before frosting.

All-American Apple Pie Cupcakes

Plan a trip to an orchard or the farmers' market and make a double batch of your own pie filling. Use half for a pie and half for these cupcakes.

INGREDIENTS | **SERVES 24**

1 18.25-ounce box yellow cake mix

¼ cup water

1 egg

2 tablespoons prepared pumpkin pie spice mix

1 15-ounce can apple pie filling

1 12-ounce tub cream cheese frosting

1. Preheat oven to 350°F. Line a muffin tin with paper baking cups.

2. Mix cake mix, water, egg, and spice mix with an electric mixer until a smooth batter forms. Fold in pie filling. Fill baking cups halfway. Bake for 23 minutes.

3. Allow cupcakes to cool on a rack before frosting.

Chocolate-Filled Angel Cakes

This light cake pairs perfectly with a chocolaty crème filling. Serve with iced tea and fresh fruit on a warm afternoon and enjoy!

INGREDIENTS | **MAKES 39 CUPCAKES**

1 18.25-ounce box angel food cake mix plus ingredients called for on box

1 3.9-ounce box instant chocolate pudding mix plus ingredients called for on box

1. Preheat oven to 375°F. Line a muffin tin with paper baking cups.

2. In a large mixing bowl, mix angel food cake according to the directions on the box. Fill baking cups ¾ full. Bake for 15 minutes or until golden.

3. Mix pudding according to the directions on the box.

4. Allow cupcakes to cool before using a cookie press to insert chocolate pudding into the center of the cupcake.

Chocolate Sundae Cupcakes

When you're really ready to pull out the stops, whip up a batch of these decadent delights.

INGREDIENTS | **MAKES 24 CUPCAKES**

1 18-ounce box white cake mix
1 cup buttermilk
¼ cup vegetable oil
4 eggs
1 12-ounce tub vanilla ice cream
Banana slices
Hot fudge ice cream topping
Whipped topping
Sprinkles (optional)
Maraschino cherries

1. Preheat oven to 350°F. Line a muffin tin with paper baking cups.

2. Combine cake mix, buttermilk, oil, and eggs in a large mixing bowl and beat using an electric mixer set to low speed until a smooth batter forms. Fill baking cups halfway.

3. Bake 15 minutes or until tops are golden. Remove from oven and allow to cool completely before frosting.

4. Place each cupcake in a dish and top with a scoop of ice cream, banana slices, fudge topping, whipped topping, sprinkles, and a cherry.

Fresh Berry Cupcakes

This eggy, creamy cake topped with light, sweet whipped topping is an amazing way to share and savor sweet, fresh berries. Pick the berries yourself to work up an appetite, or simply walk to the market to buy them fresh.

INGREDIENTS | MAKES 24 CUPCAKES

1 18-ounce box white cake mix
1 cup buttermilk
¼ cup vegetable oil
4 eggs
1 16-ounce tub nondairy whipped topping
Fresh berries

1. Preheat oven to 350°F. Line a muffin tin with paper baking cups.

2. Combine all ingredients except whipped topping and berries in a large mixing bowl and combine thoroughly using an electric mixer. Fill baking cups halfway.

3. Bake 15 minutes or until tops are golden. Remove cupcakes from the oven and allow to cool completely. Frost cupcakes with nondairy whipped topping.

4. Top with fresh-sliced berries.

Grande Ganache Cupcakes

Ganache belongs not just to the pages of gourmet magazines and ultra-complicated cookbooks. Home cooks can create the taste, too, and with fairly simple ingredients.

INGREDIENTS | MAKES 24 CUPCAKES

1 18-ounce box chocolate cake mix

1 cup buttermilk

¼ cup vegetable oil

4 eggs

1 cup whipping cream

1 12-ounce package bittersweet chocolate pieces

1. Preheat oven to 350°F. Line a muffin tin with paper baking cups.

2. Combine cake mix, buttermilk, oil, and eggs in a large mixing bowl and beat using an electric mixer set to low speed until a smooth batter forms. Fill baking cups halfway.

3. Bake about 15 minutes or until tops are golden. Allow cupcakes to cool completely.

4. Meanwhile, to make the ganache, bring whipping cream to a boil in a saucepan over medium heat. Remove pan from heat and add chocolate without stirring.

5. Allow chocolate to melt into cream for 5 minutes. Stir until smooth. Allow to cool for 15 minutes before using to frost cupcakes.

Carrot Cake Cupcakes

*This favorite cake has lots of healthy tidbits hiding in it. It's a great
way to get your vegetables without tasting them.*

INGREDIENTS | SERVES 24

¼ cup yellow raisins

¼ cup dark raisins

1 tablespoon hot tap water

1 18.25-ounce box carrot cake mix plus
  ingredients called for on box

1 cup shredded carrots

½ cup walnuts, chopped

1 12-ounce tub ready-to-spread frosting

1. Combine raisins and hot water. Cover. Set aside.

2. Preheat oven to 350°F. Line a muffin tin with paper baking cups.

3. Prepare batter according to cake mix instructions for cupcakes. Gently fold plumped raisins, shredded carrots, and nuts into batter.

4. Pour batter into muffin tin and bake for the length of time indicated on the package. Allow cupcakes to cool completely before removing from muffin tin.

5. Frost completely cooled cupcakes. Garnish with a piece of shredded carrot.

Candied Apple Cupcakes

It's hard to enjoy a caramel apple with a mouth full of dentures or braces.
This easy-to-enjoy recipe lets the whole family celebrate autumn without worry.

INGREDIENTS | SERVES 12

1 18.25-ounce box spice cake mix plus
   ingredients called for on box
2 cups apples, finely chopped
20 caramel cubes
3 tablespoons milk

1. Preheat oven to 350°F. Line a muffin tin with paper baking cups.

2. Prepare batter according to cake mix instructions. Fold in chopped apples. Fill baking cups ¾ full. Bake for 20 minutes. Remove from oven and allow to cool.

3. Cook caramels and milk in a double boiler, stirring constantly. Smooth caramel mixture over cupcakes.

Brownie Cakes

Not quite a brownie, not quite a cupcake, but definitely the best of both worlds.
Pumpkin gives this dessert a lovely texture and flavor with less fat.

INGREDIENTS | MAKES 24 CUPCAKES

1 18.25-ounce box devil's food cake mix
1 15-ounce can pumpkin
⅔ cup water
1 12-ounce tub chocolate frosting

1. Preheat oven to 325°F. Spray muffin tins with nonstick cooking spray.

2. Combine cake mix, pumpkin, and water in a large mixing bowl. Beat using an electric mixer for 2 minutes. Spoon batter into muffin tins. Bake for 40 minutes.

3. Cool cupcakes and frost.

House Mouse Cupcakes

Create the sweetest mouse ever in the house and add a little character to your afternoon treat.

INGREDIENTS | **MAKES 24 CUPCAKES**

1 18.25-ounce box chocolate cake mix plus ingredients called for on box

24 small round chocolate mint cookies, halved

1 12.6-ounce bag round candy-covered chocolates

Thin strings of black licorice

24 scoops chocolate ice cream

1. Preheat oven to 375°F. Line a muffin tin with paper baking cups.

2. Prepare batter and bake according to cake mix instructions for cupcakes. Remove cupcakes from oven and allow to cool completely.

3. Remove cupcakes from paper cups.

4. Using halved round cookies for ears, candies for eyes and nose, and licorice for whiskers, decorate cupcakes to resemble mice. Place on a cookie sheet and freeze.

5. Serve with ice cream.

Rainy Day Cupcakes

Sometimes a treat is all about the presentation. This wiggly, colorful treat brightens up a rainy day like few other cupcakes can.

INGREDIENTS | SERVES 24

1 18.25-ounce white cake mix plus
  ingredients called for on box
1 cup boiling water
1 3-ounce box blue gelatin
1 16-ounce tub thawed whipped topping
Blue-colored sugar
Cocktail parasols to decorate

1. Preheat oven to 350°F. Line a muffin tin with paper baking cups.

2. Prepare batter according to cake mix instructions. Spoon batter into cups. Bake according to instructions.

3. Allow cupcakes to cool completely before poking with skewers, creating 8 holes per cupcake. Boil water and dissolve gelatin in it completely.

4. Spoon gelatin over cupcakes so that mixture fills in the holes. Chill cupcakes in the refrigerator for 4 hours so that gelatin sets.

5. Frost with whipped topping and sprinkle with colored sugar. Garnish each cupcake with parasol.

Pudding-Topped Cupcakes

The flavors in this treat are simple, familiar, and delicious. Bake them when you need a taste of childhood.

INGREDIENTS | MAKES 12 CUPCAKES

1 18.25-ounce box cake mix plus ingredients called for on box

1 cup milk

1 3.9-ounce package instant pudding mix

3½ cups nondairy whipped topping

1. Prepare and bake cupcakes according to cake mix instructions.

2. Combine milk and pudding mix in a large mixing bowl, whisking to blend. Fold in whipped topping and combine thoroughly.

3. Use pudding mixture to frost completely cooled cupcakes.

Whipping Cream

Whipped topping is great when you're in a hurry, but for a super-luscious treat make your own whipped cream. It's easy!

INGREDIENTS | 1 CUP

1 cup whipping cream

½ tablespoon vanilla

2 tablespoons sugar

Add all ingredients to a chilled mixing bowl. Beat with an electric mixer set to medium speed until you reach the desired consistency.

Strawberry Cheese Cupcakes

The light, sweet richness of mascarpone adds a European touch to this otherwise simple cupcake. This recipe would work with any flavor of jam. Get creative. Try seasonal favorites.

INGREDIENTS | **MAKES 24 CUPCAKES**

1 18.25-ounce box white cake mix
2 cups mascarpone cheese
2 eggs
⅓ cup strawberry preserves

1. Preheat oven to 350°F. Line a muffin tin with paper baking cups.

2. Combine all ingredients except preserves in a large mixing bowl and mix well using a wooden spoon. Fill baking cups halfway, reserving about ⅓ of the batter.

3. Drop ½ teaspoon preserves into the center of each cupcake and then cover with remaining batter.

4. Bake for 25 minutes or until cupcakes spring back when gently touched. Cool cupcakes on wire racks.

Berry Crème Cupcakes

There are no artificial colors in this sweet pink dessert. Try it with different berries to get different hues and different tastes.

INGREDIENTS | MAKES 24 CUPCAKES

1 16-ounce package frozen strawberries
1 18.25-ounce box white cake mix
3 egg whites
2 tablespoons vegetable oil
1 16-ounce tub nondairy whipped topping

1. Thaw frozen berries, drain package, and reserve liquid.

2. Preheat oven to 350°F. Line a muffin tin with paper baking cups.

3. Combine cake mix, egg whites, and oil in a large bowl and beat with an electric mixer until a smooth batter forms. Fold in drained berries. Fill baking cups halfway.

4. Bake for 19 minutes. Remove from oven. As cupcakes cool, mix strawberry liquid and whipped topping. Top completely cool cupcakes with this mixture.

CHAPTER 11

For Chocolate Lovers

Ultra-Chocolate Cake

This simply sweet chocolate cake is a great foundation for other recipes.
It can be embellished with nuts or bits of candy.

INGREDIENTS | SERVES 8

1 3.9-ounce package chocolate pudding
plus ingredients called for on box

1 18.25-ounce box chocolate cake mix

½ cup semisweet chocolate chips

½ cup sweetened shaved coconut
(optional)

Whipped topping

1. Preheat oven to 350°F. Grease a cake pan. Set aside.

2. Make pudding according to package instructions. While pudding is still hot, blend in dry cake mix.

3. Blend with a whisk or an electric mixer until batter is free of lumps. Turn batter into pan.

4. Layer chocolate chips and coconut onto batter. Bake for 35 minutes. Serve warm with whipped topping.

Rich Chocolate Bundt Cake

Consider a side of strawberries, raspberries, or whipped topping
to bring out the chocolate flavors in this cake.

INGREDIENTS | SERVES 12

1 18.25-ounce box devil's food cake mix

1 3.9-ounce box instant chocolate
pudding

2 cups sour cream

5 eggs

1 teaspoon almond extract

1 cup butter, melted

2 cups semisweet chocolate chips

1. Preheat oven to 350°F. Grease a bundt pan. Set aside.

2. In a large mixing bowl, blend cake mix, pudding mix, sour cream, eggs, extract, and butter with an electric mixer set to medium speed.

3. Gently fold in chocolate chips with a wooden spoon. Turn batter into the pan. Bake for 50 minutes. Cool cake before inverting onto wire rack.

Chocolate Upside-Down Cake

*On the surface, this is a simple chocolate sheet cake, but underneath
it's a gooey, luscious, chocolate delight.*

INGREDIENTS | SERVES 12

1 cup sweetened flaked coconut

1 cup chopped nuts

1 18.25-ounce box German chocolate
  cake mix

⅓ cup olive oil

1¼ cups water

3 eggs

1 pound confectioners' sugar

1 cup margarine

1 8-ounce package cream cheese

1 cup semisweet chocolate chips

1. Preheat oven to 375°F. Grease a 13" x 9" inch pan. Layer coconut and nuts in the pan, evenly covering the bottom.

2. Mix cake mix, oil, water, and eggs in a large mixing bowl using an electric mixer set to medium speed. Stop when the batter is smooth and free of lumps.

3. Spoon batter over coconut and nuts. Bake for 45 minutes or until a toothpick comes out clean.

4. As cake bakes, mix confectioners' sugar, margarine, and cream cheese in a mixing bowl. Beat mixture with an electric mixer until light and smooth.

5. When cake is baked, remove from oven and invert onto a serving dish. Frost with cream cheese mixture and sprinkle with chocolate chips.

Classic Chocolate Trifle

This traditional favorite is picture perfect and lovely when served in a footed glass bowl—but that's not the only way to do it. Try different food-safe glass containers. Get creative.

INGREDIENTS | SERVES 12

1 18.25-ounce box chocolate cake mix plus ingredients called for on box

1 3.9-ounce box instant chocolate pudding plus ingredients called for on box

1 8-ounce tub whipped topping

4 toffee or solid chocolate candy bars

1. Prepare and bake cake according to cake mix instructions. Cool cake. Cut into cubes.

2. Make instant pudding according to instructions on the package; cool.

3. Break candy into small pieces.

4. Layer half the cake cubes in the glass bowl. Follow with half the pudding. Add half the whipped topping and top with half the candy. Repeat one more time to fill bowl.

5. Chill until ready to serve.

Chocolate Sandwich Cookies

For an extra-fancy finish roll the cookies through a saucer filled with colored sugar or sprinkles. The sprinkles will stick to the filling and create a fun decorative strip.

INGREDIENTS | SERVES 10

1 18.25-ounce box chocolate cake mix

1 egg, room temperature

½ cup butter

1 12-ounce tub vanilla frosting

1. Preheat oven to 350°F. Cover a cookie sheet with a layer of parchment paper. Set aside.

2. In a large mixing bowl, combine cake mix, egg, and butter. Use an electric mixer to create a smooth, uniform batter.

3. Roll cookie dough into 1" balls and place them on cookie sheet. Press each ball with a spoon to flatten. Bake for 10 minutes.

4. Allow cookies to cool completely before sandwiching a layer of frosting between two cookies.

Cocoa-Cola Cake

The orange extract tucked in the mix adds a fragrant sweetness that sings of spring. Consider sugared orange rinds to decorate this cake. Cut them into small pieces and sprinkle them on the cake or use the curved whole rinds to create designs in the frosting.

INGREDIENTS | SERVES 12

1 18.25-ounce box devil's food cake mix
3 eggs
1⅓ cups cola
½ cup olive oil
1 tablespoon orange extract
1 teaspoon vanilla extract
Frosting

1. Preheat oven to 350°F. Grease a cake pan. Set aside.

2. In a large bowl, combine cake mix, eggs, cola, oil, orange extract, and vanilla extract. Beat with an electric mixer set to medium speed to form a smooth batter.

3. Pour batter into cake pan. Bake for 30 minutes or until a toothpick comes out clean. Cool cake on a wire rack before frosting.

Hot Chocolate Cake

Mix cake batter and bake it in your favorite mugs. They're easy to hold and eat.

INGREDIENTS | SERVES 12

1 18.25-ounce box chocolate cake mix plus ingredients called for on box
1 16-ounce tub frozen whipped topping
Sprinkles or small marshmallows for garnish

Mexican Mocha

For an unexpected flavor add an octagon of Mexican hot chocolate, which you can find in the world food section of most grocery stores. Melt the chocolate in the milk you plan to add to the batter. The cinnamon and other spices will add a warming, unexpected flavor.

1. Preheat oven to 350°F. Butter 12 oven-safe mugs.

2. Mix cake batter according to cake mix instructions for cupcakes. Pour batter into mugs. Bake according to instructions for cupcakes.

3. Remove from oven and serve warm with a generous dollop of whipped topping. Garnish with sprinkles or marshmallows.

Micro-Mug Cake for One

*Mix the batter and refrigerate it. Then microwave a cake in your
favorite mug whenever you want a warm sweet treat.*

INGREDIENTS | SERVES 12

1 18.25-ounce box chocolate cake mix
  plus ingredients called for on box
Marshmallow fluff

1. Mix batter according to instructions on the package; put in an airtight container and refrigerate.

2. Fill a mug halfway full with batter. Microwave on high for 3 minutes. Remove and dot with marshmallow fluff. Allow to stand 2 minutes before eating.

Sweet Layers Chocolate Cake

*When creating poke cakes, work with the idea of creating a waffle-like top in the cake.
The point is to poke holes that allow liquid to soak into the cake completely.*

INGREDIENTS | SERVES 12

1 18.25-ounce box chocolate cake mix
  plus ingredients called for on box
1 6-ounce jar caramel ice cream topping
1 7-ounce can unsweetened condensed
  milk
1 8-ounce tub nondairy whipped
  topping, thawed
8 candy bars, chopped or broken into
  bits

1. Prepare and bake cake according to instructions for a 9" × 13" cake.

2. Remove cake from oven and let cool for 10 minutes before poking holes in the top of the cake with a long-pronged fork or skewer.

3. Pour caramel and then condensed milk over cake, filling all the holes. Let the cake stand until it has cooled completely.

4. Frost with whipped topping and sprinkle with candy bar pieces. Refrigerate until ready to serve.

Lower-Fat Chocolate Cake

This lower-fat recipe saves calories on the butter and oil, allowing you to savor a slice of cake without guilt. For a low-fat frosting, combine fat-free instant pudding and fat-free whipped topping. Frost the cake and chill before serving.

INGREDIENTS | SERVES 12

1 18.25-ounce box chocolate cake mix

⅓ cup low-fat applesauce

1¼ cups water

1 12-ounce tub low-fat prepared frosting or whipped topping

1. Preheat oven to 350°F. Grease and flour cake pan. Set aside.

2. Mix all ingredients in a large mixing bowl for 2 minutes using an electric mixer. Turn batter into pan. Bake according to cake mix instructions.

3. Cool cake before frosting.

Crock-o-Late Cake

A slow cooker pot can be a valuable helper on a busy day. Just mix your recipe, pop it in the slow cooker, and go about your day. When you come home, a warm cake will be waiting for you and the house will smell fantastic.

INGREDIENTS | SERVES 12

1 18.25-ounce box chocolate cake mix

1 2-ounce package instant chocolate pudding

4 eggs

1 cup water

2 cups sour cream

¾ cups vegetable oil

1 cup semisweet chocolate chips

1. Grease a 4-quart slow cooker.

2. In a medium bowl, mix cake and pudding mixes. In a large bowl, mix eggs, water, sour cream, and oil.

3. Slowly add the dry ingredients to the wet ingredients as you beat the batter with an electric mixer set on medium speed. Add chocolate chips and stir by hand to thoroughly incorporate.

4. Turn batter into slow cooker. Cover and cook on low for 6 hours. Cake is done if it springs back when lightly touched. If it doesn't, cook in 15-minute increments until it is done.

Sandwich Cookie Cake

This cake can't be dunked in a glass of milk, but it's just as tasty as your favorite sandwich cookies. The creamy filling is the sweet note that makes this cake a special event in and of itself.

INGREDIENTS | SERVES 12

1 18.25-ounce box devil's food cake mix

1 3.9-ounce box instant chocolate pudding

1 cup vegetable oil

1 cup sour cream

4 eggs

½ cup skim milk

2 teaspoons vanilla extract

2 cups mini semisweet chocolate chips

Sandwich Cookie Cake Frosting (page 177)

1. Preheat oven to 350°F. Grease and flour cake pans. Set aside.

2. In a large mixing bowl, combine all ingredients except chocolate chips and frosting, mixing with an electric mixer on medium until batter is entirely smooth.

3. Fold in chocolate chips. Turn batter into two round cake pans. Bake for 45 minutes or until a toothpick comes out clean.

4. As cake bakes, mix one batch of Sandwich Cookie Cake Frosting.

5. Remove cake from oven and allow to cool before turning one layer onto the serving platter. Spread the top of this first layer with a generous helping of frosting.

6. Invert the second layer on top of the frosting, creating a sandwich. Use the rest of the frosting to cover the cake.

Sandwich Cookie Cake Frosting

The best part of the sandwich cookie is the crème filling. A batch of this creamy frosting adds that beautiful layer of sweetness to your chocolate confection.

INGREDIENTS | SERVES 12

1 cup solid vegetable shortening

4½ cups confectioners' sugar

¼ teaspoon sea salt

2 teaspoons vanilla extract

⅓ cup unsweetened, heavy whipping cream

1. In a stainless steel mixing bowl, using an electric mixer set to medium speed, beat vegetable shortening until light and fluffy. Slowly add sugar and continue to beat.

2. Add salt, vanilla extract, and whipping cream, continuing to beat. Turn the electric mixer to high speed and beat until light and fluffy. Frost your cake.

Coconaise Cake

Mayonnaise is a great way to add light egg and oil to your recipe. Try it for a rich, light crumb that doesn't taste like a mix cake. Serve this cake with fresh raspberries or strawberries. The flavors complement chocolate famously, and the lightness of the fruit is lovely with the richness of the cake.

INGREDIENTS | SERVES 12

1 box chocolate cake mix

1 cup mayonnaise

1 cup water

3 eggs

1 teaspoon ground cinnamon

2 tablespoons cocoa powder

1 12-ounce tub prepared chocolate frosting

1. Preheat the oven to 350°F. Grease and flour cake pans. Set aside.

2. Combine cake mix, mayonnaise, water, eggs, cinnamon, and cocoa powder in a large mixing bowl. Beat batter smooth with an electric mixer set to medium speed.

3. Turn cake batter into pans. Bake for 25 minutes or until fork comes out clean. Allow cake to cool completely before frosting.

Movie Night Brownies

There's no secret to this simple recipe. With just four ingredients and only a few easy steps, they're quick enough to whip up while the previews are playing. You can frost them, sprinkle them with confectioners' sugar, or serve them with a scoop of ice cream.

INGREDIENTS | SERVES 12

1 3.9-ounce package instant vanilla pudding plus ingredients called for on box

2 cups whole milk

1 18.25-ounce box chocolate cake mix without pudding

2 cups semisweet chocolate chips

1. Preheat oven to 350°F.

2. Make pudding, whisking to combine thoroughly.

3. Slowly add cake mix to the pudding mixture. Fold in chocolate chips. Turn batter into a jellyroll pan and bake for 15 to 20 minutes.

4. Allow to cool slightly before cutting into bars.

Chocolate Cake Batter Ice Cream

This is a great way to enjoy the taste of fresh cake batter and homemade ice cream. It's easy to do with an ice-cream maker. Serve with whipped cream, chocolate syrup, or both! Top with fruit or sprinkles for an extra-special presentation.

INGREDIENTS | SERVES 8

1 cup whole milk, chilled

¾ cup sugar

2 cups whipping cream, chilled

1 teaspoon vanilla extract

⅔ cup cake mix

1. Whisk milk and sugar together in a stainless steel mixing bowl until well incorporated. Add whipping cream and vanilla extract. Continue to whisk.

2. Slowly add cake mix, whisking to avoid lumps. Put mixture in an ice-cream maker and continue according to manufacturer's instructions.

Malt Shoppe Chocolate Cake

Love a malt? This is the cake that captures the flavor. Serve with a shake or vanilla ice cream for that malt shop, sock-hop flavor.

INGREDIENTS | SERVES 14

1 18.25-ounce box chocolate cake mix
1 cup malted milk powder
1⅓ cups water
3 eggs
½ cup butter, softened
½ gallon ice cream, softened
1 16-ounce jar hot fudge ice cream topping
1 cup malted milk balls

1. Preheat oven to 350°F. Grease cake pans. Set aside.

2. Combine dry cake mix and malted milk powder in a large mixing bowl and whisk to combine completely. Slowly add water, eggs, and butter.

3. Beat batter for 1 minute using an electric mixer set to medium speed. Turn batter into cake pans. Bake for 40 minutes or until a toothpick comes out clean.

4. Allow cakes to cool completely. Mark the center of the cake with toothpicks all the way around. Using the toothpicks as your guide, cut the cake in half horizontally.

5. Line a cake pan with plastic wrap. Alternate layers of cake and softened ice cream to fill pan. Wrap in plastic wrap and freeze until ready to serve.

6. Garnish with hot fudge and malted milk balls.

Turtle Skillet Cakes

These griddle cakes aren't for breakfast, but they're a perfect treat for pajama parties or snowy nights. Cuddle up with these and a cup of something warm for a decadent delight.

INGREDIENTS | SERVES 14

1 18.25-ounce box devil's food cake mix plus ingredients called for on box

1 tablespoon butter

4 1-ounce pieces semisweet baking chocolate

1 12-ounce jar caramel ice cream topping

Whipped topping

Equipment

Some recipes call for elaborate baking equipment, but this recipe uses something you probably already have: a skillet. This method of baking will work on many basic cake recipes. If you're just learning to bake and aren't ready to invest in expensive equipment, try making this recipe in a thin-walled skillet.

1. Preheat oven to 350°F.

2. Make cake batter according to cake mix instructions.

3. Melt butter in an oven-safe iron or nonstick skillet over medium heat. Gently tilt the skillet to make sure the butter covers the bottom of the pan.

4. Turn batter into the skillet and bake in the oven, uncovered, for 30 minutes. Remove skillet from oven and allow cake to cool.

5. Run a knife around the edge of the pan to loosen cake slightly. Then invert the pan onto the cooling rack and allow the cake to fall free.

6. Grate, shave, or chop the chocolate into small pieces. In a small microwave-safe bowl, mix chocolate pieces and half the caramel topping.

7. Microwave the chocolate/caramel mix for 40 seconds or until melted. Stir. Pour over cake. Add a thin layer of reserved caramel sauce. Top with whipped topping.

Chocolaty Coconut Cake

Sure, there are other chocolate cake recipes, but how many of them offer the combination of moistening pudding and rich coconut? Serve this with warm tea or hot cocoa.

INGREDIENTS | **SERVES 12**

1 18.25-ounce box devil's food cake mix plus ingredients called for on box

1 3.9-ounce box instant chocolate pudding

1 cup milk

1 16-ounce tub whipped topping, thawed

Mini semisweet chocolate chips

½ cup sweetened, flaked coconut

Keep Your Cool

Cakes frosted with whipped topping hold their shape and their frosting better if they stay refrigerated. Not only do they hold consistency better; they also remain easy to slice. Drizzle with chocolate syrup for an extra-rich decorative touch.

1. Preheat oven to 350°F.

2. Mix cake batter according to cake mix instructions. Pour batter into a bundt pan and bake according to instructions.

3. Meanwhile, in a medium-sized stainless steel bowl, whisk pudding mix and milk together for 2 minutes. Fold in whipped topping and chocolate chips.

4. Remove cake from oven and let cool completely before inverting onto a serving platter. Frost cake with whipped topping mixture. Sprinkle with coconut.

Chocolate Zucchini Cake

Zucchini adds moistness and texture to your chocolate cake. Bake this every year when the garden harvest comes in or after your first trip to the farmers' market.

INGREDIENTS | SERVES 12

¾ cup butter, softened

3 eggs

1 teaspoon vanilla extract

¼ teaspoon almond extract

1 cup sour cream

1 18.25-ounce box chocolate cake mix with pudding

1 medium zucchini, grated

1 12-ounce tub prepared chocolate frosting

Zucchini Peels

Some cooks peel zucchini before grating, but others maintain that the peel contains most of the nutrients. Both are perfectly acceptable. If, however, you decide to use the peel in your cake, please take the time to thoroughly wash the zucchini. Conventional farming can leave pesticides and waxes on the squash that you may not want in your cake.

1. Preheat oven to 325°F. Grease and flour a bundt pan. Set aside.

2. In a large mixing bowl, cream butter, eggs, vanilla extract, and almond extract. Slowly incorporate the sour cream. Add cake mix. Fold in grated zucchini.

3. Spoon batter into the cake pan and shake until batter is level. Bake 45 minutes or until a toothpick comes out clean.

4. Cool cake completely before inverting pan onto serving platter. Frost cake with prepared frosting.

Mexican Chocolate Cake

South of the border, people add a little spice to their cocoa. Cinnamon is the secret ingredient, but some cooks also add a quick and very scant dash of cayenne pepper for heat.

INGREDIENTS | SERVES 12

1 18.25-ounce box chocolate cake mix

1 teaspoon cinnamon

1½ cups water

½ cup vegetable oil

4 eggs

1 cup semisweet chocolate chips

3 tablespoons butter

Condensed Milk Caramel

Boil a pot of water. Remove the label (but not the lid) from a can of sweetened condensed milk and boil the can for 20 minutes, keeping the pot covered. Reduce the heat and simmer, still covered, for 90 minutes. Allow the can to cool, remove the lid, and drizzle the caramel over the cake.

1. Preheat oven to 350°F. Grease and flour a bundt pan. Set aside.

2. In a large mixing bowl combine cake mix, cinnamon, water, oil, and eggs. Combine with an electric mixer. Fold in chocolate chips. Pour into pan.

3. Bake for 35 minutes or until a toothpick comes out clean. Drizzle warm cake with Condensed Milk Caramel.

Chocolate Latte Cake

Skip the coffee shop and enjoy the sophisticated flavor of a latte fresh from your own oven. The ingredients are simple, but the results are stellar.

INGREDIENTS | SERVES 12

2 tablespoons butter
1½ cups graham cracker crumbs
1 18.25-ounce box devil's food cake mix
¾ cup semisweet chocolate morsels
1½ cups whipping cream
1½ teaspoons instant coffee crystals
⅓ cup confectioners' sugar

1. Preheat oven to 350°F. Grease and flour cake pans. Set aside.

2. Mix melted butter and graham cracker crumbs and set aside to cool.

3. Prepare cake batter according to cake mix instructions for a two-layer cake. Pour into two cake pans.

4. Sprinkle butter/crumb mixture and chocolate morsels over batter before baking. Bake for 35 minutes. Remove from oven and allow to cool.

5. In a stainless steel bowl, beat whipping cream, instant coffee crystals, and confectioners' sugar until stiff peaks form.

6. Turn one layer of cake onto a serving plate. Spread cream mixture on top and sides. Add top layer and frost remainder of cake with cream mixture. Chill until ready to serve.

Peanut Butter Fudge Brownies

Cake mix makes chewy and thick brownies with a wonderful flavor. The ground chocolate adds creaminess. Be careful to not overbake these brownies.

INGREDIENTS | SERVES 36

1 18.25-ounce package dark chocolate cake mix

½ cup dark chocolate chips, ground

½ cup peanut butter

2 eggs

¼ cup water

1 16-ounce tub ready to spread vanilla frosting

⅓ cup peanut butter

2 cups powdered sugar

¼ cup cocoa

3 tablespoons water

¼ cup peanut butter

¼ cup butter

1 teaspoon vanilla

1. Preheat oven to 350°F. Spray a 13" × 9" pan with nonstick baking spray containing flour and set aside. In large bowl, combine cake mix, ground chocolate, ½ cup peanut butter, eggs, and water and mix until combined. Beat for 40 strokes, then spread into prepared pan.

2. Bake for 26–31 minutes or until brownies are just set. Cool completely on wire rack.

3. In same bowl, combine powdered sugar and cocoa and mix well. In small microwave-safe bowl, combine water, peanut butter, and butter; microwave on high until butter melts, about 1 minute. Pour into powdered sugar mixture, add vanilla, and beat until smooth.

4. Immediately pour over peanut butter filling and gently spread to cover. Let stand until frosting is firm, then cut into bars.

Chocolate Angel Cakes

*This fabulous recipe tastes like a scratch cake. The little cakes are still a
lot of work, but cake mix and ready-made frosting help a lot.*

INGREDIENTS | YIELDS 20 CAKES

1 18.25-ounce package chocolate cake
mix

1 cup water

⅓ cup oil

2 eggs

¾ cup semisweet chocolate chips,
ground

3 16-ounce cans ready to spread
chocolate frosting

2–3 cups finely chopped pecans

Flavor Variations

You can change the flavor of this simple
recipe in many ways. Use white cake mix,
white chocolate chips, and white frosting.
A spice cake can be used, also with white
chocolate chips and butter frosting. Or mix
and match; make a white cake and frost it
with chocolate frosting. You get the idea!

1. Preheat oven to 350°F. Spray a 9" × 13" pan with
   nonstick baking spray containing flour and set aside.

2. In large bowl, combine cake mix, water, oil, and eggs
   and blend. Beat two minutes at high speed. Fold in the
   finely ground chocolate chips. Spread into prepared
   pan.

3. Bake for 35–45 minutes or until toothpick inserted in
   cake comes out clean. Let cake cool completely on
   wire rack.

4. Cut cake into 20 pieces and remove from pan, one at
   a time. Frost the little cakes on all sides and roll in the
   chopped pecans to coat.

Mocha Mud Bundt Cake

This is a sophisticated cake for the latte-lovers in your life. As with all bundt cakes, this is easy to make and easy to carry.

INGREDIENTS | SERVES 12

1 18.25-ounce box cake mix

4 eggs

½ cup vegetable oil

1 16-ounce tub sour cream

½ cup Kahlua

1 8-ounce package semisweet chocolate chips

Whipped topping for garnish

Nutmeg for garnish

1. Preheat oven to 350°F. Grease a bundt pan and set aside.

2. Mix together cake mix, eggs, oil, sour cream, and Kahlua. Mix until batter is smooth. Fold in chocolate chips. Turn batter into cake pan.

3. Bake for 1 hour. When the cake is done, the top will spring back after being touched lightly. Allow cake to cool slightly before inverting onto serving platter.

4. Garnish with whipped topping and sprinkles of nutmeg.

CHAPTER 12

Holiday Favorites

Fruitcake

Fruitcakes are best when flavors are allowed to mingle. Traditionally, cakes would age for weeks in a dark, cool closet. You don't need to go that far. A day or two in your nice, clean fridge will work wonders! Use fruit-flavored brandy if possible.

INGREDIENTS | SERVES 8

Fruitcake

1 18.25-ounce box yellow cake mix

1 3.9-ounce box vanilla pudding mix

⅔ cup pineapple juice

¼ cup brandy

½ cup vegetable oil

4 large eggs

1 cup pecans, crushed

1 cup chopped dates

½ cup chopped maraschino cherries

½ cup chopped candied pineapple

Whole pecans for garnish

Glaze

1 cup confectioners' sugar

2 to 3 tablespoons brandy

1. Preheat oven to 350°F. Grease and flour a 10" tube pan. Set aside.

2. Pour cake mix into a bowl. Fold in pudding mix, pineapple juice, brandy, and oil. Mix for 3 minutes or until batter is smooth. Add eggs, beating continuously.

3. Stir in pecans and all fruit. Pour batter into cake pan. Top with a few whole pecans. Bake for 50 minutes or until a fork comes out clean.

4. Cool for 15 minutes in the pan, then remove to a rack to cool thoroughly. Mix Glaze and drizzle over cooled cake. Cover in plastic wrap and age in refrigerator for one or two days.

Rum Cake

This variation on a favorite rum cake is a little less boozy than the original, but you can add more if you like. Not all of the alcohol will bake out of this recipe, so people sensitive to alcohol should proceed with caution. Top with Rum Cake Glaze (page 192).

INGREDIENTS | SERVES 12

1 cup chopped walnuts
1 18.25-ounce box yellow cake mix
1 3.9-ounce box instant vanilla pudding mix
4 eggs
½ cup milk
½ cup canola oil
¼ cup Bacardi dark rum

1. Preheat oven to 325°F. Generously grease and flour a bundt pan, even if it is nonstick. Set aside.

2. Generously layer nuts in the bottom of the pan. (When liquid batter is added, they'll float to the top.)

3. Beat together cake mix, pudding mix, eggs, milk, oil and dark rum for 3 minutes. Turn batter into the bundt pan. Gently bang pan on counter to even out batter.

4. Bake for 1 hour. Remove from oven and let cake rest in bundt pan for 2 hours. When cake is cool, turn it out onto a platter.

Rum Cake Glaze

You could make the cake without the glaze, but why would you? It's where the rummy yummy lives! A dollop of whipped topping is the perfecting touch.

INGREDIENTS | YIELDS 1 CUP

½ cup butter
¼ cup water
1 cup sugar
½ cup dark rum

1. Melt butter in a saucepan over low heat. Slowly whisk in water and sugar. Bring to a boil; boil for 5 minutes. Remove pan from burner and stir in rum, using a spoon with a long handle.

2. Poke holes in the baked Rum Cake with a wooden skewer or long-pronged fork.

3. Pour glaze generously into holes, just as you would syrup into the holes of a waffle.

Cozy Cakes

For a traditional taste, wrap the rum cake in cheesecloth and let it set for a few days. The longer the cake rests, the better it is. For exactly this reason, it's the perfect addition for a care package.

Minute Macaroons

These are great for the holidays and any other time hungry friends gather together. They are very portable, so keep this recipe top of mind when planning for potlucks.

INGREDIENTS | MAKES 20 MACAROONS

1 18-ounce box vanilla cake mix
⅓ cup butter
2 tablespoons room-temperature water
1 teaspoon vanilla extract
1 egg, slightly beaten
1½ cups sweetened flaked coconut
½ cup dark chocolate chips

1. Preheat oven to 350°F. Lightly butter a 13" × 9" pan and set aside.

2. Pour cake mix into a large bowl. Crumble butter into mix until fully incorporated. Stir in water. Mix in vanilla. Add egg and gently fold in coconut. Turn into cake pan.

3. Bake for 18 minutes. Let cool for 20 minutes. Melt chocolate chips in a warm double boiler or small saucepan. Drizzle over top of cookies. Chill for 2 hours. Cut into bars.

Cherry Sugar Plums

These sweet, fruity, nutty treats are easy, economical, and a hit at cookie swaps and holiday parties everywhere. Substitute grenadine for water in this recipe for an extra cherry kick.

INGREDIENTS | MAKES 24 COOKIES

1 18-ounce box cherry cake mix
2 eggs
½ cup butter
1 tablespoon water
¼ cup walnuts, chopped
Confectioners' sugar

1. Combine all ingredients except confectioners' sugar in a bowl. Spoon into 1" balls. Chill in the refrigerator for 2 hours. Preheat oven to 375°F.

2. Remove cookies from fridge. Place confectioners' sugar in a paper bag and add cookies. Shake very gently to coat. Place onto an ungreased cookie sheet by spoonfuls. Bake for 12 minutes. Cool on rack.

Kitschy Pixie Poke Cake

Get out your pixie ornaments and your Chipmunks albums. This tried, true, and much-loved recipe will transport you to a time when it was chic to bake with gelatin dessert mix!

INGREDIENTS | SERVES 12

1 18.25-ounce white cake mix plus ingredients called for on box

2 cups boiling water, divided

1 3-ounce box cherry or strawberry gelatin dessert

1 3-ounce box lime gelatin dessert

1 9-ounce tub whipped topping

Versatile Holiday Treat

Use red, white, and blue gelatin for an Independence Day party or pink and green gelatin for a Southern-style sorority get-together. This cake is a crowd pleaser, and it can be adjusted to fit almost any event simply by choosing the appropriate color of gelatin.

1. Bake cake according to instructions on box for layer cake. Remove from oven and allow cake to cool.

2. Pierce layers with skewers or fork either at regular intervals or in a pattern of your choice.

3. Mix 1 cup boiling water with red gelatin; stir until completely dissolved. Pour over one pierced cake layer. Repeat with green gelatin; pour over the other layer.

4. Chill both layers for 4 hours or overnight. Rest cake pans in a shallow container of warm water. Once warm, invert one layer onto a serving plate. Frost with half of the whipped topping. Repeat with remaining layer.

5. Chill for 2 hours. Decorate cake and top with an ornament if desired.

Day-Glo Valentine Cake

Give a big beautiful valentine to someone special this year! This brightly colored Valentine's Day treat is sure to get some love. The brighter the gelatin and food coloring you use, the better.

INGREDIENTS | SERVES 12

1 18-ounce box white cake mix
1 3-ounce package instant gelatin
1 cup milk
3 large eggs
½ cup butter, melted
2 teaspoons vanilla extract
1 tub prepared white frosting
Food coloring

1. Preheat oven to 350°F. Generously butter and flour two cake pans: one round (9") and one square (9"). Set aside.

2. Combine cake mix, gelatin, milk, eggs, butter, and vanilla extract with an electric mixer on low speed.

3. Increase speed to medium and beat for an additional 3 minutes or until batter is free of lumps and completely blended.

4. Pour batter into pans and bake according to box instructions for two layers. Remove cakes from oven and invert onto cooling racks.

5. Allow cakes to cool to room temperature. Place square cake on serving surface so that it looks like a diamond.

6. Cut the round layer in half and place the halves on either side of the diamond's upper edges to make a heart. Combine frosting and food coloring. Frost cake.

Chocolate-Covered-Cherry Brownies

This dessert boasts all the decadence of chocolate-covered cherries in a rich, chewy, easy-to-bake brownie!

INGREDIENTS | MAKES 9 BROWNIES

1 18.25-ounce box of the most decadent brownie mix you can find plus ingredients called for on box (except for liquid)

1 6-ounce jar of maraschino cherries

1 1.55-ounce bar dark chocolate

1. Prepare brownies according to the directions on the box, substituting the liquid from the jar of cherries for the liquid called for in the cake mix instructions. If there isn't enough liquid from the cherries, add water to reach desired amount.

2. Top with maraschino cherries and squares of chocolate. Bake according to instructions on box. Let cool.

Green Beer Cake

What's more St. Patrick's Day than green beer? Nothing! This cake can almost certainly drive the snakes out of Ireland, but just in case it can't, raise a pint to good St. Patrick and enjoy the day!

INGREDIENTS | SERVES 12

1 18-ounce box yellow cake mix

1 3.9-ounce package instant vanilla pudding mix

1 cup beer

Green food coloring

¼ cup vegetable oil

4 eggs

Frosting

1. Preheat oven to 350°F. Grease and flour a 10" bundt pan. Set aside.

2. Blend cake mix and pudding mix in a large bowl with a wooden spoon. Color beer as green as you like using green food coloring. Stir beer and oil into batter.

3. Add eggs. Beat mixture with electric mixer set to high speed. When mixture is thick and creamy, pour into pan. Bake for 55 minutes.

4. Cool in pan for 15 minutes. Invert cake onto cooling rack. Cool cake completely. Frost as desired.

Leprechaun Cupcakes

These green snacks are too cute for words! They're easy to whip up for a St. Patrick's Day party.

INGREDIENTS | MAKES 24 CUPCAKES

1 package white cake mix

4 eggs

1 cup vegetable oil

1 cup lemon-lime soda

1 3.9-ounce package pistachio instant pudding mix

1 batch Top o' the Cupcake to You Icing (below)

1. Preheat oven to 350°F. Line a muffin tin with paper baking cups. Set aside.

2. Mix all ingredients except frosting in a large bowl. Beat together for 3 minutes with an electric beater set on medium speed. Fill muffin cups ½ full. Bake for 30 minutes.

3. Cool completely. Remove from muffin pan. Frost and serve.

Top o' the Cupcake to You Icing

Even cupcakes like to participate in the wearing o' the green on St. Patrick's day.
Dress yours up in the luck of the Irish and take a big, sweet bite.

INGREDIENTS | MAKES 1½ CUPS

1 3.9-ounce package pistachio instant pudding mix

1½ cups milk

1 8-ounce container nondairy whipped cream

Mix pudding and milk for 2 minutes using electric mixer on low speed. Fold in nondairy whipped topping.

Sparkling Lavender Garden Party Cupcakes

The light citrus flavor and glittery magical sprinkles make these cupcakes perfect for tea parties.

INGREDIENTS | **MAKES 24 CUPCAKES**

Juice of 1 lemon

Water

1 18-ounce box lemon-flavored cake mix

¼ cup vegetable oil

3 eggs

2 tablespoons lavender buds (reserve a small amount for garnish)

Zest of 1 lemon

1 16-ounce tub white frosting

Candied lemon peel for garnish

Pink sprinkles for garnish

1. Preheat oven to temperature specified in cake mix instructions. Line a muffin tin with paper baking cups. Set aside.

2. Combine lemon juice and enough water to reach amount of water called for in the cake mix instructions.

3. Empty dry cake mix into a large mixing bowl. Add water/juice, oil, eggs, most of lavender buds, and lemon zest to taste. Beat for 2 minutes using a mixer set to high speed.

4. Fill muffin cups ½ full. Bake according to the cake mix instructions. Remove cupcakes from oven when they are just slightly brown around the edges.

5. Frost while warm so that frosting melts to a glaze. Sprinkle with a few lavender buds. Add candied lemon peel for garnish. Dust with sprinkles.

Easter Coconut Cake

You can re-create the taste of the classic Betty Crocker Easter Bunny Cake with this simple coconut cake recipe. Decorate it with Easter candy for a cake so sweet you'll forget what's in your basket.

INGREDIENTS | SERVES 12

1 18.25-ounce box white cake mix, plus ingredients called for on box

1 12-ounce can cream of coconut

1 14-ounce can sweetened condensed milk

1 8-ounce container nondairy whipped topping

1 cup shredded coconut

1. Bake cake according to the directions on the box. Meanwhile, thoroughly mix the cream of coconut and sweetened condensed milk.

2. Poke holes in cake at even intervals with a wooden skewer or a long-pronged fork. Pour coconut/condensed milk mixture over cake and let soak 8 hours.

3. Smooth whipped topping over cake and sprinkle with shredded coconut.

Summer Celebration Berry Cake

Nothing says summer like the taste of fresh berries. Bake some on the cake and serve some fresh as a garnish for a seasonal treat that's sure to please.

INGREDIENTS | SERVES 8

3 eggs

¼ cup sugar

⅓ cup safflower oil

1 cup sour cream

Zest and juice of 2 lemons

1 18.25-ounce yellow cake mix with pudding

2 cups fresh, cleaned blueberries

Confectioners' sugar

1. Preheat oven to 350°F. Grease a bundt cake pan.

2. Beat eggs and sugar until light and frothy. Continue to beat and add oil, sour cream, lemon zest, and lemon juice. Mix until very smooth.

3. Fold in cake mix bit by bit. Mix until well blended. Add blueberries. Pour batter evenly into cake pan. Bake for 50 to 60 minutes. Top with confectioners' sugar.

Pesach Banana Cake for Passover

This recipe is used with permission from Torahwomen.com. It's one of their favorite Passover recipes.

INGREDIENTS | **SERVES 6–8**

1 12-ounce box Manischewitz yellow cake mix

¼ cup water

2 eggs

1 cup mashed or puréed ripe bananas

⅓ cup semisweet chocolate chips

Kosher for Passover confectioners' sugar for garnish (optional)

Whipped cream (dairy meal) for garnish (optional)

Nondairy whipped topping (meat meal) for garnish (optional)

1. Preheat oven to 350°F. Spray an 8" or 9" square or round cake pan with nonstick cooking spray.

2. Beat together all ingredients except the chocolate chips and optional ingredients for 1–2 minutes until smooth.

3. Pour into prepared cake pan and sprinkle chocolate chips over top. Bake until cake springs back when gently pressed, about 25–35 minutes.

4. Remove from oven and leave cake in pan to cool for 15 minutes, then transfer to wire rack to cool completely.

5. Dust with confectioners' sugar if desired. Cut cake into slices. Serve each piece with a dollop of whipped cream or nondairy whipped topping if desired.

Dulce de Leche Cream Cake

This traditional cake is found in almost every Mexican bakery. Its milky sweetness makes it a favorite for Cinco de Mayo celebrations.

INGREDIENTS | SERVES 8

1 18.25-ounce box yellow cake mix plus ingredients called for on box

1 14-ounce can sweetened condensed milk

⅓ cup caramel ice cream topping

2 cups heavy whipping cream

1 teaspoon vanilla extract

¼ cup confectioners' sugar

⅓ cup sliced almonds, toasted

1. Bake cake in a square pan according to the cake mix instructions. Remove cake from oven and let cool for 5 minutes. Invert onto cooling rack and cool completely.

2. Meanwhile, pour condensed milk into a microwave-safe bowl and microwave for 2 minutes. Gently stir condensed milk.

3. Return to microwave and cook 2 more minutes on medium power. Continue to microwave in 5-minute intervals for 20 minutes, whisking gently between intervals.

4. When condensed milk is thick and the color of light caramel, stir in caramel topping. Let caramel mixture cool for 10 minutes. Frost cake with this mixture.

5. Beat whipping cream in a large mixing bowl until it forms soft peaks. Fold in vanilla and confectioners' sugar. Beat until stiff peaks form. Spoon whipped cream over cake.

6. Garnish with toasted almonds. Chill for 2 hours. Serve with rich coffee.

Great Pumpkin Cake

*This structured cake makes a great holiday centerpiece and is sure
to be admired by ghost, goblins, and ghouls of all stripes!*

INGREDIENTS | **SERVES 9**

2 18.25-ounce boxes yellow cake plus
   ingredients called for on box
Orange food coloring
1 12-ounce tub white frosting
Fruit Roll-Up
1 Hostess Ho Ho

1. Prepare cake mixes according to cake mix instructions. Pour into 2 bundt cake pans and bake according to instructions. Invert cakes onto cooling rack. Mix orange food coloring into white frosting.

2. When cool, place one cake rounded side down onto a serving plate. Line upward edge of cake with orange frosting.

3. Place second bundt cake (right side up) on top of the first cake so that together they form a round, pumpkin-like shape.

4. Frost entire cake using up-and-down strokes. Cut Fruit Roll-Up into eye and mouth shapes. Lay shapes on cake to make a face.

5. Place Ho Ho in the round indentation in the top of the cake to look like a stem.

Pumpkin Patch Cake

*The tastes of autumn star in this cake. For an extra-special treat,
pick the pumpkin yourself and create your own purée.*

INGREDIENTS | **SERVES 12**

1 18.25-ounce box spice cake mix
1 can pumpkin purée
1 cup mayonnaise
3 eggs
1 12-ounce tub cream cheese frosting

1. Preheat oven to 350°F. Grease cake pan.

2. Combine all ingredients. Turn batter into pan. Bake 35 minutes or until fork comes out clean. Cool completely. Frost with cream cheese frosting.

Thanksgiving Pie Dump Cake

*This is a great recipe to pass family style or share at potluck dinners. It travels
well and is a warm, sweet, comforting dish that's sure to please.*

INGREDIENTS | **SERVES 12**

4 eggs
1 teaspoon cinnamon
1 cup sugar
1 14-ounce can pumpkin purée (not pie filling)
1 12-ounce can evaporated milk
1 18-ounce box yellow cake mix
1 cup butter
1 cup pecans
1 recipe Whipping Cream (page 166)

1. Preheat oven to 350°F. Grease a casserole dish.

2. Beat eggs, cinnamon, sugar, pumpkin, and evaporated milk in a large mixing bowl with a wooden spoon. Pour into casserole dish.

3. Layer dry yellow cake mix on top of pumpkin mixture. Dot with pats of butter. Garnish with pecans. Bake for 1 hour. When cool, top with whipping cream.

Pecan Pie Casserole

Pecan pie is a buttery, gooey, favorite cold-weather treat. Here you enjoy all the rich flavor of the pie, without needing to bake a crust from scratch. It's simple enough to make any weeknight, but yummy enough for holiday dinners.

INGREDIENTS | SERVES 12

1 18.25-ounce box yellow cake mix
4 eggs, divided use
½ cup butter, melted
1½ cups light corn syrup
½ cup dark brown sugar, packed
1 teaspoon vanilla
1½ cups chopped pecans

1. Preheat oven to 325°F. Grease a casserole dish.

2. Combine cake mix, 1 egg, and butter. Mix well. Set aside ½ cup of this mixture and pour remaining batter into casserole dish. Bake for 15 minutes.

3. Combine reserved batter, remaining 3 eggs, and the rest of ingredients in a bowl. Mix. Layer this mixture on top of baked layer and return to the oven for 50 minutes.

4. Cool and serve casserole style.

Fresh from the Bog Cranberry Cobbler

Thanksgiving is the perfect time to celebrate the tart, colorful cranberry. Paired with cherry filling, it offers a refreshingly tangy taste after a Thanksgiving feast.

INGREDIENTS | SERVES 12

1 18.25-ounce box white cake mix
1 teaspoon cinnamon
¼ teaspoon nutmeg
1 cup butter, softened
1 cup chopped walnuts (optional)
1 15-ounce can cherry pie filling
1 16-ounce can whole berry cranberry sauce
1 recipe Whipping Cream (page 166)

1. Preheat oven to 350°F.

2. Mix cake mix and spices in a large bowl. Crumble in butter. Sprinkle nuts into batter.

3. In a separate bowl, mix pie filling and cranberry sauce. Pour fruit mixture into casserole dish. Layer dry mixture over the top.

4. Bake for 50 minutes or until barely golden brown. Top generously with whipped cream.

Cranberry Bundt Cake

Sweet lemon zip and tangy cranberries blend together nicely in this creamy bundt cake.
Add a little orange flavoring, extract, or juice to the whipped topping
for a sweet citrus taste that complements cranberries beautifully.

INGREDIENTS | SERVES 15

1 18.25-ounce box lemon cake mix
1 3-ounce package cream cheese
¾ cup milk
4 eggs
1¼ cups chopped cranberries
4 eggs
¼ cup sugar
Whipped topping

1. Preheat oven to 350°F. Grease a bundt pan.

2. In a large mixing bowl, combine cake mix, cream cheese, and milk. Beat for 2 minutes with an electric mixer.

3. In a separate bowl, combine cranberries and sugar. Add eggs. Fold berry mixture into batter. Pour into bundt pan. Bake for 55 minutes.

4. Serve slightly warm with a dollop of whipped topping.

Cranberry Cream Cake

Vanilla has been a favorite since ancient times. With extra vanilla flavor and crunchy whole cranberries, this cake boasts a rich taste and texture worthy of your wildest daydreams.

INGREDIENTS | SERVES 12

1 18.25-ounce box French vanilla cake mix
1 3.9-ounce box instant vanilla pudding
4 eggs
1 cup vanilla yogurt
¼ cup vegetable oil
1 8-ounce can whole berry cranberry sauce

1. Preheat oven to 350°F. Butter and flour a 9" × 13" pan.

2. Mix cake mix, pudding, eggs, yogurt, and oil in a large bowl. Beat for 2 minutes with an electric mixer. Spread more than half the batter in the pan.

3. Spoon cranberry sauce over batter in pan. Top with remaining batter. Bake for 45 minutes. Cool before serving.

CHAPTER 13

Local and Organic

Organic Carrot Cake

This wholesome, organic, less-sweet treat is a great choice for families looking to beat the sugar blues.

INGREDIENTS | SERVES 12

1 18.25-ounce box organic carrot cake mix

1 cup organic carrots, grated

¼ cup organic applesauce

½ cup purified water

Icing a Carrot Cake

Traditionally, carrot cakes are iced with sour cream frosting, but it's also lovely with a simple glaze. Use a fork to mix 4 tablespoons organic butter with ½ cup organic confectioners' sugar and 2 teaspoons organic vanilla extract. You'll have the cool sweetness of the icing without oversweetening the cake.

1. Preheat oven to 350°F. Butter a round 9" cake pan.

2. Scrub carrots with a vegetable brush but do not peel.

3. Mix cake mix, grated carrots, applesauce, and water in a large mixing bowl. Combine contents gently with a wooden mixing spoon until batter is moist.

4. Bake for 45 minutes.

Turnip Spice Cake

Warm, mashed turnips soothe the winter soul. Mashing turnips is easy. Simply scrub the turnips, cut into chunks, boil in water, and mash using a fork or ricer.

INGREDIENTS | SERVES 8

1 18.25-ounce box spice cake mix plus ingredients called for on box

1 turnip, boiled, mashed, and cooled

1 cup raisins

4 tablespoons organic butter, melted

½ cup organic confectioners' sugar

1. Prepare and bake cake according to cake mix instructions, folding in mashed turnip and raisins after wet ingredients.

2. Allow cake to cool slightly. Whisk butter and confectioners' sugar together with a fork. Drizzle cake with glaze.

Rhubarb Upside-Down Cake

Rhubarb is best when accompanied by something sweet. Vanilla and butter fit the bill nicely. Feel like adding a little extra summer? Toss in a few ripe, sweet strawberries.

INGREDIENTS | SERVES 6

3 tablespoons organic butter, melted

1 cup sugar

1 pound rhubarb, chopped

1 18.25-ounce box white cake mix plus ingredients called for on box

1. Preheat oven according to cake mix instructions. Butter an 8" square cake pan.

2. Combine melted butter and sugar and fold into chopped rhubarb. Transfer mixture to cake pan; spread evenly.

3. Mix batter according to cake mix instructions and pour over rhubarb mixture. Bake for 35 minutes.

4. Remove cake from oven and invert onto serving platter immediately. Spoon any remaining fruit or syrup remaining in pan onto top of cake.

Easy Rhubarb Upside-Down Cake

This recipe is from Leah Jewison, president of the Mankato Area Growers Association. She knows beautiful rhubarb when she sees it.

INGREDIENTS | SERVES 8

1 cup brown sugar

3 cups rhubarb, chopped

1 18.25-ounce box yellow cake mix plus ingredients called for on box

1. Preheat oven according to cake mix instructions. Butter a 9" × 13" cake pan.

2. Sprinkle brown sugar across the bottom of the pan. Layer chopped rhubarb on top of brown sugar.

3. Prepare batter according to cake mix instructions. Pour over rhubarb. Bake according to instructions. Allow cake to cool, then invert onto serving platter.

Strawberry-Rhubarb Crumble

Strawberries and rhubarb are the taste of summer. If you've never cooked with rhubarb before, give it a try. It has a reddish color and is sold in long stalks.

INGREDIENTS | SERVES 8

1½ cups fresh rhubarb, cut into 1" pieces

1 quart fresh strawberries, hulled and quartered

Juice of 1 lemon

½ cup sugar

½ cup flour

Pinch salt

1 18.25-ounce box white cake mix

½ cup organic butter

Whipped cream, fresh cream, or ice cream to garnish (optional)

1. Preheat oven to 375°F.

2. Combine rhubarb, strawberries, lemon juice, sugar, flour, and salt in a casserole dish and mix gently but completely with a wooden spoon.

3. Layer cake mix over fruit.

4. Cut butter into pats and use to dot the top layer evenly.

5. Bake for 45 minutes, or until fruit bubbles up and top layer is golden.

6. Garnish with whipped cream, fresh cream, or ice cream if desired.

Rhubarb Tea

You can make your own lovely rhubarb tea. Simply juice the rhubarb stalks, strain the juice through cheesecloth, and strain off any froth. Mix 2 cups rhubarb juice with 6 cups water, and sweeten with 2 cups sugar. Serve over ice and garnish with fresh mint.

Sauerkraut Black Forest Cake

If you're lucky enough to have a vendor who sells homemade sauerkraut at your local farmers' market, use some of it to try this tasty treat!

INGREDIENTS | SERVES 12

1 18.25-ounce package devil's food cake mix

⅔ cup water

3 eggs

½ cup vegetable oil

1 cup sauerkraut

1 15-ounce can cherry pie filling

1 recipe Whipping Cream for garnish (page 166)

1. Preheat oven to 350°F. Grease and flour cake pans. Set aside.

2. Beat cake mix, water, eggs, and oil in a large mixing bowl, using an electric mixer set to high speed until all ingredients are completely incorporated. Gently fold in sauerkraut.

3. Turn batter into pans and bake for 30 minutes or until the center of the cake bounces back when touched gently.

4. Allow cake to cool for 15 minutes in the pan before turning out onto a wire rack.

5. Top with cherry pie filling and a dollop of whipped topping.

Chocolate Beet Cake

Fresh beets are irresistibly beautiful when you see them at the farmers' market. The challenge comes when cooking them at home. Don't let them languish in the crisper—pop them in a cake.

INGREDIENTS | SERVES 8

1 18-ounce package chocolate cake mix plus ingredients called for on box

3 cups organic beets, shredded

4 tablespoons organic butter, melted

½ cup organic confectioners' sugar

About Beets

Beets are high in vitamins A and C and well worth using. To prepare, simply scrub beets with a vegetable scrubber and shred with a grater or food processor. (Skip peeling to benefit from the trace minerals that live near the surface of the vegetable.) Remember, beet juice stains. Wear gloves and work with steel utensils whenever possible.

1. Prepare and bake cake according to cake mix instructions, folding beets in as you add wet ingredients.

2. Allow cake to cool slightly. Whisk butter and confectioners' sugar together with a fork. Drizzle cake with glaze.

Pumpkin Bread

*Whether the pumpkin is from the patch or from a can, it adds
wholesome nutrition and sweet, moist flavor to a cake.*

INGREDIENTS | SERVES 8

1 18.25-ounce box yellow cake mix

2 cups Baking Pumpkin (page 212)

½ cup organic molasses

4 eggs

1 teaspoon cinnamon

1 teaspoon ground nutmeg

1 cup chopped pecans (optional)

⅓ cup dried cranberries or raisins

Buying Pumpkin

Look for pie pumpkins or other small
pumpkins with thicker walls when you're
choosing one for baking. Most jack-o'-lan-
tern pumpkins are bred for other uses. Do
not bake your jack-o'-lantern if it is more
than one day old; it may not be safe.

1. Preheat oven to 350°F. Grease two 9½" loaf pans.

2. Combine all ingredients in a large mixing bowl and
   mix well with an electric mixer set to medium speed.
   Divide mixture evenly between the pans and bake for
   1 hour.

3. Allow to cool before turning out of pans.

Baking Pumpkin

Baking with pumpkin is easier than you might think. Simply divide this recipe's yield into batches of 2 cups (equivalent to the amount found in a can) and freeze in resealable plastic bags until ready to bake.

INGREDIENTS | YIELDS 4 CUPS

Pumpkin

Water

Oven-Baked Pumpkin

If you don't have a steamer, you can halve the pumpkin and bake it in the oven. Simply place it cut-side down in a pan filled with 1" water. Bake at 350°F for 50 minutes and proceed with Step 2.

1. Wash pumpkin and cut in half. Place 1 pumpkin half in a steamer; if it is too big, cut to fit. Steam each half for 20 minutes or until tender.

2. Allow pumpkin to cool before peeling off rind or scooping out flesh.

3. Purée pumpkin flesh and strain out excess water through a cheesecloth-lined strainer.

Spicy Squash Cake

Prepare the squash as you would the Baking Pumpkin (page 212).

INGREDIENTS | **SERVES 12**

1 18-ounce box spice cake mix plus ingredients called for on box (except water)

2 cups butternut squash, cooked and mashed

1 12-ounce tub prepared cream cheese frosting

1. Prepare batter according to cake mix instructions, substituting squash for water. Add a touch of water if batter appears too dry. Bake according to instructions.

2. Allow cake to cool before frosting.

Fresh Berry Lemon Cake

Share this cake with friends each year to celebrate the first harvest of berries from the backyard. Keep the recipe special by making it a once-a-year ritual.

INGREDIENTS | **SERVES 8**

1 18.25-ounce box lemon cake mix

1 teaspoon baking powder

1 cup fresh berries

1 cup sour cream

4 eggs

1 tablespoon oil

Lemon zest to taste

Additional berries and whipped cream (optional)

1. Preheat oven to 350°F. Grease and flour a bundt pan.

2. Combine cake mix and baking powder in a large mixing bowl. In a separate bowl, mix berries, sour cream, eggs, oil, and lemon zest. Fold dry ingredients into wet.

3. Turn batter into the bundt pan and bake for 45 minutes. Allow cake to cool slightly before turning onto rack or serving plate.

4. Serve with fresh berries and whipped cream if desired.

Harvest Squash Cobbler

Butternut squash is a versatile vegetable. It's beautiful steamed or puréed and it's just as lovely baked in a beautiful spice cake. Spice and ginger add zip to this dessert.

INGREDIENTS | SERVES 8

1 large butternut squash
2 cups sugar
2 teaspoons cinnamon
2 teaspoons pumpkin pie seasoning
1 teaspoon ground ginger
1 12-ounce can evaporated milk
4 eggs
1 18.25-ounce box yellow cake mix
1 cup organic butter, melted
Whipped topping for garnish

Add-Ins and Variations

Keep your favorite recipes fresh and exciting by adding a little something unexpected now and then. Pecans, brown sugar, and dried fruit are fun add-ins. Try them or anything else you have on hand.

1. Preheat oven to 350°F.

2. Halve the butternut squash. Clean out the seeds and microwave squash for 10 minutes. Peel and cut squash into 1" cubes. Place in a 9" × 13" pan.

3. Combine sugar, spices, evaporated milk, and eggs and pour over the squash. Crumble dry cake mix over both these layers and top liberally with melted butter.

4. Bake for 45 minutes. Serve warm with a dollop of whipped topping.

Sunshine State Cake

If you're lucky enough to have fresh organic oranges growing near you, pick them and get baking. Whether they're straight from the yard or the market, citrus is a beautiful choice for dessert.

INGREDIENTS | SERVES 8

2 eggs

1 18.25-ounce box yellow cake mix

1 3.9-ounce package instant yellow pudding mix

¾ cup water

½ cup cooking oil

⅓ cup fresh-squeezed orange juice

2 cups confectioners' sugar

3 oranges for garnish

1. Preheat oven to 350°F. Grease and flour a tube pan.

2. In a mixing bowl, beat eggs, cake mix, pudding mix, water, and oil with an electric mixer and turn into the pan. Bake for 50 minutes.

3. Allow cake to cool completely in pan.

4. As cake cools, make a glaze by boiling orange juice and sugar in a small saucepan, stirring in fresh orange zest to taste.

5. When cake is completely cool, remove it to a serving platter, drizzle with glaze, and garnish with fresh orange slices.

Juiciest Poke Cake

Consider using more than one juice to form your glaze. Try adding a dash of pomegranate or strawberry for a colorful burst of flavor.

INGREDIENTS | SERVES 8

1 18.25-ounce box orange-flavored cake mix plus ingredients called for on box

2 cups confectioners' sugar

⅓ cup fresh-squeezed citrus juice

2 tablespoons butter, melted

1 tablespoon butter

Citrus zest

Citrus fruit for garnish

1. Prepare and bake cake according to package instructions. Poke holes in the cake with a clean skewer. Combine sugar, juice, butter, and water to form a glaze.

2. Pour glaze over cake and allow cake to cool completely. Garnish with zest and sections of fruit.

A Is for Apple Cake

Got a field trip to the orchard planned? Bake this cake when you get back as you talk over your favorite memories of the day. Try Piñata, Braeburn, or Gala apples for baking.

INGREDIENTS | SERVES 8

½ cup chopped walnuts

1 18.25-ounce box spice cake mix

1 3.9-ounce box butterscotch instant pudding mix

4 eggs

½ cup vegetable oil

½ cup cold water

3 medium fresh organic apples, cored, peeled, and chopped

1 cup dried cranberries

Confectioners' sugar for garnish

1. Preheat oven to 325°F. Butter a tube pan and sprinkle the bottom with chopped walnuts.

2. Combine cake mix, pudding, eggs, oil, and water in a large mixing bowl using an electric mixer set to medium speed.

3. Gently fold in apples and dried cranberries so they are distributed evenly throughout the batter. Pour into pan and bake for 55 minutes.

4. Invert cake onto wire rack to cool. Sprinkle with confectioners' sugar.

Ginny Sawyer's Freezer Preserves

Making preserves is an easy family project that will provide sweet delights all the year through. Serve for dessert and again on warm toast with a thick layer of butter.

INGREDIENTS | **MAKES 7½ PINTS**

3 cups berries

5 cups sugar

5 tablespoons pectin

1 cup water

1. Wash, stem, and crush berries. Mix with sugar and let stand 30 minutes.

2. Mix pectin and water; bring to a boil and boil for 1 minute. Stir into berry mixture. Stir with a wooden spoon for 2 minutes.

3. Put in freezer-safe containers, leaving ½ inch air at the top. Let stand 24 hours to set, and then freeze. Thaw when ready to serve.

Farmers' Market Trifle

Have an overabundance of fresh fruit? What a wonderful dilemma! This recipe is one of many creative ways you'll find to celebrate and enjoy the taste of summer.

INGREDIENTS | SERVES 6–8

1 18.25-ounce box organic angel food cake mix plus ingredients called for on box

½ cup organic milk

½ cup organic vanilla yogurt

1 3.9-ounce box organic instant pudding mix

4 cups peaches or other juicy fresh fruit

Fresh whipped cream

Get Your Fruit Ready

There's much more to storing fruit than stashing it in the fridge. Most fruits will turn grainy and wilt if they get much cooler than 30°F. Citrus fruit has an even lower tolerance level for cold temperatures. Many fruits will do just fine—and even continue to ripen—outside the fridge. If you're just waiting a day or two to eat them, consider displaying fruit in a bowl in the kitchen.

1. Prepare and bake angel food cake according to cake mix instructions.

2. As cake bakes, combine milk, yogurt, and pudding mix in a large bowl using an electric mixer set to high speed. Let stand 10 minutes.

3. When cake is baked and cooled, cut into bite-sized cubes.

4. Place a layer of cake cubes in the bottom of a large glass bowl, follow with a layer of fresh fruit, and top with milk mixture. Repeat until bowl is nearly full.

5. Top with whipped cream. Keep cool until ready to serve.

Organic Grasshopper Brownies

A healthier take on an indulgent favorite, this is an ideal choice to satisfy your sweet tooth without abandoning your commitment to eating organic.

INGREDIENTS | SERVES 12

1 10-ounce box organic chocolate biscotti mix

2 large eggs

5 tablespoons organic butter, melted

Organic chocolate morsels

3 tablespoons organic peppermint flavor

Shopping Organic

Finding organic ingredients has never been easier. Organic mixes are readily available online as well as in co-ops and at grocers everywhere. You often pay a premium and you might have to go a little out of your way for these ingredients, but the taste and purity are worth it!

1. Preheat oven to 350°F. Grease and flour 8" × 8" cake pan. Set aside.

2. In a large mixing bowl, combine biscotti mix, eggs, butter, chocolate morsels, and peppermint flavor.

3. Use an electric mixer set to medium speed to combine ingredients. Pour batter into pan. Bake for 25 minutes.

Fruit Stand Jam Cake

This lovely dessert is one of the many simple ways to enjoy the taste of beautifully fresh fruit. With only two ingredients, it's easy to bake up any time you've got a hankering.

INGREDIENTS | SERVES 15

1 18.25-ounce box white cake mix marked "just add water"

1 12-ounce jar freezer preserves

1. Preheat oven to 350°F. Grease a bundt pan.

2. Combine preserves and cake mix in a large mixing bowl. Mix using a wooden spoon; do not expect a smooth batter. Pour into pan. Bake for 25 minutes.

Zucchini Cake

Zucchini is a delicate squash that is in season during mid- and late summer in most climates. Try to use fresh zucchini immediately and avoid refrigerating if possible. Zucchini hates the cold!

INGREDIENTS | SERVES 8

1 18.25-ounce box devil's food cake mix
1 teaspoon ground cinnamon
3 eggs
1¼ cups apple juice
1 cup organic zucchini, shredded
4-ounce cream cheese, softened
2 teaspoons lemon juice
Zucchini peel

1. Preheat oven to 350°F. Flour and grease a 10" tube pan.

2. Combine cake mix, ground cinnamon, and eggs and beat for 2 minutes. Shred zucchini using a large-holed grater or a food processor. Fold zucchini in gently.

3. Turn batter into pan and spread evenly. Bake for 55 minutes.

4. Allow cake to cool. Mix softened cream cheese and lemon juice for frosting. Frost cake and garnish lightly with zucchini zest.

Smoothie Splash Pound Cake

Need a little boost of antioxidants or vitamin C on a cold night? Bake a pound cake with a hidden punch!

INGREDIENTS | **SERVES 12**

1 16-ounce box organic pound cake mix
¾ cup organic smoothie
2 eggs
3 lemons
2 limes
¼ cup packed brown sugar

1. Preheat oven to 350°F. Grease a loaf pan.

2. Mix cake mix, smoothie, and eggs according to cake mix instructions. Bake according to package directions.

3. Allow cake to cool in the pan on a wire rack for 15 minutes before turning onto a serving platter. Juice lemons and limes and stir in brown sugar to make glaze. Use to top the cake.

CHAPTER 14

Vegetarian Cakes

DIY Vegan Cake Mix

A great way to ensure wholesome and vegan cake is to add all the ingredients yourself. On a rainy day, make up a few batches of cake mix and enjoy simple baking later.

INGREDIENTS | MAKES 5 CUPS

3 cups flour
2 cups sugar
8 tablespoons cocoa
2 teaspoons baking soda
2 teaspoons salt

1. Combine all ingredients. Stir to mix. Store in an airtight container.

2. To bake cake, preheat oven to 375°F. Combine mix, 2 cups water, 1½ teaspoons vanilla, 2 tablespoons vinegar, and ¾ cup canola oil. Bake for 30 minutes.

Converting Recipes

Cooking vegan doesn't always mean abandoning all your favorite old recipes. In some cases you'll be able to replace dairy milk with soy milk, butter with margarine, and eggs with Ener-G Egg Replacer or banana.

Super Quick Vegan Cookies

Vegan treats don't have to take tons of time and a lengthy list of ingredients. There are great shortcuts; this recipe is one of them.

INGREDIENTS | MAKES 24 COOKIES

1 18.25-ounce box vegan cake mix
1 cup unsalted vegan margarine
3 teaspoons Ener-G Egg Replacer
4 tablespoons warm water
1½ cups vegan chocolate chips (optional)

1. Mix all ingredients in a bowl. Chill at least 1 hour or overnight.

2. Preheat oven to 350°F.

3. Drop batter onto nonstick cookie sheet in small balls. Bake for 12 minutes or until golden brown. Remove from sheet and place on cooling rack.

Vegan Pumpkin Cookies

This classic vegan treat for autumn days goes great with a steaming mug of coffee.

INGREDIENTS | **MAKES 24 COOKIES**

2 boxes spice cake mix
1 29-ounce can organic pumpkin purée
2 cups vegan chocolate chips (optional)

1. Preheat oven to 350°F.

2. Mix all ingredients thoroughly. Drop by spoonfuls onto a nonstick cookie sheet. Bake for 10–12 minutes. Cool on a rack.

Vegan Yellow Cake Sugar Cookies

This is a great base for iced holiday cookies or cutouts.

INGREDIENTS | **MAKES 24 COOKIES**

1 18-ounce box vegan yellow cake mix
3 teaspoons Ener-G Egg Replacer
4 tablespoons warm water
¼ cup oil
½ cup brown sugar

1. Preheat oven to 350°F.

2. Mix all ingredients well. Gather up dough and roll out on a well-floured surface. Cut with a biscuit cutter or the top edge of a drinking glass.

3. Transfer with spatula to nonstick cookie sheet. Bake for 8–10 minutes or until golden. Cool.

Famous Vegan Fizz Cake

*Ask a vegan for a cake mix recipe and you'll undoubtedly hear about the simple soda cake.
This amazing recipe calls for only two ingredients and is very easy to bake.
It's a great go-to staple any time you need a vegan treat.*

INGREDIENTS | SERVES 12

1 18-ounce box vegan cake mix
1¼ cups non-diet soda

1. Preheat oven according to cake mix instructions. Lightly grease cake pan or bundt pan with vegan margarine or a vegan spray.

2. Gently stir together cake mix and soda. Do not overstir; you want to preserve the soda's fizz. Pour mixture into pan.

3. Bake according to cake mix instructions.

Vegan Chocolate Fizz Bundt Cake

*Whip up the taste of an old-fashioned chocolate cola for a truly decadent desert. This is a
convenient vegan treat that's easy to keep on hand to satisfy cravings for something sweet.*

INGREDIENTS | SERVES 12

1 18.25-ounce box chocolate cake mix
1 12-ounce can cola
Vegan Bundt Cake Glaze (page 227)

1. Preheat oven according to cake mix instructions. Lightly grease cake pan or bundt pan with vegan margarine or a vegan spray.

2. Gently stir together cake mix and soda. Do not overstir; you want to preserve the soda's fizz. Pour mixture into pan.

3. Bake according to cake mix instructions. Cool and frost with Vegan Bundt Cake Glaze.

Vegan Bundt Cake Glaze

A milk-free chocolate glaze adds a bit of super-sweetness to your vegan bundt cake. Easy to make and fun to drizzle, there's no reason not to try this wonder recipe.

INGREDIENTS | **SERVES 12**

¼ cup melted vegan chocolate chips
¾ cup rice milk

Mix melted chocolate chips and rice milk together. Drizzle over cake.

Vegan Cherry Cola Cake

Committing to a vegan diet doesn't mean giving up all your favorite fast foods. Here's a way to satisfy a soda craving without downing a whole can.

INGREDIENTS | **SERVES 12**

1 18-ounce box chocolate cake mix
1 12-ounce can cherry cola
Vegan Bundt Cake Glaze (above)

1. Preheat oven according to cake mix instructions. Lightly grease cake pan or bundt pan with vegan margarine or a vegan spray.

2. Gently stir together cake mix and soda. Do not overstir; you want to preserve the soda's fizz. Pour mixture into pan.

3. Bake according to cake mix instructions. Cool and frost with Vegan Bundt Cake Glaze.

Vegan Spice Cake

Simple fizz cake gets a little fancy in this still-simple recipe. Four ingredients are all it takes to bake up a beautiful cake.

INGREDIENTS | **SERVES 12**

1 18-ounce box chocolate cake mix

1 12-ounce can Dr. Pepper

2 cups raisins

Vegan Bundt Cake Glaze (page 227)

1. Preheat oven according to cake mix instructions. Lightly grease cake pan or bundt pan with vegan margarine or a vegan spray.

2. Gently stir together cake mix and soda. Do not overstir; you want to preserve the soda's fizz. Stir in raisins. Pour mixture into pan.

3. Bake according to cake mix instructions. Frost with Vegan Bundt Cake Glaze.

Fancy Red Fizz Cake

For anyone with egg, nut, or dairy allergies, this recipe is a lifesaver. This simple cake is bright, cheery, pleasing, and safe for those who need to steer clear of allergens. Just to be on the safe side, be sure to double-check for allergens in the ingredients listed on the cake mix box.

INGREDIENTS | **SERVES 12**

9.9-ounce box allergen-free white cake mix

2 tablespoons unsweetened cocoa

1 12-ounce can ginger ale or other clear soda

2 teaspoons vanilla extract

Red food coloring

1 12-ounce tub cream cheese or chocolate frosting

1. Preheat oven according to cake mix instructions.

2. Sift cake mix and cocoa in a bowl. Add soda and beat with an electric mixer. Add vanilla. Add food coloring.

3. Pour into a pan and bake according to cake mix instructions. Frost with cream cheese or chocolate icing.

Chocolate Pumpkin Muffins

This quick and easy recipe is good to try for people who have food allergies, or for groups of young children.

INGREDIENTS | SERVES 24

1 29-ounce can organic pumpkin purée
1 16.4-ounce box dairy- and egg-free organic chocolate cake mix

1. Preheat oven according to cake mix instructions. Line muffin tins with paper baking cups.

2. Blend pumpkin purée into cake mix. Pour into muffin tins. Bake according to cake mix instructions for muffins.

Vegan Vanilla Icing

This vegan royal icing is perfect for fancy wedding and birthday cakes, so you can celebrate in style and stay true to your vegan lifestyle.

INGREDIENTS | MAKES 4 CUPS

2 cups Crisco
1 cup icing sugar
½ cup water
1 tablespoon vanilla

Combine all ingredients with electric mixer on low speed for 1 minute. Scrape sides of bowl. Mix for another minute.

Vegan Chocolate Frosting

The creamy, buttery taste of this rich, fudgy frosting will fool people into thinking it's not really vegan.

INGREDIENTS | 8 CUPS

1 cup vegan margarine
1 cup unsweetened cocoa powder
5⅓ cups confectioners' sugar
½ cup water
2 teaspoons vanilla

1. Mix vegan margarine and cocoa powder with electric mixer set to low speed. Slowly introduce confectioners' sugar and water, alternating between the two.

2. Mix at a slightly higher speed until desired consistency is achieved. Add vanilla.

Vegan Dump Cake

Dump cake is a favorite potluck treat, and now it's been modified to serve to your vegan friends too! Using this recipe as a template, you can veganize other dump cake recipes in this book.

INGREDIENTS | SERVES 12

1 can crushed pineapple
1 can blueberry pie filling
1 18.5-ounce box Duncan Hines yellow cake mix
½ cup vegan margarine
1 tablespoon brown sugar

1. Preheat oven according to cake mix instructions. Grease a pan.

2. Pour pineapple into prepared pan. Layer in blueberry pie filling. Top with cake mix. Dot with chunks of margarine. Bake according to cake mix instructions. Allow to cool. Sprinkle with brown sugar.

Vegan Applesauce Cake

This dish is easy to bake, simple to serve, and easy to transport. Take it along and watch it disappear.

INGREDIENTS | SERVES 12

1 tablespoon flour
1 18.5-ounce box Duncan Hines yellow
  cake mix
⅓ cup organic applesauce
3 bananas, mashed
1¼ cups water

1. Preheat oven to 350°F.

2. Add flour to cake mix and sift. Add applesauce and bananas. Stir in water. Pour into nonstick pan. Bake according to package directions.

Sugar Cake

Combine gooey brown sugar and light yellow cake for this lovely, versatile dessert.
Serve with sliced peaches or other fleshy fruits for an extra luscious treat.

INGREDIENTS | SERVES 8

½ cup soy margarine
½ cup brown sugar
½ cup soy milk
1 18.5-ounce box Duncan Hines yellow
  cake
Sugar Cake Topping (page 232)

1. Preheat oven to 350°F. Lightly grease a sheet cake pan.

2. Melt margarine in saucepan over low heat. Whisk in brown sugar and soy milk. Remove from heat. Pour into sheet cake pan.

3. Layer cake mix on top of the brown sugar mixture. Shake pan to even out mixture. Bake for 10 minutes. Remove from pan. Cool on rack.

4. Frost with Sugar Cake Topping.

Sugar Cake Topping

With only two ingredients to keep on hand, this frosting can be
ready to go in a snap any time the urge to bake strikes.

INGREDIENTS | **SERVES 8**

1 3-ounce package instant vanilla
pudding

1 16-ounce tub nondairy whipped
topping

Mix pudding and nondairy whipped topping gently.
Spread onto cake. Keep cake cool until ready to serve.

Vegan Brownie Bites

Sometimes a tiny bite of sweetness is just enough to satisfy your
sweet tooth. These are great for lunches or snacks.

INGREDIENTS | **SERVES 24**

1 18.25-ounce box vegan chocolate cake
mix

1 29-ounce can organic pumpkin purée

2 cups vegan chocolate morsels

1 cup chopped walnuts

1. Preheat oven to 350°F.

2. Use an electric mixer to combine cake mix and
   pumpkin until completely incorporated. Fold in
   chocolate morsels and walnuts.

3. Drop by spoonfuls onto nonstick baking sheet. Bake
   for 10 minutes. Cool on a wire rack.

Eggless Yellow Cake

This is the perfect recipe for vegetarians who are okay with milk but want to avoid eggs. This basic yellow cake recipe is a perfect canvas for your creative touch. Consider adding chocolate chips, butterscotch pieces, candies, or fresh fruit to this recipe.

INGREDIENTS | SERVES 12

1 3-ounce box vanilla pudding (not instant)
2 cups milk
1 18.5-ounce box Duncan Hines yellow cake mix
1 12-ounce tub prepared frosting

1. Preheat oven to 350°F. Butter and flour a 13" × 9" × 2" baking pan. Set aside.

2. Mix pudding and milk.

3. In a large mixing bowl combine pudding and dry cake mix. Use an electric mixer to blend until batter is completely smooth.

4. Pour into pan and bake for 25 minutes. Allow cake to cool completely before frosting.

Vegan Strawberry Shortcake

Bake up this not-too-sweet treat on a beautiful summer day. For a lighter, spongier cake, substitute yellow cake mix for Bisquick. For a richer, thicker dessert, substitute Vegan Brownie Bites (page 232) for biscuits.

INGREDIENTS | SERVES 4

4 sliced strawberries
½ cup sugar
2¼ cups Bisquick
⅔ cup soy milk
½ cup vegan margarine
Vegan whipped topping

1. Preheat oven to 450°F.

2. Mix sliced strawberries with sugar in a large mixing bowl. Set aside. In a separate bowl, mix Bisquick, soy milk, and margarine until a smooth dough forms.

3. Drop by spoonfuls onto nonstick cookie sheet. Bake 9 minutes or until slightly golden.

4. Remove from oven and let biscuits cool thoroughly before topping with strawberries and whipped topping.

CHAPTER 15

Special Diets and Allergies

Basic DIY Cake Mix

Want to enjoy the convenience of baking with a mix but need to keep an eye out for allergens and other problematic ingredients? Make your own cake mix. This mix will keep three weeks in the refrigerator and three months in the freezer.

INGREDIENTS | MAKES 12 CUPS

7½ cups sifted flour

1 tablespoon salt

4½ cups sugar

4 tablespoons double-acting baking powder

¾ cup unsalted butter

1. Combine all ingredients except butter in a large mixing bowl and mix well.

2. Cut butter into fine pats and run through a food processor with 2½ cups of the flour mixture. Stop when the mixture is quite fine.

3. Combine processed mixture with remaining flour mixture. Mix thoroughly. Place 4 cups mixture in each of 3 resealable plastic bags for future use.

4. Label and refrigerate or freeze mixture until ready to use.

Yellow Cake from DIY Mix

Yellow cake is a staple of many of the recipes in this book. This basic cake will taste similar to yellow cakes made from mixes but will not include dyes, preservatives, and other ingredients that can spark allergic reactions.

INGREDIENTS | SERVES 8–12

4 cups Basic DIY Cake Mix (above)

1 cup skim milk

2 teaspoons vanilla

¼ cup unsalted butter, softened

3 eggs

1. Preheat oven to 350°F. Grease and flour cake pans. Set aside.

2. Pour cake mix into a large bowl. Make a well in the center. Add skim milk, vanilla, and butter. Beat for 3 minutes or until a smooth batter forms. Add eggs and thoroughly combine. Pour into pans.

3. Bake for 35 minutes or until the center of the cake springs back when lightly touched.

White Cake from DIY Mix

This recipe for white cake provides a beautiful base for frosted birthday and wedding cakes. It's simpler than baking from scratch, but you can control your own ingredients.

INGREDIENTS | SERVES 8–12

4 cups Basic DIY Cake Mix (page 236)
1 cup skim milk
2 teaspoons vanilla
¼ cup unsalted butter, softened
3 egg whites

1. Preheat oven to 350°F. Grease and flour cake pans. Set aside.

2. Pour cake mix into a large bowl. Make a well in the center. Add skim milk, vanilla, and butter. Beat for 3 minutes or until a smooth batter forms. Add egg whites and thoroughly combine. Pour into a pan.

3. Bake for 35 minutes or until the center of the cake springs back when lightly touched.

Spice Cake from DIY Mix

Create your own warm, spicy, nourishing cakes with this spectacular combination. Add a little more of your favorite flavors for a blend that's all your own.

INGREDIENTS | SERVES 8–12

4 cups Basic DIY Cake Mix (page 236)
1 teaspoon freshly ground cinnamon
½ teaspoon ground allspice
¼ teaspoon ground cloves
1 cup skim milk
2 teaspoons vanilla
¼ cup unsalted butter, softened
3 eggs

1. Preheat oven to 350°F. Grease and flour cake pans. Set aside.

2. Mix cake mix and spices in a large bowl. Make a well in the center. Add milk, vanilla, and butter. Beat for 3 minutes or until a smooth batter forms. Add eggs and thoroughly combine. Pour into a pan.

3. Bake for 35 minutes or until the center of the cake springs back when lightly touched.

Strawberry Cake from DIY Mix

This simple strawberry cake contains sugar and spice and everything nice, so it's perfect for a girly cake—but the boys like the taste, too!

INGREDIENTS | SERVES 8–12

4 cups Basic DIY Cake Mix (page 236)

2 teaspoons vanilla

3 egg whites

1 cup skim milk

1 10-ounce package frozen strawberries, thawed

¼ cup softened, unsalted butter

1. Preheat oven to 350°F. Grease and flour cake pans. Set aside.

2. Pour cake mix into a large bowl. Make a well in the center. Add skim milk, strawberries, and butter. Beat for 3 minutes or until a smooth batter forms. Add vanilla and egg whites; thoroughly combine. Pour into cake pans.

3. Bake for 35 minutes or until the center of the cake springs back when lightly touched.

"Flour" to Make Gluten-Free DIY Cake Mix

Substitute this mixture for flour in the DIY Cake Mix recipes to create gluten-free cake mixes. It is easier than ever to find gluten-free baking mixes and baked goods, but it's just as easy to create your own mixes and use them to try other recipes in this book.

INGREDIENTS | 6 CUPS

3 cups finely ground brown rice flour

1 cup potato starch

½ cup tapioca flour

1¼ teaspoons xanthan or guar gum

Sift all ingredients together and blend thoroughly. Substitute for flour in DIY cake mix recipes.

Dye- and Milk-Free Chocolate Frosting

This recipe is free of milk, dye, nuts, and other common allergens.
It's a yummy and safe bet for food-sensitive folks.

INGREDIENTS | **4 CUPS**

½ cup allergy-safe margarine, softened
½ cup unsweetened cocoa
2⅔ cups confectioners' sugar
¼ cup water
1 teaspoon pure organic vanilla extract

Beat margarine using an electric mixer set to low speed. Add other ingredients and mix until completely incorporated. Use to top a cooled cake.

No-Dye Red Velvet Cake

Love red velvet cake but worried about food coloring allergies? Here's
a naturally sweet solution rich in color, texture, and flavor.

INGREDIENTS | **SERVES 8**

1 18.25-ounce box white cake mix plus ingredients called for on box
1 cup canned puréed cooked beets
1 teaspoon vanilla extract
1 12-ounce tub prepared cream cheese frosting

1. Preheat oven according to cake mix instructions.

2. Mix batter according to instructions, adding in beets and vanilla before mixing batter. Bake according to instructions. Allow to cool completely. Frost.

Chocolate Cake from DIY Mix

Finally, easy-to-bake chocolate cake without all the colors and artificial flavors! Starting with DIY Mix makes it easy. Selecting your own ingredients makes it wholesome.

INGREDIENTS | **SERVES 8–12**

4 cups Basic DIY Cake Mix (page 236)

1 cup plus 2 tablespoons skim milk, divided

2 teaspoons vanilla

¼ cup unsalted butter, softened

3 eggs

2 squares unsweetened chocolate, melted

3 tablespoons cocoa powder

1. Preheat oven to 350°F. Grease and flour cake pans. Set aside.

2. Pour cake mix into a large bowl. Make a well in the center. Add 1 cup skim milk, vanilla, and butter. Beat for 3 minutes or until a smooth batter forms.

3. Add remaining 2 tablespoons skim milk, melted chocolate, and cocoa powder. Beat using an electric mixer until batter and chocolate are fully incorporated. Add eggs and thoroughly combine. Pour batter into cake pans.

4. Bake for 35 minutes or until the center of the cake springs back when lightly touched.

Cherrybrook Kitchen's Chocolate Cake
with Raspberry Filling

This is a fruity, chocolaty recipe that's egg and dairy free. It's safe for many diets and delicious too.

INGREDIENTS | SERVES 8

2 boxes Cherrybrook Kitchen Chocolate Cake mix and ingredients called for on box

1 box Cherrybrook Kitchen Chocolate Frosting mix and ingredients called for on box

½ cup seedless raspberry preserves

½ pint fresh raspberries

1. Prepare and bake cake according to package instructions for two layer cakes. Set cake aside to cool.

2. While cake is cooling, prepare chocolate frosting according to package instructions. Set aside.

3. Place one cake on a serving platter and spread with a thin layer of frosting.

4. Top with raspberry jam, leaving a ½" border around the edge to ensure that jam doesn't run over the sides.

5. Place second cake round on top of the first and frost top and sides with remaining frosting. Arrange berries as desired on top of cake.

6. Chill cake until ready to serve.

Gluten-Free Vanilla Cake

Baking can be the trickiest part of observing a gluten-free diet. Gluten-free mixes make it easy, delicious, and almost foolproof.

INGREDIENTS | SERVES 6

1 15-ounce box Gluten-Free Pantry Old Fashioned cake mix

1 3.9-ounce box instant vanilla pudding

½ cup sugar

5 eggs

½ cup olive oil

¾ cup orange or cranberry juice

1½ teaspoons vanilla extract

1. Preheat oven to 350°F. Flour and grease cake pan. Set aside.

2. Combine cake mix, pudding mix, and sugar in a medium bowl. In a separate bowl, combine eggs, olive oil, juice, and vanilla extract in a mixing bowl and combine thoroughly using an electric mixer set to high speed. Add dry ingredients and thoroughly incorporate. Turn batter into prepared cake pan.

3. Bake for 45 minutes, or until a toothpick comes out clean. Allow cake to cool completely before frosting.

Where to Find Gluten-Free Mixes

If you have a health food store nearby, you have a go-to spot for gluten-free mixes. Your grocer may also carry one or two. If neither of these options work for you, try the Internet. Many reputable online merchants can deliver these mixes right to your door.

Allergy-Friendly Icing

When you know what's in your icing, it's easier to avoid allergens like milk and eggs. Use a splash of coffee for a warm brown color, beets for pinks and reds, blueberries for blue, strawberries for flavorful pinks, and lemon for the lightest of yellow tints.

INGREDIENTS | SERVES 8

1 pound confectioners' sugar

2 tablespoons water

1 cup solid vegetable shortening

1 tablespoon vanilla extract

1 teaspoon butter flavoring

1 tablespoon meringue powder (optional)

1. Sift confectioners' sugar into a large mixing bowl. Cream remaining ingredients in a separate bowl.

2. Combine mixtures using an electric mixer set to medium speed for 2 minutes or until creamy and all ingredients are fully incorporated.

Sugar-Free Frosting

This recipe works for diabetics or others who are looking to limit their sugar intake. But don't let the low sugar content fool you—it's as sweet and delicious as you want it to be.

INGREDIENTS | 4 CUPS

1 1.4-ounce package sugar-free instant vanilla pudding

1¾ cups milk

1 8-ounce package cream cheese

1 8-ounce tub frozen light whipped topping, thawed

1. In a steel mixing bowl, mix pudding mix and milk until lumps are gone. Set aside until mixture thickens.

2. Use an electric mixer to beat cream cheese until spreadable. Add pudding mixture to cream cheese and combine using electric mixer.

3. Fold in whipped topping and keep cool (not frozen) until ready to use.

Gluten-Free Peach Cobbler

This is a gluten-free recipe the whole family will want to share. Peaches and spice bake up with a buttery cake crust that just begs for a dollop of whipped topping or vanilla ice cream.

INGREDIENTS | SERVES 8

1 quart canned peaches with liquid

2 cups gluten-free cake mix

½ cup soy milk

1 teaspoon cinnamon

½ teaspoon nutmeg

½ cup Fleischmann's margarine

1. Preheat oven to 350°F.

2. Pour canned peaches and liquid into a casserole dish.

3. Combine cake mix, soy milk, and spices in a small mixing bowl. Spoon this mixture on top of peaches in dish.

4. Cut margarine into pats and dot the top of the casserole. Bake for 15–20 minutes or until top looks golden brown.

Diabetic-Friendly Hearth-Spice Angel Food Cake

Angel food cake is a staple of many healthier diets. The delicate blend of spices in this recipe adds a little kick for variety.

INGREDIENTS | SERVES 6

1 teaspoon cinnamon

1 teaspoon ground ginger

½ teaspoon ground nutmeg

1 18.25-ounce box angel food cake mix plus ingredients called for on box

Mix spices into dry cake mix. Prepare cake according to instructions on the package. Let cake cool in the pan before inverting onto a wire rack.

Diabetic Carrot Cake

While cakes can be made lower in sugars, they are not usually lower in carbohydrates. Enjoy them in moderation, taking special care to avoid cake recipes that contain fruit juice, which quickly raises blood sugar.

INGREDIENTS | SERVES 6

1 18.25-ounce box spice cake mix

1 12-ounce can diet lemon-lime soft drink

½ cup shredded carrots

½ cup raisins

½ cup nuts, chopped

1. Preheat oven to 350°F. Grease and flour cake pan. Set aside.

2. Combine cake mix and diet soda, using electric mixer to blend completely. Fold in carrots, raisins, and nuts. Bake according to cake mix instructions. Allow cake to cool.

Diabetic Lemon Cake

Substituting diet soda for eggs and oil saves calories but lets the sweet flavor and tender texture shine right through. Add a splash of lemon juice to some sugar-free whipped topping to frost your fully cooled cake.

INGREDIENTS | SERVES 6

1 18.25-ounce box lemon cake mix

1 12-ounce can lemon-lime diet carbonated soft drink

1. Preheat oven to 350°F. Grease and flour cake pan. Set aside.

2. Combine cake and soft drink to create a smooth batter. Turn batter into the cake pan. Bake according to cake mix instructions.

Egg- and Dairy-Free Yellow Cake

Three convenient ingredients stocked in your pantry means you're ready to bake anytime company stops by—or whenever the mood strikes.

INGREDIENTS | SERVES 6

1 18.25-ounce box Duncan Hines Moist Deluxe Yellow Cake mix plus ingredients called for on box except eggs

6 teaspoons Ener-G Egg Replacer

8 tablespoons warm water

1 tub Duncan Hines French Vanilla Creamy Home-Style Frosting

Preheat oven to 350°F. Bake cake according to package instructions, substituting egg replacer and water for egg. Allow cake to cool completely before frosting with an egg- and dairy-free frosting.

Orangey Angel Cookies

These bright and yummy cookies are a tempting treat that can fit safely into a diabetic diet. Citrus adds a bright sweetness and the soda gives the dessert a celebratory color. Try this with sodas that don't contain any artificial colors.

INGREDIENTS | SERVES 28

1 14½-ounce box angel food cake mix

½ cup diet orange soda

¼ teaspoon almond extract

1. Preheat oven to 350°F. Lightly treat cookie sheets with cooking spray.

2. Combine cake mix, orange soda, and almond extract in a large mixing bowl using an electric mixer set to medium speed. Mix to form a smooth, fully incorporated dough.

3. Spoon dough onto cookie sheets. Bake for 8 minutes. Remove from baking sheet to a wire rack for cooling. Serve and enjoy.

Diabetic-Friendly Sweet Treat

Finding a sweet indulgence that fits into a diabetic diet can be tricky. This one makes the choice easy and helps keep cravings under control. One serving equals 1 starch, 1 fruit, and 2 fats.

INGREDIENTS | SERVES 12

1 18.25-ounce box white cake mix

1¾ cups sugar-free orange soda, divided use

¼ cup vegetable oil

2 eggs

1 1.3-ounce envelope dry whipped topping mix

1. Preheat oven to 350°F. Grease and flour a 13" × 9" cake pan.

2. In a large mixing bowl, beat cake mix, 1¼ cup orange soda, oil, and eggs for 3 minutes to form a smooth batter. Turn batter into cake pan and bake for 35 minutes.

3. Allow cake to cool before inverting onto a wire rack to cool completely.

4. Meanwhile, beat whipped topping mix and remaining ½ cup soda until stiff peaks form. Frost cake and store chilled until ready to serve.

APPENDIX A

Cake Decorating

Basic Tools and Techniques

Most of the recipes in this book call for you to simply frost the cake. But if you really want to show off your creation, knowing how to decorate your cake will come in handy. First, there are a few necessary tools you'll want to keep around your kitchen.

To create designs or write words on your cake, you can buy decorating bags made of vinyl or even disposable plastic bags for more convenience. Spoon your frosting into the bag, filling it about halfway. Twist the top of the bag to seal and then squeeze firmly to move the frosting out through the decorating tip and onto your cake. It will take a bit of practice to become comfortable with the technique. A great way to practice using the different tips is to make designs on a sheet of waxed paper.

Some of the tools that you may want to collect are:

- Couplers—allow you to change decorating tips quickly and easily
- Fine writing tips—great for outlining parts of the cake, making scrolls and small dots, and writing
- Star tips—make nice mounds to put dragees on and create shells and other decorative effects
- Larger writing tips—great for polka dots and filling in larger areas with color
- Paintbrushes—can be used for applying egg yolk paint or corn syrup
- Toothpicks—can be used to move color or create a chevron effect when you drag them through stripes of thin frosting
- Special tools that allow you to make intricate sculptures with marzipan and fondant are fun to learn to use and will help you make spectacular decorated desserts.

Once the cake is decorated, set it aside to allow the frosting to harden before storing; this will keep the designs from smearing. A final garnish may be created by using products like luster dust or edible glitter to enhance the decorated cookie. Some people even use edible gold leaf for very special decorated cookies.

Edible gold and silver have been used for years all over the world. It is available in the United States, but the Food and Drug Administration (FDA) says that it has not been approved for human consumption. Edible gold and silver has been in use since before there was an FDA, so it was never submitted for premarket approval.

Dusting and Stenciling Techniques

One of the easiest ways to decorate is to sift a fine coating of cocoa powder or confectioners' sugar onto your dessert. This technique is sometimes called dusting. To take this technique one step further, you can create a design on the top of your dessert by sifting cocoa powder or confectioners' sugar through a stencil.

1. You can use a paper doily as a stencil, or you can create a custom stencil by cutting a design out of sift paper or light cardboard.
2. If the top of your dessert is dry, you can lay the stencil directly on top. Place the cocoa powder or confectioners' sugar in a fine mesh sieve and gently tap, rather than shake, a thin even layer over the stencil. Take care to use a minimal amount. You want an even coverage, but if you use too much, the design will blur when you remove the stencil. Then slowly lift the stencil up, being careful not to disturb the design.
3. If the top of your dessert is moist or sticky, rig a frame that will hold the stencil above your dessert. You can do this by placing the dessert in a pan that is slightly larger and taller, or by arranging glasses or boxes around the dessert, upon which the stencil can rest.

If you've never used a stencil, it's a good idea to practice first by stenciling onto waxed paper. Once you've stenciled a few desserts, you'll have a feel for how much cocoa powder or confectioners' sugar to use and what stenciled designs look best.

Two more tips: Use alkalized ("Dutch-processed") cocoa powder for dusting and stenciling; it has a softer flavor. And don't be shy about blending cocoa powder and confectioners' sugar together. Adding ground nuts or spices provides varied effects and flavors.

Chocolate Drizzles

This decorating technique works best on a cake that has already been covered with a smooth glaze. It creates an artistic random effect, like raindrops hitting your window on a windy day.

1. To prevent some of the mess this technique can create, set up a splatter shield by covering your immediate working area, including the walls, with waxed paper.
2. Melt couverture (chocolate rich in cocoa butter), stirring until smooth. While the chocolate is warm and very fluid, dip a fork in it, and quickly flick the fork over your dessert. Continue flicking in different directions until most of the chocolate has left the fork.
3. Dip the fork in the chocolate again and repeat until you achieve the effect you desire. With some desserts, you may want a light coverage, while with other desserts you may want more.
4. Allow the dessert to set in a cool room, or place in the refrigerator for 3 to 5 minutes.
5. When you're finished, place the waxed paper onto which the excess chocolate has fallen in the refrigerator until set.
6. Peel the bits of chocolate off the waxed paper and store to melt and use again, or save to break up and sprinkle on other desserts instead of the chocolate flavored sprinkles grocery stores sell.

Piping

Perhaps one of the most widely used decorating techniques is piping. This can be used to create a wide variety of designs, including initials.

This technique requires a pastry bag fitted with a writing tip or a squeeze bottle with a very small opening. You can do this with frosting, royal icing, and special piping gels. If you want chocolate piping, use high-quality couverture for the best results. Melt the chocolate and place it in the pastry bag while it's still warm.

1. The easiest, and most popular, designs for piping are straight or diagonal lines, crosshatches, and swirls.
2. If you want very fine lines, choose a tip with a very small opening, make sure your piping material is very warm and fluid, and work quickly.
3. If you prefer heavier lines, let the material cool a bit and work more slowly, or select a tip with a slightly larger opening.
4. If the base glaze or coating on your dessert has not yet set, the material you pipe on top will melt into the base. If you want the decoration to sit on top of the base, wait until the base has set to decorate.

As with stenciling, if you've never piped before, practice on waxed paper.

Filigree

This is a lovely decoration that's surprisingly simple to do if you have a template. Filigree is a design piped in a delicate, usually loopy, design, and placed vertically or horizontally on a dessert. It can be made using royal icing or melted chocolate. You can even create multidimensional decorations by piping flat pieces and gluing them together with melted chocolate.

1. The easiest way to create filigree is to place a picture of the design you'd like to duplicate on a flat surface under a sheet of waxed paper or cooking-grade acetate.
2. Place the filigree material in a pastry bag fitted with a writing tip and trace the design. Allow the filigree to set in a cool room, or refrigerate for 3 to 5 minutes.
3. Carefully remove the filigree from the waxed paper or acetate with a metal spatula. Try not to touch the piece too much; this prevents fingerprints and melting.
4. Place on a cake or store in an airtight container in a cool place. If you need to stack the pieces, place a piece of waxed paper between each layer.

Appliqués

Similar to filigree or stained glass, with this decoration you pipe an outline of an object (for example, a butterfly) and then color in the center.

1. Place a picture of the object you want to copy on a cookie sheet or jelly-roll pan under a sheet of waxed paper or acetate.
2. Place melted chocolate or icing in a pastry bag fitted with a writing tip. Outline the object.
3. Allow the outline to set in a cool room, or refrigerate for 3 to 5 minutes.
4. Place melted chocolate or icing of another color in a pastry bag fitted with a writing tip. Lightly fill in the area within the outlines with chocolate.
5. Quickly lift and tap the cookie sheet after you fill each small object or each area of a larger object; the newly piped material should spread and flatten, filling in any small gaps.
6. Refrigerate for 3 to 5 minutes, or until set.
7. Carefully remove the appliqués from the waxed paper or acetate with a metal spatula.
8. Handle and store these decorations as you would filigree.

Grated Chocolate

Grated chocolate can be folded into a batter, much like chocolate chips, or used to decorate desserts or drinks.

1. Chill a bar or block of couverture. Line a jellyroll pan with waxed paper.
2. Draw the chocolate over the holes of a stainless-steel hand-held grater onto the waxed paper.
3. Store the grated chocolate in an airtight container in a cool place.

Shaved Chocolate

Shaving chocolate with a vegetable peeler or a knife is one way of creating chocolate curls.

1. To create the smallest chocolate curls: Chill a bar or block of couverture. Line a jellyroll pan with waxed paper.
2. Prop the chocolate on the edge of the jellyroll pan so that the curls will fall onto the waxed paper. Draw a vegetable peeler over the chocolate lightly and quickly.
3. For slightly larger curls: Allow the chocolate to warm slightly at room temperature. Draw the vegetable peeler over the chocolate a little more slowly, applying a little more pressure.
4. For wider chocolate curls: Prop a block of chocolate on the edge of a jellyroll pan lined with waxed paper.
5. Place a large chef's knife at the base of the chocolate block. Hold the handle of the knife with one hand and the tip of the blade with the other, so the blade of the knife is parallel to the surface of the chocolate. (If you've never used this technique, place a cardboard sleeve over the tip of the knife so you don't cut yourself.)
6. Draw the knife up from the base of the chocolate block. Once again, the temperature of the chocolate and the amount of pressure you apply will determine the size and weight of the shaved curls.
7. Store shaved chocolate in an airtight container, in a cool place.

Chocolate Curls

The other method for creating chocolate curls is to spread and scrape melted chocolate. With this technique, you can use one type of chocolate, creating solid color curls, or you can blend chocolate of different colors, creating marbled, feathered, or striped curls. For a scraping tool you can use a spatula, chef's knife, plastic putty knife, or almost anything with a clean, dry straight edge.

1. For this technique you will need stainless-steel cookie sheets or jellyroll pans with perfectly flat, clean backs. Warm the pans on a low heat in your oven. This prevents the melted chocolate from cooling too quickly while spreading a thin layer. Be careful not to let the pans get too hot; you should be able to handle them without oven mitts.
2. To create solid color curls: Spread the melted chocolate in a thin (approximately ⅛-inch-thick), even layer on the back of the warmed pans. Tap the pans gently to release air bubbles and to smooth the finish.
3. Refrigerate for about 15 to 20 minutes, or until set. Remove from the refrigerator and warm at room temperature until you can scrape the chocolate without it cracking or splintering. If it gets too warm, refrigerate it for a few more minutes.
4. The size and shape of the curls depends on the scraping tool you use, the temperature of the chocolate, and the angle at which you scrape. The wider the blade or straight edge, the wider the chocolate curls. The softer the chocolate, the tighter the curl. The sharper the angle of your blade, the tighter the curl. For example, to create chocolate cigarettes, scrape at a 45-degree angle.
5. Secure the pan so it will not slide or shift as you scrape. Place your scraping tool at the top of the pan and gently slide your scraping tool over the chocolate. Place the curls on your dessert or in an airtight container layered with sheets of waxed paper.

Striped Chocolate Curls

1. To create curls with thin stripes: Warm the pans.
2. Spread a thin layer of chocolate on the back of a pan. Chill until set.
3. Scrape a series a fine lines into the chocolate using a pastry comb. If you're having trouble keeping the lines straight, place a metal ruler or straight edge alongside the chocolate to guide your pastry comb.
4. Lift and gently tap the excess chocolate onto waxed paper to recycle.
5. Spread a contrasting color of melted chocolate over the remaining chocolate lines. Refrigerate until set and scrape.
6. For wider stripes: Melt contrasting colors of chocolate separately. Using pastry bags fitted with plain ¼-inch tips, pipe parallel stripes of

chocolate about ¼ inch apart on the back of warmed pans. Using a spatula, carefully spread the lines so they blend together. Proceed as you would for solid color curls.

7. For random stripes: Melt contrasting colors of chocolate separately. Spread a thin layer of chocolate on the back of a warmed pan. Randomly drizzle a contrasting color of chocolate on top. Proceed as you would for solid color curls.

Feathered Chocolate Curls

1. To create a feathered effect: Warm the pans.
2. Spread a thin layer of chocolate on the back of a pan.
3. Working quickly with a contrasting color of chocolate, pipe evenly-spaced parallel lines of chocolate, using a pastry bag fitted with a writing tip.
4. Using a toothpick or small sable paintbrush, gently run a line perpendicularly from left to right through one of the piped lines. Change direction, running a line from right to left, through the next piped line. Repeat, alternating directions, until all the lines are feathered.
5. Tap, chill, and scrape, as you would for solid color curls.
6. To create feathered hearts: Pipe or spoon small circles of chocolate in a parallel line. Run a toothpick or brush through the center of the circles to create a line of hearts. Tap, chill, and scrape, as you would for solid color curls.

Marbled Chocolate Curls

1. To create a marbled effect: Warm the pans.
2. Spread a thin layer of chocolate on the back of a pan.
3. Working quickly with a contrasting color of chocolate, lightly pipe random lines or swirls of chocolate using a pastry bag fitted with a writing tip. (Or drizzle the contrasting color on top.)
4. Using a toothpick or small sable paintbrush, gently swirl the chocolates together.
5. Tap, chill, and scrape, as you would for solid color curls.

Chocolate Fans

Chocolate fans can be made with pure chocolate for a crisp look, or with chocolate dough for a softer look. In either case, they can be made in a variety of sizes and designs.

1. Warm a pan, melt and spread the chocolate, and chill as you would for solid, striped, feathered, or marbled chocolate curls.
2. After chilling, brace the pan to prevent it from shifting as you work. Hold the bottom of a spatula or straightedge blade in one hand and the top edge in the other, at a slight angle (about 10 degrees) to the pan.
3. Scrape sections of the chocolate in a slight arc, or fan shape, with one end of the scraper moving faster than the other. One side of the fan should have soft ruffles, while the other should come together in a tight gather. Gently pinch the gathered end before chilling again to set.

Chocolate Leaves

Chocolate leaves are fairly simple and fun to make. They can also be made in a variety of shapes and sizes to reflect the season or theme of your dessert. They can be scattered, placed symmetrically, or even clustered in a large, open, rose bloom shape.

Be careful to use leaves of edible plants that are clean, dry, and free of pesticides.

1. Line several cookie sheets or jellyroll pans with waxed paper.
2. Paint the top (shiny side) of the leaves with melted chocolate, using a paintbrush, small pastry brush, or your finger. Be careful not to get any chocolate on the edges of the leaves, which will make it more difficult to peel the leaf off after the chocolate has set.
3. Place the leaves chocolate side up on the waxed paper. Refrigerate until set.
4. Gently peel the fresh leaves off the chocolate leaves, and place on your dessert, or store in an airtight container layered with waxed paper.

Chocolate Cutouts

Chocolate cutouts can turn a simple dessert into something special. They can also help you incorporate a theme into your dessert.

1. Proceed as you would for solid, striped, feathered, or marbled chocolate curls.
2. Refrigerate for a few minutes, until firm but not yet set.
3. If you are using metal cookie cutters to create shapes, gently press the cookie cutters into the chocolate. If you need squares, rectangles, or triangles, score the chocolate with a knife. Chill until set.
4. Remove from refrigerator, fit the cookie cutters (or knife) into the preformed shapes, and gently cut through the chocolate. Place on your dessert, or store in an airtight container, layered with waxed paper.

APPENDIX B

Substitutions and Conversions

Common Baking Substitutions

Allspice: For each teaspoon, use ½ teaspoon cinnamon, ¼ teaspoon ginger, and ¼ teaspoon cloves.

Baking powder: For each teaspoon, use ½ teaspoon cream of tartar and ¼ teaspoon baking soda.

Beer: For each cup, use 1 cup chicken broth.

Brandy: For each ¼ cup, use 1 teaspoon imitation brandy extract plus enough water to make ¼ cup.

Brown sugar: For each cup, use 1 cup granulated sugar plus ¼ cup molasses (decrease amount of liquid in recipe by ¼ cup).

Butter (salted): For each cup, use 1 cup margarine.

Butter (unsalted): For each cup, use 1 cup shortening.

Buttermilk: For each cup, place 1 tablespoon lemon juice or vinegar in the bottom of a measuring cup and fill with milk. Let stand 5 minutes.

Cardamom: Use an equal amount of ginger.

Cheddar cheese: For each cup, use 1 cup Colby Cheddar or Monterey Jack cheese.

Chocolate (semisweet): For each ounce, use 1 ounce unsweetened chocolate plus 4 teaspoons sugar.

Chocolate (unsweetened): For each ounce, use 3 tablespoons unsweetened cocoa and 1 tablespoon melted butter.

Cinnamon: Use ½ the amount of nutmeg.

Cloves: Use double the amount of cinnamon and a little cayenne pepper.

Cocoa: For each ¼ cup, use 1 ounce unsweetened chocolate.

Corn syrup: For each cup, use 1 cup granulated sugar and ¼ cup water; bring to a boil and boil 1 minute. Set aside.

Cream (half and half): For each cup, use 1 tablespoon vegetable oil or melted butter and enough whole milk to make a cup.

Cream (heavy): For each cup, use ¾ cup milk and ⅓ cup butter.

Cream (light): For each cup, use ¾ cup milk and 3 tablespoons butter.

Cream (whipped): For each cup, use 1 cup frozen whipped topping, thawed.

Cream cheese: For each cup, use 1 cup pureéd cottage cheese.

Cream of tartar: For each teaspoon, use 2 teaspoons lemon juice.

Egg: For each egg, use 2 egg whites or 2 egg yolks or ¼ cup egg substitute.

Evaporated milk: For each cup, use 1 cup light cream.

Gelatin: For each tablespoon, use 2 teaspoons agar.

Ginger: Use an equal amount of cinnamon and a pinch of cayenne pepper.

Granulated sugar: For each cup, use 1 cup brown sugar.

Honey: For each cup, use 1¼ cups granulated sugar and ¼ cup water.

Lemon juice: For each teaspoon, use ½ teaspoon vinegar.

Lemon zest: For each teaspoon, use ½ teaspoon lemon extract.

Lime juice: For each teaspoon, use 1 teaspoon vinegar.

Lime zest: For each teaspoon, use 1 teaspoon lemon zest.

Margarine: For each cup, use 1 cup shortening and ½ teaspoon salt.

Mayonnaise: For each cup, use 1 cup sour cream or plain yogurt.

Milk (whole): For each cup, use 1 cup soy milk or rice milk.

Molasses: For each cup, use ½ cup honey, ½ cup brown sugar, and ¼ cup water.

Nutmeg: Use ½ the amount of cinnamon and ¼ amount of ginger.

Orange juice: For each tablespoon, use 1 tablespoon lemon or lime juice.

Orange zest: For each tablespoon, use 1 teaspoon lemon juice.

Parmesan cheese: For each ½ cup, use ½ cup Asiago or Romano cheese.

Pepperoni: For each ounce, use 1 ounce salami.

Pumpkin pie spice: For each teaspoon, mix ½ teaspoon cinnamon, ¼ teaspoon ginger, ⅛ teaspoon cloves, and ⅛ teaspoon grated nutmeg.

Raisins: For each cup, use 1 cup dried cranberries.

Ricotta cheese: For each cup, use 1 cup dry cottage cheese.

Rum: For each tablespoon, use ½ teaspoon rum extract plus enough water to make 1 tablespoon.

Semisweet chocolate chips: For each cup, use 1 cup chocolate candies.

Shortening: For each cup, use 1 cup butter.

Sour cream: For each cup, use 1 cup plain yogurt.

Sweetened condensed milk: For each 14-ounce can, use ¾ cup granulated sugar, ½ cup water, and ⅛ cup dry powdered milk; boil and cook, stirring frequently, until thickened, about 20 minutes.

Vegetable oil: For each cup, use 1 cup applesauce.

Vinegar: For each teaspoon, use 1 teaspoon lemon or lime juice.

Wine: For each cup, use 1 cup chicken broth.

Yogurt: For each cup, use 1 cup sour cream.

U.S. Volume Equivalents

1½ teaspoons	=	½ tablespoon				
3 teaspoons	=	1 tablespoon				
2 tablespoons	=	1 ounce	=	⅛ cup		
8 ounces	=	16 tablespoons	=	1 cup		
2 cups	=	1 pint	=	16 ounces		
2 pints	=	1 quart	=	4 cups	=	32 ounces
4 quarts	=	1 gallon	=	16 cups	=	128 ounces

U.S. Volume to Metric Volume

¼ teaspoon	=	1.23 ml
½ teaspoon	=	2.5 ml
¾ teaspoon	=	3.7 ml
1 teaspoon	=	4.9 ml
1½ teaspoons	=	7.5 ml
2 teaspoons	=	10 ml
3 teaspoons	=	15 ml
⅛ cup	=	30 ml
¼ cup	=	60 ml
½ cup	=	120 ml
¾ cup	=	180 ml
1 cup	=	240 ml
2 cups	=	480 ml
2¼ cups	=	540 ml

2½ cups	=	600 ml
2¾ cups	=	660 ml
3 cups	=	720 ml
4 cups	=	960 ml
4 quarts	=	3.8 l

U.S. Weight Measurements to Metric Weight Measurements

½ ounce	=	14 grams
1 ounce	=	29 grams
1½ ounces	=	43 grams
2 ounces	=	57 grams
4 ounces	=	113 grams
8 ounces	=	227 grams
16 ounces	=	454 grams
32 ounces	=	907 grams
64 ounces	=	1.8 kilograms

Vegan Substitutions

Cooking vegan doesn't always mean abandoning all your favorite old recipes. In some cases you'll be able to replace milk with soy milk, butter with margarine, and eggs with Ener-g Egg replacer, or banana. (Use one banana per egg called for in recipe.)

It's also possible to find vegan cake mixes.

P.E.T.A., the organization famous for protecting animals and animal rights, keeps a list of vegan convenience foods on its website under the name "Accidentally Vegan." On this list you will find a few cake mixes, pudding mixes, and prepared frosting that are readily available in most groceries and completely vegan. Unexpected listings include:

- Duncan Hines California Walnut Brownie Mix

- Duncan Hines Creamy Home-Style Frosting (Chocolate)

- Duncan Hines Creamy Home-Style Frosting (Classic Vanilla)

- Duncan Hines Creamy Home-Style Frosting (French Vanilla)

- Ghirardelli Chocolate Chip Cookie Mix

- Jell-O Instant Pudding (Pistachio)

- Jell-O Instant Pudding (Banana Creme)

- Jell-O Instant Pudding (Chocolate)

- Jell-O Instant Pudding (Lemon)

- Jell-O Instant Pudding (Vanilla)

APPENDIX C

Glossary

Baking pan

A flat pan, usually metal, that may or may not have a lip around the edge.

Beat

To make a mixture smooth by briskly stirring with a whisk, spoon, or electric beater.

Blend

To gently mix ingredients until they are completely mixed.

Boil

To bring a liquid to the temperature that causes bubbles to rise to the surface and break in a steady stream.

Cream

To beat butter or shortening until it has a light, fluffy consistency. Air is incorporated into the fat so the texture is lighter and fluffier.

Drizzle

To quickly pour a glaze over a baked item randomly and in a thin stream.

Dust

To lightly coat a baked good with powdered sugar.

Extract

Flavoring products that are made from the essential oil of a plant. These concentrated oils are generally suspended in alcohol.

Examples are: vanilla, anise, almond, lemon, mint. Extracts are higher quality than flavorings and are preferred in these recipes.

Flavoring

Imitation extracts which are created in laboratories from chemicals. A flavoring does not have to contain any part of the item it mimics and is often completely artificial.

Fold

To gently mix ingredients. Generally, the dry ingredients are sifted over the top of the whipped or beaten ingredients and then a rubber spatula is used to cut through the mixture. The spatula is then moved across the bottom and brought up the other side, folding the mixture back on itself.

Food Coloring

Food-grade dyes which are used to tint various foods. Paste food colors are the best, and give the most intense color.

Glaze

A thin type of frosting that is used to add extra flavor to a cookie or cake.

Gluten

A protein present in all flour, but especially in wheat flour. It provides an elastic structure for baked goods. Many people are allergic to it and must not eat it.

Gluten-free baking mix

A baking mix that is free of gluten and nonallergenic.

Pipe

To force frosting or filling through a pastry bag.

Shortening

A solid fat made from vegetable oils. Shortening has been criticized for the high amounts of trans fatty acids it has had in the past. Manufacturers are now making it without the trans fats, or with reduced trans fats. You can also get organic shortenings that have no trans fats.

Sift

To shake flour or powdered sugar through a sifter to make it light and fluffy and to remove lumps.

Vanilla bean

Vanilla beans are the seed pods of a special orchid plant from which vanilla is made. It can be placed in a canister with sugar to flavor the sugar.

Whip

To beat a food, usually cream or egg whites, rapidly enough to incorporate air and cause the food to double or triple in volume.

Zest

The outer, colored portion of a citrus fruit. It is grated and added to foods to flavor them.

APPENDIX D

Resources

All Recipes

This site has an uncountable number of recipes, and each recipe has an area for comments so you can find out if it worked for other people or not. Excellent search features and other user-friendly items make this online cookbook invaluable.
http://allrecipes.com

Bakers' Nook

Thousands of pans, decorations, and cookie cutters to help you create incredible baked goods.
www.shopbakersnook.com

Bakespace

Bakespace is a social networking site for foodies. Socialize, have your questions answered, and find new recipes as well as new friends.
http://bakespace.com

Baking Delights

This site is where I post my own recipes on at least a daily basis and answer readers' questions.
www.bakingdelights.com

Converting Recipes

This is an excellent resource for those who do not use the same measurements as those used in the United States. You can easily convert any recipe with these charts.
www.jsward.com/cooking/conversion.shtml

Cook's Thesaurus

Thousands of suggestions for food substitutions in one place. A great resource.
www.foodsubs.com

Daring Bakers Blog Roll

This site lists over 1,000 blogs of the members of Daring Bakers. Daring Bakers is a group of bloggers that create the same challenging recipe every month. The recipes that you will find on the various sites are top notch.
http://thedaringkitchen.com/member-blogs

Group Recipes

Another networking site for people who love to cook. Plenty of recipes to choose from.
www.grouprecipes.com

Kitchen Kraft

Kitchen Kraft is a huge site with every item imaginable to make your baking more creative, easier, and more fun.
www.kitchenkrafts.com

Nutritional Information Calculator

Enter the ingredients of any recipe and find out the calories, carbs, proteins, and other nutritional information.
http://recipes.sparkpeople.com/recipe-calculator.asp

Penzeys Spices

Wonderful, fresh spices and herbs for your cooking and baking needs.
http://penzeys.com/cgi-bin/penzeys/shophome.html

Wilton

Baking supplies of all types. A huge variety of paste food colorings, icing bags, decorator tips, and inspiration.
www.wilton.com

Cookies
and
Brownies

Introduction to Cookies and Brownies

THE EARLIEST RECORD OF cookie-type treats were small cakes that were made in seventh-century Persia. These small cakes spread to Europe during the Crusades, and by the fourteenth century cookies were well known in Italy and France, and their popularity had begun to spread to the rest of Europe.

In the 1600s immigrants brought cookies to America. The word "cookie" actually came from *koekje*, the Dutch word for "small cake." Cookies were saved for holidays and special occasions because it was difficult and expensive to get the ingredients to make them. There weren't many varieties of cookies, but many of them are still popular today:

- Gingerbread
- Lebkuchen
- Jumbles
- Macaroons

Before vanilla was commonly available, cookies were flavored with rose water. The leavener that was most often used was a type of ammonia made from the antlers of a deer. While butter was used at times, it was more likely to be lard that provided the fat in the cookies. Lard was the more readily available of the two at this time.

In the late 1800s, technology was creating new ways of doing things. Sugar and certain spices were easier to get and women had a bit more leisure time. With the ability to more accurately regulate the temperature of their ovens, bakers were able to create different textures, shapes, and varieties of cookies. Bar cookies became popular among busy farm women in the early twentieth century as a way to make the family a treat quickly. During the depression, "no-bake" cookies allowed families to satisfy a sweet tooth with readily available dried fruits and nuts. The popularity of these cookies increased during the 1940s as rationing limited the availability of ingredients like sugar and chocolate.

Creating Memories and Building Relationships

The first baking that most people do is often some sort of cookie. Making a habit of baking cookies with your children is an excellent way to create memories and build relationships. Children as young as two or three enjoy helping by mixing ingredients, arranging the cooled cookies on a plate, or even using a cookie cutter to cut the dough. By age six, children love to decorate cookies with colored sugar, sprinkles, and frosting; they are able to use their creativity and create unique cookies. They can learn to measure the ingredients and help to mix the dough. Your children will have fun while building self-esteem and even increasing their math skills.

Don't wait for a rainy day to make some cookies. Choose a recipe, gather your family together, and enjoy some quality time while creating a mouth-watering snack.

CHAPTER 19

Cookie Baking Basics

Successful cookie baking is a skill that anyone can learn. Like any type of cooking or baking, there are techniques that need to be learned. Having a basic understanding of the ingredients, equipment, and methods of measuring and mixing is an essential part of creating the perfect cookie every time. Once the cookies are baked, knowing how to decorate them and store them allows any baker to create professional-looking cookies for any occasion. Before choosing a recipe, read through Chapter 1 to ensure success.

Ingredients for Success

All cookies have the same basic ingredients:

- Flour
- Sugar
- Fat
- Flavoring
- Leavening

It is the variations in these ingredients that produce the differences in the many varieties of cookies. Once you know how the ingredients affect the finished cookie, you can create numerous variations for any recipe and get a predictable result every time.

Flour

There are different types of flour for different types of baking. Most cookie recipes call for all-purpose flour. All-purpose, or white, flour is not as delicate as cake flour and has more protein. This means that it can develop gluten and become tough if mixed for too long. Most recipes will direct you to stir in the flour rather than beating it in so the cookies do not come out tough.

You can substitute whole-wheat flour for part of the all-purpose flour in most recipes if you want. However, too much whole-wheat flour will make your cookies heavy so beware of a ratio higher than 50/50 wheat to white. If you have an allergy to wheat or gluten, you can substitute a good gluten-free baking mix for the flour in almost any recipe.

Sugar

Sugar is what adds the sweetness to the cookie. It also works with the other ingredients to create the individual texture of each type of cookie. This is why when you try to substitute a low-calorie sweetener for sugar in a recipe the texture is often not what you expected. It is usually better to use a recipe written specifically for sugar-free cookies than to try to adapt an old favorite.

White sugar allows the flavor of the cookie to come through, while brown sugar adds a flavor all its own. Honey is sometimes substituted for sugar in recipes, but it will also change the texture of the finished product and the other liquids in the recipe will need to be decreased.

Can I substitute noncaloric sweetener for sugar in a cookie recipe?
You can substitute sugar with Splenda cup for cup without any appreciable loss of quality. Be careful, though; cookies baked with Splenda tend to bake faster and should be checked earlier than your recipe may suggest. Also, items made with Splenda do not brown.

Fat

Fat is what makes a cookie chewy, crumbly, or crisp. Butter is the preferred fat in most cookie recipes because of the delicate flavor it adds. Using all butter can make your cookies very thin, though, so if you consistently seem to have paper-thin cookies when you want thick and chewy ones, try substituting half the butter with a vegetable shortening.

Some very old, heirloom recipes will call for lard. The lard available in most grocers is not the same lard that our great-grandmothers used. If you have leaf lard available then by all means use it for a very finely textured cookie. Otherwise, substitute shortening for lard called for in the recipe.

Flavoring

Vanilla is added to almost any cookie recipe because it enhances the rest of the flavors. You can use rose water to do the same thing and give an old-fashioned flavor. One teaspoon of vanilla and ½ teaspoon of almond extract makes a nice flavor combination for butter cookies and other cookies with a lighter flavor.

Always use pure extracts for the best results. Imitation flavors do not have the same intensity as the natural flavors do. When you invest a little extra money in quality ingredients, you end up with a more delicious product.

Leavening

Leavening is the ingredient that causes baked goods to rise. In breads it is yeast and in cakes and cookies it can be either baking soda or baking powder. It is important to use the leavening called for in the recipe and measure it carefully. Too much baking soda will give your cookies a "soapy" flavor that is not at all appealing. Too much baking powder can give the cookies an acidic flavor.

You can make a baking powder substitute by using ¼ teaspoon of baking soda and ½ teaspoon cream of tartar for each teaspoon of baking powder called for in the recipe. This is single-acting, so bake immediately once you have mixed the dough together.

There are two kinds of baking powder. Single-acting baking powder begins the leavening process when it gets wet. It is very important if you are using single-acting baking powder not to allow the cookie dough to sit once the ingredients are mixed. If you don't bake the recipe immediately they won't rise in the oven and will be like rocks. Double-acting baking powder has two separate processes; the first reacts with moisture and the second reacts with heat. This allows you to mix up your dough ahead of time without losing any of the rising abilities of the baking powder.

The Zen of Measuring and Mixing

Baking cookies is actually a scientific process. Like any other formula, a recipe is written in a certain way to achieve certain results. It is important to read your recipe all the way through before beginning. Make sure you have all the ingredients on hand and in the amounts specified. Mix them in the order given in the recipe instructions. Careful mixing will mean that your cookies do not have streaks of flour or lumps of baking soda in the finished treat.

Measure for Accuracy

Accurate measurements mean that your cookies will come out the same time after time. When you know how to measure accurately there are no surprises in the finished product. Some people seem to have a knack for adding the right amount of baking powder or salt by just judging the amount. It is a risky way to bake because anyone can have an off day! Here are the methods for measuring different types of ingredients.

When you are measuring whole-wheat flour, don't sift it; just stir it lightly and then spoon into the measuring cup. Level off even with the top, as for all-purpose flour. You only need to sift whole-wheat flour when you want to remove the bran.

- Measure the flour by sifting first and then lightly spooning into a measuring cup and leveling it off even with the top. Use a butter knife to level it. Do not pack down.
- To measure sugar, just spoon into the measuring cup and level off the top.
- Brown sugar is measured by packing it down into the measuring cup. When you tip it out into your recipe it should keep its shape.
- Confectioners', or powdered, sugar should be sifted before measuring. Spoon it into a measuring cup lightly and level off with a butter knife.
- Salt, spices, baking powder, and baking soda are all measured by using the measuring spoon to scoop out the ingredient and then leveling it off gently with a butter knife.
- Cornstarch should be lightly spooned into the measuring cup and then leveled off with a knife. If your recipe calls for a tablespoon or less, use the proper measuring spoon to scoop it out of the container and proceed as for measuring salt.
- To measure flavorings like vanilla, just pour them from the bottle into the properly sized measuring spoon. The liquid should be level with the rim of the spoon.

- Milk, juice, and water are measured by pouring them into the measuring cup until the liquid is level with the top.
- Oil, honey, and syrup are measured the same way as other liquids. You may need to use a spoon to get all of the ingredient out of the measuring cup.
- Fats are measured by spooning into a measuring cup and pressing down firmly to get rid of any air pockets. Sticks of butter generally have the measurements printed on the side in tablespoon increments. One stick or ¼ pound of butter is equal to ½ cup.

If you measure the oil called for in a recipe before you measure honey, molasses, or syrup the sticky ingredient will slide right out of the measuring cup. Recipe doesn't call for oil? Lightly oil the measuring cup before measuring the honey and you will have the same easy results.

Mixing the Dough

Nearly every cookie recipe in existence uses the creaming method of mixing the dough. In this technique the fat and sugar are "creamed" together with a mixer until they are light and fluffy. Generally, the eggs and flavorings are added at this point. Once the eggs are incorporated into the butter mixture the dry ingredients are stirred in, either by hand or at low speed on a mixer.

If you are hand mixing cookie dough, it takes approximately 150–200 strokes to thoroughly cream the butter and sugar together. You will need a sturdy wooden spoon and a strong arm. It is no wonder that pioneer women had muscles!

The dough will mix up better if all the ingredients are at room temperature. The butter should not be melting, but it should not be hard, either. When the eggs are beaten in at room temperature the texture of the finished cookie is better.

Stir in the sifted dry ingredients carefully. Mix them into the butter mixture until there are no streaks of flour or lumps of baking powder. Be careful not to toughen the cookies by over mixing the dough. Once the cookie dough is finished, the remaining ingredients like chocolate chips, raisins, and nuts are stirred in with a wooden spoon.

Once the ingredients have been mixed, proceed with the recipe according to the instructions.

Sweet Necessities: Equipment and Pans

While it may be true that a poor workman blames his tools, it is also true that using quality equipment makes it easier to create perfect cookies. If at all possible, buy your tools at a restaurant supply store. You will find that the commercial pans are less expensive and of higher quality than what are commonly found in the local department store.

Why should I use shiny pans?
Shiny baking sheets allow the heat to be reflected away from the cookies and they bake more evenly without burning. Since pans do wear out, you should expect to replace them every few years. Once they have become blackened or are dull, retire them from cookie service and find another use for them.

Having an inventory of good pans and equipment will allow you to bake with confidence at a moment's notice. Some gadgets, like different-sized scoops, are not essential but do make the job easier. Other items, cookie presses for example, are total luxuries but are fun to use.

Essential Equipment

There are some things that you just can't do without when baking cookies. Following is a list of what is needed to make basic cookies. Other items, like cookie cutters, might be essential for fancier cookie baking.

- Two shiny metal baking sheets smaller than the interior of your oven. They need to leave a four-inch space all the way around the inside of the oven.
- An electric mixer is the best way to get those ingredients mixed. If you don't have one you will need a very strong arm and a wooden spoon.
- A couple of mixing bowls allow you to do more than one thing at a time.
- When you have measuring cups and spoons in several sizes your measurements will be more accurate.
- A glass measuring cup allows for the accurate measurement of liquid ingredients.
- A spatula is necessary for removing the cookies from the baking sheet.
- At least one 13" × 9" inch pan is necessary for baking brownies and bars.

If you are baking brownies or bars in a glass pan, be sure to lower the oven temperature by 25 degrees from the temperature called for in the recipe. Glass pans conduct heat more than metal pans do and the lower temperature will keep the bars from burning or becoming too dry.

Not Essential but Nice to Have

With the list above you can cook many different kinds of basic cookies, but if you want to do anything special you will need a few more pieces of equipment. Always try to buy the best quality that you can afford. Cheap items just don't last as long or work as well and there is really nothing more frustrating than having a rolling pin fall apart halfway through ten dozen Christmas cookies!

- Cookie cutters in various shapes and sizes are a necessity for cute decorated sugar cookies. You can find cutters in every shape from maple leaves to motorcycles.

- Rolling pins are important aids to creating cute cookies of all kinds. Pick up a few and choose one that is heavy but not so heavy it hurts your back or arms to use it.
- A pizelle iron is the only way to make delicate anise-flavored pizelles. The iron looks like a thin, decorative waffle iron.
- If you are planning on making Spritz cookies you will need a good cookie press.
- Pastry tubes and decorating tips allow you to be creative with the cookies that you make.
- A cooling rack allows the cookies to cool on all sides without the possibility of the bottoms getting soggy.
- A timer will keep you from getting distracted and over baking the cookies.
- A cookie press allows you to press intricate and beautiful designs into your cookies.
- Scoops in various sizes will keep the cookies uniform in size and shape.
- Silpat nonstick baking sheets are made of silicone and keep cookies from sticking to the cookie sheets without greasing them.
- Madeline pans are specially formed pans that allow you to make French madelines like a professional.

Of course, there are many other items that you could add to the list. By having some of this equipment you will be able to make beautiful cookies anytime.

Gilding the Lily: Decorating Tips

There are essentially two types of decorated cookies: the kind that are decorated before baking and the kind that are decorated after baking. The type you use is up to you; there are pros and cons for both types. The type that are decorated before baking are usually, although not always, quick to put together. A few sprinkles of colored sugar or dragees and you are done.

The kinds of cookies that are decorated after baking generally take longer and are more intricately done. They are often more beautiful than the simpler cookies. This type of decorating entails using royal icing in different colors, frostings, or even melted chocolate. Depending on the decoration the process can be tedious.

Here are some tips for beautifully decorated cookies:

- Royal icing will give the most professional look to your cookies. It dries hard and is durable.
- Use paste food colors to color the frostings, icings, and white chocolate for the best and most vivid results.
- Paint the baked and cooled cookies with corn syrup in any pattern and then sprinkle on colored sugar. The corn syrup will make the sugar stick on the patterns.
- After decorating your cookies with icing or frosting, set them aside in a safe place until the frosting or icing dries and forms a crust.
- Drizzling melted chocolate over a cookie is a wonderful embellishment.
- Always let the cookies cool completely before decorating.
- Color the raw dough with assorted food colors for colorful cookies.
- Dip part of a cookie in melted chocolate and then sprinkle with chopped nuts.

The very first decorated cookies in history are thought to be from Switzerland. Carved springerle molds were first used to stamp designs on cookies in the 1300s. These decorated cookies had scenes and pictures on them that were used to teach illiterate peasants the Bible stories.

Tools for Decorating

You can buy decorating bags made of vinyl or even disposable plastic bags for more convenience. Spoon your frosting into the bag, filling it about halfway. Twist the top of the bag to seal and then squeeze firmly to move the frosting out through the decorating tip and onto your cookie. It will take a bit of practice to become comfortable with the technique. A great way to practice using the different tips is to make designs on a sheet of waxed paper.

Some of the tools that you may want to collect are:

- **Couplers**—allow you to change decorating tips quickly and easily
- **Fine writing tips**—great for outlining parts of the cookie, making scrolls and small dots, and writing
- **Star tips**—make nice mounds to put dragees on and create shells and other decorative effects
- **Larger writing tips**—great for polka dots and filling in larger areas with color
- **Paintbrushes**—can be used for applying egg-yolk paint (recipe given in Chapter 16) or corn syrup
- **Toothpicks**—can be used to move color or create a chevron effect when you drag them through stripes of thin frosting
- **Special tools** that allow you to make intricate sculptures with marzipan and fondant are fun to learn to use and will help you make spectacular decorated desserts

Edible gold and silver have been used for years all over the world. It is available in the United States, but the Food and Drug Administration (FDA) says that it has not been approved for human consumption. Edible gold and silver has been in use since before there was an FDA, so it was never submitted for premarket approval.

Once the cookies are decorated, set them aside to allow the frosting to harden before storing; this will keep the designs from smearing. A final garnish may be created by using products like luster dust or edible glitter to enhance the decorated cookie. Some people even use edible gold leaf for very special decorated cookies.

Royal icing stores and ships well once it hardens, but buttercream does not. It is best to decorate cookies with buttercream just before serving. If you are making cookies that will be stored for a period of time or shipped, use royal icing and allow it to harden completely before packing and shipping. The icing will help seal the cookie and maintain the fresh flavor and texture.

Storing and Shipping

Most cookies store and ship very well. Cookies with dried fruit in them have better keeping qualities than delicate cookies like pizzelles because the dried fruit helps keep the cookie moist for a long period of time. Before choosing a cookie for storage or shipping, consider the type of cookie it is and the ingredients included in the recipe. This will help you decide whether or not it can be used as you wish to use it.

Storing Cookies

All cookies are not the same and have different techniques for successful storage. Always allow cookies, brownies, and bars to cool completely before packaging them for storage. If you have decorated the cookies, take the time to allow the icing to harden before you try to store them. This will keep them as beautiful as they were when you first made them. Any cookies that are properly stored should keep close to a week at room temperature.

Crisp cookies should be stored in a container that is loosely covered. This allows the moisture to be released from the container easily, stopping it from building up and making them soggy. If you have high humidity, it is actually better to store them in an airtight container to keep the moisture out.

While almost all cookies can be frozen successfully, you should never freeze meringue cookies. Freezing them will cause them to become soggy, sticky lumps when they are thawed. Instead, always keep these crisp, delicate cookies in an airtight container at room temperature in a dry place.

Soft cookies should be kept in an airtight container. This allows the moisture to be trapped in with the cookies, keeping them soft and chewy. If they begin to dry out you can add a slice of apple or a piece of bread to the container. Always keep an eye on soft cookies because they will have a tendency to mold more quickly than crisp ones. Separating the layers of cookies with wax paper will keep them from sticking to each other and make them easy to remove from the container.

When cookies are iced they should also be kept in an airtight container. Allow the icing to harden completely and layer the cookies between sheets of waxed paper. Do not make more than three layers in a container because the weight will cause the bottom layers to crumble and the icings to crack.

For long-term storage, cookies can be easily frozen. You can freeze the dough for up to twelve months or baked cookies for up to six months. Never freeze more than one kind of dough or cookie together—the different cookies will take on each other's flavors. Always wrap the cookies or dough in a couple of layers of plastic wrap and then put them in an airtight container. Cookies pick up freezer flavors very easily and this will keep your prize-winning chocolate chip cookies from tasting like the catfish your husband brought home from his last fishing trip.

> If you freeze crisp cookies and then find that when they have thawed they are no longer as crisp as you would like, you can restore the crispness by warming them up in a 300°F oven for about 5 minutes. Not only will the crisp texture be restored, but the house will smell great!

Baked cookies can be put in freezer bags and frozen, but often this results in a lot of broken cookies. It is better to layer them in a freezer container with waxed paper between the layers and over the top. The sturdy container will give support to the cookies and they will be less likely to crumble. Label the container with the type of cookie and the date they were frozen so you can keep track of them.

Shipping Cookies

Sending someone you love a box of homemade cookies is a great way to say, "I am thinking of you." Make sure that the cookies arrive in top condition by choosing a sturdy cookie recipe and packaging them well.

Packing cookies for shipping is very similar to getting them ready for freezing. Be careful to choose a sturdy cookie that will hold up to be jostled and tossed.

- Use a sturdy box and line it with waxed paper.
- Crumple sheets of waxed paper for a soft cushion and then place a layer of waxed paper over that.
- Place a layer of cookies on the waxed paper, cover with a sheet of waxed paper, and then repeat the layers.
- Do not stack the cookies more than three layers high.
- Leave enough room at the top of the box for more crumpled waxed paper.

The cookies should be packed tightly enough that they do not jiggle around. If you want to ship an assortment of cookies, be sure to wrap each type individually so the flavors don't get mixed up. Try to put a cushioning layer between the different cookie flavors to help them maintain their individuality.

Place a 3" × 5" card in the box with the recipient's name and address. Wrap it securely in brown packing paper and write the address clearly. It is a good idea to mark the box "fragile" and "perishable" in several places. If you will be sending it overseas, you should be prepared to list the contents of the box clearly. Sending the cookies priority mail will help get them there in a timely manner.

Never use popcorn, cereal, or other grains as the cushioning material when you are shipping cookies. By the time your cookies get to their destination, they could be full of weevils or other bugs. It is better to use crumpled waxed paper or plastic wrap for cushioning purposes.

Cookies that are good candidates for shipping are those that are moist and soft. Brownies, bars, and drop cookies are all good cookies to ship. Cookies with dried fruit in the ingredients will stay fresher longer than other types. Filled and frosted cookies don't ship well, with the exception of cookies that are filled with a dried-fruit filling and cookies that are iced with a hardened royal icing. Never ship any kind of cookie that has a cream cheese or dairy filling of some sort; they will spoil and can make someone sick if eaten.

Knowing how to store and ship cookies makes it easy to send a quick gift or have a cozy snack whenever you want. Keep the cookie jar full and the family happy by using your freezer to your advantage.

CHAPTER 20

All Kinds of Chips

Classic Chocolate Chip

The recipe everyone craves—a crisp outside with a chewy middle. Take these out of the oven when they are still slightly underdone for best results.

INGREDIENTS | YIELDS 24 COOKIES

½ cup unsalted butter
½ cup vegetable shortening
¾ cup sugar
¾ cup brown sugar
2 eggs
1 tablespoon vanilla extract
2¼ cups flour
1 teaspoon baking soda
2 cups chocolate chips

1. Preheat oven to 350°F. Lightly grease cookie sheets.

2. Cream butter, shortening, sugar, and brown sugar until fluffy. Add eggs one at a time; beat well after each egg is added. Beat in vanilla.

3. Combine dry ingredients; stir into butter mixture.

4. Carefully fold in chocolate chips.

5. Drop by teaspoonfuls about 2" apart on cookie sheets. Bake 8–10 minutes. Allow to cool on cookie sheets 10 minutes before removing.

Chip History

The chocolate chip cookie was created by accident by Ruth Wakefield, who ran the Toll House Inn with her husband near Whitman, Massachusetts. While hurriedly trying to bake a chocolate butter cookie, she chopped up a chocolate bar hoping that it would melt and produce a chocolate cookie. It did not, but the result was so good that Nestle cut a deal with her to provide her with chocolate for her inn in exchange for the rights to the recipe.

Chocolate Chocolate Chip

Mexican vanilla is a strong vanilla available in many stores. Regular vanilla extract can be substituted by adding an extra ½ teaspoon.

INGREDIENTS | **YIELDS 48 COOKIES**

1 cup unsalted butter
1 cup butter-flavored shortening
1½ cups sugar
1½ cups brown sugar
4 eggs, room temperature
1½ tablespoons Mexican vanilla extract
4 cups flour
⅔ cup Hershey's Special Dark cocoa
1½ teaspoons baking soda
1 teaspoon salt
1 cup semi-sweet chocolate chips
1 cup bittersweet chocolate chips
1½ cups chopped pecans

1. Preheat oven to 350°F.

2. Cream together butter, shortening, and sugars until light and fluffy. Add eggs and vanilla; beat well.

3. Mix dry ingredients; add to butter mixture.

4. Fold in chocolate chips and nuts. Chill 30 minutes.

5. Drop by teaspoonfuls onto baking sheets. Bake 8–10 minutes. Allow to cool slightly before removing from pan.

Tired of Chocolate Chips?

A great substitution for chocolate chips in nearly any cookie recipe is using the same amount of chocolate-covered raisins. You still get the chocolate flavor, but the raisins add sweetness and a chewy texture. Exchange them cup for cup and you will be adding extra iron as well.

Orange and Dark Chocolate Chip

These taste very much like the chocolate oranges that are so popular during the holidays.
Use a good juice orange rather than a navel orange, if possible.

INGREDIENTS | YIELDS 24 COOKIES

½ cup unsalted butter

½ cup vegetable shortening

1 cup sugar

½ cup light brown sugar

2 eggs

1½ teaspoons vanilla

Grated rind and juice of 1 medium orange

2¼ cups flour

1 teaspoon baking soda

½ teaspoon salt

2 cups bittersweet chocolate chips

1. Preheat oven to 350°F. Lightly grease cookie sheets.

2. Cream together butter, shortening, and sugars. Add eggs; beat well. Thoroughly mix in vanilla and orange juice.

3. Mix in dry ingredients and grated orange rind.

4. Carefully stir in chocolate chips.

5. Drop by teaspoonfuls on cookie sheets; bake 8–10 minutes. Cool slightly before removing from pan.

White Chocolate Chip Macadamia

The addition of the pulp and seeds scraped from the inside of the vanilla bean gives these
cookies a deep vanilla flavor. If you don't have a vanilla bean it can be omitted.

INGREDIENTS | YIELDS 36 COOKIES

1 cup unsalted butter

1 cup light brown sugar, packed

¾ cup sugar

2 eggs

2½ teaspoons vanilla

2 piece vanilla bean, split lengthwise

2¼ cups flour

1 teaspoon baking soda

½ teaspoon salt

1 cup macadamia nuts

1 cup white chocolate chips

1. Preheat oven to 350°F. Lightly grease baking sheets.

2. Cream together butter and sugars. Add eggs and vanilla. Scrape insides of vanilla bean into butter mixture; set aside 30 minutes so flavors blend.

3. Stir together dry ingredients; blend into butter mixture.

4. Fold in macadamia nuts and white chocolate chips.

5. Drop by rounded teaspoons onto prepared baking sheets. Bake 8–10 minutes. Cool 10 minutes before removing from baking sheets.

Double Chocolate Toffee Chip

*These rich cookies are reminiscent of a toffee bar. If you can't find the toffee pieces,
just use 8 ounces of Heath bars coarsely chopped.*

INGREDIENTS | YIELDS 24 COOKIES

½ cup unsalted butter

½ cup shortening

2 teaspoons vanilla

¾ cup sugar

¾ cup dark brown sugar

2 eggs

2 cups flour

½ cup cocoa

1 teaspoon baking soda

1 teaspoon salt

1 cup Heath Toffee pieces

2 cups white chocolate chips

1 cup chopped hazelnuts

1. Preheat oven to 350°F. Lightly grease cookie sheets.

2. Cream together butter, shortening, vanilla, and sugars. Add eggs; beat well.

3. Mix dry ingredients together; stir into butter mixture.

4. Fold in toffee, white chocolate chips, and hazelnuts. Chill 30 minutes to 1 hour.

5. Bake 8–10 minutes, or until just barely done for a chewy cookie. Allow to cool on cookie sheet 10 minutes before removing.

Just Chill

If you like a cookie that is a little thicker without being cakey, try chilling the dough for 30 minutes or so before baking. Drop them by teaspoonfuls on cold baking sheets. The cookies will have less of a tendency to flatten out when they are baking.

Chocolate Chunk Cookies

*By cutting up a chocolate bar you will often get a better-quality chocolate
and can control the size of the chunks in the cookies.*

INGREDIENTS | **YIELDS 36 COOKIES**

½ cup unsalted butter, softened

½ cup shortening

1 cup sugar

¾ cup dark brown sugar

2 eggs, room temperature

2 teaspoons vanilla extract

2¼ cups flour

½ teaspoon cinnamon

1 teaspoon baking soda

1 teaspoon salt

12 ounces chocolate chunks, or 12 ounces good-quality chocolate cut in chunks

1. Preheat oven to 375°F. Lightly grease cookie sheets.

2. Cream together butter, shortening, and sugars. Add eggs and vanilla.

3. Mix together dry ingredients; stir into butter mixture.

4. Fold in chocolate chunks; chill 30 minutes.

5. Drop by large, rounded tablespoonfuls on prepared cookie sheets. Bake 15–18 minutes. Cool in pan 10 minutes; remove from pan to finish cooling.

Ice Cream Sandwiches

Two large cookies are a treat when you sandwich them together with your favorite flavor of ice cream. Try chocolate or vanilla ice cream in chocolate chip cookies or chocolate ice cream in peanut butter cookies. Just soften the ice cream a little before you put them together.

Cherry Chocolate Chip

If you like chocolate-covered cherries you are sure to love these cookies. Maraschino cherries can be thoroughly drained and chopped and used in place of dried cherries.

INGREDIENTS | **YIELDS 48 COOKIES**

⅓ cup peanut oil
⅓ cup unsalted butter
½ cup sugar
½ cup brown sugar
1 egg
1 teaspoon almond extract
2 teaspoons vanilla
2 cups flour
½ teaspoon baking soda
½ teaspoon salt
½ cup chopped almonds
1½ cups chocolate chips
½ cup dried cherries

1. Preheat oven to 375°F. Lightly grease cookie pans.

2. Cream together oil, butter, egg, sugars, almond extract, and vanilla.

3. Stir together dry ingredients; beat into butter mixture.

4. Fold in nuts, chips, and cherries.

5. Drop by rounded teaspoonfuls on prepared baking sheets. Bake 10–12 minutes. Cool slightly before removing from pan.

Tres Amigos Chocolate Chips

The three amigos in these rich cookies are the combination of different types of chocolate chips and chocolate chunks. You can add a cup of chopped pecans or walnuts if you like.

INGREDIENTS | **YIELDS 18 COOKIES**

1½ cups unsalted butter
¾ cup white sugar
¾ cup brown sugar, packed
2 eggs
1½ teaspoons vanilla extract
1¾ cups flour
1 teaspoon baking soda
1 cup white chocolate chips
1 cup milk chocolate chunks
1 cup bittersweet chocolate chips

1. Melt the butter; pour into mixing bowl. Allow to cool.

2. Add both types of sugar; beat until mixture is creamy. Add eggs, one at a time, beating well after each addition. Add vanilla and beat well.

3. Combine dry ingredients; stir into butter mixture until well blended. Add chips and chunks. Chill overnight.

4. Preheat oven to 325°F. Cover a cookie sheet with parchment.

5. Drop by ⅛ cup measure about 2" apart on the cookie sheet. Bake for 10 to 12 minutes. Allow to cool before removing from the cookie sheets.

Cranberry White Chocolate Chip

Cranberry White Chocolate cookies are great anytime, but are especially festive on a platter of Christmas treats.

INGREDIENTS | YIELDS 48 COOKIES

1 cup unsalted butter
1 cup light brown sugar, packed
1 cup sugar
2 eggs
2 tablespoons grated orange peel
1 teaspoon vanilla
3 cups flour
1 teaspoon baking soda
1½ cups white chocolate chips
2 cups dried cranberries
1 cup walnuts, chopped

1. Preheat oven to 375°F. Lightly grease cookie sheet.

2. Cream together unsalted butter and both sugars until fluffy. Beat in egg, orange peel, and vanilla

3. Stir dry ingredients together; stir into creamed mixture.

4. Stir in white chocolate walnuts, and dried cranberries. Chill 30 minutes. Drop by rounded teaspoonfuls onto cookie sheets.

5. Bake 8–10 minutes; do not overcook. Allow to cool on cookie sheet 10 minutes before removing.

Dazzle Them with Drizzle

A drizzle of chocolate or white chocolate is a nice finishing touch on almost any cookie. Just melt 1 cup of chocolate chips with 1 tablespoon of corn syrup. Allow mixture to run off a fork while moving it quickly back and forth over the cookie.

Aztec Chocolate Chip

The addition of chipotle adds a unique, smoky flavor to these cookies along with some heat. If you can't find dried chipotle you may substitute cayenne pepper.

INGREDIENTS | YIELDS 48 COOKIES

1 cup unsalted butter

1½ cups sugar

2 eggs

1 teaspoon vanilla

2 cups all-purpose flour

⅔ cup Hershey's Special Dark cocoa powder

½ teaspoon salt

1 teaspoon ground cinnamon, preferably Vietnamese

½ teaspoon soda

2 cups bittersweet chocolate chips

2 teaspoons dried chipotle, chopped fine

1. Preheat oven to 350°F. Lightly grease cookies sheets.

2. Beat butter, sugar, eggs, and vanilla until light and fluffy.

3. Mix dry ingredients together; add to butter mixture, blending well.

4. Stir in the chocolate chips and chipotle. Drop by rounded tablespoonfuls on prepared cookie sheets.

5. Bake 8–10 minutes. The cookies should be very slightly undercooked. Allow to cool on baking sheets 5 minutes before removing from pan.

Know Your Cinnamon

There are several kinds of cinnamon besides the generic mix available on most grocers' shelves. By using the Vietnamese, Chinese, Ceylon, or Korintje Cassia varieties of cinnamon you can make interesting changes in the way a finished cookie tastes. The Vietnamese is the spiciest while the Chinese has the mildest flavor.

Lavender White Chocolate Drops

Lavender has a citrus taste that is hard to describe. Always be sure to use food-grade lavender buds, or if you grow your own lavender, be sure not to spray it with pesticides. These cookies, with their flecks of purple, are a perfect accompaniment to tea.

INGREDIENTS | **YIELDS 36 COOKIES**

½ cup vegetable shortening

½ cup unsalted butter

½ cup brown sugar

1 cup sugar

2 eggs

1 tablespoon vanilla

1 tablespoon grated lemon peel

2¼ cups all-purpose flour

1 teaspoon baking soda

1–2 tablespoons dried food-grade lavender flowers

2 cups white chocolate chunks or chips

1. Preheat oven to 350°F. Cover cookie sheets with parchment.

2. Cream together shortening, butter, and sugars until light and fluffy. Beat in eggs, vanilla, and lemon peel.

3. Mix dry ingredients; stir into butter mixture until well blended.

4. Stir in lavender and white chocolate.

5. Drop by teaspoonfuls onto cookie sheet; bake 8–10 minutes.

6. Allow to cool for 5 minutes on cookie sheets before removing to finish cooling.

Royal Flavor

Queen Elizabeth 1 loved the flavor of lavender so much that she ordered lavender conserve to be served with every meal. Lavender should be used sparingly; too much of it and your dishes will have a bitter taste. The intensity of the taste can vary from plant to plant and from season to season, so always err on the side of less rather than more.

Blueberry White Chocolate Chippers

This is an unusual combination that will make any blueberry lover in your house happy. The lemon peel can be replaced with finely chopped candied ginger if you like something with a little zip.

INGREDIENTS | **YIELDS 48 COOKIES**

½ cup unsalted butter

½ cup shortening

¾ cup sugar

¾ cup brown sugar, packed

2 eggs

1 teaspoon vanilla

2 tablespoons grated lemon peel

2¼ cups all-purpose flour

¼ teaspoon freshly grated nutmeg

1 teaspoon baking soda

½ teaspoon salt

1 cup dried blueberries

1½ cups white chocolate chips

Parchment Alternative

If you don't have parchment paper, you can simply grease and then flour the cookie sheet. The cookies will be more likely to hold their shape during baking. Whenever you are baking cookies with chocolate chips or candied fruit this method will keep the bottoms from burning too easily.

1. Preheat oven to 350°F. Line a cookie sheet with parchment.

2. Cream together butter, shortening, and both sugars. Add eggs, vanilla, and lemon peel; beat until well blended.

3. Mix dry ingredients together; stir into creamed mixture. Blend well; add dried blueberries and white chocolate chips.

4. Drop by generous, rounded teaspoonfuls onto parchment baking sheets. Keep cookies about 2" apart. Bake 8–10 minutes, removing from oven when just barely done.

5. Cool on pans 5 minutes; remove to cool completely.

Chocolate Peanut Butter Chip

Chocolate and peanut butter are a classic combination. These cookies are made a little bigger than usual to satisfy those giant cravings. For more chocolate flavor add ½ cup of dark chocolate chips when you add the peanut butter chips.

INGREDIENTS | YIELDS 30 COOKIES

½ cup butter
½ cup vegetable shortening
1½ cups sugar
2 teaspoons vanilla
2 eggs
2 cups all-purpose flour
⅔ cup cocoa powder
¾ teaspoon baking soda
½ teaspoon salt
2 cups peanut butter chips

1. Preheat oven to 350°F. Lightly grease cookie sheets.

2. In a mixing bowl, cream together butter, shortening, sugar, and vanilla until light and fluffy. Beat in eggs.

3. Combine dry ingredients; blend into butter mixture. Stir in peanut butter chips.

4. Drop by heaping tablespoons onto baking sheets. Bake 10–12 minutes, or until just set.

5. Allow cookies to cool on baking sheets 5 minutes before removing to finish cooling.

Peanut Butter Passion

Peanut butter was first introduced to the general public at the 1904 World's Fair. It quickly gained fans, and by 1915 it was being featured in cookies. It is so popular today that over half of the peanut crop in the United States is made into peanut butter.

Easy Drop Cookies

Whoopie Pies

Whoopie Pies are a traditional Pennsylvania Dutch treat popular throughout Pennsylvania and up into New England. They consist of two large-sized cookies with a cream filling. The cookie is cake-like rather than crunchy, and those people who love them will settle for nothing else.

INGREDIENTS | **YIELDS 16 COOKIES**

2⅔ cups all-purpose flour

½ cup Hershey's Special Dark cocoa

1 teaspoon baking powder

1 teaspoon baking soda

1 teaspoon salt

½ cup hot coffee

½ cup sour milk

1½ cups sugar

½ cup shortening

2 eggs

1 teaspoon vanilla

Cream Filling for Whoopie Pies (page 555)

1. Preheat oven to 350°F. Grease a large cookie sheet.

2. Combine flour, cocoa, baking powder, baking soda, and salt; set aside.

3. Combine coffee and sour milk; set aside.

4. Beat sugar and shortening until fluffy. Add eggs and vanilla blend well. Starting with the flour mixture, add flour and sour milk mixture alternately. End with flour.

5. Drop by generous, rounded tablespoonfuls onto baking sheet. Flatten slightly with wet fingertips. Bake 10–12 minutes, or until cookies spring back when touched lightly. Cool completely before filling.

Pumpkin Whoopie Pies

These are delicious all year, but they are a special treat when the first crisp breezes of autumn start pulling the leaves from the trees. Use the filling recipe given or substitute the Buttercream (page 546) and fold in some finely chopped, candied ginger.

INGREDIENTS | YIELDS 18 COOKIES

3 cups all-purpose flour

1 teaspoon baking powder

1 teaspoon baking soda

1 teaspoon salt

1½ teaspoons cinnamon

1 teaspoon ginger

½ teaspoon ground cloves

½ teaspoon freshly grated nutmeg

2½ cups brown sugar

1 cup vegetable oil

2 eggs

2 cups solid-pack pumpkin

1 teaspoon vanilla

1 recipe Cream Cheese Filling for Pumpkin Whoopie Pies (page 556)

1. Combine flour, baking powder, baking soda, salt, cinnamon, ginger, cloves, and nutmeg in a mixing bowl; set aside.

2. Cream together sugar, oil, eggs, pumpkin, and vanilla.

3. Add dry ingredients; mix well.

4. Drop by rounded tablespoons onto ungreased cookie sheets. Bake at 350°F 10–12 minutes. When done, centers of cookies will quickly spring back when pressed lightly.

5. Cool thoroughly before filling.

Freezing Whoopie Pies

Because Whoopie Pies are a soft cookie, they can be filled and frozen successfully. In fact, a great way to do this is to wrap the finished cookies individually in plastic wrap and place them carefully in a freezer container. Grab a cookie out of the container and place it in a lunch bag while stile frozen. It will be just right at lunchtime—thawed but still cool.

Vanilla Whoopie Pies

This vanilla version of Whoopie Pies is a little more delicate than the chocolate version, but no less wonderful. Adding the seeds and pulp from the inside of a vanilla bean intensifies the flavor and adds a nice visual effect.

INGREDIENTS | **YIELDS 18 COOKIES**

2 cups sugar
½ cup unsalted butter
½ cup vegetable shortening
3 eggs
1 teaspoon vanilla
4 cups all-purpose flour
2 teaspoons baking soda
3 teaspoons baking powder
1 teaspoon cream of tartar
1 teaspoon cider vinegar
1 cup buttermilk
¼ cup half-and-half
2 split vanilla bean, optional
Cream Filling for Whoopie Pies
(page 555)

1. Preheat oven to 350°F. Lightly grease cookie sheets.

2. Cream sugar, butter, and shortening together until fluffy. Add eggs one at a time, beating well after each addition. Stir in vanilla. Scrape vanilla bean pulp into creamed mixture.

3. Combine dry ingredients; set aside.

4. Combine vinegar, buttermilk, and half-and-half. Add to creamed mixture, alternating with flour mixture. Begin and end with flour mixture.

5. Drop by rounded tablespoons onto prepared cookie sheets. Bake 10–12 minutes. Cool thoroughly before filling with Cream Filling for Whoopie Pies.

Shortening Makes Them Durable

You will notice that almost all of the recipe for Gobs, Whoopie Pies, and similar cookies call for shortening rather than butter. This is because shortening makes the cookies hold up better; they are more easily transported without crumbling. That durability makes them great for sending in school lunches.

Chocolate-Peanut Butter Whoopie Pies

If you love peanut butter, this is the perfect choice for an afternoon snack. For an even more amazing cookie, glaze the top with the Chocolate Glaze (page 548).

INGREDIENTS | YIELDS 18 COOKIES

2⅔ cups all-purpose flour

½ cup Hershey's Special Dark cocoa

1 teaspoon baking soda

1 teaspoon baking powder

½ teaspoon salt

½ cup shortening

1½ cups sugar

2 eggs

1 teaspoon vanilla

1 cup sour milk

Peanut Butter Filling for Whoopie Pies (page 556)

1. Preheat oven to 375°F. Line cookie sheets with parchment.

2. Mix flour, cocoa, baking soda, baking powder, and salt together; set aside.

3. Cream, shortening and sugar until fluffy. Add eggs one at a time. Stir in vanilla.

4. Combine dry ingredients; add alternately with milk, to creamed mixture. Begin and end with dry ingredients.

5. Drop by rounded tablespoons on parchment. Bake 10 minutes. Allow to cool completely before filling with Peanut Butter Filling.

Why Whoopie Pies?

Whoopie pies were originally a way for Amish cooks to use the batter that was left over from cake baking. The cookies were packed in children's school lunches. The common story is that when the children opened their lunches and saw the cookies, they would yell, "Whoopie!"

Gobs

So, what is the difference between Whoopie Pies and Gobs? Nothing! Gobs are just another name for Whoopie Pies. This version produces a more cake-like cookie because of the use of cake flour.

INGREDIENTS | **YIELDS 24 COOKIES**

2 cups sugar

½ cup unsalted butter

2 eggs

1 cup boiling water

½ cup cocoa

4 cups cake flour

2 teaspoons baking soda

Pinch of salt

½ teaspoon baking powder

1 cup buttermilk

Cream Filling for Whoopie Pies (page 555)

1. Preheat oven to 375°F. Line cookie sheets with parchment.

2. Cream butter and sugar until fluffy. Add eggs one at a time.

3. Mix boiling water into cocoa, stirring until it is a smooth paste; cool. Add to creamed mixture; blend well.

4. Add dry ingredients, alternating with buttermilk. Begin and end with buttermilk.

5. Bake 10 minutes, or until top springs back when touched lightly. Allow to cool completely before filling.

Classic Oatmeal Cookies

These are the chewy, old-fashioned oatmeal cookies that you remember from childhood. Leave them plain or add any (or all!) of the optional ingredients—they are delicious any way you make them. Be careful not to overbake.

INGREDIENTS | YIELDS 60 COOKIES

¾ cup vegetable shortening

1 cup packed brown sugar

½ cup sugar

1 egg

1 teaspoon vanilla

¼ cup water

3 cups old-fashioned oatmeal, uncooked

1 cup flour

1 teaspoon salt

½ teaspoon baking soda

1 cup coconut, optional

1 cup raisins, optional

1 cup pecans or walnuts, optional

1. Preheat oven to 350°F. Lightly grease cookie sheets.

2. Beat together shortening and sugars until light and fluffy. Beat in egg, vanilla, and water.

3. Combine dry ingredients; stir into creamed mixture. Add any optional ingredients at this time.

4. Drop by rounded teaspoons onto prepared cookie sheets. Bake 12–15 minutes.

5. Allow to cool 5 minutes before removing from cookie sheet.

It all Started with Quaker Oats

The now-famous Quaker Oatmeal Cookie recipe was first published during World War II. Since butter was in very short supply, the recipe was developed using shortening and was so popular that there was never a reason to change the ingredient to butter once rationing was over.

Oatmeal Cream Pies

These are basically just oatmeal Whoopie Pies. The cookie is a bit more prone to crumbling than the other types of Whoopie Pies, so handle with care. Different fillings can be used successfully, including the Date Filling (page 550).

INGREDIENTS | **YIELDS 20 COOKIES**

½ cup unsalted butter
¼ cup vegetable shortening
2 cups brown sugar
2 eggs
1 teaspoon baking soda
3 tablespoons boiling water
½ teaspoon salt
2 cups flour
2 cups quick-cooking oatmeal
1 teaspoon cinnamon
1 teaspoon baking powder
Cream Filling for Whoopie Pies (page 555)

1. Preheat oven to 350°F. Line cookies sheets with parchment.

2. Cream butter, shortening, and sugar until fluffy. Add eggs; beat well.

3. Combine baking soda and water; add to creamed mixture, beating in carefully.

4. Combine dry ingredients; stir into creamed mixture.

5. Drop by rounded tablespoons onto parchment-lined cookie sheets. Bake 10–12 minutes. Cool completely before filling.

Raisin Nut Cookies

Some people prefer the raisins be plumped when they go into the dough, others prefer the chewier quality of the dried raisins. See which you prefer.

INGREDIENTS | **YIELDS 36 COOKIES**

1 cup water
2 cups raisins
3½ cups all-purpose flour
1 teaspoon baking powder
1 teaspoon baking soda
1 teaspoon salt
1 teaspoon ground cinnamon
½ teaspoon freshly ground nutmeg
½ cup butter, softened
½ cup shortening
1 cup white sugar
¾ cup brown sugar
1 teaspoon vanilla
2 eggs
1 cup coarsely chopped walnuts

1. Bring the water to a boil; remove from heat. Place raisins in a bowl with water, cover; set aside to cool.

2. Preheat oven to 375°F. Lightly grease cookie sheets.

3. Combine dry ingredients; set aside.

4. Cream butter, shortening, and sugars until fluffy. Beat in vanilla and eggs. Stir in raisins along with any water left on them. Blend in flour mixture and nuts.

5. Drop by tablespoons onto baking sheets; bake 12–15 minutes. Allow to cool 5 minutes before removing from baking sheet.

Frosted Chocolate Drops

Frosted chocolate drops are an old-fashioned favorite. They can be frosted with either the Mocha Butter Frosting (page 553) or the Caramel Fudge Frosting (page 551).

INGREDIENTS | YIELDS 36 COOKIES

¼ cup shortening
¼ cup butter
1 cup sugar
1 egg
1 teaspoon vanilla
¾ cup sour milk
1¾ cups all-purpose flour
½ cup cocoa
½ teaspoon salt
½ teaspoon baking soda
1 cup chopped walnuts

1. Preheat oven to 400°F. Line cookie sheets with parchment.

2. Cream shortening, butter, and sugar until light and fluffy. Beat in egg, vanilla, and sour milk.

3. Combine dry ingredients; stir in with walnuts.

4. Drop by rounded teaspoon onto baking sheets. Bake 8–10 minutes. Cool completely.

5. Frost tops with frosting and garnish with a walnut half.

Sour Milk

If you don't happen to have soured milk or buttermilk on hand, you can make your own. Just add 1 tablespoon white vinegar to 1 cup of milk and allow it to stand at room temperature for 10 minutes. The acids in the vinegar will sour the milk and it can be easily used in your recipe.

Black Forest Cookies

Black forest cake is a popular dessert made with dark chocolate, cherries, and whipped cream. Cream Cheese Frosting is used to give the cookie an authentic Black Forest flavor. It can be omitted if you like.

INGREDIENTS | **YIELDS 36 COOKIES**

1 cup all-purpose flour

¼ cup Hershey's Special Dark Cocoa powder

1 teaspoon baking powder

Pinch of salt

1 cup bittersweet chocolate, chopped

½ cup unsalted butter

¾ cup sugar

2 eggs

1 cup dried cherries, soaked in kirsch if desired

2 cups dark chocolate chunks

Cream Cheese Frosting (page 550)

1 cup coarsely chopped bittersweet chocolate for garnish

1. Preheat oven to 350°F. Line cookie sheets with parchment.

2. Stir flour, cocoa, baking powder, and salt together.

3. Melt bittersweet chocolate and butter together until smooth. Remove from heat; allow to cool to room temperature. Beat in sugar and eggs until very smooth.

4. Stir in flour mixture until blended; do not overmix. Add cherries and chocolate chunks. Chill 30 minutes.

5. Drop by rounded teaspoonfuls onto baking sheets. Bake 10–12 minutes; do not over bake. Cool 5 minutes; remove from cookie sheet to cool completely. Frost tops with Cream Cheese Frosting and garnish with coarsely chopped chocolate.

Chocolate Toffee Cookies

These huge cookies are rich and full of buttery toffee flavor. They are a bit like a brownie and a bit like a cookie. Watch them carefully; the bottoms burn easily.

INGREDIENTS | **YIELDS 18 COOKIES**

¾ cup all-purpose flour

1 teaspoon baking powder

Pinch of salt

1 pound bittersweet chocolate, chopped

¼ cup unsalted butter

2 cups packed brown sugar

4 eggs

1 tablespoon vanilla

1 teaspoon butter flavor

1½ cups Heath bars, chopped coarsely

1 cup almonds, chopped and toasted

1. Combine dry ingredients; set aside.

2. Melt chocolate and butter together. Cool to room temperature. Beat sugar and eggs until thick and lemony, 5 minutes. Add vanilla, butter favoring, and chocolate mixture.

3. Stir in dry ingredients, blending well. Fold in toffee and almonds. Cover and chill overnight.

4. Next day, preheat oven to 350°F. Line a baking sheet with parchment. Drop cookies by ¼ cup scoops 3" apart on baking sheets. Bake 15 minutes, or until tops are dry and cracked but not overdone. Cool completely.

Butterscotch Cookies

These can be served plain, of course. If you want a little extra shazzam, when serving this cookie glaze it with the Confectioners' Glaze (page 547) and sprinkle with more pecans.

INGREDIENTS | YIELDS 48 COOKIES

2½ cups all-purpose flour
1 teaspoon baking soda
½ teaspoon baking powder
½ teaspoon salt
½ cup unsalted butter
1½ cups dark brown sugar, packed
2 eggs
2 teaspoons vanilla
1 cup whole buttermilk (not skim or low fat)
1 cup chopped pecans

1. Preheat oven to 350°F. Lightly grease baking sheets.

2. Stir dry ingredients together; set aside.

3. Cream together butter and brown sugar until light and fluffy. Beat in eggs and vanilla.

4. Add dry ingredients alternately with buttermilk. Mix well after each addition. Stir in the pecans.

5. Drop by rounded teaspoons onto prepared baking sheets. Bake 10–12 minutes; do not overbake. Cool for a few minutes before removing from baking sheets.

Light or Dark?

The only difference between light brown and dark brown sugars is the amount of molasses added to each; which you use in your recipe is largely a personal preference. The dark brown sugar will give a richer flavor that may be overpowering in some cookies.

Walnut Clusters

These cookies are rich with flavor. Pecans, hickory nuts, macadamias, hazelnuts, and even pistachios can be substituted for the walnuts if you wish.

INGREDIENTS | **YIELDS 30 COOKIES**

½ cup all-purpose flour
Pinch of salt
¼ teaspoon baking powder
¼ cup unsalted butter
½ cup sugar
1½ ounces melted unsweetened chocolate
1 egg
2 teaspoons vanilla
2 cups walnuts, chopped

1. Preheat oven to 375°F. Cover baking sheets with parchment.

2. Sift dry ingredients together.

3. Cream butter and sugar until light and fluffy. Add in chocolate, egg, and vanilla; beat until smooth.

4. Blend in flour mixture and walnuts. Drop by teaspoonfuls onto baking sheets. Bake 8–10 minutes. Allow to cool slightly before removing from sheets.

Three Leaf Clovers

You can make an unusual cookie using three different types of drop cookie dough. Just drop about ½ teaspoon of each flavor of dough in a clover shape on the cookie sheet. Gently push the dough together so that they will adhere when baked. Each recipe you choose should have a similar baking temperature and time.

Old-Fashioned Date Hermits

Date Hermits are a long-keeping cookie because of the amount of dried fruit in the recipe. They will stay fresh for up to two weeks if stored properly.

INGREDIENTS | YIELDS 72 COOKIES

3 cups flour
1 teaspoon baking soda
1 teaspoon cloves
½ teaspoon salt
1 teaspoon cinnamon
1 cup butter
1½ cups brown sugar
3 eggs, beaten
1 tablespoon unsulfured molasses
1 cup chopped walnuts
1 tablespoon grated orange rind
1 cup chopped dates
1 cup raisins

1. Preheat oven to 400°F. Line baking sheets with parchment.

2. Mix together dry ingredients; set aside.

3. Cream butter and sugar until light and fluffy. Add eggs and molasses; beat until smooth.

4. Blend in flour mixture. Fold in walnuts, orange rind, dates, and raisins. Chill 30 minutes.

5. Drop by teaspoonfuls onto baking sheets. Bake 7–10 minutes, or until golden.

Great for Shipping

Hermits are a very sturdy, very moist cookie great for shipping. It is one of the better cookies to ship if you are sending a care package overseas because of the amount of dried fruit in the recipe. Want to send someone an assortment? See Chapter 7 for more cookies that ship well.

Frosted Ginger Creams

Reminiscent of gingersnaps, but not quite, these spicy cookies are the perfect ending to a chilly day. They are softer and more cake like than gingersnaps. For the best flavor, serve with coffee and some great conversation.

INGREDIENTS | YIELDS 72 COOKIES

1 cup sugar

½ cup shortening

2 eggs

½ cup unsulfured molasses

1 teaspoon baking soda

1 cup hot, black coffee

3 cups all-purpose flour

1 teaspoon ginger

1 teaspoon cinnamon

1 teaspoon cloves

1 cup raisins

¼ cup finely chopped crystallized ginger

Glaze

Mix the juice and grated rind of 1 orange mixed with enough confectioners' sugar to make it spreadable. (Start with 1 cup on the confectioners' and add more as needed.)

1. Preheat oven to 350°F. Grease baking sheets.

2. Cream sugar and shortening until light and fluffy. Add eggs one at a time, mixing well after each. Stir in molasses.

3. Dissolve baking soda in coffee; stir into egg mixture.

4. Combine dry ingredients and stir into egg mixture. Fold in raisins.

5. Drop by teaspoonful onto baking sheets. Bake 20 minutes, or until done. Frost with glaze while still warm.

Sour Cream Sugar Cookies

These cookies are a soft and cake-like, not too sweet, drop sugar cookie.
These are very easy to do, with no rolling or cutting.

INGREDIENTS | **YIELDS 60 COOKIES**

5 cups cake flour
1 teaspoon baking soda
2 teaspoons baking powder
¼ teaspoon freshly grated nutmeg
½ teaspoon salt
1 cup unsalted butter
1 cup sugar
2 eggs, room temperature
2 cups sour cream
1 teaspoon vanilla

Uniform Sizes

The best size ice cream scoops to use for drop cookie dough are # 80 or # 90. Scoop the dough out of the bowl with the scoop, pressing the dough firmly into the scoop. Release it onto the prepared cookie sheet. Each cookie will be uniform in size and texture because they will bake at the same rate.

1. Preheat oven to 375°F. Grease cookie sheets.

2. Sift dry ingredients together; set aside.

3. Cream butter and sugar until fluffy. Beat in eggs and vanilla.

4. Add flour mixture and sour cream alternately to mixture. Drop by teaspoons on prepared cookie sheets.

5. Bake 12–15 minutes, until golden. Allow to cool a few minutes on cookie sheets before removing to cool completely.

CHAPTER 22

Brownies and Bars

Chewy Chocolate Brownies with Pecans

If you don't have two 9" × 9" baking pans for this recipe, you can use a 13" × 9" pan. The brownies will be thicker and take a little longer to bake.

INGREDIENTS | **YIELDS 32 BROWNIES**

6 ounces unsweetened chocolate, chopped

1 cup butter

2 cups sugar

1 cup brown sugar

⅔ cup light corn syrup

6 eggs

2 cups all-purpose flour

2 cups chopped pecans

32 pecan halves for garnish

Keep That Chewy Texture

Bar cookies are a quick-to-put-together snack. Be careful not to overbake them or they will be dry and crumbly. Generally, for a chewy texture the cookies should be removed from the oven when they are just barely done; they will continue to cook a little as they cool.

1. Preheat oven to 350°F. Grease two 9" square baking pans.

2. Melt chocolate in butter. Beat in sugars and corn syrup; beat at medium speed 2 minutes, until well blended. Add eggs one at a time, beating 1 minute after each one.

3. Stir in flour and pecans. Spoon batter into pans. Arrange pecan halves in rows over tops of batter.

4. Bake 40 minutes, or until done but still slightly doughy in center.

5. Cool completely and cut into squares.

Butterfinger Brownies

The rich flavor of Butterfinger adds a nice touch to these moist brownies. Set aside about ¼ cup of the chopped Butterfinger to sprinkle on the top of the batter before baking if you wish.

INGREDIENTS | **YIELDS 36 BROWNIES**

8 ounces bittersweet chocolate, chopped

1 cup butter

2 cups sugar

4 eggs

2 teaspoons vanilla

1½ cups flour

Pinch of salt

4 Butterfinger candy bars, coarsely chopped

1. Preheat oven to 350°F. Grease a 13" × 9" pan.

2. Melt chocolate and butter together. Spoon into bowl of a mixer; beat in sugar. Add eggs one at a time, blending well after each. Stir in vanilla.

3. Fold in flour and salt until well blended and no streaks of white show.

4. Fold in chopped Butterfinger bars.

5. Spoon into pan; bake 35–40 minutes. Cool completely before cutting into bars.

Quick Tip for Easy Cutting

If you can never cut bar cookies in straight, even lines, here is a solution: Use a ruler and a pizza cutter! Just place the ruler gently on top of the baked bars and follow the lines of the ruler with the pizza cutter. The bars will be cut evenly every time.

Cookie Dough Brownies

These brownies are done in three separate layers—the brownie, the cookie dough, and the glaze. They are very rich, so you may be able to get double the yield given.

INGREDIENTS | **YIELDS 18 BROWNIES**

Brownie Layer

1½ cups flour

½ teaspoon of salt

½ cup Hershey's Dark cocoa

1 cup vegetable oil

2 cups sugar

2 teaspoons vanilla

4 eggs

Cookie Dough Layer

1 cup unsalted butter

1 cup brown sugar

½ cup sugar

2 teaspoons vanilla

2 tablespoons milk

2 cups flour

1 recipe Chocolate Glaze (page 548)

Remove Bar Cookies Easily

To remove bar cookies more easily, just be sure and take the corner cookie first. Once the corner is out it is a simple matter to slip a fork under each remaining cookie and carefully remove it from the pan. For layered bars, like Cookie Dough Brownies, it will also be easier if the bars are well chilled.

Brownie Layer

1. Grease a 13" × 9" pan and set aside. Preheat oven to 350°F.

2. Combine 1½ cups flour, ½ teaspoon salt, and ½ cup cocoa; set aside.

3. Mix 1 cup oil, 2 cups sugar, vanilla, and eggs; mix 3 minutes at medium speed.

4. Spread in prepared pan; bake 25 minutes; do not overbake.

5. Cool completely before proceeding.

Cookie Dough Layer

1. Mix 1 cup butter, 1 cup brown sugar, ½ cup sugar, 2 teaspoons vanilla, 2 tablespoons milk, and 2 cups flour in a mixer until well blended and smooth.

2. Spread thickly over cooled brownies. Cover and place in refrigerator 1 hour.

3. Spread glaze over cooled cookie dough layer.

4. Cover with plastic wrap; chill until set.

5. Cut into bars. Refrigerate unused portions.

Rocky Road Brownies

For extra chocolate flavor in these Rocky Road Bars, try adding 1 cup of bittersweet chocolate chunks to the brownie batter.

INGREDIENTS | YIELDS 12 BROWNIES

1 cup miniature marshmallows
1 cup chocolate chips
½ cup chopped pecans
½ cup butter
1 cup sugar
2 eggs
1 teaspoon of vanilla
½ cup cocoa
½ teaspoon baking powder
Pinch of salt
½ cup flour
1 recipe Chocolate Glaze (page 548)

1. Preheat oven to 350°F. Grease a 9" square baking pan.

2. Stir together marshmallows, chocolate chips, and nuts; set aside.

3. Microwave butter on high 1 minute, or until melted. Beat in sugar, eggs, and vanilla.

4. Add dry ingredients; blend well. Spoon batter into prepared pan; bake 20 minutes.

5. Sprinkle marshmallow mixture over top; continue to bake until marshmallows have softened and puffed slightly. Remove from oven. Cool; drizzle glaze over top. Cut into squares with a wet knife.

Substituting Margarine for Butter

When baking cookies, you can substitute stick margarine for an equal amount of butter; however, the texture will be less crisp and flavorful. Never substitute light margarine or the butter or margarine that comes in a tub for sticks of butter. It is whipped and does not contain the right amount of fat.

Chipotle Brownies

Deep chocolate, cinnamon, and smoky chipotle add a south-of-the-border twist to these brownies. Adjust the chipotle to suit your own tastes, but be careful—it is hot.

INGREDIENTS | YIELDS 12 BROWNIES

2 sticks unsalted butter

2 ounces unsweetened chocolate, chopped

2 ounces bittersweet chocolate, chopped

1 cup sugar

½ cup light brown sugar

4 eggs

1 teaspoon cinnamon

¾ teaspoon ground chipotle pepper

1 cup all-purpose flour

1. Preheat oven to 325°F. Grease 9" × 9" pan.

2. Melt butter and chocolates in microwave, stirring often. Cool.

3. Beat sugars and eggs into melted chocolate mixture.

4. Blend in dry ingredients.

5. Spoon into pan; bake 30–35 minutes, or until center is set. Cool completely and cut into squares.

Chocolate Chip Brownies

The little pockets of chocolate chips in these brownies make them perfect for the chocolate lover. You can also add 1 cup of pecans or walnuts if you would like.

INGREDIENTS | YIELDS 12 BROWNIES

1¼ cups butter

1 cup cocoa

2 eggs

1 teaspoon vanilla

1½ cups sugar

1 cup all-purpose flour

2 cups chocolate chips

1. Preheat oven to 325°F. Grease 9" × 9" pan.

2. Melt butter; stir in cocoa powder to make a smooth paste. Cool.

3. Beat in eggs, vanilla, and sugar until smooth.

4. Stir in flour and chocolate chips; make sure it is well blended. Spoon dough into prepared pan.

5. Bake about 30 minutes, or until center is set. Cool completely before cutting into bars.

Which Rack?

For bar cookies of all types, the rack should be put in the center of the oven. This will allow the air to circulate and the bar cookies to bake more evenly. For best results, only bake one batch of cookies at a time. The heat will stay more uniform and the bars will bake more evenly.

Triple Layer Chocolate-Peanut Butter Brownies

Here is another very rich brownie. The first layer must be completely cool before you proceed with the next steps. Chill well before cutting and keep these refrigerated.

INGREDIENTS | YIELDS 24 BROWNIES

Base Layer

¾ cup unsalted butter

12 ounces bittersweet chocolate, chopped

1¼ cups sugar

4 eggs

2 teaspoons vanilla

½ teaspoon salt

1 cup all-purpose flour

Peanut Butter Layer

1 cup peanut butter

¼ cup unsalted butter

¾ cup powdered sugar

Pinch of salt

1 tablespoon milk

1 teaspoon vanilla

Glaze

¼ cup unsalted butter

8 ounces bittersweet chocolate, chopped

Base Layer

1. Preheat oven to 350°F. Grease 13" × 9" pan.

2. Melt ¾ cup unsalted butter and 12 ounces of chocolate in microwave, stirring often.

3. Whisk in sugar until well blended and smooth. Beat in eggs one at a time, beating well after each. Add 2 teaspoons vanilla, ½ teaspoon salt, and flour. Mix until very well blended.

4. Spoon into prepared pan; bake 30–35 minutes, or until a toothpick comes out with just a few crumbs clinging to it.

5. Cool completely before proceeding.

Peanut Butter Layer

1. Combine peanut butter and ¼ cup butter; mix until smooth and creamy.

2. Stir in powdered sugar, salt, milk, and vanilla.

3. Spoon peanut butter onto cooled brownie base; chill.

Glaze

1. Melt butter and 8 ounces of chopped chocolate together. Mix until smooth.

2. Pour and smooth over chilled peanut butter layer. Chill brownies covered for several hours before cutting.

Retro Blondies

These butterscotch-flavored brownies have been a favorite with kids and adults alike for decades. Omit the nuts if you want to. Sprinkle the tops of the Blondies with some confectioners' sugar just before serving for a sweet touch.

INGREDIENTS | YIELDS 16 BROWNIES

2 cups flour
1 teaspoon baking powder
1 teaspoon salt
¼ teaspoon baking soda
½ cup unsalted butter
1 cup brown sugar, packed
2 eggs
1 teaspoon vanilla
1 cup chocolate chips
1 cup pecans or walnuts

1. Preheat oven to 325°F. Grease 9" square pan. (Glass works best for this recipe.)

2. Sift together dry ingredients; set aside. Melt butter and brown sugar together, stirring until smooth. Let cool to room temperature.

3. Add eggs one at a time, beating well after each addition. Stir in vanilla.

4. Fold in dry ingredients, nuts, and chocolate chips until well blended and there are no streaks of flour in the dough.

5. Bake 30–35 minutes, or until a toothpick inserted in the center comes out with just a few crumbs clinging to it. Cool and cut into squares.

Coconut Praline Bars

Use light brown sugar when you make the praline topping for this bar. Dark brown sugar will overpower the delicate flavors.

INGREDIENTS | YIELDS 36 BARS

Crust
1½ cups all-purpose flour
⅔ cup confectioners' sugar
¾ cup butter

Topping
¼ cup all-purpose flour
2 cans sweetened condensed milk
4 cups flaked coconut
2 teaspoons vanilla
½ cup butter
½ cup brown sugar
1 cup chopped pecans

1. Preheat oven to 350°F. Butter 13" × 9" pan and set aside.

2. Mix 1½ cups flour and confectioners' sugar; blend butter in until mixture is crumbly.

3. Press firmly into prepared pan; bake 10 minutes.

4. Mix condensed milk, ¼ cup flour, vanilla, and coconut. Spread over bars; return to oven 10 minutes.

5. Melt butter and brown sugar together in a pan; cook, stirring, until mixture is no longer grainy; do not overcook. Pour quickly over bars and sprinkle with pecans. Chill.

Key Lime Bars

*The addition of rose water to these tangy bars takes them from average to incredible;
it adds a delicate flavor that is hard to describe. Rose water is available at
many health food stores, Middle Eastern markets, or online.*

INGREDIENTS | **YIELDS 24 BARS**

Crust

1½ cups all-purpose flour

½ cup powdered sugar

¾ cup unsalted butter,
room temperature

½ teaspoon vanilla

1 teaspoon rose water

Topping

4 eggs

1½ cups sugar

½ cup key lime juice

1 tablespoon all-purpose flour

1 tablespoon grated lime peel

Powdered sugar for dusting

1. Preheat oven to 350°F. Butter 13" × 9" pan.

2. Combine 1½ cups flour and ½ cup powdered sugar. Add butter, vanilla, and rose water. Cut in with your fingers until it looks like coarse crumbs.

3. Gently but firmly press flour and sugar mixture into bottom of pan; bake 20 minutes, or until golden brown.

4. Whisk eggs, 1½ cups sugar, lime juice, 1 tablespoon flour, and lime peel in a bowl; blend well.

5. Pour into crust; bake 20 minutes more, or until mixture is set. Cool. Sift powdered sugar over top before serving.

Key Limes

Key limes are a particularly tangy, small lime that grows on Key West, Florida. The juice is often available year round in your grocery store next to the lemon and lime juices. It is a little more expensive than regular lime juice, but the taste is worth it. Fresh key limes are sometimes available during the summer months.

Lemon Bars

Instead of dusting the finished bars with confectioners' sugar, put several gingersnap cookies in a food processor and turn into crumbs. Sprinkle the crumbs over the top of the bars.

INGREDIENTS | **YIELDS 24 BARS**

Crust

1½ cups all-purpose flour
¼ teaspoon ginger
⅔ cup confectioners' sugar
¾ cup butter

Topping

6 eggs
1¾ cups white sugar
⅓ cup flour
¾ cup fresh lemon juice
2 tablespoons grated lemon peel
Confectioners' sugar for sprinkling

1. Preheat oven to 350°F. Butter 13" × 9" pan and set aside.

2. Combine flour, ginger, and ⅔ cup of confectioners' sugar. Blend in butter with fingers until it resembles coarse crumbs.

3. Press into pan; bake 20 minutes, or until golden.

4. Whisk together eggs, sugar, ⅓ cup flour, lemon juice, and lemon peel until foamy. Pour over hot bars.

5. Return to oven and bake 20–25 minutes, or until set. Cool completely. Dust with confectioners' sugar.

Lemon Bars and More!

Nearly any citrus fruit that you like can be substituted in lemon bars measure for measure. Grapefruit, orange, lemon, lime, and tangerine all make delicious bars. If you are using a fruit like orange or tangerine that is already sweet, either use a little less sugar or add ¼ cup of lemon juice for ¼ cup of the orange juice called for in the recipe.

Raspberry Dreams

This is a versatile bar that can be flavored a number of ways. Dried fruit purées and other jams and preserves can be substituted for the raspberry with equally delicious results.

INGREDIENTS | YIELDS 16 BARS

1½ cups all-purpose flour
½ teaspoon salt
½ cup unsalted butter
¼ cup sugar
2 eggs, separated
1 cup seedless raspberry jam
½ cup sugar
1 teaspoon vanilla

Meringue and Humidity

If the day is very hot and humid, choose a recipe that does not include meringue. Very humid days will often keep the meringue from holding the volume. The result will be a thin, sticky meringue. Some of this can be overcome by using cream of tartar as a stabilizer, but all in all it is best not to make meringues under these conditions.

1. Preheat oven to 350°F. Sift together flour and salt; set aside.

2. Cream butter and ¼ cup sugar until light and fluffy. Add egg yolks; beat until well blended.

3. Mix in flour mixture. It will be crumbly. Press firmly into 9" square pan. Spread jam evenly over top.

4. Beat egg whites until foamy. Gradually add ½ cup of sugar; beat until stiff, glassy peaks form. Blend in vanilla. Spread over raspberry jam.

5. Bake 30 minutes. Cool completely before cutting into bars.

Espresso Brownies

These brownies are full of the great taste of espresso. For even more flavor, frost cooled brownies with the Mocha Butter Frosting (page 553).

INGREDIENTS | YIELDS 36 BROWNIES

1¼ cups all-purpose flour

¼ teaspoon baking soda

Pinch of salt

1 cup sugar

½ cup unsalted butter

¼ cup strong, dark roast coffee

¼ cup light corn syrup

12 ounces bittersweet chocolate, chopped

3 eggs

2 teaspoons vanilla

8 ounces dark chocolate, chopped

½ cup chocolate-covered coffee beans, coarsely chopped in a processor

1. Butter 9" × 13" pan; set aside. Mix together flour, baking soda, and salt; set aside. Preheat oven to 325°F.

2. Combine sugar, butter, coffee, and corn syrup in a microwave-safe bowl. Bring to a boil; add bittersweet chocolate. Allow to stand without stirring for a few minutes.

3. Beat chocolate mixture until smooth. Add eggs and vanilla, and then flour mixture. Fold in chopped chocolate and coffee beans.

4. Spoon batter into pan. Bake 40–45 minutes.

5. Let come to room temperature then chill, covered, overnight. Cut into bars.

Coffee Beans

Coffee beans are a great way to add flavor to cookies and brownies. When freshly roasted, the beans are crunchy and can be used in place of nuts in many of your recipes. You can grind them in the grinder or crush them with a rolling pin for a coarser product.

The Best Brownies Ever

This decadent brownie is so smooth, so rich, and so delicious that you won't believe it.
You can add nuts, M&M's, or any other ingredient you want, but try them
with no additions the first time. They are that good.

INGREDIENTS | **YIELDS 12 BROWNIES**

1½ cups sugar

¾ cup unsalted butter, melted

1 teaspoon vanilla

2 eggs

1 teaspoon rose water

¾ cup all-purpose flour

½ cup dark cocoa

¼ teaspoon salt

1. Butter a 9" square pan; set aside. Preheat oven to 350°F.

2. Cream sugar and melted butter until smooth. Add eggs one at a time, beating well after each addition. Add vanilla and rose water.

3. Combine dry ingredients and stir into the butter mixture.

4. Spread in pan; bake 30 minutes. Take brownies out of oven when they are just slightly underdone.

5. Cool completely before cutting.

Cranberry Walnut Blondies

These are wonderful plain, but adding the Cream Cheese Frosting
(page 550) takes them to a brand-new level.

INGREDIENTS | **YIELDS 12 BROWNIES**

½ cup unsalted butter, melted

1 cup brown sugar

1 egg

1 teaspoon vanilla

Pinch salt

1 cup flour

1 cup dried cranberries

½ cup chopped walnuts

½ cup white chocolate chips

1. Butter 8" × 8" pan. Preheat oven to 350°F.

2. Mix melted butter with brown sugar; beat until smooth, then add egg and vanilla.

3. Add salt and flour; stir until well blended. Fold in cranberries, walnuts, and white chocolate chips.

4. Bake 20–25 minutes. Cool completely before cutting.

Caramel-Filled Brownies

These brownies have bits of gooey caramel within the rich brownie. Don't try to cut or eat these when they are hot—you could be badly burned by the hot caramel.

INGREDIENTS | **YIELDS 16 BROWNIES**

1 box German chocolate cake mix

¾ cup melted butter

⅓ cup evaporated milk

¼ cup chopped pecans

14 ounces caramels

½ cup evaporated milk

2 cups bittersweet chocolate chips

Chill for Texture

Try keeping the brownie batter well covered in the refrigerator overnight and baking it the next day. Doing this allows the flavors to develop and the gluten in the flour to relax. The next day, just preheat the oven and bake as instructed. The brownies will be more flavorful and have a better texture.

1. Preheat oven to 350°F. Butter 9" × 13" pan; set aside.

2. Mix cake mix with butter, ⅓ cup evaporated milk, and chopped pecans. Press ⅓ of the mixture gently into pan; bake 6 minutes, or until set.

3. Remove wrappers from caramels and microwave with ½ cup evaporated milk, stirring until caramels are melted.

4. Remove brownies from oven; sprinkle chocolate chips over top. Spoon melted caramel over chocolate chips. Crumble remaining brownie dough over top of all. Bake 15 more minutes.

5. Chill for several hours before cutting.

Graham Cracker Chews

*For a variation on this recipe, add ½ cup white chocolate chips and
½ cup chocolate chips in with the nuts.*

INGREDIENTS | **YIELDS 24 BARS**

Crust

1½ cups graham cracker crumbs
2 tablespoons all-purpose flour
½ cup unsalted butter

Topping

2 eggs, beaten
1 teaspoon vanilla
1½ cups brown sugar
½ cup chopped pecans

When to Cut the Bars?

Most bar cookies should be cut when they have cooled completely. Brownies, Blondies, and any other bar that is soft should be cut when completely cool for the very best results. Bars that are crunchy when they have cooled need to be cut while still warm to look their best.

1. Preheat oven to 350°F. Butter 9" × 9" pan; set aside.

2. Combine 1½ cups of graham cracker crumbs and flour in a bowl. Add butter with your fingers until mixture is crumbly. Press crumbs into pan; bake 30 minutes.

3. Mix eggs and vanilla in a bowl until frothy.

4. Blend remaining ingredients together; stir into egg mixture. Pour over baked crust.

5. Bake 20 minutes, or until set. Cool completely.

Butter Bars

This is an easy recipe. You can add variety by just using different flavors of cake mix. You can also add coconut, chocolate chips, and other things to the filling.

INGREDIENTS | YIELDS 36 BARS

1 box yellow cake mix
1 egg
1 stick butter, melted
8 ounces cream cheese, room temperature
2 eggs
1 teaspoon vanilla
1 pound confectioners' sugar
1 stick unsalted butter, melted

1. Preheat oven to 350°F. Grease 9" × 13" pan; set aside.

2. Combine cake mix, egg, and butter; press into pan.

3. Beat cream cheese, eggs, vanilla, and confectioners' sugar until very smooth.

4. Add butter slowly with mixer running on low speed.

5. Pour over cake mixture; bake about 40–45 minutes; do not overbake! Cool completely before cutting. Store butter bars in the refrigerator.

Pan Sizes

Always try to use the same pan size that is used in the recipe. If the pan is too large, the bars can come out too crisp and dry. If the pan is too small the bars may be burned on the edges and raw in the middle.

Six Layer Bars

These are a tropical twist on a traditional favorite. To make the traditional bars, just substitute pecans for macadamia nuts and chocolate chips for white chocolate.

INGREDIENTS | YIELDS 12 BARS

¾ cup butter, melted
1½ cups cinnamon graham cracker crumbs
1⅓ cups sweetened condensed milk
1½ cups sweetened flaked coconut
1½ cups macadamia nuts, chopped
1½ cups white chocolate chips

1. Preheat oven to 350°F.

2. Pour melted butter in 9" square pan; sprinkle graham cracker crumbs over it.

3. Carefully drizzle condensed milk over crumbs. Spread gently with a spatula.

4. Top with coconut, macadamia nuts, and white chocolate chips. Press lightly to pack down ingredients.

5. Bake 25–30 minutes. Cool before cutting into bars.

Chocolate Squares

Add 3 tablespoons grated orange peel to the butter cookie layer of these bars.
It adds the classic orange-and-chocolate combination that just can't be beat.

INGREDIENTS | **YIELDS 24 SQUARES**

Crust

2 cups all-purpose flour

½ cup powdered sugar

⅔ cup unsalted butter

Topping

4 eggs

3 ounces unsweetened chocolate

1¼ cups sugar

1 teaspoon baking powder

2 teaspoons vanilla

1. Preheat oven to 350°F. Butter 13" × 9" pan.

2. Combine flour, powdered sugar, and butter. Cut in butter until mixture looks like crumbs. Press into pan; bake 20 minutes.

3. Beat remaining ingredients together. Pour over base layer. Bake 20–25 minutes, or until set.

4. Cool completely before cutting into bars.

Finish It

Many bar cookies have a frosting or glaze on them, but some do not. To make the plain bars look more finished, you can use a sugar shaker to dust them with powdered sugar or a combination of powdered sugar and cocoa. By doing this, you can add a little flavor and make the bars more attractive.

Chocolate Chip Brittle Cookies

These irregularly shaped bars are halfway between a cookie and a candy. Do not omit the nuts in this recipe, although you can use different nuts if you wish.

INGREDIENTS | **YIELDS 48 COOKIES**

1 cup unsalted butter
1 cup sugar
2 teaspoons vanilla
2 cups all-purpose flour
1 teaspoon salt
12 ounces chocolate chips
1 cup toasted almonds

How to Toast Almonds

Toasting nuts gives them a better, deeper flavor. Nuts of any sort are very easy to toast for your recipes. Just spread the nuts on a cookie sheet in one layer and bake in a 375°F oven for 10 minutes or so. Watch them carefully so that they don't burn.

1. Preheat oven to 375°F.

2. Cream together butter, sugar, and vanilla. Beat in flour and salt.

3. Stir in almonds and half of the chocolate chips.

4. Press gently into 15" × 10" jelly roll pan; bake 20–25 minutes. Cool.

5. Microwave rest of chocolate chips until melted. Drizzle over cookies. Break in irregular pieces.

Tiramisu Brownies

This recipe used finely grated chocolate as a final garnish to these rich Tiramisu bars. A more traditional finish would be dusting the top with sifted cocoa powder.

INGREDIENTS | **YIELDS 36 BROWNIES**

1 cup cake flour
¼ cup espresso powder
1 cup unsalted butter
12 ounces bittersweet chocolate
1⅓ cups sugar
6 eggs
1 pound mascarpone cheese
¼ cup sugar
2 teaspoons vanilla
2 eggs
¼ cup finely grated chocolate

1. Preheat oven to 350°F. Butter 13" × 9" baking dish. Combine cake flour and espresso; set aside.

2. Melt butter and chocolate, stirring until smooth. Cool slightly. Beat in sugar. Add eggs one at a time, beating well after each addition.

3. Fold in cake flour mixture. Pour into pan, spreading evenly.

4. In another bowl, whisk together cheese, ¼ cup of sugar, and vanilla. Pour over brownie batter in pan. Bake 35–40 minutes, or until top is set. Cool. Dust with grated chocolate and cut into bars.

Maple Pecan Sticky Bars

These go great with coffee for an energy boost on a chilly afternoon. You can substitute hickory nuts or walnuts for the pecans for slightly different flavors.

INGREDIENTS | YIELDS 12 BARS

Crust

½ cup unsalted butter

¼ cup sugar

1 egg yolk

1½ cups all-purpose flour

Topping

½ cup maple syrup

⅓ cup packed light brown sugar

¼ cup whipping cream

¼ cup unsalted butter

1 teaspoon vanilla

1⅓ cups coarsely chopped pecans

1. Preheat oven to 350°F. Butter 9" × 9" pan; set aside.

2. Beat butter, sugar, and egg yolk in a bowl. Add flour; mix until dough begins to clump up and hold together. Press dough into bottom and slightly up sides of pan. Bake 20 minutes. Cool.

3. Combine syrup, sugar, cream, and butter in a sauce pan. Bring to a boil, stirring constantly; boil 30 seconds. Remove from heat; mix in vanilla and nuts.

4. Pour into baked crust. Bake until center is bubbling, about 15 minutes.

5. Cool completely and chill overnight before using.

Conga Bars

This recipe reportedly appeared in the Chicago Tribune *early in the twentieth century. Conga Bars are a lot like a Blondie, but the texture is chewier. Here, Brazil nuts are added for a more exotic flavor.*

INGREDIENTS | YIELDS 24 BARS

2¾ cups all-purpose flour

2½ teaspoons baking powder

½ teaspoon salt

⅔ cup melted butter

2 cups brown sugar

3 eggs

2 teaspoons vanilla

1 cup chopped Brazil nuts or other nuts

6 ounces chocolate chips

1 cup coconut, optional

1. Preheat oven to 350°F. Butter 10" × 15" jelly roll pan.

2. Sift together flour, baking powder, and salt; set aside.

3. Pour butter into a mixing bowl. Add sugar; whisk until you can no longer feel sugar granules. Add eggs one at a time, beating well after each addition.

4. Blend in vanilla. Stir in flour mixture until smooth. Fold in remaining ingredients.

5. Spread in pan; bake 25–30 minutes. Cool and cut into bars.

S'Mores Brownies

Nearly everyone has had a S'more by a campfire at one time or another. These taste like the real thing. For easiest handling, chill the finished brownies before cutting and then let them come back up to room temperature.

INGREDIENTS | **YIELDS 9 BROWNIES**

Crust

1 cup graham cracker crumbs
1 tablespoon sugar
⅓ cup melted butter

Topping

¾ cup unsalted butter
½ cup dark cocoa
2 eggs
1 cup sugar
1 teaspoon vanilla
⅔ cup all-purpose flour
¼ teaspoon salt
½ teaspoon baking powder
2 cups mini marshmallows

1. Preheat oven to 350°F. Butter 8" × 8" pan.

2. Mix graham cracker crumbs with sugar and melted butter. Press firmly into bottom of pan; bake 8 minutes.

3. Melt butter; whisk in cocoa until very smooth. Cool. Beat in eggs, sugar, and vanilla. Combine flour, salt, and baking powder; blend in.

4. Pour over cooked graham cracker crust. Bake 20–25 minutes, until set.

5. Top with marshmallows. Broil until marshmallows are golden brown. This will only take 2-3 minutes at most. Watch carefully. Cool.

Marshmallow Topping

When your plain brownies do not look quite finished, mini marshmallows make a great topping. They work on almost any brownie and you can add chocolate chips or nuts as well. Jut sprinkle on a layer of marshmallows, add the nuts and chips if you want them, and broil for a few minutes until the top is golden and the marshmallows are melted.

Mississippi Mud Brownies

*Rich and decadent, you can substitute walnuts for the pecans and add
1 cup of coconut to the frosting if you like.*

INGREDIENTS | YIELDS 24 BROWNIES

4 ounces unsweetened chocolate

1 cup unsalted butter

2 cups sugar

4 eggs

1 cup all-purpose flour

Pinch of salt

1 cup chopped pecans

3 ounces unsweetened chocolate

½ cup evaporated milk

½ cup unsalted butter

½ teaspoon vanilla extract

4½ cups confectioners' sugar

3 cups mini marshmallows

Chocolate Bloom

Heat and humidity can cause chocolate to get a discoloration called bloom. The white bloom caused by heat does not change the taste of the chocolate, so you can still use it. The grayish bloom caused by high humidity does change the taste of the chocolate, and it is best to throw it away.

1. Preheat oven to 350°F. Grease 13" x 9" pan; set aside.

2. Chop the 4 squares of chocolate. Melt butter in microwaveable bowl and stir in chocolate until melted. Cool.

3. Beat sugar into chocolate mixture. Beat in eggs one at a time. Add flour and salt; blend until smooth. Fold in pecans.

4. Spread in prepared pan; bake 25–30 minutes, or until a toothpick comes out with only a few crumbs clinging to it.

5. Chop the remaining chocolate. Bring milk to a simmer in microwave; add butter and chocolate, stirring until chocolate is completely melted. Cool slightly. Add vanilla; beat in confectioners' sugar until frosting is smooth but can still be poured.

6. Spread marshmallows over warm brownies and quickly pour frosting over it. Cool and cut into bars.

Pecan Pie Bars

These taste just like pecan pie, but they are so easy. You can sprinkle 1 cup of chocolate chips over the crust before pouring on the filling for a chocolaty variation.

INGREDIENTS | **YIELDS 36 BARS**

Crust

3 cups all-purpose flour

½ cup white sugar

½ teaspoon salt

1 cup unsalted butter

Topping

1½ cups light corn syrup

4 eggs

¾ cup white sugar

¾ cup brown sugar

¼ cup unsalted butter, melted

1½ teaspoons vanilla

3 cups chopped pecans

1. Preheat oven to 350°F. Line 10" × 15" jelly roll pan with parchment, allowing it to overhang sides and ends slightly.

2. Stir together flour, ½ cup sugar, and salt. Cut in 1 cup butter until mixture resembles coarse crumbs. Press firmly into the pan.

3. Bake 20 minutes.

4. Mix together corn syrup, eggs, remaining sugars, 3 tablespoons of butter, and vanilla; whisk until smooth. Stir in pecans. Pour over hot crust.

5. Bake 25 minutes, or until set. Cool completely before cutting into bars.

Pecans

Pecans are a delicious addition to cookies and brownies. The do have a high fat content and will become rancid over time. Pecans in the shell keep much longer; once the nuts have been shelled they will keep four months in the refrigerator or eight months in the freezer. Keep them well wrapped; the pecans will take on other flavors if they are not sealed in an airtight container.

Sunshine Dream Bars

This recipe has been a favorite of many since Pillsbury came out with it in 1963.
The original calls for walnuts, but here pistachios add a mellow flavor.

INGREDIENTS | YIELDS 36 BARS

Crust

1 cup all-purpose flour

⅓ cup sugar

2 teaspoons grated lemon peel

¼ cup unsalted butter, softened

2 ounces cream cheese, softened

Filling

6 ounces cream cheese, softened

⅓ cup sugar

2 eggs

1 teaspoon grated lemon peel

2 tablespoons lemon juice

2 tablespoons flour

1 teaspoon baking powder

½ teaspoon salt

1 cup firmly packed brown sugar

2 eggs

1 teaspoon vanilla

1 cup chopped pistachios

1. Preheat oven to 350°F. Butter 13" × 9" pan; set aside.

2. Combine flour, sugar, lemon peel, butter, and 2 ounces cream cheese. Blend with fingers until mixture is crumbly.

3. Press into pan. Bake 12–15 minutes, until crust is light brown.

4. Combine the remaining 6 ounces cream cheese, sugar, eggs, lemon peel, and juice. Pour over crust.

5. Combine flour, baking powder, and salt. Beat brown sugar, eggs, and vanilla until smooth. Stir in flour mixture. Fold in ¾ cup pistachios. Spoon topping over filling; sprinkle with remaining ¼ cup nuts. Bake 25–30 minutes. Cool completely before cutting into bars.

Pistachios: A Favorite Throughout History

Pistachios were well known in ancient times for their delicate flavor. They are one of the two nuts mentioned in the Bible, and were the choice of kings and queens in the middle ages. The unique flavor goes especially well with citrus or chocolate. Shelling them is tedious, so buy them already shelled if possible.

Marshmallow Fudge Bars

Brownies, marshmallows, and rice crispy treats all in one, these bars are sure to be a big hit at your house. The nuts can be omitted if you prefer.

INGREDIENTS | **YIELDS 36 BARS**

1⅓ cups all-purpose flour
½ teaspoon baking powder
¼ teaspoon salt
¼ cup cocoa
¾ cup unsalted butter
1½ cups sugar
3 eggs
1 teaspoon of vanilla
½ cup chopped nuts
4 cups mini marshmallows
1 cup peanut butter
¼ cup unsalted butter
2 cups chocolate chips
2 cups crisp rice cereal

1. Preheat oven to 350°F. Butter 10" × 15" jelly roll pan; set aside.

2. Combine flour, baking powder, salt, and cocoa; set aside.

3. Cream ¾ cup butter and sugar. Add eggs and vanilla; beat until fluffy. Add flour mixture; blend well. Fold in nuts.

4. Spread in pan; bake 15 minutes. Spread marshmallows over top; return to oven just until marshmallows melt, about a minute or so. Spread over bars with a knife dipped in hot water. Cool.

5. Combine peanut butter, butter, and chocolate in a microwave-safe bowl. Melt together on medium power, stirring often until smooth and blended. Stir in rice cereal; spread over bars. Chill.

Substituting with Marshmallow Cream

In recipes that use marshmallows, you can easily substitute marshmallow cream if the marshmallows are to be melted anyway. Just use 1 cup of marshmallow cream to replace 1 cup of marshmallows. Everything else is the same. Marshmallow cream works especially well when you are putting another layer over the marshmallow layer.

Hoosier Peanut Bars

This is for you if you love peanuts. You can also use the honey roasted peanuts for a slightly different flavor; just substitute them in the exact measure.

INGREDIENTS | YIELDS 18 BARS

2 cups all-purpose flour
1 teaspoon baking soda
2 teaspoons baking powder
½ teaspoon salt
½ cup unsalted butter
½ cup sugar
1½ cups brown sugar, divided
2 eggs, separated
1 teaspoon vanilla
3 tablespoons water
1 cup milk chocolate chips
1½ cups chopped salted peanuts

More about Meringues

Egg whites will refuse to whip up properly is there is any oil at all on the bowl. Take a minute to rinse your clean mixing bowl and beaters with lemon juice or white vinegar to cut any greasy residue that might be there.

1. Preheat oven to 325°F. Butter and flour 13" × 9" baking dish.

2. Sift together flour, baking soda, baking powder, and salt; set aside.

3. Cream together butter, sugar, and ½ cup brown sugar until light and fluffy. Add egg yolks and vanilla; beat well. Add water and flour mixture to make a stiff dough. Press dough into bottom of prepared pan. Sprinkle with chocolate chips.

4. In a clean bowl, beat egg whites until foamy. Gradually add remaining 1 cup brown sugar, beating until stiff and glassy. Spread over chocolate; sprinkle peanuts over top.

5. Bake 35 minutes. Cool.

Cherry Coconut Bars

*These bars are wonderful just the way they are, but for a chocolaty variation
add ½ cup chocolate or white chocolate chips.*

INGREDIENTS | **YIELDS 36 BARS**

¾ cup all-purpose flour

¼ cup finely ground almonds or
almond flour

¼ cup confectioners' sugar

¼ cup all-purpose flour

½ teaspoon baking powder

¼ teaspoon salt

½ cup cold, unsalted butter

2 eggs

1 cup sugar

1 teaspoon vanilla

¼ teaspoon almond extract

¾ cup chopped toasted almonds

½ cup quartered maraschino cherries

½ cup flaked coconut

1. Preheat oven to 350°F. Grease 13" × 9" pan; set aside.

2. Combine ¾ cup flour, ground almonds, and confectioners' sugar. Blend in butter with fingers until it turns into crumbs. Press into pan firmly. Bake 10–12 minutes.

3. Combine ¼ cup flour, baking powder, and salt in a bowl; set aside.

4. Beat eggs, sugar, vanilla, and almond extract until well blended. Stir in flour mixture. Stir in almonds, cherries, and coconut; pour over crust.

5. Bake 20–25 minutes, or until firm. Cool completely.

Maraschino Cherries

Maraschino cherries are sweet cherries that have been preserved in sugar syrup and dyed, usually with Red #40. They add a beautiful color and sweetness to cookies and other desserts, but some people are sensitive to the dye. If you prefer a more natural cherry, in most cases, you can substitute dried cherries for the maraschinos.

By Cracky Bars

*These are just perfect the way they are, but if you want some variety
then try them with pecans and white chocolate chips.*

INGREDIENTS | YIELDS 9 BARS

1¾ cups flour
1 teaspoon salt
¼ teaspoon baking soda
¾ cup unsalted butter
1 cup sugar
3 eggs
⅓ cup half-and-half
1 teaspoon vanilla
1 ounce unsweetened chocolate, melted
¾ cup chopped walnuts
9 whole graham crackers
¾ cup chocolate chips

1. Preheat oven to 375°F. Grease 8" × 8" pan; set aside.

2. Sift together flour, salt, and baking soda; set aside.

3. Cream butter and sugar until light and fluffy. Add eggs one at a time, blending well after each addition. Mix half-and-half and vanilla, add alternately with flour mixture to creamed mixture.

4. Mix melted chocolate and walnuts to ⅓ of batter; spread in pan. Top with crackers.

5. Mix chocolate chips with remaining batter. Spread over crackers; bake 30 minutes. Cool completely.

Applesauce Oat Bars

*Thick, homemade applesauce works the best in this recipe. If you are using commercial
applesauce and it is runny, just cook it for a few minutes to thicken it up.*

INGREDIENTS | YIELDS 9 BARS

1¼ cups quick oats
1¼ cups flour
1 cup brown sugar
¾ cup unsalted butter
1 cup applesauce
2 tablespoons sugar
1 teaspoon cinnamon
½ teaspoon cloves
1 cup chopped walnuts

1. Preheat oven to 350°F. Butter 8" × 8" pan; set aside.

2. Mix oats, flour, and brown sugar. Blend in butter with fingers until mixture is crumbly. Press half mixture in bottom of prepared pan.

3. Mix apple sauce, remaining sugar, cinnamon, and cloves. Spoon sauce over dough, leaving ½" border all around.

4. Combine rest of crumb mixture with chopped walnuts; sprinkle over apple sauce. Pat down gently.

5. Bake 40 minutes. Cool completely.

Date Squares

Date squares are full of old-fashioned goodness. You can add variety to this recipe by substituting dried apricots, figs, apples, or peaches for the dates.

INGREDIENTS | **YIELDS 24 SQUARES**

3½ cups quick-cooking oats

2 cups brown sugar

1½ cups butter, melted

3 cups all-purpose flour

1 cup sugar

1 cup water

2 cups chopped dates

Confectioners' sugar for dusting

Buying Dates

You will usually find three types of dates at the store: whole dates for cooking; chopped dates; and whole gourmet dates for eating, not cooking. If you have a choice, buy the dates that are already cut up; dates are very sticky and hard to cut. If you do cut your own, dust them with confectioners' sugar to make it easier.

1. Preheat oven to 350°F. Butter 13" × 9" baking pan.

2. Combine oats, flour, and brown sugar. Add butter; combine by hand until crumbly. Spread half in pan.

3. Combine sugar, water, and dates in a saucepan. Bring to boil; simmer 1 minute, stirring constantly. Remove from heat.

4. Spread date mixture over crumb mixture in pan. Sprinkle with remaining crumbs.

5. Bake 25 minutes. Cool completely. Sift confectioners' sugar over top before serving.

Dulce de Leche Bars

These sweet bars should be stored in the refrigerator if they are not eaten right away.
For a praline flavor, add 2 cups chopped pecans over the caramel layer.

INGREDIENTS | **YIELDS 36 BARS**

2 cups all-purpose flour
1 teaspoon baking soda
1 teaspoon salt
1 cup butter, softened
1 cup firmly packed brown sugar
2 eggs
1½ teaspoons vanilla
1 (14-ounce) package caramels
½ cup heavy cream

Dulce de Leche: Sweet Milk

Dulce de leche is a combination of milk and sugar that is slowly cooked for hours. It is popular in many desserts and can be used as a sauce. Making it with caramels and heavy cream is cheating a bit...but so much easier. For the real thing, check your grocer's Latin food section.

1. Preheat oven to 350°F. Butter 13" × 9" pan; set aside.

2. Sift flour, baking soda, and salt into a bowl; set aside.

3. Beat butter and brown sugar until fluffy. Add eggs and vanilla; beat until smooth. Stir in flour mixture. Spread half of dough in prepared pan. Bake 8 minutes. Allow to cool while preparing caramel mixture.

4. Melt caramels with cream in microwave, stirring often. Reserve ¼ cup caramel mixture; pour rest over baked layer. Crumble remaining dough over top.

5. Bake 25 minutes, or until golden. Cool completely. Drizzle reserved caramel over top.

Pumpkin Bars with Cream Cheese Frosting

This is a great bar that goes quickly at autumn bake sales. Try adding ¼ cup of chopped candied ginger to the frosting for a sweet and spicy flavor.

INGREDIENTS | SERVES 40

2 cups all-purpose flour

4 teaspoons baking powder

½ teaspoon salt

1 teaspoon cinnamon

1 teaspoon freshly grated nutmeg

1 teaspoon ginger

½ cup butter

1 cup brown sugar, packed

¼ cup sugar

4 eggs

1 pound mashed pumpkin

Cream Cheese Frosting (page 550)

1. Butter 15" × 10" jelly roll pan; set aside. Preheat oven to 350°F.

2. Sift flour, baking powder, salt, and spices; set aside.

3. Cream together butter, brown sugar, and sugar until light and fluffy. Add eggs one at a time, beating well after each. Blend in pumpkin.

4. Stir dry ingredients into creamed mixture; blend well. Spread mixture evenly into pan.

5. Bake 30–35 minutes, or until top springs back when lightly touched. Cool completely before frosting.

Softening Brown Sugar

Brown sugar can get rock hard at times; it does this when improper storage allows the moisture to evaporate. To soften it up, just add a slice or two of fresh bread and seal the bag. The next day the bread will be extremely stale, but the brown sugar will be soft and easy to work with.

Raspberry Crumb Bars

If you like nuts, ½ cup of chopped toasted almonds is a great addition to this bar. Just sprinkle them over the top before baking.

INGREDIENTS | **SERVES 36**

Crust

2 cups all-purpose flour

½ cup brown sugar, packed

¼ teaspoon salt

1 cup unsalted butter, softened

Topping

2 cups white chocolate chips, divided

1 (14-ounce) can sweetened condensed milk

⅓ cup seedless raspberry jam

1. Preheat oven to 350°F. Butter 13" x 9" pan; set aside.

2. Mix flour, brown sugar, and salt together. Blend in butter with your fingers until crumbly. Firmly press 1¾ cups of flour mixture into prepared pan; reserve rest. Bake 10 minutes.

3. Microwave 1 cup white chocolate and condensed milk in a microwave-safe bowl until melted, stirring every few seconds.

4. Spread milk mixture over hot crust. Sprinkle remaining crumb mixture over top. Drop teaspoonfuls of raspberry jam here and there over crumb mixture; sprinkle with remaining white chocolate chips.

5. Bake 25–30 minutes, or until set. Cool.

Hawaiian Pineapple Bars

When using crushed pineapple in this recipe, make sure it is drained very well. Place in a colander and gently press out any remaining juice after draining; if it is too wet, the crust layer will be soggy.

INGREDIENTS | **SERVES 36**

Crust

2 cups flour

1 cup sugar

1 cup unsalted butter

Cream Layer

1 pound cream cheese, room temperature

¼ cup heavy cream

2 teaspoons vanilla

2 cups crushed pineapple, drained

⅓ cup sugar

Topping

2 cups coconut

1 tablespoon brown sugar

3 tablespoons melted unsalted butter

1. Preheat oven to 350°F. Lightly butter bottom of 13" × 9" pan.

2. Mix flour and 1 cup sugar. Blend in butter with fingers until mixture is crumbly. Pat firmly into bottom of prepared pan. Bake 15 minutes. Cool.

3. Beat cream cheese, ⅓ cup sugar, and cream. Add vanilla; blend well. Stir in pineapple; spread over bottom layer.

4. Mix coconut, brown sugar, and melted butter. Spread over cream layer.

5. Bake 15 minutes. Store in refrigerator.

CHAPTER 23

Shaped Cookies

Snickerdoodles

Snickerdoodles are a perfect cookie to bake with children. Even the smallest child loves to roll the balls in the cinnamon-and-sugar mixture.

INGREDIENTS | **YIELDS 36 COOKIES**

1 cup unsalted butter

1½ cups sugar

2 eggs

2¾ cups all-purpose flour

1 teaspoon baking soda

2 teaspoons cream of tartar

Pinch of salt

2 tablespoons white sugar

2 teaspoons ground cinnamon

Snickerdoodles

Snickerdoodles are a slightly spicy cookie with a unique texture and taste. This is largely due to the use of the cream of tartar as part of the leavening. The first recipe for Snickerdoodles is thought to have been published in 1901; not one of the oldest cookie recipes in America, but certainly one of the best.

1. Beat together butter and 1½ cups sugar until smooth. Add eggs one at a time, beating well after each one. Combine flour, baking soda, cream of tartar, and salt; stir into butter mixture. Blend well. Chill 30 minutes.

2. Preheat oven to 400°F. Line a cookie sheet with parchment.

3. Mix cinnamon and sugar together on a plate. Roll dough into small balls the size of a walnut. Roll each ball in sugar mixture; place 2" apart on cookie sheet.

4. Bake 8 minutes.

5. Cookies will flatten out as they cool.

Old-Fashioned Gingersnaps

These spicy cookies are both chewy and crisp. For a spicier cookie, add about ¼ teaspoon of cayenne pepper. It gives heat to the cinnamon without adding flavor.

INGREDIENTS | **YIELDS 36 COOKIES**

2 teaspoons baking soda
¼ teaspoon salt
2 cups flour
1 teaspoon cinnamon
1 teaspoon ginger
¼ teaspoon cloves
¼ cup shortening
½ cup butter
1 egg
1 cup sugar
1 cup unsulfured molasses
Sugar for rolling

1. Sift together baking soda, salt, flour, cinnamon, ginger, and cloves; set aside.

2. Cream shortening, butter, and 1 cup of sugar. Blend in molasses and egg.

3. Add dry ingredients to creamed mixture; blend well. Cover and chill 30 minutes or longer.

4. Preheat oven to 375°F. Butter baking sheets.

5. Shape dough into walnut-sized balls; roll in sugar. Place 2" apart on baking sheets; bake 12 minutes. Cool completely.

About Molasses

There are usually several different kinds of molasses on the shelves at the grocery store, and it can be confusing to try and figure out which one to use. For most dessert baking, unsulfured molasses is the best choice. It has a milder flavor and less of an aftertaste than blackstrap molasses. It is extracted from the sugar cane without the use of sulfur dioxide.

Lemon Crinkles

Lemon crinkles are a lemony cookie with the texture of a gingersnap or snickerdoodle. They are great as the sandwich part of an ice cream sandwich.

INGREDIENTS | **YIELDS 48 COOKIES**

⅓ cup unsalted butter
1 cup sugar
2 eggs
3 tablespoons lemon juice
1½ teaspoons lemon extract
3½ cups flour
2½ teaspoons baking powder
¼ teaspoon baking soda
1 teaspoon grated lemon peel
¼ teaspoon freshly grated nutmeg
½ teaspoon salt
Sugar for rolling

1. Preheat oven to 375°F. Lightly grease baking sheets.

2. Cream butter and sugar together; beat in eggs. Add lemon juice and lemon extract.

3. Mix dry ingredients and stir them into the butter mixture, blending well.

4. Roll dough into walnut-sized balls. Roll in sugar; place 2" apart on baking sheet.

5. Bake 10 minutes. Remove from oven and gently press down tops while still warm.

Chocolate Snowballs

Chocolate snowballs are a crunchy, crumbly, chocolaty cookie that are wonderful in a holiday assortment. Cookies must be completely cool before they are rolled in the powdered sugar or else the sugar will melt off.

INGREDIENTS | **YIELDS 48 COOKIES**

1¼ cups unsalted butter
⅔ cup sugar
2 teaspoons vanilla
2 cups flour
½ teaspoon salt
½ cup cocoa
Confectioners' sugar

1. Cream butter, sugar, and vanilla together until creamy.

2. Mix flour, salt, and cocoa. Blend dry mixture into butter mixture. Chill 2 hours or overnight.

3. Preheat oven to 350°F.

4. Form small balls; place on ungreased baking sheet. Bake 15 minutes.

5. Cool, then roll in confectioners' sugar.

Rose Crackle Cookies

Rose water is an old-fashioned flavor that is regaining popularity. It is sweetly floral and very delicate. For a tea or bridal shower, roll these cookies in pink sugar crystals.

INGREDIENTS | YIELDS 60 COOKIES

1 cup unsalted butter

2 cups sugar

2 eggs

½ teaspoon vanilla

1 teaspoon rose water

2⅔ cups flour

1 teaspoon cream of tartar

1 teaspoon baking soda

½ teaspoon salt

Sugar with a few drops of rose water in it for rolling

1. Cream butter and 2 cups of sugar until light and fluffy. Add eggs one at a time, beating well after each addition. Add vanilla and rose water; beat until smooth.

2. Blend dry ingredients; stir into butter mixture. Chill 2 hours.

3. Preheat oven to 350°F.

4. Roll tablespoons of cold dough into balls; roll in sugar. Place 2" apart on ungreased baking sheets

5. Bake 20 minutes. Cool completely.

Baking with Flowers

There are many flowers that add unique flavors to baked goods. The three most popular are rose, lavender, and violet, but even the lowly pansy is edible and can be used in cakes, cookies, breads, and salads. Give your recipes more beauty and versatility with ingredients from your garden.

Chai Chocolate Crackles

If you love Chai, these spicy, chocolaty cookies are the perfect treat.
For a little more heat, add ¼ teaspoon of cayenne.

INGREDIENTS | YIELDS 48 COOKIES

½ cup unsalted butter

2 cups sugar

4 eggs

2 cups all-purpose flour

2 teaspoons baking powder

½ teaspoon salt

1 teaspoon cardamom

½ teaspoon cracked black pepper

¾ cup Hershey's Special Dark cocoa

Confectioners' sugar

1. Cream butter and sugar together. Add eggs one at a time, beating well after each.

2. Sift dry ingredients together; blend into butter mixture. Cover tightly; chill at least 30 minutes.

3. Preheat oven to 300°F. Lightly grease cookie sheet.

4. Using a teaspoon to measure, roll dough into balls. Roll in confectioners' sugar to coat thoroughly. Place 2" apart on baking sheet.

5. Bake 18–20 minutes. Cool completely.

Flavoring with Chai

Chai is a very popular tea spiced with a number of different spices. The most common are: cardamom, black pepper, ginger, cloves, cinnamon, nutmeg, and anise. Cardamom is always included in Chai and gives it its unusual flavor. You can add any combination of these spices to almost any cookie recipe for a delicious Chai flavor.

Chipotle Chocolate Pixies

The chipotle adds a smoky, slow burn to these cookies that many people find pleasant.
If you don't like the heat, you can leave out the chipotle for a fantastic pixie cookie.

INGREDIENTS | **YIELDS 48 COOKIES**

½ cup unsalted butter

1¾ cups sugar

¼ cup brown sugar

4 eggs

2 cups all-purpose flour

2 teaspoons baking powder

½ teaspoon salt

¾ cup Hershey's Special Dark cocoa

¼–½ teaspoon chipotle

Confectioners' sugar

1. Cream butter and sugars together. Add eggs one at a time, beating well after each.

2. Sift dry ingredients together; blend into butter mixture. Cover tightly; chill at least 30 minutes.

3. Preheat oven to 300°F. Lightly grease cookie sheet.

4. Using a teaspoon to measure, roll dough into balls. Roll in confectioners' sugar to coat thoroughly. Place 2" apart on baking sheet.

5. Bake 18–20 minutes. Cool completely.

Chipotle and Chocolate

Chipotle is a smoked hot pepper that is dried, and it adds a smoky spice to many foods. Paired with chocolate, it is a unique combination of flavors that is exciting and addicting at the same time. Start off slowly when using chipotle; it can become too hot very quickly.

Mexican Wedding Cakes

Be sure that you grind the nuts into a flour-like substance and not a paste. To do this, add 1–2 tablespoons of the flour called for to the nuts when grinding in the food processor.

INGREDIENTS | YIELDS 48 COOKIES

1 cup unsalted butter, room temperature

½ cup confectioners' sugar

2 teaspoons vanilla extract

2 cups all-purpose flour

1 cup pecans, toasted and ground

¼ teaspoon ground cinnamon

1 cup confectioners' sugar

Working with Rich Doughs

Mexican Wedding cookies, Russian Tea Cakes, and Pecan Sandies are all similar types of dough—they must be shaped when icy cold. For the best results, only work with ⅓ of the dough at a time, leaving the rest in the refrigerator until it is needed. Save some of the dusting sugar to sift over the cookies just before serving.

1. Beat butter until creamy. Add ½ cup confectioners' sugar and vanilla; beat until mixture is well blended. Stir in flour and pecans. Cover with plastic wrap; chill thoroughly, at least 1 hour.

2. Preheat oven to 350°F. Line cookie sheet with parchment. Mix ¼ teaspoon of cinnamon and 1 cup of confectioners' sugar; set aside.

3. Roll dough by 2 teaspoonfuls in hands and form into crescents. Place on cookie sheets about 1" apart.

4. Bake 18–20 minutes, or until bottoms are golden.

5. Cool cookies about 5 minutes on baking sheet. Roll in cinnamon-sugar mixture to coat completely. Allow to cool. Store tightly covered for no more than 2–3 days.

Russian Chai Tea Cakes

Russian tea cakes are delicate and crumbly cookies given an exotic flavor by your favorite Chai. If you are making these ahead to freeze, freeze them without the confectioners' sugar coating.

INGREDIENTS | YIELDS 36 COOKIES

1 cup walnuts
2 cups all-purpose flour
2 teaspoons loose Chai tea blend
1 cup unsalted butter
1 teaspoon vanilla extract
½ cup confectioners' sugar
Confectioners' sugar for dusting

1. Preheat oven to 350°F.

2. Put walnuts, 2 tablespoons of flour, and Chai in a blender; pulse until walnuts are chopped finely but are not yet a paste.

3. Cream butter and vanilla until well blended. Add ½ cup confectioners' sugar and remaining flour until blended. Fold in walnut mixture.

4. Roll by teaspoonfuls into balls; place 2" apart on cookie sheets. Bake 12 minutes. Cool.

5. Roll balls gently in confectioners' sugar to coat.

Pecan Tassies

Dainty pecan tarts are perfect for baby showers or Christmas trays. Drizzle the tops with melted chocolate for a tasty garnish.

INGREDIENTS | YIELDS 36 COOKIES

1¼ cups unsalted butter
8 ounces cream cheese
2⅓ cups all-purpose flour
2 eggs
1½ cups packed light brown sugar
2 tablespoons melted butter
½ teaspoon vanilla
Pinch of salt
1 cup pecans, chopped

1. Preheat oven to 350°F.

2. Beat butter and cream cheese until blended. Stir in flour until mixture forms a smooth, soft dough. Roll in small balls; push into small tart or mini muffin pans, forming a tart shell.

3. Blend eggs, brown sugar, remaining butter, vanilla, and salt. Stir in pecans.

4. Fill each crust about ⅔ full with nut mixture; be careful not to overfill.

5. Bake 15–18 minutes. The filling will have puffed up and the shell will be golden brown. Cool; remove from pans carefully.

Maple Snickerdoodles

These are chewy Snickerdoodles that have big maple flavor. If you can't find the maple sugar, you can add ¼ teaspoon of maple flavoring to ¼ cup light brown sugar.

INGREDIENTS | **YIELDS 36 COOKIES**

2 cups all-purpose flour
1½ teaspoons baking powder
¼ teaspoon baking soda
1½ teaspoons ground cinnamon
¼ cup unsalted butter
¼ cup vegetable shortening
1 cup sugar
3 tablespoons real maple syrup
1 egg
½ cup sugar
¼ cup maple sugar

1. Preheat oven to 350°F. Stir together dry ingredients; set aside.

2. Cream butter, shortening, 1 cup of white sugar, and maple syrup until light and fluffy. Add egg; beat well. Stir in dry ingredients until well blended.

3. Mix ½ cup of sugar and maple sugar in a small saucer. Roll dough into balls and then into sugar mixture.

4. Place on baking sheet; bake 8–10 minutes. Cookies should still look slightly underdone.

5. Cool on cookie sheets 5 minutes. Remove and cool completely.

Baking with Maple Syrup

Maple syrup comes in several grades and classifications. Generally, you will find the Grade-A, extra-fancy maple syrup in the stores. This is lighter syrup, great for pancakes but not the best for baking. If you can find a B-grade syrup, when baking it will add a more intense flavor to your foods.

Pecan Sandies

If a flavoring called Vanilla Butter Nut is available at your grocery store, use 1 teaspoon of that in place of 1 teaspoon of the vanilla. It gives a buttery and nutty flavor that enhances these cookies.

INGREDIENTS | YIELDS 48 COOKIES

½ cup unsalted butter

½ cup mild-flavored vegetable oil

¼ cup white sugar

¼ cup brown sugar

½ cup confectioners' sugar

1 egg

2 teaspoons vanilla

2 cups all-purpose flour

½ teaspoon baking soda

½ teaspoon cream of tartar

½ teaspoon salt

1 cup chopped pecans

¼ cup turbinado sugar

1. Cream together butter and oil until very well blended. Beat in sugar and brown sugar until very smooth. Beat in confectioners' sugar and egg. Stir in vanilla.

2. Combine dry ingredients; stir into creamed mixture. Fold in pecans. Chill overnight.

3. Preheat oven to 375°F.

4. Roll teaspoons of dough into balls and then roll in turbinado sugar. Flatten slightly with a glass dipped in turbinado sugar. Place 2" apart on cookie sheets.

5. Bake 10–12 minutes, or until edges are golden brown. Cool.

Turbinado Sugar

Turbinado sugar is a natural cane sugar that has much bigger crystals than regular sugar. Because of the larger crystals, it creates an exceptionally nice finish on cookies and adds a little flavor. It can be found in the natural foods section of your grocer or in many health food stores.

Peanut Butter Blossoms

This recipe used the old-fashioned Hershey's Kisses, but consider trying one of the new versions: caramel filled, almond, Hershey's Hugs, or your own favorite.

INGREDIENTS | YIELDS 48 COOKIES

¼ cup shortening
¼ cup unsalted butter
¾ cup peanut butter
⅓ cup sugar
⅓ cup light brown sugar
1 egg
2 tablespoons milk
1½ teaspoons vanilla
1½ cups all-purpose flour
1 teaspoon baking soda
½ teaspoon salt, optional
Sugar or turbinado sugar for rolling
48 chocolate Kisses

To Grease...or Not to Grease

While most cookies need a greased cookie sheet, cookies with a lot of fat in them spread too much on a greased or buttered baking sheet. If the recipe does not specify, then it usually means the cookie sheet should be ungreased. If you are in doubt, you can always use parchment paper or a silpat.

1. Heat oven to 350°F. Remove foil from Kisses.

2. Beat shortening, butter, and peanut butter in a large bowl until very well blended. Beat in sugars, egg, milk, and vanilla until fluffy.

3. Add flour, baking soda, and salt; mix until well blended. Shape into 1" balls and roll in sugar.

4. Place 2" apart on an ungreased cookie sheet. Bake 8–10 minutes, or until golden.

5. Remove from oven and immediately press a Kiss firmly in the center of each cookie. The sides will crack, but this is part of the charm of the cookie. Allow to cool completely.

Peanut Butter Cookies

Classic peanut butter cookies are everyone's childhood favorite. They can be made with crunchy or creamy peanut butter, your choice. Either way is delicious.

INGREDIENTS | **YIELDS 72 COOKIES**

2½ cups all-purpose flour
1 teaspoon baking powder
1 teaspoon baking soda
1 teaspoon salt
½ cup unsalted butter
½ cup vegetable shortening
1 cup peanut butter
1 cup sugar
1 cup firmly packed brown sugar
2 eggs, beaten
1 teaspoon vanilla

Peanut Butter Sandwich Cookies

A great variation on peanut butter cookies is to sandwich them together with either the Ganache (page 544) or a mixture made up of equal amounts of peanut butter and honey. Just spoon a layer of the desired filling on the flat bottom side of the cookie and top it with another cookie, flat side toward center.

1. Preheat oven to 350°F. Stir together dry ingredients; set aside.

2. Cream butter, shortening, and peanut butter until smooth. Add sugars; blend well. Beat in eggs and vanilla.

3. Stir in flour mixture; blend well.

4. Shape dough into 1" balls. Place on an ungreased cookie sheet 2" apart. Flatten with a fork dipped in flour. Flatten in other direction to create little squares on dough.

5. Bake 8–10 minutes for chewy cookies and 12–14 minutes for crispy cookies. Cool.

Molasses Cookies

Do not use any other type of molasses for this recipe except unsulfured, preferably Grandma's brand. The molasses can give a bitter flavor to the cookies if it isn't the right kind.

INGREDIENTS | YIELDS 72 COOKIES

2¼ cups all-purpose flour
2 teaspoons baking soda
1 teaspoon ground cinnamon
¾–1 teaspoon ground ginger, according to taste
½ teaspoon ground allspice
½ teaspoon ground cloves
¼ teaspoon cayenne pepper or chipotle
½ teaspoon salt
½ cup vegetable shortening, room temperature
½ cup unsalted butter, room temperature
1 cup packed dark brown sugar
1 egg
½ cup unsulfured molasses
Sugar for cookie tops

1. Preheat oven to 375°F. Whisk dry ingredients together.

2. Beat together shortening, butter, and brown sugar until creamy. This will take about 3 minutes with a stand mixer or 6 minutes with a handheld. Add egg and molasses; beat well.

3. Stir in flour mixture carefully. Roll into 1" balls.

4. Dip one end of each ball in sugar; place on ungreased baking sheet, sugar side up.

5. Bake 10–12 minutes. Tops will crackle as they cool if they are not overbaked.

Nutmeg Butterballs

Freshly grated nutmeg makes all the difference in these buttery cookies. Whole nutmegs are available in the spice aisle at the grocers. Just run one across a grater until you have enough for your recipe.

INGREDIENTS | YIELDS 48 COOKIES

1 cup unsalted butter
½ cup sugar
1 teaspoon vanilla
1⅓ cups chopped pecans
2 cups all-purpose flour
½ cup confectioners' sugar
2 teaspoons freshly ground nutmeg

1. Cream butter and sugar until light and fluffy. Add vanilla and pecans.

2. Add flour; blend well. Chill dough 30 minutes or more.

3. Preheat oven to 325°F. Lightly grease baking sheets.

4. Shape teaspoonfuls of dough into balls. Place 2" apart on cookie sheets. Bake 15–20 minutes.

5. Combine confectioners' sugar and nutmeg. Roll warm cookies in mixture until coated.

Coconut Oat Cookies

Toasting half of the coconut in this recipe and using organic coconut oil adds a deep coconut flavor. If you can't get organic coconut oil, just use shortening in place of it.

INGREDIENTS | YIELDS 48 COOKIES

1 cup flaked coconut
¾ cup shortening
¼ cup organic coconut oil
1 cup unsalted butter
2 cups packed brown sugar
2 cups white sugar
4 eggs
2 teaspoons vanilla
4 cups all-purpose flour
2 teaspoons baking powder
2 teaspoons baking soda
4 cups old-fashioned oatmeal
1 cup flaked coconut

1. Preheat oven to 350°F. Lightly grease cookie sheets.

2. Toast 1 cup of coconut in the microwave, stirring every minute and watching it carefully to prevent burning. The coconut should be a light, golden brown. This will take approximately 3-5 minutes.

3. Cream shortening, coconut oil, butter, and sugars. Add eggs and vanilla; beat until blended.

4. Stir together dry ingredients. Add to shortening mixture. Fold in remaining 1 cup coconut and toasted coconut.

5. Drop by teaspoons onto baking sheet. Bake 8–10 minutes, or until golden; do not overbake.

Organic Coconut Oil

Organic, cold pressed, pure virgin coconut oil is very different from what you may find in the oil section of your store. It has a fresh coconut scent and light flavor, and is very good for you. It can be used as a substitute for butter in cookies, but always keep it cold because coconut oil melts at room temperature.

Molten-Middle Truffle Cookies

Try substituting mini marshmallows for the caramel. Use one marshmallow in place of the caramel when forming the cookies.

INGREDIENTS | YIELDS 48 COOKIES

12 ounces bittersweet chocolate

¼ cup unsalted butter

14 ounces sweetened condensed milk

1 teaspoon vanilla

2 cups flour

½ cup finely chopped pecans

24 caramels, cut in half

¼ cup sugar

Sweetened Condensed Milk

Sweetened condensed milk, like Eagle Brand, is not the same as evaporated milk. It is milk with the water removed and sugar added. You can make your own by mixing 1 cup instant dry milk with ⅔ cup sugar, ⅓ boiling water, and ¼ cup butter. Process in a blender and store in the refrigerator. This makes the same amount as 1 can.

1. Preheat oven to 350°F.

2. Melt chocolate and butter, stirring often. Stir until chocolate is completely melted and mixture is smooth. Blend in condensed milk and vanilla. Stir in flour and pecans, mixing to a stiff dough

3. Roll 1 tablespoon of dough around each caramel half. Be sure that none of the caramel is showing. Roll in sugar.

4. Place 1" apart on cookie sheets.

5. Bake 6–8 minutes, or until cookies are shiny. Allow to cool completely before storing.

Chocolate Turtle Cookies

Just like the candy only with a cookie bottom, these turtle cookies will be a favorite in your house. Substitute any chocolate for the milk chocolate called for in this recipe.

INGREDIENTS | SERVES 36

¾ cup unsalted butter
¾ cup powdered sugar
2 tablespoons heavy cream
1 teaspoon vanilla
2 cups flour
25 caramels, unwrapped
3 tablespoons heavy cream
3 tablespoons unsalted butter
½ cup powdered sugar
1 cup pecans, chopped
½ cup milk chocolate chips
1 tablespoon unsalted butter
1 teaspoon vanilla
2 tablespoons powdered sugar

1. Combine ¾ cup butter, ¾ cup powdered sugar, 2 tablespoons cream, and 1 teaspoon vanilla. Beat until smooth; then add flour. Seal in an airtight package; chill several hours or overnight.

2. Preheat oven to 325°F.

3. Roll teaspoons of dough into 1" balls. Place on an ungreased cookie sheet and flatten to about ¼" thickness with the bottom of a glass. Bake 8–10 minutes, until set and light golden brown. Cool completely.

4. In microwave on medium power, melt caramels with 3 tablespoons cream and 3 tablespoons butter. Stir in ½ cup powdered sugar and chopped nuts. Place a spoonful on top of each cooled cookie.

5. In microwave-safe bowl, place milk and semisweet chocolate chips along with 1 tablespoon butter. Microwave on medium power 1–2 minutes, stirring once during cooking time, until melted and smooth. Stir in 1 teaspoon vanilla and 2 tablespoons powdered sugar until smooth. Spoon a small amount of chocolate mixture over caramel mixture. Cool.

Cinnamon Snaps

The dough needs to be chilled for two hours to be easy to work with, but for a better flavor and texture keep these chilled overnight. The gluten relaxes and will make your cookies more tender.

INGREDIENTS | YIELDS 60 COOKIES

½ cup unsalted butter

½ cup shortening

2 cups sugar

2 eggs

1 teaspoon vanilla

2⅔ cups all-purpose flour

1 teaspoon cream of tartar

1 teaspoon baking soda

½ teaspoon salt

2 teaspoons cinnamon

½ cup sugar mixed with 1 tablespoon cinnamon, for rolling cookies

1. Cream butter, shortening, and 2 cups of sugar until light and fluffy. Add eggs one at a time, beating thoroughly after each egg. Add vanilla.

2. Mix dry ingredients together; stir in until well blended. Chill 2 hours.

3. Preheat oven to 350°F.

4. Using a tablespoonful of dough, roll into balls, then roll in cinnamon-sugar mixture. Place on an ungreased baking sheet about 2" apart.

5. Bake 20 minutes. Remove from oven when just barely done; allow to cool.

Crinkle-Topped Cookies

The secret to making perfect crinkle-topped cookies every time is to remove the cookies from the oven before they are completely done. As the cookies cool, the tops settle and create the cracks and crinkles that make these cookies just the right texture. The sugar melts slightly in the oven, giving the cookies a delicate crackly crust.

Almond Delights

You can buy almonds blanched or easily do it yourself. Just pour boiling water over raw almonds and set aside for a few minutes. Using your fingers, slip the skins off the almonds and allow them to dry.

INGREDIENTS | YIELDS 60 COOKIES

2 cups all-purpose flour
1 cup confectioners' sugar
Dash salt
¼ teaspoon baking powder
¼ teaspoon baking soda
1 cup unsalted butter
1 egg yolk
½ teaspoon vanilla
½ teaspoon almond extract
3 tablespoons heavy cream
60 blanched almonds

1. Sift flour, confectioners' sugar, salt, baking powder, and baking soda; set aside.

2. Cream butter until light and fluffy. Add egg yolk, vanilla, and almond extract; blend well.

3. Stir in flour mixture. Chill at least 1 hour.

4. Preheat oven to 375°F. Grease baking sheets.

5. Roll dough into ½" balls. Place 2" apart on baking sheets. Brush lightly with cream; press an almond into each. Bake 10–12 minutes, or until just golden.

Snow Drops

These pretty cookies can be an elegant addition to parties during the holiday season. They're a delicious treat year-round, too.

INGREDIENTS | YIELDS 60 COOKIES

1 cup unsalted butter
2 teaspoons vanilla
¼ cup confectioners' sugar
2 cups cake flour
1 cup chopped toasted almonds
1 teaspoon water
1 cup confectioners' sugar, sifted

1. Beat butter, vanilla, water, and ¼ cup confectioners' sugar until creamy. Add flour and nuts.

2. Chill overnight.

3. Preheat oven to 400°F. Line a baking sheet with parchment.

4. Scoop out a teaspoon of cookie dough and roll into a small ball. Repeat for each cookie.

5. Bake 10–12 minutes. Roll in remaining confectioners' sugar while still hot.

Melting Moments

The cornstarch makes these delicate cookies literally melt in your mouth.
They can be stored for up to two weeks, but do not ship well.

INGREDIENTS | **YIELDS 36 COOKIES**

1½ cups all-purpose flour

½ cup cornstarch

¼ teaspoon salt

1 cup unsalted butter, room temperature

¼ cup confectioners' sugar, sifted

1 teaspoon vanilla extract

1 cup confectioners' sugar, sifted, for topping

Homemade Vanilla

Pure vanilla has a taste that imitation vanilla just can't match. Make your own at home with a few vanilla beans and some brandy. Just split open 5 vanilla beans and add them to 1 pint of good-quality brandy. Allow to stand in a dark, cool place for several (4–6) months, shaking often. It can be used after a month, but has the most intense flavor after six months.

1. Sift together flour, cornstarch, and salt.

2. Cream butter and ¼ cup confectioners' sugar until light and fluffy. Blend in vanilla extract. Add flour mixture; stir well.

3. Chill several hours, tightly sealed.

4. Preheat oven to 350°F. Line a baking sheet with parchment.

5. Form dough in 1 balls; place on baking sheet 1" apart. Bake 12–14 minutes, until cookies start to brown on edges. Cool slightly. Roll in remaining confectioners' sugar.

Lemon Bon Bons

The frosting should be divided and tinted several pastel colors to make these pretty cookies. You can substitute pecans for the pistachios.

INGREDIENTS | **YIELDS 36 COOKIES**

1 cup unsalted butter
⅓ cup confectioners' sugar
¾ cup cornstarch
1 teaspoon grated lemon peel
1¼ cups all-purpose flour
½ cup pistachios, finely chopped

Frosting

1 cup confectioners' sugar
1 teaspoon unsalted butter, melted
2 tablespoons lemon juice
Food coloring

1. Beat butter and sugar until light and fluffy. Add cornstarch, lemon peel, and flour; blend well. Chill overnight.

2. Preheat oven to 350°F. Line a baking sheet with parchment.

3. Roll cookie dough in 1" balls. Roll in pistachios; place on baking sheet. Flatten with bottom of a glass. Bake 12–15 minutes.

4. Meanwhile, prepare frosting. Mix frosting ingredients until smooth. Divide into equal parts; tint each a different color.

5. Frost tops of cooled cookies with frosting.

Paste Food Coloring for More Colorful Cookies

Paste food coloring is a thick food coloring that allows you to create deeper, more intense colors in frostings and glazes. Just dip a toothpick in the desired color and stir into the frosting. Continue this way, adding a little at a time until you reach the color you want.

Tea Dainties

Delicate cookies are unusual with the distinct flavor of Earl Grey tea. An easy way to blend the tea to a powder is to place it with ¼ cup of the flour in a blender.

INGREDIENTS | **YIELDS 36 COOKIES**

1 cup unsalted butter

½ cup confectioners' sugar

¼ teaspoon salt

2 tablespoons Earl Grey tea, ground to a powder

1 teaspoon orange peel, grated

2¼ cups all-purpose flour

¾ cup finely chopped pecans, if desired

1. Cream butter and sugar until light and fluffy. Add remaining ingredients; blend well.

2. Chill overnight.

3. Preheat oven to 400°F. Line a baking sheet with parchment.

4. Roll dough into 1" balls; place on baking sheets.

5. Bake 10–12 minutes. Cool.

Tea Cookies

Tea cookies can really be any type of cookie that is made in a diminutive size. They are generally a delicate texture and light flavor, and that makes them perfect to serve with other delights on a tea tray. Tea cookies do not tend to ship well because of their delicate nature; however, they generally keep well at room temperature for up to two weeks.

Chocolate Thumbprints

Beautiful and delicate but with a triple-chocolate kick, these chocolate thumbprints are a nice accompaniment to an after-dinner espresso or cup of tea.

INGREDIENTS | YIELDS 24 COOKIES

½ cup unsalted butter

⅔ cup sugar

1 egg

2 tablespoons heavy cream

1 teaspoon vanilla

1 cup all-purpose flour

⅓ cup cocoa

¼ teaspoon salt

1 cup sugar for rolling

1 recipe Ganache (page 544)

24 unwrapped chocolate Kisses

Easy Freeze-y

For the quickest cookies ever, form your cookie dough and place it on baking sheets as if you were going to bake them. Freeze them completely on the baking sheets. When they are totally frozen, remove from the sheets and toss into a freezer bag. You can then remove exactly the number of cookies that you need to bake, pop them in the oven, and have freshly baked cookies in less than fifteen minutes, with no mess at all.

1. Cream butter, sugar, egg, cream, and vanilla. Combine flour, cocoa, and salt; blend into creamed mixture. Chill 2 hours.

2. Preheat oven to 350°F. Line a baking sheet with parchment.

3. Roll chilled dough into 1" balls; roll in sugar. Place on cookie sheet. Press thumb gently in center of each cookie.

4. Bake 10–12 minutes.

5. When cookies are removed from oven, press centers again with thumb. Quickly add ¼ teaspoon Ganache in indentation, then press 1 chocolate Kiss on top of each cookie. Cool completely.

Rich Chocolate Teas

These tea cookies are from a vintage recipe. Use the darkest cocoa you can find for the richest chocolate flavor. You can substitute ¼ cup freshly ground espresso beans for the walnuts.

INGREDIENTS | YIELDS 36 COOKIES

1 cup unsalted butter, room temperature
1 teaspoon vanilla
1 cup powdered sugar
Pinch salt
¼ cup cocoa
1 tablespoon water
2¼ cups all-purpose flour
1 cup finely chopped walnuts
1 cup confectioners' sugar for rolling finished cookies in

1. Cream butter, vanilla, and powdered sugar until smooth. Stir in rest of ingredients until well blended. Chill at least 2 hours.

2. Preheat oven to 300°F.

3. Roll dough into tablespoon-sized balls. Place on ungreased baking sheets.

4. Bake 15–20 minutes, or until done.

5. Cool. Roll in confectioners' sugar.

Rollo Cookies

These cookies can be a bit messy to make, but the melting caramel middles make them totally worthwhile. If you can't get turbinado sugar you can substitute white sugar, but the results won't be quite so spectacular.

INGREDIENTS | YIELDS 48 COOKIES

1 cup unsalted butter
1 cup sugar
1 cup brown sugar, packed
2 eggs
1 teaspoon vanilla
2½ cups all-purpose flour
¾ cup cocoa
1 teaspoon baking soda
1 bag of Rollo candies, unwrapped
Turbinado sugar for rolling

1. Cream butter, sugars, eggs, and vanilla. Stir in flour, cocoa, and baking soda. Chill overnight.

2. Preheat oven to 350°F. Line a baking sheet with parchment.

3. Take a tablespoon of dough and roll it around a Rollo candy, enclosing it completely. Roll in turbinado sugar.

4. Place on baking sheets; bake 10 minutes, until done.

5. Cool completely. The middles of these are very hot when they come out of the oven.

Petticoat Tails

Petticoat Tails are rumored to get their name from the French chefs that worked for Mary Queen of Scots. They called the cookies they made for her Petit Gautelles, or "little cakes." This was anglicized by the Scots, and we know them as Petticoat Tails.

INGREDIENTS | YIELDS 60 COOKIES

1 cup unsalted butter

1 cup confectioners' sugar

1 teaspoon vanilla

2½ cups all-purpose flour

¼ teaspoon salt

The Many Variations of Short-bread Cookies

Shortbread can be formed in many ways: It can be chilled and rolled like pie dough and then cut into wedges; made into logs of dough, chilled, and sliced; or pressed down with a glass cup or cookie press. You can dip one side in melted chocolate, roll in sugar or nuts before baking, or sandwich two baked cookies together with a filling. However you make these versatile cookies, they are sure to disappear fast.

1. Cream together butter, confectioners' sugar, and vanilla. Blend in flour and salt. Wrap; chill overnight.

2. Preheat oven to 400°F.

3. Roll teaspoons of dough into balls; place on cookie sheets.

4. Press down with the bottom of a glass dipped in sugar until cookies are ⅛" thick.

5. Bake 8–10 minutes, or until lightly browned.

CHAPTER 24

Rolled Cookies

Mrs. T's Sugar Cookies

The actual yield of cookies in this recipe will vary with the size of the cookie cutters. These cookies are easy to roll, and don't get tough when they are overworked like some cookies. It makes this a great recipe for cooking with kids.

INGREDIENTS | YIELDS 36 COOKIES

2 cups sugar

1½ cups unsalted butter, melted

4 eggs, beaten

1 tablespoon vanilla

5 cups all-purpose flour

1½ teaspoons baking powder

1. Whisk sugar into melted butter; let cool until lukewarm. Add eggs and vanilla. Stir in flour and baking powder.

2. Chill overnight, well covered.

3. Preheat oven to 375°F. Lightly grease baking sheets.

4. Roll dough out to about ⅛ thick on a lightly floured surface. Cut into desired shapes; sprinkle with sugar if desired.

5. Bake 8–10 minutes. Cookies will be very light in color with golden edges. Let cool; decorate as desired.

Painting Sugar Cookies

Sugar cookies can be decorated in a variety of ways. One of the most unusual is to paint the cookies before baking with Egg Yolk Paint (page 549) and food color paint. Use clean paintbrushes and rinse and blot dry between colors. With this technique you can make everything from tie-dye cookies to recreating actual paintings if you have the time and patience.

Butterscotch Cookies

If you like crunchy cookies, leave these old-fashioned treats in the oven for the full 10 minutes, checking often to make sure they do not scorch.

INGREDIENTS | YIELDS 36 COOKIES

1 cup brown sugar

½ cup butter, softened

1 egg, beaten

1 teaspoon vanilla

½ teaspoon salt

1¾ cups flour

½ teaspoon baking powder

¼ teaspoon baking soda

Pinch freshly grated nutmeg

1. Cream brown sugar and butter until fluffy. Add egg and vanilla; beat well.

2. Whisk dry ingredients together; stir into butter mixture.

3. Chill overnight.

4. Preheat oven to 350°F. Roll out dough on lightly floured surface. Cut into shapes.

5. Bake 8–10 minutes. Allow to cool before removing from baking sheets.

Basic Butter Cookies

For a little change of flavor, you can substitute orange juice,
lemon juice, or lime juice for the milk in this recipe.

INGREDIENTS | **YIELDS 36 COOKIES**

1 cup unsalted butter, room temperature
1 cup sugar
1 egg
1 tablespoon vanilla
2 tablespoons cream or milk
2½ cups all-purpose flour
1 teaspoon baking powder

1. Combine butter and sugar; mix until creamy. Add egg, vanilla, and milk; blend well.

2. Add dry ingredients; stir to blend. Chill at least 3 hours, or overnight.

3. Preheat oven to 400°F. Line a cookie sheet with parchment.

4. On a floured surface, roll out dough to ¼" thickness. Roll ⅓ of dough at a time, keeping remaining dough chilled.

5. Cut with cookie cutters; transfer to baking sheet. Bake 6–10 minutes. Cool completely.

Brown Sugar Cookies

Sugar cookies with a praline flavor are a wonderful treat anytime. Give the cookies
even more flavor by substituting vanilla-butter-nut flavoring for the vanilla.

INGREDIENTS | **YIELDS 36 COOKIES**

⅔ cup vegetable shortening
⅔ cup unsalted butter
1 cup sugar
1 cup packed brown sugar
2 eggs
2 teaspoons vanilla extract
3¼ cups all-purpose flour
1 teaspoon baking soda
1 teaspoon salt
Chopped pecans

1. Mix shortening, butter, and sugars until creamy and light. Add eggs one at a time. Add vanilla to shortening mixture; blend well.

2. Sift dry ingredients; add to mixture. Blend well; blend in pecans.

3. Shape dough into 1½" diameter log. Wrap in wax paper; chill thoroughly. Dough will keep up to 1 month in refrigerator.

4. Preheat oven to 375°F. Slice dough ½" thick; place on ungreased baking sheets.

5. Bake 8–10 minutes. Cool completely.

Chocolate Rolled Cookies

This dough is quite soft and can be challenging to work with; be sure to chill it overnight. If you are rolling it out on a warm day, keep the bowl of dough in the refrigerator until it is needed.

INGREDIENTS | **YIELDS 36 COOKIES**

3 ounces unsweetened chocolate

1 cup unsalted butter

1 cup sugar

1 egg

1 teaspoon vanilla

2 cups all-purpose flour

1 teaspoon baking soda

Pinch of salt

Sugar for sprinkling

Wax Paper Trick

If the cookie dough seems to be difficult to work with, try this trick: Roll chilled dough out between sheets of wax paper. Cut into shapes as desired, but leave on the wax paper. Place the paper in the freezer for several minutes to chill. Remove the chilled shapes to the cookie sheet with a spatula.

1. Microwave chocolate and butter in a microwave-safe container until butter is melted. Stir chocolate until it is blended and smooth.

2. Blend in sugar until smooth; blend in egg and vanilla. Whisk together dry ingredients; add to butter mixture.

3. Cover tightly; chill overnight.

4. Preheat oven to 375°F. Line baking sheets with parchment paper. Roll dough on a lightly floured surface and cut into shapes. Sprinkle with sugar if desired.

5. Bake 8–10 minutes. Cool completely.

Gingerbread Men

This is very soft dough; be sure to keep it well chilled and allow plenty of room on the cookie sheet for the dough to spread.

INGREDIENTS | YIELDS 36 COOKIES

1 cup packed dark brown sugar

¾ cup sugar

½ cup vegetable shortening

2 eggs

¼ cup molasses

½ teaspoon vanilla

2 cups all-purpose flour

1 teaspoon baking soda

1 teaspoon baking powder

1½ teaspoons ginger

1 teaspoon salt

1 teaspoon cinnamon

¼ teaspoon white pepper or cayenne

¼ teaspoon ground cloves

Turbinado sugar for sprinkling

1. Cream together sugars and shortening until fluffy. Add eggs, molasses, and vanilla.

2. Whisk together dry ingredients until smooth; add to shortening mixture. Blend well. Chill overnight.

3. Preheat oven to 300°F. Place parchment on cookie sheets.

4. Roll dough ⅛" thick on heavily floured surface. Cut with floured cookie cutters and transfer to parchment. Sprinkle with turbinado sugar if desired.

5. Bake 15–18 minutes, or until done.

Spice It Up

Adding cayenne, chipotle, black pepper, or white pepper to a cookie may seem a little odd, but the spice enhances the flavors of the cinnamon and cloves in the cookie. Which pepper you use will depend on how spicy you like your gingerbread. Grated orange peel is a nice addition to any type of spice cookie, as well.

Lavender Diamonds

Lavender has an unusual flowery-citrus flavor that goes well with lemon or vanilla.
Both are used here to give the cookies a complex yet mellow flavor.

INGREDIENTS | YIELDS 24 COOKIES

1½ cups butter, room temperature

⅔ cup sugar

¼ cup confectioners' sugar

1 tablespoon lavender flowers, chopped fine

1 teaspoon lemon zest

1 teaspoon vanilla

2½ cups all-purpose flour

½ cup cornstarch

¼ teaspoon salt

1. Cream butter and sugars. Add lavender, lemon zest, and vanilla; blend well.

2. Whisk dry ingredients together; blend into butter mixture. Chill dough overnight.

3. Preheat oven to 325°F. Line a baking sheet with parchment.

4. Roll out chilled dough ¼" thick on floured surface. Cut into diamonds; place on baking sheets. Sprinkle with sugar.

5. Bake 15–20 minutes, or until done.

Baking with Lavender

Lavender is a very fragrant herb often used in cooking and baking. You can make a delicious lavender sugar by placing 1 tablespoon of lavender flowers in a cheesecloth bag and sealing it with 2 cups of sugar for a day or so. The sugar will pick up the lavender flavor and is delicious as a garnish on top of cookies.

Animal Crackers

For the best flavor, use old-fashioned oats rather than the quick or instant oats for this recipe—just be sure to grind it to a fine powder in the blender. Make certain that the blender is totally dry, or you will have paste.

INGREDIENTS | **YIELDS 36 COOKIES**

½ cup oatmeal
¼ teaspoon salt
¾ cup flour
¼ teaspoon baking soda
¼ cup unsalted butter, softened
¼ cup buttermilk
2 teaspoons honey
¼ teaspoon maple extract

Cookies as a Teaching Tool

You can use cookies to teach your pre-schooler his alphabet or numbers. Instead of using animal cookie cutters, you can buy number or alphabet cutters. This enables your child to learn with all of his senses: saying the letter; touching the letter; seeing the letter; smelling the letter; and finally, eating it.

1. Preheat oven to 400°F. Do not grease cookie sheets.

2. Grind oatmeal in blender until it is like flour. Mix in rest of dry ingredients.

3. Cut in butter until mixture is like coarse crumbs. Add buttermilk, honey, and maple extract. Gather into a ball; knead lightly.

4. Roll about ⅛" thick; cut with animal-shaped cookie cutters. Place on baking sheet.

5. Bake 10–12 minutes, or until golden. Cool completely.

Easy Homemade Graham Crackers

Whole-wheat graham flour is different than whole-wheat flour. You may be able to find it in the natural foods section of your grocery store. If not, it is available on the Internet. Bob's Red Mill has wonderful graham flour and it is usually easy to find.

INGREDIENTS | **YIELDS 48 CRACKERS**

¾ cup unbleached all-purpose flour

1½ cups whole-wheat graham flour

1 teaspoon baking powder

½ teaspoon baking soda

½ teaspoon salt

¼ teaspoon ground cinnamon

¼ cup sugar

¼ cup brown sugar

½ cup cold unsalted butter, cut into pieces

¼ cup honey

¼ cup cold water

1 teaspoon vanilla or maple extract

1. In a food processor, mix together dry ingredients and sugars. Pulse until blended.

2. Add butter; pulse until mixture resembles coarse crumbs. Add honey, water, and extract; mix until dough forms a ball.

3. Roll dough ½" thick between 2 sheets of waxed paper. Chill 1 hour.

4. Preheat oven to 350°F. Line a baking sheet with parchment. Roll chilled dough ⅛" thick; cut into desired shapes, or squares. Prick holes in crackers with a fork; sprinkle turbinado sugar over tops.

5. Bake 15 minutes, or until lightly browned. Cool crackers completely.

Cream Cheese Cut Outs

This is a soft, sticky type of dough that can be hard to work with. Chill overnight in the refrigerator and work with ¼ of the dough at a time. Use lots of powdered sugar to roll them out.

INGREDIENTS | **YIELDS 72 COOKIES**

1 cup unsalted butter

8 ounces cream cheese

1 cup sugar

½ teaspoon almond extract

1 teaspoon vanilla

1 egg

2¾ cups all-purpose flour

½ teaspoon salt

Confectioners' sugar for rolling

1. Combine butter, sugar, and cream cheese; beat until well blended. Add almond extract, vanilla, and egg; beat until smooth. Add dry ingredients. Chill overnight.

2. Preheat oven to 375°F. Line a baking sheet with parchment.

3. Roll dough out to ⅛" thickness on a surface that has been dusted with confectioners' sugar.

4. Cut into desired shapes; place on baking sheets. Sprinkle with sugar if desired.

5. Bake 7–10 minutes. Cool completely; frost, if desired.

Peanut Butter Shapes

*Cut these cookies into rounds and sandwich them together with
a little of the Ganache filling from page 544.*

INGREDIENTS | **YIELDS 48 COOKIES**

½ cup unsalted butter

½ cup creamy peanut butter

1 egg

½ cup sugar

½ cup firmly packed brown sugar

1½ cups all-purpose flour

¾ teaspoon baking soda

⅛ teaspoon salt

Peanut Butter Facts

Peanut butter can get rancid quickly in hot weather. For the best taste, keep the peanut butter chilled in the refrigerator during the summer months. This is especially true with natural peanut butter. An added bonus: Chilled peanut butter is much easier to measure and remove from the measuring cup.

1. Beat butter and peanut butter together until smooth. Add egg and sugars.

2. Mix in dry ingredients until well blended. Cover tightly; chill overnight.

3. Preheat oven to 350°F. Line a baking sheet with parchment.

4. On a floured surface, roll dough ⅛" thick. Cut out desired shapes; place on baking sheet. Sprinkle with turbinado sugar.

5. Bake 8–10 minutes. Cool completely.

Cheery Cherry Refrigerator Rolled Cookies

This dough will keep for one week in the refrigerator; freeze for longer storage. Refrigerator roll cookies are the original slice-and-bake cookie—homemade convenience.

INGREDIENTS | YIELDS 48 COOKIES

½ cup butter

½ cup shortening

8 ounces cream cheese

1 cup sugar

2½ cups flour

½ teaspoon salt

½ cup chopped maraschino cherries

½ cup chopped pecans, optional

Orange marmalade

Maraschino cherry halves

1. Cream butter, shortening, and cream cheese together. Add sugar; beat well. Blend in flour and salt; stir in chopped cherries and pecans, if desired.

2. Shape dough into rolls 2" in diameter; wrap with waxed paper. Chill.

3. Preheat oven to 400°F. Grease cookie sheets.

4. Cut in ⅛ slices; place on cookie sheet. Top with ⅛ teaspoon orange marmalade and a cherry half.

5. Bake 6–8 minutes.

Cutting Refrigerator Roll Cookies

Refrigerator roll cookies can be a real time saver. By keeping a roll or two in the refrigerator and freezer, you will always be prepared for a quick treat. You can slice off just the amount of cookies you want to bake at a time so they are always warm and fresh.

Chocolate Thin Mint Cookies

If you are addicted to the Girl Scout thin mint cookies, you will love these.
Peppermint oil is a flavoring available at most candy and cake supply stores.

INGREDIENTS | **YIELDS 36 COOKIES**

½ cup unsalted butter
1 cup confectioners' sugar
1 teaspoon vanilla
1 cup cocoa
½ teaspoon salt
1¾ cups all-purpose flour
12 ounces bittersweet chocolate chips
Peppermint oil

1. Cream butter until light and fluffy. Add confectioners' sugar and vanilla; blend well.

2. Stir in cocoa, salt, and flour. Shape into 2" diameter logs; wrap in wax paper. Chill overnight.

3. Preheat oven to 350°F. Line a baking sheet with parchment. Cut cookie dough as thin as possible without breaking. Bake 10 minutes.

4. Melt chocolate chips in microwave, stirring often, until melted. Add peppermint oil a drop at a time until you are happy with the flavor. Dip cooled cookies completely in chocolate coating; place on clean parchment to set.

Sand Tarts

These old-fashioned cookies should be rolled out and cut very thin, only ⅛"–1⁄16".
Use plenty of confectioners' sugar to keep them from sticking.

INGREDIENTS | **YIELDS 84 COOKIES**

1 cup unsalted butter
2 cups sugar
3 eggs
1 teaspoon vanilla
4 cups flour
Confectioners' sugar for rolling
3 egg whites
1 cup sugar
1 tablespoon cinnamon
Pecan halves

1. Cream butter and 2 cups of sugar together until fluffy. Beat in eggs and vanilla; blend well. Stir in flour. Chill dough overnight.

2. Preheat oven to 325°F. Lightly grease a baking sheet.

3. Roll dough out on a surface covered with powdered sugar. Cut into rounds.

4. Beat egg whites until foamy. Mix 1 cup sugar and cinnamon. Brush top of each cookie with egg-white mixture; sprinkle with cinnamon-sugar mixture. Top with a pecan half.

5. Bake 10–12 minutes. Cool completely.

Filled Maple Leaf Cookies

Maple-leaf cookie cutters are available at many baking supply stores as well as online. The number of cookies you actually get from this recipe will depend on the size of the cutters you use.

INGREDIENTS | **YIELDS 12 COOKIES**

1 cup unsalted butter

1 cup sugar

¼ cup light brown or maple sugar

2 eggs

1 tablespoon vanilla

1 teaspoon maple extract

¼ cup maple syrup

2½ cups all-purpose flour

½ teaspoon baking soda

¾ teaspoon baking powder

½ teaspoon salt

Maple sugar for sprinkling

1 recipe Vanilla Filling (page 554) with 1 teaspoon of maple flavoring added

1. Cream butter and sugars until light and fluffy. Add eggs one at a time. Beat in vanilla, maple extract, and syrup.

2. Combine flour, baking soda, baking powder, and salt; stir into butter mixture. Wrap and chill several hours or overnight.

3. Preheat oven to 375°F. Line a baking sheet with parchment.

4. Roll out dough ⅛" thick on floured surface; cut with cookie cutters. Make sure you have an even number of cookies. Place on pan; sprinkle with maple sugar.

5. Bake 8–10 minutes, or until done. Cool completely; spread flat side on one cookie with filling. Add another cookie to make a sandwich.

Ice Cream Sandwiches

If you don't have access to the dark cocoa called for in this recipe, you can use any good-quality cocoa. The flavor may not be as intense, but it will still be very good.

INGREDIENTS | YIELDS 18 SANDWICHES

½ cup unsalted butter

½ cup vegetable shortening

⅔ cup sugar

½ cup brown sugar

1 egg

2 tablespoons espresso

½ cup Hershey's Special Dark cocoa powder

3 cups all-purpose flour

½ teaspoon baking soda

¼ teaspoon salt

1 half-gallon ice cream in your favorite flavor

Filling Ice Cream Sandwiches

There are many fabulous combinations when it comes to ice cream sandwiches. Choose one of the following to put in the middle: coffee, mint chocolate chip, chocolate, peanut butter cup, Oreo, vanilla, butter pecan. Any one of them will taste great. For a garnish, roll the sides of the sandwich in mini M&M's, colored jimmies, or other colorful candies.

1. Cream butter, shortening, and sugars. When mixture is very light and fluffy, add egg and coffee; blend well.

2. Sift dry ingredients together; stir into butter mixture. Blend well. Knead together until smooth and dough is very stiff. Wrap and chill overnight.

3. Preheat oven to 350°F. Line a baking sheet with parchment.

4. Roll dough out on floured surface; cut into rounds or any desired shape. Bake 6–8 minutes. Cool completely.

5. Spoon softened ice cream generously on flat side of 1 cookie. Top with another cookie, flat side down. Press down gently. Wrap and freeze.

Chinese Almond Cookies

*For a richer, but less delicate, flavor substitute ½ cup light
brown sugar for an equal amount of the white sugar.*

INGREDIENTS | **YIELDS 48 COOKIES**

4 cups all-purpose flour

4 teaspoons baking powder

1 teaspoon baking soda

2½ cups sugar

2 cups unsalted butter

2 eggs

1 tablespoon almond extract

Almonds for garnish

Egg wash

Sugar for sprinkling

Egg Wash

An egg wash is nothing more than an egg
mixed with a teaspoon of water and
beaten. Use it to give glossy color to your
baked goods. It also helps sugar crystals
adhere to the cut cookies as they are baking. Just gently brush the egg mixture over
the cookies before baking.

1. Sift dry ingredients and sugar together. Cut in butter until it is blended in and the mixture looks like coarse crumbs. Add eggs and almond extract. Form into 1½" diameter log; roll in wax paper. Chill overnight, or for several hours.

2. Preheat oven to 350°F. Lightly grease baking sheets.

3. Slice logs into ½" rounds; place on baking sheet.

4. Brush with egg wash; place an almond in center of each cookie. Sprinkle with sugar, if desired.

5. Bake 12–15 minutes, but do not allow to brown. Cool completely.

Key Lime Cutouts

Key limes are tiny limes that grow on the Florida Keys. They are sometimes available seasonally, but most often you will find the juice near the other citrus juices in the grocery store. Regular limes may be substituted if necessary.

INGREDIENTS | YIELDS 48 COOKIES

1 tablespoon peanut oil

1½ teaspoons key lime zest

⅓ cup key lime juice

1¾ cups all-purpose flour

½ teaspoon baking soda

½ teaspoon baking powder

⅛ teaspoon salt

½ cup unsalted butter

⅔ cup sugar

1½ teaspoons vanilla extract

½ teaspoon lemon extract

Sugar for sprinkling

1. Preheat oven to 350°F. Line a baking sheet with parchment. Combine oil and lime zest; set aside. In a microwave-safe bowl, microwave lime juice on high until it is reduced to 3 tablespoons. Time will vary according to many factors, including humidity. Plan on about 5 minutes. You can also reduce the juice on top of the stove. Let cool.

2. Sift dry ingredients together; set aside. Cream butter and sugar until fluffy. Add oil mixture, vanilla, lemon extract, and lime reduction. Stir in dry ingredients until well blended.

3. Dough should be somewhat stiff. If not, chill 30 minutes.

4. Roll dough out ¼" thick between sheets of waxed paper. Place in freezer about 10 minutes to firm up. Cut with cookie cutters; transfer to lined baking sheets. If dough begins to be too soft, put back in freezer to chill a few minutes. Sprinkle with sugar.

5. Bake 8–10 minutes, or until done.

Maple Sugar Cookies

These are a subtle-tasting maple cookie and not too sweet. For more maple flavor, you can increase the maple flavoring to 2 teaspoons.

INGREDIENTS | **YIELDS 48 COOKIES**

½ cup unsalted butter

½ cup vegetable shortening

¾ cup light brown sugar

2 eggs

½ cup grade-B maple syrup

1 teaspoon maple flavoring

4 cups all-purpose flour

2 teaspoons cream of tartar

1 teaspoon baking soda

½ teaspoon salt

Confectioners' Glaze (page 547), flavored to taste with maple flavoring, about ¼ teaspoon.

Extra Cookie Sheets

Ideally, you should have three cookie sheets: one for the dough; one in the oven; and one cooling and ready for the next batch. In real life this isn't always the case, but you can easily remedy that: Just use sheets of parchment the same size as your baking sheets. When one batch of cookies is done, pull the parchment off the baking sheet and replace with the cookie-filled parchment.

1. Cream butter and shortening until blended. Add brown sugar; beat until fluffy. Blend in eggs, syrup, and maple flavoring.

2. Sift dry ingredients; stir into butter mixture. Gather into a ball. Cover with plastic wrap; chill several hours, or overnight.

3. Preheat oven to 350°F. Lightly grease a cookie sheet.

4. Roll dough out on a lightly floured surface. Keep dough you are not working with in refrigerator. Cut into shapes; transfer to baking sheet.

5. Bake 10–12 minutes, or until golden brown. Cool and glaze.

Ganache-Filled Stars

This is a rich cookie that is more of a dessert than a snack. Keep filled cookies refrigerated, tightly covered.

INGREDIENTS | YIELDS 12 COOKIES

1¼ cups unsalted butter

½ teaspoon almond flavoring

⅔ cup sugar

1¾ cups ground almonds

2 cups all-purpose flour

Ganache (page 544)

1 cup chocolate chips, melted

Rolling the Dough

For very tender cookie dough, you can use confectioners' sugar rather than flour for rolling. The confectioners' sugar will not cause the cookies to become tough like rolling them with flour can. It does add a little sweetness, so do this only with cookies that are not overly sweet to begin with.

1. Cream butter, almond flavoring, and sugar together until light and fluffy.

2. Grind almonds with a little of the flour until they are a finely ground; do not let them become pasty. Add almonds and remaining flour to butter mixture; blend well. Chill overnight.

3. Preheat oven to 350°F. Line a baking sheet with parchment. Roll dough out to ¼" thickness on a surface covered with confectioners' sugar. Cut into star shapes.

4. Bake 10–15 minutes, or until golden at the edges. Cool completely.

5. Cover flat side of 1 cookie with Ganache. Place another cookie over it, flat side down. Drizzle with melted chocolate chips.

Key Lime-and-Strawberry Sandwich Cookies

The finished cookies will need to be kept refrigerated once chilled. If you choose to use the cream cheese frosting, just add 1 tablespoon key lime juice and 1 teaspoon lime zest for flavoring. Either way, these cookies are delicious.

INGREDIENTS | YIELDS 30 COOKIES

1½ cups unsalted butter

1 cup sugar

1 egg

2 packages (4-serving size) strawberry gelatin

1½ teaspoons vanilla

3½ cups flour

1 teaspoon baking powder

Lime Curd (page 546) or Cream Cheese Frosting (page 550)

Varying Flavors

Any flavor of gelatin can be used for these sandwich cookies. Try orange or raspberry gelatin with Ganache filling (page 544), lemon with vanilla filling, or even cherry with almond filling. The cookies are very colorful, and they make a great party food. You can also add a festive touch by rolling the logs in the gelatin powder or colored sprinkles so when you cut the cookies the edges are decorated.

1. Cream butter and sugar until light and fluffy. Add egg, 1½ packages of gelatin, and vanilla; blend well.

2. Sift flour and baking powder together; blend into creamed mixture. Form into a 2" diameter roll; wrap in wax paper. Chill overnight.

3. Preheat oven to 400°F. Line a baking sheet with parchment.

4. Slice cookies ¼" thick; place on parchment. Sprinkle half of cookies with remaining gelatin. Bake 8–10 minutes, or until done. Cool completely.

5. Spread chosen filling on one cookie and top with another. Refrigerate until ready to serve.

White Velvet Cutouts

You can easily change the flavor of these cookies by substituting almond extract for the vanilla and leaving out the lemon zest.

INGREDIENTS | **YIELDS 36 COOKIES**

1 cup unsalted butter
3 ounces cream cheese
1 cup sugar
1 egg yolk
1 teaspoon clear vanilla
1 teaspoon lemon zest
2½ cups all-purpose flour
Confectioners' sugar for rolling

1. Cream butter, cream cheese, and sugar together until light and fluffy. Blend in egg yolk, vanilla, and lemon zest. Stir in flour. Chill overnight.

2. Preheat oven to 350°F. Line baking sheets with parchment.

3. On a surface covered with confectioners' sugar, roll dough out ¼" thick. Cut into desired shapes with cookie cutters.

4. Bake 12 minutes, or until edges are golden. Cool.

Buttermilk Butterflies

It is important to use full-fat buttermilk in this recipe for best flavor and texture. If you can't get whole buttermilk, use half buttermilk and half sour cream.

INGREDIENTS | **YIELDS 60 COOKIES**

5 cups flour
2 cups sugar
2 teaspoons baking powder
1 teaspoon freshly grated nutmeg
1 teaspoon salt
½ cup shortening
1 cup thick buttermilk
3 eggs
2 teaspoons vanilla
1 teaspoon baking soda

1. Mix flour, sugar, baking powder, nutmeg, and salt. Cut in shortening until mixture looks like coarse crumbs.

2. Mix buttermilk, eggs, vanilla, and baking soda. Stir into flour mixture until it forms a ball. Chill 1 hour, or overnight.

3. Preheat oven to 375°F. Line baking sheets with parchment.

4. Roll dough out on a floured surface to ¼" thick. Cut in butterfly shapes. Sprinkle with sugar; arrange on baking sheets.

5. Bake 15 minutes, or until done. Cool completely.

CHAPTER 25

The Best Cookies for Shipping

Peanut Butter Cookies

This recipe is full of peanut flavor. If you are a peanut butter fanatic, try adding 1 cup of peanut butter chips, 1 cup of chocolate chips, or a mixture of the two.

INGREDIENTS | **YIELDS 48 COOKIES**

½ cup butter
½ cup shortening
1 cup creamy peanut butter
1 cup sugar
1 cup packed brown sugar
2 eggs
1½ teaspoons vanilla extract
2½ cups all-purpose flour
1 teaspoon baking soda
1 teaspoon salt

Shipping Peanut Butter Cookies

If you are shipping cookies overseas, they need a little extra insurance against breakage. Just wrap two cookies with the bottom sides together in plastic wrap. Place carefully in your package and repeat with the rest of the cookies. The cookies will give each other support and be less likely to break.

1. Preheat oven to 375°F. Lightly grease cookie sheets.

2. Cream butter, shortening, and peanut butter until well blended. Add sugars; beat until fluffy. Add eggs and vanilla; blend.

3. Stir in dry ingredients.

4. Drop dough by rounded tablespoons onto prepared baking sheets. Flatten with tines of a fork dipped in flour. Push down horizontally then vertically to create raised squares.

5. Bake 8–10 minutes, or until set but not hard. Cool on baking sheets 5 minutes before removing.

Oatmeal Raisin Cookies

Part of the reason these cookies ship so well is the moisture from the raisins. If you do not like raisins, substitute dried cranberries, dates, or other dried fruit.

INGREDIENTS | **YIELDS 36 COOKIES**

½ cup butter
¾ cup vegetable shortening
½ cup sugar
¾ cup brown sugar
1 egg
1½ teaspoons vanilla
1½ cups all-purpose flour
1 teaspoon baking soda
1 teaspoon cinnamon
1 teaspoon freshly ground nutmeg
1 teaspoon salt
3 cups old-fashioned oats
1½ cups raisins

1. Preheat oven to 375°F.

2. Beat butter, shortening, and sugars until fluffy. Add egg and vanilla; blend well.

3. Sift flour, baking soda, cinnamon, nutmeg, and salt. Stir into butter mixture. Blend in oats and raisins.

4. Drop by teaspoons onto prepared baking sheet.

5. Bake 8–10 minutes. Cool a few minutes before removing from baking sheet. Cool completely before wrapping to ship.

Boxes in Boxes

You can buy different-sized boxes at many office supply stores. If you are shipping several different types of cookies, it may be worth it to buy separate small boxes for each and fit them all in the main box. This will keep your cookies from sharing flavors as well as give them more protection during mailing.

Brown-Eyed Susans

This cookie is very similar to Chocolate Thumbprints (page 377), but the filling holds up much better for shipping. Almond extract can be substituted for the vanilla.

INGREDIENTS | YIELDS 60 COOKIES

1 cup butter
1 teaspoon vanilla
¼ cup sugar
2 cups all-purpose flour
½ teaspoon salt
Sugar for rolling
1 cup confectioners' sugar
2 tablespoons cocoa
1 tablespoon strong hot coffee
½ teaspoon vanilla

1. Preheat oven to 375°F.

2. Beat butter, vanilla, and sugar until very light. Blend in flour and salt.

3. Shape teaspoons of dough into balls; roll in sugar. Place on baking sheet. Press thumb in center to make an indentation.

4. Bake 8–10 minutes, or until golden. Remove from oven and press center down again if necessary. Cool.

5. Combine confectioners' sugar and cocoa. Add hot coffee and vanilla; stir until smooth. Use to fill depression in each cookie.

Brown-Eyed Kisses

There are many ways to do Brown-Eyed Susan cookies. Instead of using the filling in the recipe, you can use one of the varieties of Hershey's Kisses and press down into the warm cookies. Return to the oven for 1 minute, then cool completely. These also ship well, although sometimes the Kiss falls out of the depression in the cookie.

Hermits

For the very best flavor, allow these cookies to ripen a day or two at room temperature. The flavors blend together and the taste is much better.

INGREDIENTS | YIELDS 48 COOKIES

½ cup unsalted butter
1 cup sugar
¼ cup vegetable shortening
¼ cup unsulfured molasses
1 egg
1 teaspoon cinnamon
1 teaspoon ground ginger
¼ teaspoon freshly grated nutmeg
½ teaspoon cloves
½ teaspoon baking soda
2 cups all-purpose flour
¼ teaspoon salt
1 cup raisins
1 cup chopped pecans
¼ cup candied ginger, chopped

1. Preheat oven to 350°F. Line a baking pan with parchment paper.

2. Cream together butter, sugar, and shortening until creamy. Add molasses and egg; blend well.

3. Sift together dry ingredients. Stir into butter mixture. Blend in raisins, pecans, and candied ginger.

4. Drop by teaspoons onto prepared sheets.

5. Bake 8–10 minutes. Cool completely.

Peanut Butter M&M's Bars

Use the seasonally colored M&M's for different seasons. If the recipient of these loves peanut butter, it is worth it to substitute the peanut butter M&M's for the regular kind.

INGREDIENTS | YIELDS 24 BARS

½ cup unsalted butter
⅔ cup peanut butter
1 cup packed dark brown sugar
1 egg, beaten
1 teaspoon vanilla
1¼ cups all-purpose flour
½ teaspoon baking soda
¼ teaspoon salt
2 cups M&M's candies

1. Preheat oven to 350°F. Grease 13" × 9" pan.

2. Cream butter, peanut butter, and sugar until smooth. Blend in egg and vanilla.

3. Combine dry ingredients; mix until crumbly.

4. Stir in M&M's; press firmly into pan.

5. Bake 20–25 minutes. Cool completely.

Cuccidati

The filling for these cookies should be made three days ahead of time;
it gives the flavors time to blend and mellow.

INGREDIENTS | **YIELDS 48 COOKIES**

1 pound figs

½ pound raisins

1 pound walnuts

1 pound dates

1 orange

1 cup brown sugar

¼ teaspoon black pepper

2 teaspoons cinnamon

1½ cups water

2 ounces brandy

¾ cup butter

½ cup sugar

2 eggs

1½ tablespoons orange juice

Zest from 1 orange

1 teaspoon vanilla

3 cups flour

2 teaspoons baking powder

Confectioners' Glaze (page 547)

1. Grind dried fruits, nuts, and whole orange. Add brown sugar, black pepper, cinnamon, and ½ cup water; simmer 15 minutes. Remove from heat; stir in brandy. Cover and let stand 3 days.

2. Cream ¾ cup butter with ½ cup sugar until light. Add eggs; beat until well blended. Add orange juice, zest, and vanilla. Mix flour and baking powder; stir in. Chill 1 hour.

3. Preheat oven to 375°F. Line a baking sheet with parchment. Roll dough out on a surface dusted with confectioners' sugar. Cut in 3" wide strips.

4. Place filling down middle of each strip; fold over. Press edges together to seal filling inside. Cut on a diagonal about every 1½". Place on baking sheet.

5. Bake 10–12 minutes. Cool completely. Cover with glaze. Place in an airtight container, separating each layer with wax paper. Allow to ripen 5 days.

Brandy

The brandy in Cuccidati helps preserve the cookies a long time. Years ago, before refrigeration, people often used brandy or other alcohol in their mincemeat and fruit-cakes because of its power to keep the food from going bad. You may substitute whiskey or rum if you like, but be sure to use the amount of alcohol called for to achieve the best results. Because of the alcohol, these cookies should not be sent to military personnel in the Middle East.

Chinese Chews

Chinese Chew cookies started showing up in cookbooks in the early 1950s. From there, they made their way into school cafeterias. Offer a plate of these to nearly any baby boomer and they will immediately tell you how their mom made them.

INGREDIENTS | **YIELDS 24 BARS**

2 eggs
1 cup sugar
½ cup all-purpose flour
½ teaspoon baking powder
¼ teaspoon salt
1 cup chopped dates
1 cup chopped pecans
¼ cup coconut
1 teaspoon vanilla
Confectioners' sugar for rolling

1. Preheat oven to 350°F. Grease 13" × 9" baking pan.

2. Beat eggs until light and lemon colored. Add sugar; blend well.

3. Stir in dry ingredients, dates, nuts, coconut, and vanilla; mix well. Turn into prepared pan.

4. Bake 30 minutes. Cool.

5. Cut into squares; roll in confectioners' sugar.

Chinese Chew Variation

Some of the oldest recipes call for you to cut the bars into squares while still warm and roll the warm, baked cookies into logs or balls before rolling in the confectioners' sugar. This results in a dense, very chewy cookie that is rather small. Either way, Chinese Chews are delicious.

Oh Henry! Bars

While these bars do ship beautifully, you may want to refrain from sending them in the summer months. Separate the layers with waxed paper for best results.

INGREDIENTS | **YIELDS 24 BARS**

4 cups oats
½ cup sugar
1 cup brown sugar
1 cup melted unsalted butter
6 ounces chocolate chips
1 cup crunchy peanut butter

1. Preheat oven to 350°F. Grease 13" × 9" pan.

2. Mix oats, sugar, and brown sugar in a bowl. Pour butter over all; stir to blend.

3. Press firmly into pan; bake 20 minutes. Cool completely.

4. Melt chocolate and peanut butter together, stirring until well blended. Pour over cooled crust.

5. Cool completely before cutting into bars.

Raisin Cookies

For a unique flavor to these cookies, try substituting the water with an equal amount of your favorite tea. Earl Grey, with its delicate citrus flavor, is perfect.

INGREDIENTS | **YIELDS 36 COOKIES**

¼ cup unsalted butter
¼ cup vegetable shortening
½ cup brown sugar
¼ cup sugar
1 egg
1 teaspoon vanilla
1½ cups all-purpose flour
½ teaspoon baking soda
½ teaspoon salt
3 tablespoons water
¾ cup raisins
½ cup chopped walnuts

1. Preheat oven to 375°F.

2. Cream together butter, shortening, and sugars until fluffy. Add egg and vanilla; blend well.

3. Whisk dry ingredients together to blend; add alternately with water to butter mixture. Stir in raisins and walnuts.

4. Drop teaspoon-size mounds of dough 2" apart on baking sheet.

5. Bake 8–10 minutes; do not overcook. Cool completely.

Hot-Buttered Rum Bars

For a great variation on these bars, add 1 cup of pecans, walnuts, or macadamia nuts when you add the butterscotch chips to the batter before baking.

INGREDIENTS | YIELDS 24 BARS

⅔ cup unsalted butter

½ cup sugar

¼ cup brown sugar

3 eggs

¼ cup half-and-half

¼ cup rum

1½ cups flour

1 teaspoon cinnamon

1 teaspoon ginger

½ teaspoon freshly ground nutmeg

¼ teaspoon cloves

¼ teaspoon salt

⅔ cup butterscotch chips

1. Preheat oven to 350°F. Lightly grease 9" × 9" square pan.

2. Beat butter and sugars until light and creamy. Add eggs, cream, and rum.

3. Stir together dry ingredients; blend into butter mixture.

4. Stir in butterscotch chips. Spread evenly in pan.

5. Bake 25–30 minutes. Cool completely before cutting into bars.

Mailing Bar Cookies

An easy solution to mailing bar cookies is to bake them in an aluminum foil pan. Allow them to cool completely in the pan. Lay wax paper down on the surface of the cookie, then wrap the whole pan in aluminum foil or plastic wrap. The bar cookies will be unlikely to break in transit, and because they are uncut, they will stay fresh longer.

Mudslides

These chocolaty cookies are almost overwhelming. For even more chocolate flavor, substitute ½ pound of dark chocolate for ½ pound of the milk chocolate.

INGREDIENTS | **YIELDS 48 COOKIES**

6 ounces unsweetened chocolate
8 ounces bittersweet chocolate
8 ounces semisweet chocolate
⅓ cup unsalted butter
⅔ cup all-purpose flour
2 teaspoons baking powder
½ teaspoon salt
5 eggs
1¾ cups sugar
1 teaspoons vanilla
1 teaspoon strong espresso
1 pound milk chocolate chips

Tip for Melting Chocolate

When melting chocolate, be sure that everything is clean and dry. The smallest bit of water in your chocolate will cause it to seize up and become impossible to work with. For best results, microwave on low heat stirring every minute or so until the chocolate is soft. Remove from the microwave and continue to stir until it has melted completely.

1. Preheat oven to 400°F. Line baking sheets with parchment.

2. Melt unsweetened chocolate, bittersweet chocolate, and semisweet chocolate together with butter in a microwave-safe bowl. Stir every minute until smooth.

3. Sift dry ingredients; set aside. Beat eggs, sugar, vanilla, and espresso until light and fluffy.

4. Blend in flour mixture until just combined. Stir in chocolate chips.

5. Drop by generous teaspoon on baking sheets; bake 8–10 minutes; do not overbake. The tops will be cracked.

Raspberry-White Chocolate Blondies

Dried raspberries are often available at the natural food store. They are tangy and full of intense raspberry flavor. If you can't find them, you can substitute dried blueberries.

INGREDIENTS | **YIELDS 16 BARS**

½ cup unsalted butter

12 ounces white chocolate chunks

2 eggs

½ cup sugar

½ teaspoon almond extract

1 cup flour

½ teaspoon salt

½ cup dried raspberries

½ cup chopped toasted almonds

1. Preheat oven to 325°F. Grease and flour 8" square pan.

2. Melt butter in a microwave-safe bowl. Add half of white chocolate chunks.

3. Beat eggs and sugar until well blended. Stir in butter mixture and almond extract.

4. Add flour and salt; stir until blended. Stir in dried raspberries, remaining chocolate chunks, and almonds.

5. Bake 20 minutes, or until bars are light golden brown and a tester comes out clean. Do not overcook.

Cranberry Oatmeal Cookies

Any dried fruit or mixture of dried fruit is great in these chewy cookies. Quick oats can be substituted for the old-fashioned oats if necessary.

INGREDIENTS | **YIELDS 24 COOKIES**

½ cup unsalted butter

½ cup vegetable shortening

¾ cup packed brown sugar

¾ cup sugar

2 eggs

1 teaspoon vanilla

2¼ cups old-fashioned oats

2 cups all-purpose flour

1 teaspoon baking soda

1 teaspoon baking powder

½ teaspoon salt

2 cups dried cranberries

2 tablespoons orange zest

1 cup chopped pecans

1. Preheat oven to 350°F. Line a baking sheet with parchment.

2. Beat butter, shortening, sugars, eggs, and vanilla together until creamy.

3. Whisk dry ingredients together; add to butter mixture, blending well.

4. Mix in dried cranberries, orange zest, and pecans.

5. Drop by generous teaspoonfuls on baking sheet; bake 10–12 minutes, or until done. Cookies should be slightly undercooked when they come out of oven. Cool completely.

Snickers Bar Brownies

Nearly any candy bar can be substituted for the Snickers bars in this recipe. Milky Way bars are an especially good substitute if the recipient has a peanut allergy.

INGREDIENTS | YIELDS 16 BROWNIES

2 ounces unsweetened chocolate

1 ounce bittersweet chocolate

½ cup unsalted butter

1 cup sugar

2 eggs

1 teaspoon vanilla

¾ cup all-purpose flour

½ teaspoon baking powder

¼ teaspoon salt

3 Snickers bars, chopped coarsely

Flouring the Pan

Many brownie recipes, as well as cake recipes, call for you to grease and flour the pan. This can look unsightly on chocolate items, leaving white streaks on the finished product. Get around this by flouring the pan with sifted cocoa powder. It will blend right in with the brownies or cake.

1. Preheat oven to 350°F. Grease and lightly flour inside of 9" square baking pan.

2. Melt unsweetened chocolate and bittersweet chocolate together. Stir until smooth; allow to cool slightly.

3. Cream butter and sugar together until light and fluffy. Add eggs one at a time. Add vanilla and melted chocolate; blend well.

4. Add dry ingredients, blending just until completely mixed. Quickly stir in chopped candy bars.

5. Spread in prepared pan; bake 30–35 minutes. Cool completely.

Vanilla Bean Sugar Cookies

The vanilla sugar for these takes about three days to complete, so plan ahead when making these intense vanilla treats. Place about 2 inches of vanilla bean in the container with the cookies before shipping for even more flavor.

INGREDIENTS | YIELDS 48 COOKIES

2¼ cups sugar
3 Tahitian or Madagascar vanilla beans
1¼ cups unsalted butter
1 egg
1 teaspoon vanilla extract
½ teaspoon cream of tartar
3 cups all-purpose flour
¼ teaspoon salt

Don't Throw Away the Vanilla Bean Pods!

Vanilla beans are expensive, and it is a waste to scrape out the seeds and throw the pods away. The pods actually have even more flavor than the seeds. After using the seeds, place the pods into a sugar, tea, or coffee canister for a touch of vanilla flavor in these items. When the pod has little or no scent left, add it to home-made potpourri.

1. Mix sugar and one vanilla bean, cut in half. Place in an airtight container; set aside 3 days.

2. Preheat oven to 350°F. Line a baking sheet with parchment.

3. Cream butter and 1¼ cups of vanilla sugar until fluffy. Cut all 3 vanilla beans lengthwise and scrape seeds and pulp into mixing bowl. Add egg and vanilla extract; beat until completely blended.

4. Stir dry ingredients into creamed mixture. Form into balls; roll balls in remaining vanilla sugar. Place on prepared baking sheets. Flatten gently with a press or glass dipped in vanilla sugar.

5. Bake 8–10 minutes, or until edges start to turn golden. Cool.

Butterscotch Chip Cookies

For more of a butter-brickle flavor, add about ½ cup chopped toasted pecans for ½ cup of the toffee pieces. You can also omit the toffee and use pecans instead.

INGREDIENTS | **YIELDS 24 COOKIES**

½ cup unsalted butter
½ cup butter-flavor shortening
¾ cup sugar
¾ cup light brown sugar
2 eggs
2½ teaspoons vanilla
2¼ cups all-purpose flour
1 teaspoon baking soda
1 teaspoon salt
2 cups butterscotch chips
1 cup toffee pieces

1. Preheat oven to 350°F. Lightly grease baking sheets.

2. Cream butter and shortening together until well blended. Add sugars; beat until light and fluffy. Add eggs and vanilla; beat well.

3. Mix dry ingredients together; add to butter mixture. Stir until well blended.

4. Fold in butterscotch chips and toffee pieces, and pecans if you are using them.

5. Drop by rounded teaspoonfuls on baking sheets; bake 8–10 minutes. Cool. Do not overbake these cookies; they should be slightly soft in the middle when they come from the oven.

Peanut Butter Temptations

These mouthwatering treats should be made in nonstick mini muffin pans for ease of removal. Silicone mini muffin pans also work well.

INGREDIENTS | **YIELDS 36 COOKIES**

½ cup packed brown sugar
½ cup white sugar
½ cup unsalted butter
½ cup creamy peanut butter
1 egg
½ teaspoon vanilla
1¼ cups flour
¾ teaspoon baking soda
½ teaspoon salt
36 mini peanut butter cups, unwrapped and chilled

1. Preheat oven to 375°F. Spray mini muffin pans lightly with baking spray.

2. Cream together brown sugar, white sugar, and butter. Blend in peanut butter, egg, and vanilla.

3. Sift dry ingredients together; blend into creamed mixture then shape dough into 1" balls; press into mini muffin pans. Bake 8–10 minutes.

4. Immediately press a peanut butter cup in center of each cookie after removing from oven. Press gently but firmly until only the top of peanut butter cup is showing, even with cookie top. Allow to cool completely.

Carrot Cake Cookies

These cookies taste remarkably like carrot cake. The flavor improves after standing, so allow them to mellow for at least a day before eating them. Glaze them with Confectioners' Glaze (page 547) for a nice finish.

INGREDIENTS | **YIELDS 36 COOKIES**

½ cup unsalted butter

1 cup brown sugar

2 eggs

1 teaspoon of vanilla

1 (8-ounce) can crushed pineapple, well drained

¾ cup grated carrots

1 cup raisins

2 cups all-purpose flour

1 teaspoon baking powder

½ teaspoon baking soda

½ teaspoon salt

2 tablespoons cinnamon

½ teaspoon cloves

¼ teaspoon ginger

½ cup white chocolate chips

1 cup chopped walnuts

1. Preheat oven to 350°F. Line a baking sheet with parchment paper.

2. Cream together butter and sugar. Beat in eggs and vanilla.

3. Stir in pineapple, carrots, and raisins.

4. Whisk dry ingredients together; blend in. Stir in white chocolate chips and walnuts.

5. Drop by rounded teaspoonfuls on prepared baking sheets; bake 15–20 minutes. Allow cookies to cool.

Add a Little Extra

When you are shipping cookies and baked goods, always add a little extra something for good measure. A magazine, special book, coffee, or box of tea will tell the recipient that you are thinking of them. Best of all, in the event that something goes awry with the cookies, they will still have a treat. Be careful though; adding strongly scented candles or potpourri can make the cookies taste like the potpourri.

Vanilla Bean-White Chocolate Chip Cookies

For more vanilla flavor, place the vanilla bean in the ¾ cup of sugar the day before you want to use it.

INGREDIENTS | **YIELDS 24 COOKIES**

½ cup unsalted butter
½ cup shortening
¾ cup light brown sugar
¾ cup sugar
2 eggs
1 teaspoon vanilla
1 (3) Mexican vanilla bean
2¼ cups flour
1 teaspoon baking soda
1 teaspoon salt
2 cups white chocolate chips
1 cup macadamia nuts, chopped

1. Preheat oven to 350°F. Lightly grease baking sheets.

2. Cream together butter, shortening, and sugars. Add eggs, vanilla, and seeds and pulp from inside of vanilla bean; mix well.

3. Whisk together dry ingredients; blend into creamed mixture. Stir in white chocolate chips and macadamia nuts.

4. Drop by teaspoonfuls on prepared baking sheet.

5. Bake 8–10 minutes, or until cookies are almost done. Remove from oven and allow to cool completely. Cookies centers will finish baking as they cool.

Chubby Hubby Cookies

These big cookies are full of sweet and salty flavors. The pretzels should be in small chunks, not chopped so fine they are powdered. Try to achieve pieces about the size of chocolate chips.

INGREDIENTS | **YIELDS 60 COOKIES**

2 cups unsalted butter
1 cup sugar
1 cup brown sugar
2 eggs
2 tablespoons vanilla
4 cups all-purpose flour
1 tablespoon baking soda
12 ounces chocolate chips
1 package peanut butter chips
1 cup salted peanuts, chopped
2 cups coarsely crushed pretzels

1. Preheat oven to 350°F.

2. Cream butter and both sugars together until light and fluffy. Blend in eggs one at a time, then the vanilla.

3. Whisk flour and baking soda together; stir into creamed mixture.

4. Stir in chocolate and peanut butter chips, chopped peanuts, and pretzels.

5. Drop by heaping tablespoonfuls on an ungreased baking sheet. Bake 10–13 minutes. Middles will still be soft. Allow to cool a few minutes before removing from baking sheet.

CHAPTER 26

No-Bake Cookies

Oatmeal Fudgies

These easy cookies are very sweet and rich. You can press the hot mixture into a 9" square pan to cool and then cut into bars. Make them easy to remove by lining the pan with waxed paper.

INGREDIENTS | **YIELDS 36 COOKIES**

2 cups sugar

½ cup unsalted butter

⅔ cup evaporated milk

3 tablespoons cocoa

½ teaspoon salt

1 cup crunchy peanut butter

4 cups old-fashioned rolled oats

1½ teaspoons vanilla

1. Bring sugar, butter, and evaporated milk to a rolling boil, stirring constantly. Boil 3 minutes, stirring constantly.

2. Remove from heat; quickly stir in remaining ingredients.

3. Drop by tablespoonfuls onto waxed paper; cool.

Assemble Your Ingredients

When making no-bake cookies, you will be working against the clock. These recipes go together fast! Have your ingredients and anything else called for in the recipe assembled and in place before you start the recipe. Always read the recipe all the way through and make sure you understand the steps before beginning.

Krispie Kritters

*These are exactly as you remember them from your childhood. They
don't keep well, so make them and eat them the same day.*

INGREDIENTS | YIELDS 18 BARS

3 tablespoons unsalted butter
1 (10-ounce) package marshmallows
6 cups crispy rice cereal

Variations

Krispy Kritters are a bar with many variations. Use the cocoa or fruit-flavored rice
cereals for a different flavor. Add M&M's,
pecans, crushed pretzels, or almost any
other candy or nut that you can think of. At
Christmas, the melted marshmallow mixture can be tinted with green food coloring, or use various pastel colors for Easter.

1. Grease 13" × 9" pan.

2. Melt butter in a saucepan over medium heat. Add
   marshmallows; stir until completely smooth and well
   blended.

3. Stir in crisp rice cereal; blend quickly.

4. Spoon into prepared pan; press down firmly with
   buttered hands.

5. Let cool; cut into bars.

Edible Play Dough

*Toddlers love to play in their food, and this play dough allows them to do just that.
Set out edible embellishments like raisins and M&M's to make it more fun.*

INGREDIENTS | YIELDS 4 SERVINGS

1 cup smooth peanut butter
½ cup honey
2 cups powdered sugar
1 teaspoon vanilla

1. Mix all ingredients together until smooth and pliable.
   You will need to use your hands.

2. Store in an airtight container; mixture does not need
   to be refrigerated.

Playing with Your Food

The edible play dough stores nicely at
room temperature. Once a child has gotten
his hands into the play dough, it should be
eaten or discarded. Even the cleanest
hands can harbor harmful bacteria that will
multiply over time. It is a good idea to separate the dough into portions and keep
each portion sealed in a snack-sized bag.

Cereal Cookies

Kids will have a great time putting these bars together, but it is best if an adult does the microwaving. The caramels get very hot and could burn someone badly.

INGREDIENTS | **YIELDS 32 BARS**

1 (14-ounce) bag caramels, unwrapped
¼ cup unsalted butter
¼ cup water
8 cups oat flour, O's type cereal
1 (6.5 ounce) can salted peanuts
6 ounces milk chocolate chips

1. Spray a 3-quart microwaveable casserole dish with cooking spray. Spray a 13" × 9" pan with cooking spray; set aside.

2. Arrange caramels in a layer over bottom. Sprinkle butter pieces over caramels; pour water over all.

3. Microwave on high, stirring every minute, for 6 minutes, or until mixture is smooth.

4. Quickly stir in cereal and peanuts. Stir until cereal is well covered with caramel. Stir in chocolate chips.

5. Press into prepared pan; let cool.

Granola Cookies

These nutritious cookies make a great breakfast on the go if you leave out the chocolate chips. Just don't tell anyone that they are good for you.

INGREDIENTS | **YIELDS 36 COOKIES**

½ cup packed brown sugar
1 teaspoon vanilla
¼ cup honey
¼ cup unsalted butter
3 cups of your favorite granola
½ cup bran flakes cereal
½ cup dried raisins or cranberries
½ cup chopped toasted almonds or pecans
¾ cup chocolate chips, optional
½ cup coconut, optional

1. Grease 13" × 9" pan. Set aside.

2. On medium heat, bring brown sugar, vanilla, honey, and butter to a boil. Lower heat; simmer and stir 2 minutes, until sugar is completely dissolved.

3. Cool completely.

4. Mix rest of ingredients together in a large bowl. Pour brown sugar mixture over all; stir to coat evenly.

5. Press into pan firmly. Refrigerate 2–3 hours. Cut into bars.

Baby Ruth Bars

Baby Ruth bars have been around for over seventy years and are still going strong. This homemade version is deliciously close to the original in taste.

INGREDIENTS | YIELDS 32 BARS

½ cup sugar

½ cup brown sugar

1 cup white corn syrup

1 cup peanut butter

6 cups cornflakes, crushed coarsely

1 cup milk chocolate chips

3 ounces butterscotch chips

1 cup chopped salted peanuts

1. Grease 13" × 9" pan.

2. Heat sugar, brown sugar, corn syrup, and peanut butter in a pan over medium heat; mix until smooth.

3. Combine remaining ingredients.

4. Pour peanut butter mixture over cereal mixture; stir to coat evenly.

5. Press into prepared pan; cool completely.

Storing No-Bake Cookies

Baby Ruth Bars should be stored in an airtight container. Put them in the container in layers with wax paper between each of the layers. Keep the container in a cool, dry place to maintain freshness, but do not keep in the refrigerator. Refrigerating or freezing changes the texture of these bars.

Ohio Buckeyes

You can use your favorite type of chocolate with this; milk chocolate, semisweet, dark, or bittersweet chocolate work equally well in these treats. You can even mix the types of chocolate, if you wish.

INGREDIENTS | **YIELDS 60 COOKIES**

1½ cups creamy peanut butter
½ cup unsalted butter
½ teaspoon vanilla
3 cups sifted confectioners' sugar
60 toothpicks
4 cups high-quality chocolate
2 teaspoons vegetable shortening, no substitutions

About Paraffin Wax

Some recipes call for a little paraffin to be added to chocolate when dipping. This is to stabilize the chocolate and make it shiny when set. Pure vegetable shortening is a better choice: Paraffin contains trace amounts of toxins and is really not healthy for you.

1. Line a baking sheet with wax paper; set aside. Combine peanut butter, butter, and vanilla until well blended and smooth. Add confectioners' sugar; beat until well mixed.

2. Roll mixture into ¾" balls; place on waxed paper. Place a toothpick in each ball to aid in dipping. Place on wax paper-lined baking sheet. Freeze 30 minutes.

3. Melt chocolate and shortening together in microwave, stirring until blended and smooth, about 3 minutes.

4. Dip each frozen peanut butter ball in melted chocolate, leaving top of peanut butter showing. Work quickly. Place back on waxed paper.

5. Remove toothpick. Smooth over hole left from toothpick with your finger. Chill 2 hours.

Strufoli

These small balls of fried cookie dough are a special treat in some Italian families during the Christmas and Easter holidays. While they do puff up quite a bit during frying, no one can eat just one. This recipe will serve eight people, but beware, they will clamor for more.

INGREDIENTS | SERVES 8 PEOPLE

2½–3 cups all-purpose flour
½ cup sugar
½ teaspoon salt
2 teaspoons baking powder
4 eggs, beaten
2 tablespoons lemon zest
¼ cup unsalted butter
1½ cups honey
¾ cups toasted almonds, chopped
Candy sprinkles, optional

Deep Frying

When you are deep frying pastries and cookies, always start out with clean oil. A light type of oil with a high smoking point such as peanut oil is best. Allow the oil to reach the indicated temperature and then fry the dough a little at a time. When the dough begins to brown too quickly, it is time to change the oil.

1. Set electric fryer for 375°F. Melt butter; set aside.

2. Mix 2½ cups flour, sugar, salt, and baking powder in a large bowl. Make a well in center and add eggs, lemon zest and melted butter.

3. Stir with a large spoon until dough leaves sides of bowl. Knead in rest of flour ½ cup at a time, until dough is no longer sticky.

4. Break off sections of dough; roll into pencil-sized logs. Cut into ¼" long pieces; set aside. Roll pieces into balls; fry until golden.

5. Bring honey to a boil; boil gently 3 minutes. Add fried dough; stir until well coated. Remove balls from honey with a slotted spoon. Place on a platter; sprinkle with remaining ingredients. Shape into a tall cone, wreath, or other shape while still warm. Cool completely.

Bird's Nest Cookies

These quick cookies are adorable at Easter time. Place a single cookie in a small, clear cellophane bag and tie with a pastel organza ribbon for giving as gifts.

INGREDIENTS | **YIELDS 24 COOKIES**

12 ounces butterscotch chips
¼ cup peanut butter
2 cups chow mein noodles
1 cup salted peanuts
Assorted jelly beans or candy-covered chocolate eggs

1. Line a baking sheet with wax paper.

2. Place butterscotch chips and peanut butter in microwave; melt, stirring often, about 3 minutes.

3. Stir in chow mein noodles and peanuts; coat well.

4. Drop by teaspoonfuls on baking sheet.

5. Press centers down with your thumb; add jelly beans or chocolate eggs to make it resemble a nest. Let cool completely.

M&M's Granola No Bakes

You can use the peanut butter-filled M&M's or mini M&M's for variety in these chewy no-bake bars.

INGREDIENTS | **YIELDS 36 BARS**

½ cup packed brown sugar
2 tablespoons honey
1 teaspoon vanilla
¼ cup unsalted butter
3 cups granola
1 cup M&M's
1 cup mini marshmallows
½ cup salted peanuts, chopped

1. Grease 13" × 9" pan; set aside.

2. Combine brown sugar, honey, vanilla, and butter in a pan. Bring to a boil; simmer 2 minutes. Set aside.

3. Combine remaining ingredients in a bowl.

4. Pour cooled honey mixture over M&M's mixture; stir to coat thoroughly.

5. Spoon into prepared pan; press down gently. Chill at least 1 hour before cutting into bars.

Orange Balls

It is worth it to buy the pistachios already shelled. Shelling them is very time consuming and hard on the fingers.

INGREDIENTS | **YIELDS 24 BALLS**

12 ounces vanilla wafer cookies, crushed
1 pound confectioners' sugar
¾ cup melted unsalted butter
½ cup chopped toasted pistachios
6 ounces frozen orange juice, thawed
Coconut for rolling

1. Line a baking sheet with wax paper.

2. Mix all ingredients except coconut.

3. Form into balls; roll in coconut until coated.

4. Chill.

5. These should be kept refrigerated or frozen. Bring to room temperature before serving.

Coating with Coconut

When you need to coat something with coconut, it is easiest if you grind the coconut up a little first. In order to do this, put it in the food processor with about 2 tablespoons of confectioners' sugar and pulse a few times until the coconut is in small pieces but not ground into a powder.

Honey Oat Bran Bars

You can use plain bran flakes or raisin bran instead of the oat bran flakes. If using raisin bran flakes, just omit the raisins called for in the recipe, unless you like a lot of raisins.

INGREDIENTS | **YIELDS 16 BARS**

4 cups oat bran flakes
½ cups chopped toasted pecans
½ cup raisins
⅓ cup unsalted butter
⅓ cup honey
⅓ cup firmly packed brown sugar

1. Grease 9" × 9" square pan; set aside.

2. Mix cereal, nuts, and raisins in a large bowl; set aside.

3. Bring butter, honey, and brown sugar to a boil over medium heat, stirring constantly.

4. Boil 5 minutes, continuing to stir constantly.

5. Pour over cereal mixture; stir to coat evenly. Spoon into prepared pan; press down gently. Cool 1 hour before cutting into bars.

S'Mores Bars

You can make these in less than 30 minutes, start to finish. Chocolate chips can be substituted for the chunks if desired.

INGREDIENTS | **YIELDS 24 BARS**

6 cups sweetened graham cereal
3 cups mini marshmallows
2 cups milk chocolate chunks
1 cup light corn syrup
½ cup sugar
¼ cup unsalted butter

1. Spray 13" × 9" pan with cooking spray.

2. Combine cereal, marshmallows, and chocolate chunks in a large bowl; set aside.

3. Combine corn syrup and sugar; bring to a boil, stirring constantly.

4. Remove from heat; stir in butter until completely melted.

5. Pour over cereal mixture, stirring to coat completely. Spoon into prepared pan; press down firmly. Cool 1 hour. Cut into bars.

Apricot Coconut Balls

These no-bake balls keep well stored in the refrigerator for up to a month. Layer them in an airtight container with wax paper between each layer.

INGREDIENTS | **YIELDS 96 BALLS**

4 cups dried apricots, finely chopped
4 cups coconut
2 cups chopped pecans
14 ounces sweetened condensed milk
1 cup confectioners' sugar for rolling

1. Combine ingredients in a large bowl; mix well.

2. Shape into 1" balls; roll in confectioners' sugar.

3. Refrigerate for at least an hour.

Chinese New Year Cookies

Salted peanuts or macadamia nuts can easily be substituted for the cashews if you like them better. These taste a bit like Payday candy bars.

INGREDIENTS | YIELDS 24 COOKIES

6 ounces chocolate chips
6 ounces caramels
3 ounces chow mein noodles
1 (7.5-ounce) can cashews, chopped

1. Line a baking sheet with wax paper

2. Melt chocolate chips and caramels, stirring constantly.

3. Add chow mein noodles and nuts.

4. Drop by teaspoonfuls on prepared baking sheet and chill for at least an hour.

Christmas Fruit Balls

These beautiful cookies can be rolled in confectioners' sugar if you don't like coconut. They are a wonderful addition to a holiday cookie tray.

INGREDIENTS | YIELDS 48 BALLS

¾ cup brown sugar
½ cup evaporated milk
1 cup mixed candied fruits
1 cup diced dried apricots
1 cup chopped pecans
Shredded coconut for rolling

1. Bring sugar and milk to a boil over low heat, stirring until sugar is completely dissolved.

2. Remove from heat; stir in remaining ingredients.

3. Allow to cool.

4. Shape into small balls; roll in coconut.

Rice Krispie Treats Without Marshmallows

These bars are for those who like the Rice Krispie treats but want a little extra nutrition. The corn syrup and peanut butter hold them together in a sweet, nutty glaze.

INGREDIENTS | **YIELDS 36 SQUARES**

1 cup corn syrup
½ cup sugar
½ cup brown sugar
1½ cups peanut butter
5 cups Rice Krispies

Corn Syrup Substitute

If you prefer not to use corn syrup in your cooking, you can easily make a sugar syrup to substitute. To substitute for light corn syrup, mix 2 cups of sugar and 1 cup of water. Bring to a boil and boil for 1 minute. Remove from heat. Add ½ teaspoon of vanilla if you wish. To make a substitute for dark corn syrup, use brown sugar rather than white sugar.

1. Spray 13" × 9" pan with cooking spray; set aside.

2. Bring corn syrup and sugars to a boil, stirring constantly. Stir in peanut butter.

3. Add cereal; stir until completely coated.

4. Remove from heat; spoon into prepared pan, pressing down firmly.

5. Allow to cool 1 hour. Cut into bars.

Honey Balls

These simple-to-make cookies are easy enough for preschoolers to make. Package them in small cellophane bags and tie with raffia for a sweet gift for a special teacher.

INGREDIENTS | **YIELDS 24 BALLS**

½ cup honey
½ cup peanut butter
1 cup confectioners' sugar
2 cups graham cracker crumbs

1. Combine honey, peanut butter, and confectioners' sugar.

2. Roll into small balls.

3. Roll each ball in graham cracker crumbs.

4. Store at room temperature in an airtight container.

Condensed Milk Cookies

These are chocolaty, fudgy cookies with a delicious crunch. For variety, try butterscotch, peanut butter, or white chocolate chips in this recipe.

INGREDIENTS | **YIELDS 30 COOKIES**

14 ounces sweetened condensed milk

12 ounces chocolate chips

1 cup Grape-Nuts cereal

Easy Shaping

No-bake cookies can be hard to work with because they often need to be shaped while they are hot. You can get scoops in several sizes at a restaurant supply store and easily create whatever size you need. For easy release of the dough, spray the scoop with baking spray before using. Spray again when cookies begin to stick. You will have perfectly shaped, uniform cookies every time.

1. Line a baking sheet with wax paper.

2. Heat milk in microwave until bubbles form around the edges, about 2 minutes. Do not allow to boil.

3. Add chocolate chips; stir until smooth.

4. Stir in cereal until well coated.

5. Drop by teaspoonfuls on prepared baking sheet. Cool until firm.

3 Bar Cookies

This no-bake, three-layer bar is not exactly a cake, a brownie, or a pudding.
For a chilly variation on a hot day, serve it partially frozen.

INGREDIENTS | **YIELDS 20 BARS**

¾ cup plus 1 tablespoon butter

¼ cup plus 1 tablespoon cocoa

½ cup sugar

1 teaspoon vanilla

1 egg at room temperature, beaten

2 cups graham cracker crumbs

1 cup coconut

½ cup chopped pecans

2 tablespoons whole milk

2 cups confectioners' sugar

2 tablespoons instant vanilla pudding mix

6 ounces chocolate chips

Tempering Eggs

When a recipe directs you to add eggs to a hot mixture, you must temper them or run the risk of having lumps of egg in your final product. To temper eggs, add about 1 tablespoon of hot mixture to the eggs and whisk in well. Add 3 tablespoons of the hot mixture to the eggs and whisk in. Finally, add the rest of the hot mixture, whisking the whole time to keep the eggs moving.

1. Grease 13" × 9" pan; set aside.

2. In a microwave-safe bowl, melt ½ cup of butter. Stir in cocoa and sugar. Microwave, stirring every 30 seconds, until sugar granules are gone and mixture is smooth.

3. Whisk in vanilla and egg until well blended. Stir in crumbs, coconut, and nuts. Evenly pack mixture into prepared baking dish. Chill.

4. Combine ¼ cup butter, milk, confectioners' sugar, and pudding mix. Whisk mixture until well blended; spread on crumbs.

5. Melt chocolate with remaining 1 tablespoon of butter, whisking until smooth. Pour and spread over pudding mixture. Chill 2 hours before cutting into bars.

CHAPTER 27

Just Like...

Baltimore Cookies

These cookies are very similar to the famous ones sold only in Baltimore. Use a good-quality chocolate for best results.

INGREDIENTS | SERVES 24

1 cup unsalted butter

2 cups sugar

3 eggs

1½ tablespoons vanilla

2 teaspoons baking soda

5 cups all-purpose flour

½ teaspoon salt

1 teaspoon baking powder

2 cups whole buttermilk

1 cup heavy cream

6 ounces milk chocolate, chopped

6 ounces dark chocolate, chopped

6 ounces bittersweet chocolate, chopped

1. Preheat oven to 350°F. Line a baking pan with parchment.

2. Cream butter, sugar, and eggs until light and fluffy. Add vanilla. Sift dry ingredients together; whisk into creamed mixture alternately with buttermilk.

3. Drop by heaping tablespoonfuls on prepared baking sheet. Bake 15 minutes, or until cookies spring back when touched. Cool.

4. Bring heavy cream just to a boil and remove from heat. Stir in chocolate until smooth and melted. Cool slightly. It should be thick but spreadable.

5. Smear over tops of cookies in a thick, ½" layer.

Why Mix Chocolate?

Often, the recipes in this cookbook call for several different type of chocolate mixed together. You may use just one kind or another in the same total amount; however, when chocolate is mixed it brings a more intense flavor and deeper dimension to the finished flavor. Experiment until you find the chocolate taste that suits you the best.

Coffee Shop Chocolate Fudge Squares

*Serving these warm from the oven with a scoop of coffee ice cream and a drizzle
of hot fudge sauce is absolutely decadent. Your coffee lovers will thank you.*

INGREDIENTS | **YIELDS 9 SQUARES**

½ cup unsalted butter
1 cup sugar
1 egg
2 ounces unsweetened chocolate
1 ounce bittersweet chocolate
1 cup all-purpose flour
¼ teaspoon baking powder
½ cup whole milk
½ cup chopped walnuts
1 teaspoon vanilla
1 cup confectioners' sugar
1 tablespoon unsalted butter
1 ounce unsweetened chocolate, melted
1 teaspoon vanilla extract
¼ cup espresso or strong coffee

1. Preheat oven to 350°F. Butter 9" × 9" square baking pan.

2. Cream ½ cup butter, sugar, and egg. Melt 2 ounces unsweetened chocolate with 1 ounce bittersweet chocolate in the microwave, about 1 minute. Stir until smooth, and add to butter mixture.

3. Whisk together flour and baking powder; add to chocolate mixture. Stir in milk, walnuts, and vanilla.

4. Spread in prepared pan; bake 20 minutes, or until brownies are done. Cool.

5. Mix remaining ingredients until well blended. Allow to cool; pour over cake. Spread glaze smoothly with a spatula. Let cake set; cut into bars.

Milano Cookies

*Lightly orange flavored and delicate, these cookies are sandwiched with a rich chocolate filling.
Raspberry jam or orange marmalade can be substituted for the chocolate.*

INGREDIENTS | **YIELDS 36 COOKIES**

¾ cup unsalted butter
2½ cups confectioners' sugar
6 egg whites
1 tablespoon grated orange zest
2 tablespoons vanilla extract
1½ cups flour
1 recipe Ganache (page 544)

1. Preheat oven to 350°F. Line a baking sheet with parchment.

2. Cream butter and confectioners' sugar until fluffy; add egg whites, orange zest, and vanilla.

3. Stir in flour until just blended.

4. Using ¼" decorating tip, fill a bag with dough and pipe out 2 long on baking sheet, 2" apart.

5. Bake 10 minutes, or until golden. Cool completely and sandwich together with Ganache.

Cranberry Bliss Bars

For something a little different, you can add 1 cup of chopped walnuts or pecans to the batter. Just fold them in with the dried cranberries.

INGREDIENTS | YIELDS 40 BARS

1 cup softened unsalted butter

⅓ cup granulated sugar

1 cup brown sugar

1 teaspoon vanilla

1 teaspoon orange extract

3 eggs

2 cups all-purpose flour

1½ teaspoons baking powder

1 teaspoon ground ginger

1 cup dried cranberries

¾ cup white chocolate chips

1 teaspoon orange zest

3 ounces cream cheese

2 tablespoons butter

2 teaspoons vanilla

3 cups confectioners' sugar

⅓ cup dried cranberries, chopped

2 tablespoons grated orange peel

⅓ cup white chocolate chips, chopped coarsely

½ teaspoon light oil

1. Preheat oven to 350°F. Spray 13" × 9" pan with cooking spray.

2. Beat 1 cup butter, sugar, and brown sugar until fluffy. Add extracts and eggs; beat well. Whisk dry ingredients together; stir in. Fold in 1 cup cranberries, ¾ cup white chocolate chips, and 1 teaspoon orange zest.

3. Spread in pan; bake 25–30 minutes.

4. For frosting: Blend cream cheese and 2 tablespoons of butter with vanilla extract until creamy. Add confectioners' sugar; beat until spreadable. Spread on cooled bars.

5. Mix remaining orange zest and chopped dried cranberries. Sprinkle over bars. Melt white chocolate and oil together, mixing until smooth. Drizzle over bars. Cut in 20 squares, then cut each square in half, in a triangle shape.

White Chocolate

White chocolate is not officially chocolate because it does not contain chocolate liquor. It does contain cocoa butter, which is where it gets the chocolate association. Good white chocolate should also contain sugar, milk solids, lecithin, and vanilla. Read the ingredients carefully; if it doesn't contain cocoa butter, don't buy it. It is inferior quality, made with vegetable fat.

Coffee Shop Biscotti

*Biscotti means "twice baked." These crunchy cookies are perfect
to dip in your coffee or tea for an afternoon snack.*

INGREDIENTS | **YIELDS 24 COOKIES**

2 cups all-purpose flour

1 cup sugar

1 teaspoon baking powder

1 cup chopped toasted almonds

¼ teaspoon salt

3 eggs, room temperature

½ teaspoon almond extract

1½ teaspoons vanilla extract

Cutting the Loaves of Biscotti

Biscotti is first baked in loaves then cut and baked again to achieve the crunchy texture everyone loves. The loaves are ready to cut when you can comfortably touch them and not get burned. Slice carefully on a diagonal in even slices and place the cookies flat on the baking sheet for the second baking.

1. Preheat oven to 325°F. Line a baking sheet with parchment.

2. Mix dry ingredients together.

3. Whisk eggs and extracts until foamy; add to dry ingredients. Mixture will be very thick and sticky.

4. Divide dough into 2 parts; shape into loaves 8" long and 2" high. Bake loaves 25 minutes, or until firm and golden. Cool.

5. Reduce oven to 300°F. Cut ½" thick on a diagonal; lay flat on baking sheet. Bake 20 more minutes, or until cookies are dry and crisp.

Peppermint Brownies

For a pretty presentation, color the peppermint layer pink. Be sure to chill these brownies thoroughly before cutting or the layers won't show up.

INGREDIENTS | **YIELDS 9 BROWNIES**

2 ounces unsweetened chocolate

½ cup unsalted butter

2 eggs

1 cup sugar

½ cup all-purpose flour

1½ cups confectioners' sugar

3 tablespoons unsalted butter

¼ cup cream

½–1 teaspoon peppermint extract, depending on taste

¼ teaspoon vanilla

⅓ cup cream

12 ounces chocolate chips

Crushed peppermint candies to garnish

1. Preheat oven to 350°F. Grease and flour 9" square baking dish.

2. Melt 2 ounces of chocolate with ½ cup butter. Stir until smooth. Cool.

3. Beat eggs and sugar. Blend in cooled chocolate and flour. Spread in pan; bake 20–25 minutes, or until a tester comes out clean. Cool completely.

4. Combine confectioners' sugar, 3 tablespoons of butter, ¼ cup of cream, and extracts; beat until smooth. Spread on cooled brownies. Chill until firm.

5. Bring ⅓ cup of cream to a simmer. Remove from heat. Stir in chocolate chips; stir until melted. Spread quickly over peppermint layer. Sprinkle with crushed peppermints. Chill.

Saltines

These crisp crackers are just as good with soup as the store-bought kind, maybe better. Sprinkle the tops with coarse salt, sesame seed, or leave plain.

INGREDIENTS | **YIELDS 100 CRACKERS**

2 cups all-purpose flour, whole-wheat flour, or a combination

1 teaspoon salt

½ teaspoon baking soda

¼ cup butter

1½ cups sour milk

1 egg

1. Preheat oven to 400°F. Lightly grease baking sheet.

2. Sift dry ingredients into a large bowl.

3. Cut in butter until coarse crumbs are formed. Add milk and egg; blend together.

4. Knead dough until smooth. Let rest 10 minutes. Roll very thin on a floured surface.

5. Cut in squares or other shapes; place on baking sheet and prick with a fork. Sprinkle with salt crystals if desired. Bake 10 minutes.

Sausalito Cookies

These cookies cook a little longer to achieve a crisper texture. If you like them soft and chewy, take them out a minute or two sooner. If you like them thinner and flatter, use all butter rather than part shortening.

INGREDIENTS | **YIELDS 40 COOKIES**

½ teaspoon baking powder
½ teaspoon salt
2½ cups all-purpose flour
½ cup unsalted butter
½ cup butter-flavored shortening
¾ cup brown sugar
¾ cup sugar
1 egg
1½ teaspoons vanilla
1 cup chopped macadamia nuts
12 ounces milk chocolate, chopped in large chunks

1. Preheat oven to 350°F. Lightly grease a baking sheet.

2. Whisk dry ingredients together in a bowl.

3. Beat butter and shortening until well blended. Beat in sugars until fluffy. Add egg and vanilla.

4. Add dry ingredients; blend well. Stir chocolate and nuts into dough.

5. Form 1" balls; place on baking sheet. Bake 15 minutes, or until they are done.

Twix

Shortbread topped with caramel and rich chocolate; what's not to like? For a great variation, add 1 cup chopped pecans over the melted caramel layer before you add the Ganache.

INGREDIENTS | **YIELDS 16 BARS**

Shortbread Layer
¾ cup unsalted butter
½ cup confectioners' sugar
1½ cups flour

Topping
1 (14-ounce) bag caramels
⅓ cup evaporated milk
¼ cup unsalted butter
1 recipe Ganache (page 544)

1. Preheat oven to 350°F. Lightly butter 9" square pan.

2. Blend ¾ cup butter, confectioners' sugar, and flour together until blended and crumbly. Press into bottom of pan.

3. Bake 10–15 minutes.

4. Melt caramel, evaporated milk, and ¼ cup butter together until smooth and blended. Spread over top of baked shortbread layer. Chill.

5. Spread warm Ganache over top of all. Chill. Cut into bars.

Windmill Cookies

Traditionally, this dough is shaped in a mold. If you don't have a mold you can use windmill-shaped cookie cutters.

INGREDIENTS	YIELDS 36 COOKIES

2 cups all-purpose flour

½ teaspoon baking powder

½ teaspoon salt

½ cup dark brown sugar

1 teaspoon cinnamon

½ teaspoon freshly ground nutmeg

¼ teaspoon cloves

⅛ teaspoon cardamom

⅛ teaspoon ginger

1 cup unsalted butter

¼ cup milk

Slivered almonds

1. Mix dry ingredients. Cut in butter; add milk.

2. Knead until a firm dough is formed. Chill overnight.

3. Preheat oven to 350°F. Line a baking sheet with foil.

4. Roll dough out to ¼" thickness on a floured surface. Cut with cookie cutters. Sprinkle with almonds.

5. Bake 15–20 minutes. Cool.

Windmill Cookies

Windmill cookies or Speculaas are a treat enjoyed by Dutch children on December 6, Saint Nicholas's feast day. The cookies can be made one of two ways: either rolled or sliced thin; or rolled into balls which are then rolled in sugar and flattened with the bottom of a glass. The first cookie is crispy in texture while the second is cake like.

Samoa Cookies

Melt-in-your-mouth Scottish shortbread is dipped in chocolate and then topped with caramel and coconut for an amazing taste. For best results, make the shortbread the day before you want to make these.

INGREDIENTS | YIELDS 30 COOKIES

2 cups chocolate chips

30 Scottish Shortbread cookies (page 493), baked and cooled

½ cup light corn syrup

½ cup sugar

⅓ cup unsalted butter

½ cup sweetened condensed milk

½ teaspoon vanilla

4 cups coconut, toasted

Ready a Candy Thermometer

When you are using a candy thermometer in cooking, it is important that you are able to read it accurately. Being off by even 2°F can sometimes ruin a recipe. Test your thermometer often for accuracy by placing it in a cup of boiling water. It should register 212°F. Read the thermometer by holding it up to eye level and quickly making note of the temperature.

1. Line a baking sheet with parchment. Melt chocolate chips, stirring until smooth.

2. Dip bottoms of cookies in chocolate. Place on parchment with chocolate side up. Put in refrigerator to harden.

3. Remove cookies from refrigerator. Turn them so chocolate side is down. Combine corn syrup, sugar, and butter. Heat mixture to a full boil, stirring constantly. Boil 3 minutes. Slowly add condensed milk, stirring constantly.

4. Cook over low heat until mixture registers 220°F on a candy thermometer. Remove from heat; stir in vanilla. Beat until creamy; add coconut, stirring to blend well.

5. Working quickly, place a spoonful of coconut mixture on top of cookies; gently press down with back of a spoon. Cool completely. Pipe stripes of melted chocolate across tops.

Not-Nutter Butters

Rather than flattening these with a fork as with other peanut butter cookies, try using a cookie stamp. You can find cookie stamps at many craft and baking supply stores.

INGREDIENTS | YIELDS 24 COOKIES

½ cup shortening
⅔ cup sugar
1 egg
½ teaspoon salt
3 tablespoons creamy peanut butter
½ cup oats
1 cup flour
2 tablespoons graham cracker crumbs
1 cup creamy peanut butter
1½ cups sifted powdered sugar
Milk if needed to thin filling

Fancy Sandwich Cookies

Sandwich cookies are special even when they are plain, but you can make them fancy for special days by embellishing them with chocolate. Try dipping half the cookie in melted chocolate and letting it set, or even sprinkling it with chopped nuts while the chocolate is still warm. You can also pipe stripes of melted chocolate across the top. Try different flavored chips for different cookies.

1. Preheat oven to 325°F.

2. Cream shortening and sugar together until fluffy. Add egg, salt, and peanut butter; blend well.

3. Process oats until they are a fine powder. Add with flour to shortening mixture; blend until smooth. Roll into 1" balls; place on cookie sheet. Flatten with a fork or glass dipped in sugar.

4. Bake 8–10 minutes. Cool.

5. Mix filling ingredients: graham cracker crumbs, 1 cup peanut butter, and powdered sugar. You may need to add up to ¼ cup milk, a tablespoon at a time, to get the correct consistency for spreading. Sandwich 2 cookies, flat sides together, with filling.

N'Oreos

These taste very much like Oreos. Change the flavor of the filling to come up with your own variations. Some suggestions are: coffee, chocolate, strawberry, peanut butter, or raspberry.

INGREDIENTS | **YIELDS 24 COOKIES**

1 cup Hershey's Special Dark cocoa, divided use, no substitutions

1¼ cups sugar

¾ cup unsalted butter

1 teaspoon salt

1 teaspoon espresso powder

1 egg

1 tablespoon water or coffee

1 teaspoon vanilla

1½ cups all-purpose flour

1¼ teaspoons unflavored gelatin

2 tablespoons cold water

½ cup vegetable shortening

1 teaspoon vanilla

2½ cups confectioners' sugar

1. Preheat oven to 325°F. Line baking sheets with parchment.

2. Place ¼ cup cocoa and ¼ cup sugar in a bowl; set aside.

3. Beat remaining sugar, butter, salt, and espresso until fluffy. Beat in egg, water, and vanilla. Stir in flour and remaining cocoa. Roll 2 teaspoons of dough into balls; put in sugar and cocoa mixture. Shake bowl until balls are thoroughly coated.

4. Place on baking sheets; press flat with a glass dipped in cocoa mixture. The cookies should be about ⅛" thick. Bake 18 minutes; be careful not to scorch. Cool completely.

5. Soften gelatin in water. Beat shortening, vanilla, and confectioners' sugar until smooth. Add dissolved gelatin; beat until smooth. Place a teaspoon of filling between two cookies; refrigerate. Cookies should be stored in refrigerator.

Famous A's Chocolate Chip

*These are made in small, grape-sized balls that cook into about 12 dozen
tiny cookies. For larger cookies use a rounded teaspoon.*

INGREDIENTS | **YIELDS 144 COOKIES**

½ cup unsalted butter
½ cup shortening
1 cup light brown sugar
1 cup sugar
3 eggs
1 tablespoon vanilla
1 cup cornstarch
3 cups Bisquick biscuit mix
½ cup nonfat dry milk powder
2 tablespoons espresso powder
1 tablespoon cocoa
1 cup chopped pecans
12 ounces chocolate chips
½ cup coconut, optional

1. Preheat oven to 350°F. Lightly grease baking sheets.

2. Cream butter and shortening until blended. Add both sugars; beat until creamy. Beat in eggs and vanilla.

3. Whisk dry ingredients together; stir into butter mixture. Stir in pecans, chocolate chips, and coconut, if desired.

4. Form into grape-sized balls; place on cookie sheets.

5. Bake 12 minutes, or until done.

Monster Cookies

You can make huge, bistro-style cookies by using an ice cream scoop to scoop out about ¼ cup of cookie dough and placing it 3 apart on the baking sheets. Bake the cookies for about 3–5 minutes more than called for in the original recipe. These big cookies make great ice cream sandwiches or just a generous after-school snack.

Nilla Wafers

Theses are perfect cookies to pair with traditional banana pudding or to eat with a glass of milk. An easy way to get these shaped and sized correctly is to use a pastry bag and pipe them onto the baking sheets. Make them quarter sized for the best results.

INGREDIENTS | **YIELDS 24 COOKIES**

½ cup unsalted butter
1 cup sugar
1 egg
1 tablespoon vanilla
1⅓ cups all-purpose flour
¾ teaspoon baking soda
¼ teaspoon salt
Pinch of freshly grated nutmeg, optional

1. Preheat oven to 350°F.

2. Cream butter and sugar. Beat in egg and vanilla.

3. Mix dry ingredients; blend into butter mixture.

4. Drop by teaspoon-sized cookie scoop onto ungreased baking sheets.

5. Bake 12–15 minutes, or until edges are brown.

Color Your World

Vanilla wafers are a very basic cookie. For a special effect, you can color the dough with paste food colors. With the paste colors the dough can be made either pastel or very bright colors by varying the amount of food coloring you add to the dough. You can make several colors of cookies by separating the dough into several bowls and coloring each individually.

Grandma's Molasses Cookies

These large, chewy cookies are full of old-fashioned flavor. Use turbinado sugar for rolling the balls of dough—this will give a nice crunch to the finished cookie.

INGREDIENTS | **YIELDS 24 COOKIES**

½ cup unsalted butter
½ cup shortening
¾ cup Grandma's unsulfured molasses
3 cups dark brown sugar
2 eggs
3 cups all-purpose flour
½ teaspoon salt
1 tablespoon baking soda
1½ teaspoons cinnamon
1 teaspoon cloves
1½ teaspoons ginger
½ cup chopped candied ginger, optional
½ cup sugar for rolling

1. Beat butter and shortening until blended. Beat in molasses and sugar until creamy; beat in eggs one at a time.

2. Whisk together dry ingredients. Add to creamed mixture; blend thoroughly. Stir in candied ginger, if using.

3. Chill, covered tightly, 30 minutes. Meanwhile, lightly grease baking sheets.

4. Preheat oven to 350°F. Using a tablespoon, measure out chilled dough and roll into balls. Roll balls in sugar.

5. Place dough on baking sheets. Bake 10–12 minutes, or until firm to touch but not overcooked. Cool completely.

Kit Kat Bars

These come pretty close to the candy bar. They are best when they are eaten the same day as they are made.

INGREDIENTS | **YIELDS 18 BARS**

16 ounces Club or Ritz crackers
1 cup light brown sugar
⅓ cup sugar
2 cups graham cracker crumbs
1 cup unsalted butter
½ cup milk
1 cup chocolate chips
1 cup butterscotch chips
¾ cup peanut butter

Snack Packs

If you are making cookies or bars ahead of time for school lunches, store them in snack bags by serving sizes. Place all of the snack bags in a large, food-grade container and just grab a snack bag to toss into the lunchbox when needed. The homemade cookies are healthier, tastier, and save money, too.

1. Line 13" × 9" pan with parchment. Lay a single layer of Club or Ritz crackers on bottom.

2. Mix brown sugars, sugar, graham cracker crumbs, butter, and milk. Bring to a boil; boil 5 minutes, stirring.

3. Pour half mixture over crackers; add another layer of crackers. Repeat layers once more.

4. Melt remaining ingredients together until smooth, stirring constantly. Spread over top cracker layer.

5. Chill. Cut into bars.

Zweiback

These are very much like biscotti, except that they have yeast in them to help with the rising. Use them just as you would commercial zwieback.

INGREDIENTS	YIELDS 24 COOKIES

2 tablespoons active dry yeast

2 tablespoons sugar

½ cup warm water

2 cups milk, lukewarm

1½ teaspoons salt

2 tablespoons sugar

2 egg yolks, beaten

8 cups flour, approximately

½ cup unsalted butter

1 teaspoon cinnamon

1. Dissolve yeast and 2 tablespoons of sugar in warm water.

2. Mix milk, salt, and 2 tablespoons of sugar; add to yeast mixture. Beat in egg yolks.

3. Add 3 cups flour; mix thoroughly. Continue to add flour until you have a smooth dough. Knead until dough is elastic. Set aside to rise for 1 hour.

4. Preheat oven to 400°F. Shape dough into 1½" thick loaves. Allow to rise until double. Bake 12 minutes. Cool.

5. Cut diagonally into ½" thick slices. Lay slices on a cookie sheet; brush with melted butter mixed with cinnamon. Bake 12 minutes. Let cool.

CHAPTER 28

Kids Can Bake!

Handprint Cookies

The actual yield of this recipe will depend on how big the handprints are. This is an especially fun rainy day recipe. Have some tubes of icing on "hand" to make rings, fingernail polish, and gloves.

INGREDIENTS | **YIELDS 24 COOKIES**

3 cups all-purpose flour
1 teaspoon baking soda
2 teaspoons cream of tartar
1 cup unsalted butter
2 eggs
1 cup sugar
2 teaspoons vanilla
Sugar crystals for sprinkling

Teaching Tip #1

Handprint cookies are a tasty way to teach the basics of American Sign Language. Just make cardboard templates of the alphabet and cut around them. Bake the cookies and write the corresponding letter in the palm of the hand with frosting. It's a fun way to get practice with signing.

1. Whisk flour, baking soda, and cream of tartar together. Cut in butter until it looks like coarse crumbs.

2. Beat eggs, 1 cup of sugar, and vanilla until frothy. Stir into flour mixture. Chill 30 minutes. Meanwhile, lightly grease baking sheets.

3. Preheat oven to 350°F. Divide dough into fourths. Roll each out ¼" thick on a floured surface. Carefully cut around your child's hand. Continue until all dough is used up.

4. Place on baking sheets; sprinkle with sugar. Bake 10–12 minutes.

5. Cool completely. Decorate as desired.

M&M's Cookies

M&M's cookies will be much prettier if you hold out about ⅓ of the M&M's and immediately press a few of them into the tops of the cookies when they come from the oven.

INGREDIENTS | YIELDS 48 COOKIES

1 cup unsalted butter
1 cup dark brown sugar, packed
1 cup sugar
2 eggs
2½ teaspoons vanilla
½ teaspoon salt
1 teaspoon baking powder
1 teaspoon baking soda
3 cups all-purpose flour
2 cups plain M&M's

1. Preheat oven to 350°F. Lightly grease a baking sheet.

2. Cream together butter and sugars. Add eggs one at a time, blending well after each addition. Add vanilla.

3. Whisk dry ingredients together; stir into butter mixture until blended.

4. Stir in M&M's. Drop by rounded teaspoonfuls on baking sheet.

5. Bake 8–10 minutes, or until just barely done. Remove and cool.

Thumbprint Cookies

You may substitute almost any jam for the raspberry. Apricot, cherry preserves, or poppy seed filling all add a delicious sweetness to these pretty cookies.

INGREDIENTS | YIELDS 36 COOKIES

1 cup unsalted butter
½ cup brown sugar
2 egg yolks
½ teaspoon vanilla
½ teaspoon almond
2 cups all-purpose flour
¼ teaspoon salt
1¼ cups finely chopped pecans or walnuts
½ cup raspberry jam

1. Preheat oven to 350°F. Line a baking sheet with parchment.

2. Mix butter and sugar until light and fluffy. Add egg yolks, vanilla, and almond.

3. Whisk dry ingredients together. Stir into creamed mixture until well blended. Form into 1" balls; roll in chopped nuts. Arrange on baking sheet.

4. Bake 5 minutes. Press thumb down to dent each cookie; fill indentation with jam.

5. Bake 8–10 more minutes. Remove from oven and cool completely.

Cookies on a Stick

Cookies on a stick are great for parties or to give as special-occasion bouquets. Be sure to get the stick about halfway in the cookie so that it will hold firmly.

INGREDIENTS | YIELDS 48 COOKIES

1 cup butter-flavor shortening

1 cup sugar

2 eggs

2 teaspoons vanilla

½ teaspoon almond

3 cups flour

2 teaspoons baking powder

½ teaspoon salt

1 tablespoon milk, if needed.

48 popsicle or lollipop sticks, approximately 9"–11" long

Cookie Bouquets

To make a cookie bouquet, use a basket that has dry floral foam fit into it. Place some Easter grass or other covering over the foam. Arrange baked cookies in the basket by gently pushing the sticks into the floral foam until the cookie is securely in place. Cut the lollipop sticks to different heights for a more interesting arrangement. Carefully wrap the entire basket in cellophane or tulle and secure at the top with a pretty bow.

1. Cream together shortening and sugar until fluffy. Add eggs, vanilla, and almond; beat until well mixed.

2. Mix dry ingredients together; add to creamed mixture. Add milk if dough is too dry. Chill overnight.

3. Preheat oven to 350°F. Line a baking sheet with parchment.

4. Roll dough about ⅜" thick on a lightly floured surface; cut with cookie cutters. Lay cookies on baking sheet; insert lollipop sticks halfway into cookie.

5. Bake 8–10 minutes. Cool completely. Decorate as desired.

ABC Cookies

The number of cookies you get will depend on the size of the cookie cutters. If you don't have ABC cookie cutters, you can make templates from cardboard and cut around them.

INGREDIENTS | YIELDS 36 COOKIES

¼ cup shortening

¼ cup unsalted butter

1 cup sugar

1 egg

1 teaspoon vanilla

2⅔ cups all-purpose flour

1 teaspoon baking powder

½ teaspoon baking soda

½ teaspoon salt

½ teaspoon cinnamon

¼ teaspoon freshly grated nutmeg

½ cup sour cream

1. Preheat oven to 400°F. Lightly grease baking sheets.

2. Blend shortening and butter together until creamy. Add sugar; beat until light and fluffy. Add egg and vanilla.

3. Whisk dry ingredients together; add to butter mixture alternately with sour cream, beginning and ending with flour.

4. Roll dough on a lightly floured surface; cut with cookie cutters. Place on baking sheet.

5. Bake 6–8 minutes, or until lightly browned. Cool completely.

Teaching Tip #2

Use firm, rolled cookie dough to teach geography. Just roll out the dough and cut one large cookie the shape of the country you are studying. Bake the cookie as the recipe directs, adding time as needed to make sure the cookie is completely baked. Cool. Carefully remove the cookie from the baking sheet and let your children use frosting bags and decorator tips to mark rivers, lakes, major cities, and capitals.

Ranger Cookies

These are very versatile cookies. You can change the type of cereal, the type of chips, the type of nuts, or leave them out altogether. Try making this with granola rather than cornflakes.

INGREDIENTS | **YIELDS 60 COOKIES**

1 cup shortening
1 cup sugar
1 cup brown sugar
2 eggs
1 teaspoon vanilla
2 cups all-purpose flour
2 teaspoons baking soda
1 teaspoon baking powder
½ teaspoon salt
2 cups corn flakes
2 cups quick-cooking oats
1 cup coconut
1 cup butterscotch chips
1 cup chopped pecans

1. Preheat oven to 350°F. Lightly grease cookie sheets.

2. Cream shortening and sugars until smooth. Beat in eggs and vanilla.

3. Whisk together flour, baking soda, baking powder, and salt; add to shortening mixture.

4. Fold in remaining ingredients. Drop by tablespoons on baking sheet.

5. Bake 10–12 minutes, or until done. Middles should be slightly soft.

Pink Lemonade Cookies

For more lemony flavor, you can make a lemon glaze with confectioners' sugar and some of the thawed lemonade. Just mix until it reaches the right consistency and spread on the cooled cookies.

INGREDIENTS | **YIELDS 36 COOKIES**

1 cup unsalted butter
1 cup sugar
2 eggs
3 cups all-purpose flour
1 teaspoon baking soda
1 (12-ounce) can frozen pink lemonade, thawed and divided
A few drops of red food coloring
Pink-colored sugar

1. Preheat oven to 375°F. Line a baking sheet with parchment.

2. Cream butter and sugar until fluffy. Beat in eggs.

3. Combine flour and baking soda; add to butter mixture. Add ¾ cup of lemonade and a few drops of food coloring if needed to make dough pink.

4. Drop by rounded teaspoonfuls on baking sheet.

5. Bake 8–10 minutes, or until done. Brush with more lemonade and sprinkle with sugar.

Tie-Dye Cookies

These tie-dye cookies are fun to make and to eat. Be sure to use a wide brush and paint the dough randomly for the best look. No need to chill this simple dough.

INGREDIENTS | **YIELDS 60 COOKIES**

1 cup unsalted butter
1 cup sugar
2 eggs
1½ teaspoons vanilla
3 cups all-purpose flour
½ teaspoon baking powder
½ teaspoon baking soda
Pinch of salt
3 recipes of Egg Yolk Paint (page 549). Use 3 different colors.
Clean paint brushes
Newspaper to catch drips

1. Preheat oven to 350°F. Lightly grease baking sheets.

2. Cream butter and sugar until light and fluffy. Add eggs and vanilla.

3. Sift together dry ingredients; add to creamed mixture. Blend well. Divide dough in half; roll each half out on a floured surface.

4. Using a clean brush, paint swirls and streaks of color on dough. Use a clean brush for each color. Paint until there is little or no plain dough showing. Allow to stand 10 minutes.

5. Cut dough in desired shapes; bake 10–12 minutes, or until done. Gather the scraps of dough and reroll. Cut with cutters. Repeat until all dough is used.

Easy One-Bowl Brownies

These easy brownies go together quickly and without a lot of mess. Most eight to ten year olds can make these by themselves if they have had some experience in the kitchen.

INGREDIENTS | **YIELDS 24 BROWNIES**

4 squares unsweetened chocolate

¾ cup unsalted butter

2 cups sugar

3 eggs

1 teaspoon vanilla

1 cup all-purpose flour

1 cup chopped pecans

1 cup chocolate chips

Start with Success

When your child is just beginning to bake on her own, it is good to make the shift from head chef to sous chef. By becoming her assistant, you will allow her to develop cooking skills in a safe environment while allowing her to be in charge. Celebrate her first solo cooking adventure with an apron and a whisk of her own.

1. Preheat oven to 350°F. Grease 13" × 9" pan.

2. In a large microwave-safe bowl, microwave unsweetened chocolate and butter, stirring once a minute, until butter is melted. This should take about 2 minutes. Remove from microwave; stir until chocolate is melted and smooth.

3. Stir in sugar. Blend in eggs and vanilla. Add flour, nuts, and chocolate chips.

4. Spoon into pan, smoothing top. Bake 30–35 minutes, or until a toothpick inserted in center comes out with just a few crumbs sticking to it.

5. Cool completely. Cut into bars.

Honey Raisin Bars

Wholesome honey raisin bars provide lots of B vitamins and iron. Dried cranberries can be substituted for the raisins if you like.

INGREDIENTS | YIELDS 48 BARS

¾ cup unsalted butter
½ cup sugar
½ cup brown sugar
2 eggs
½ cup honey
1 teaspoon vanilla
1 cup all-purpose flour
½ cup whole-wheat flour
1 teaspoon baking powder
1 teaspoon baking soda
1 teaspoon salt
2 teaspoons cinnamon
½ teaspoon freshly grated nutmeg
½ teaspoon allspice
¼ teaspoon cloves
¾ cup quick oats
1 cup raisins
1 cup walnuts, chopped
Confectioners' sugar for rolling

1. Preheat oven to 375°F. Lightly grease 15" × 10" jelly roll pan.

2. Cream butter and sugars until light and fluffy. Mix in eggs one at a time. Beat in honey and vanilla.

3. Whisk flours, baking powder, baking soda, salt, and spices together; gradually add to creamed mixture. Blend well; stir in remaining ingredients.

4. Spoon evenly in prepared pan; bake 18–20 minutes, or until done.

5. Cool. Cut into bars and roll in confectioners' sugar

Wholesome Whole Wheat

Whole-wheat flour is full of B vitamins. It can be substituted for part of the all-purpose flour in most cookie recipes. For every cup of all-purpose flour called for in a recipe, use ¾ cup all-purpose flour and ¼ cup of whole wheat flour. This works especially well for bar cookies.

Joe Froggers

Joe Froggers are a recipe that dates from colonial times. Use a coffee can with the ends cut out of it for a cookie cutter to create the traditional plate-sized cookies. They keep for a long time.

INGREDIENTS | **YIELDS 36 COOKIES**

3½ cups all-purpose flour
1½ teaspoons salt
1½ teaspoons ginger
1 teaspoon baking soda
½ teaspoon cloves
½ teaspoon freshly grated nutmeg
¼ teaspoon allspice
½ cup shortening
1 cup light brown sugar
1 cup molasses
⅓ cup hot coffee
2 tablespoons dark rum

1. Mix dry ingredients.

2. Beat together shortening, sugar, and molasses. Mix coffee and rum; add to shortening mixture, alternating with flour mixture. If dough is too dry, add a little water or coffee.

3. Roll dough out between 2 sheets of wax paper. Refrigerate several hours.

4. Preheat oven to 375°F. Cut dough with large round cutters; place on lightly greased baking sheets.

5. Bake 15–20 minutes for large cookies, 10–15 minutes for smaller sizes.

Cookie Pizza

*Almost anything you can imagine can be added as a topping to this pizza.
Try sprinkling with graham cracker crumbs or adding peanut butter cups.*

INGREDIENTS | YIELDS 16 COOKIES

⅓ cup unsalted butter

1 cup brown sugar

1 egg

1 tablespoon hot water

1 teaspoon vanilla

1 cup all-purpose flour

½ teaspoon baking powder

½ cup chopped walnuts

½ cup M&M's

1 cup chocolate chips

1 cup mini marshmallows

1. Preheat oven to 350°F. Grease two 9" pie pans.

2. Melt butter; combine with brown sugar in a mixing bowl. Beat at medium speed until well blended; add egg, hot water, and vanilla.

3. Whisk dry ingredients together; mix into sugar mixture. Split dough in half; spread each half in one pie pan, covering the bottom and up the sides.

4. Sprinkle each pizza with half the toppings.

5. Bake 20 minutes, or until golden. Cut each into 8 slices.

Blueberry Crumble Bars

*Many different fruits can be substituted for the blueberries. Any seasonal fresh fruit
will work well in these bars; just chop large fruit like apples in small pieces.*

INGREDIENTS | YIELDS 24 BARS

1 cup sugar

3 cups all-purpose flour

1 teaspoon baking powder

¼ teaspoon salt

Zest of one lemon

1 cup unsalted butter

1 egg

1½ tablespoons cornstarch

½ cup sugar

4 cups blueberries

2 tablespoons lemon juice

1 cup white chocolate

1. Preheat oven to 375°F. Grease 13" × 9" pan.

2. Mix 1 cup of sugar, flour, baking powder, salt, and lemon zest. Cut in butter and beaten egg until mixture resembles coarse crumbs. Press half of mixture in bottom of pan.

3. Stir together cornstarch, remaining ½ cup sugar, blueberries, and lemon juice. Spoon blueberry mixture evenly over crust.

4. Sprinkle remaining crumb mixture on top. Bake 45–50 minutes. Cool completely.

5. Melt white chocolate in microwave, stirring until smooth. Drizzle over top. Cut into bars.

Oatmeal Carmelitas

These bars are very rich. A delicious variation is to leave off the chocolate chips and add 1 cup chopped apple instead.

INGREDIENTS | **YIELDS 36 BARS**

Crust

1 cup all-purpose flour
½ teaspoon baking soda
1 cup quick-cooking oats
¾ cup brown sugar
¼ teaspoon salt
¾ cup melted butter

Topping

½ cup chocolate chips
1 cup chopped pecans
¾ cup caramel ice cream topping
3 tablespoons all-purpose flour

1. Preheat oven to 350°F. Grease 9" square pan.

2. Mix together 1 cup flour, baking soda, oats, brown sugar, salt, and melted butter; toss with a fork until crumbly. Press half mixture firmly in bottom of pan.

3. Bake 10 minutes.

4. Sprinkle chocolate chips and chopped nuts over crust. Mix caramel ice cream topping with 3 tablespoons flour. Spoon over chocolate chips.

5. Top with rest of oatmeal mixture. Bake 15 minutes. Let bars cool completely.

Chopping Nuts

If nuts need to be chopped for a recipe, you can chop them in a food processor or blender. Just add about 2 tablespoons of the flour called for in the recipe and pulse until the nuts are the size that you want. The flour will keep them from getting gummy and turning into nut butter.

Tiger Cookies

*These deep chocolate cookies have a white crackle coating. Add
2 teaspoons of espresso powder if you like a mocha flavor.*

INGREDIENTS | **YIELDS 48 COOKIES**

½ cup vegetable oil

1½ cups sugar

3 eggs

½ cup Hershey's Special Dark cocoa

1½ teaspoons vanilla

2 cups all-purpose flour

1½ teaspoons baking powder

½ teaspoon salt

Confectioners' sugar

48 Hershey's Kisses, unwrapped

1. Stir together oil and sugar. Beat in eggs, cocoa, and vanilla until mixture is smooth.

2. Whisk flour, baking powder, and salt together; blend into cocoa mixture. Chill overnight.

3. Preheat oven to 350°F. Line a baking sheet with parchment.

4. Form dough into 1" balls; roll in confectioners' sugar to coat. Bake 10–12 minutes.

5. Immediately push a Kiss on top of each cookie when they come from oven. Cool.

Why Chill the Dough Overnight?

You can often cut corners when chilling cookie dough by putting it in the freezer for thirty minutes or so to save time. This does help make the dough more workable, but allowing the dough to rest overnight allows any gluten in the dough to relax; this creates a more tender cookie. Allowing the dough to chill for a longer period of time also allows the flavors to blend and develop.

CHAPTER 29

Homemade for the Holidays

Linzer Hearts

These delicate cookies are beautiful for Valentine's Day. Substitute 1 teaspoon of rose water for the vanilla for an old-fashioned taste.

INGREDIENTS | **YIELDS 24 COOKIES**

¾ cup unsalted butter
½ cup sugar
½ teaspoon lemon rind
1 egg
½ teaspoon vanilla
¼ teaspoon almond flavoring
1½ cups finely ground almonds
2¼ cups cake flour
½ teaspoon baking powder
½ teaspoon cinnamon
1 cup raspberry jam
Confectioners' sugar for dusting

1. Cream butter. Add sugar, lemon, egg, vanilla, almond, and ground nuts; beat until creamy.

2. Whisk dry ingredients together; blend in. Chill dough overnight, tightly wrapped.

3. Preheat oven to 350°F. Line a baking sheet with parchment.

4. Roll dough on a lightly floured surface to ⅛" thickness. Cut with heart-shaped cookie cutters. Cut 3 holes in half of the cookies using a thimble. Place on cookie sheets; bake 12 minutes.

5. Heat jam; spread a layer on solid cookies. Press a cookie with holes in it on top. Fill holes with more jam. Sprinkle with powdered sugar when cool.

M&M's Cookie Mix in a Jar

Cookie mix in a jar makes wonderful gifts for any occasion. Be sure to pack the ingredients down tightly so they will fit into the jar.

INGREDIENTS | **YIELDS 36 COOKIES**

1¼ cups sugar

1¼ cups M&M's

2 cups all-purpose flour

½ teaspoon baking soda

½ teaspoon baking powder

Wide-mouth, quart Mason jar with top

Cardstock for printing instructions

Raffia

Baking instructions (page 557) to print and add to jar

1. Using a canning funnel, put sugar in jar. Use a small meat mallet to tamp it down tightly.

2. Pour M&M's in jar.

3. Mix dry ingredients; pour over M&M's. Press down firmly.

4. Screw lid on jar.

5. Copy instructions (page 557) and print on cardstock. Tie instructions to jar with raffia.

Shelf Life

Cookie mix in a jar has about a six month shelf life if kept in a cool dry place. Check the baking powder and baking soda that you use to make sure they are not near the expiration date. When there are nuts in the mix, it is better to use it within three months to be sure the nuts do not get rancid.

White Chocolate-Cranberry Cookie Mix in a Jar

*Rather than layering this in a jar, you can mix it in a zip-top bag
and put it in a pretty container with the instructions.*

INGREDIENTS | **YIELDS 18 COOKIES**

1⅛ cups all-purpose flour
½ teaspoon baking soda
½ teaspoon salt
½ cup rolled oats
⅓ cup white sugar
⅓ cup brown sugar
½ cup dried cranberries
½ cup white chocolate chips
½ cup chopped pecans
1 wide-mouth Mason jar with lid
Instructions (page 557)
Raffia
Cardstock for printing instructions

1. Layer ingredients in jar in order given. Press down between each later.

2. Put top on jar.

3. Print instructions and tie to jar with raffia.

Brownie Mix in a Jar

*Wipe the inside of the jar after adding the cocoa. If you don't, the cocoa
will coat the inside of the jar and the layers won't show up.*

INGREDIENTS | **YIELDS 24 BROWNIES**

1 teaspoon baking powder
1 teaspoon salt
1¼ cups all-purpose flour
⅔ cup cocoa powder
2¼ cups sugar
½ cup chopped pecans
1 quart-sized, wide-mouth Mason jar
Instructions (page 559)
Raffia
Cardstock for printing instructions

1. Mix together baking powder, salt, and flour. Pour into jar.

2. Add the cocoa powder. Press down firmly.

3. Add sugar.

4. Top with pecans.

5. Close jar; add raffia and printed tag.

Stained Glass Cookies

If you are going to hang these pretty cookies, poke a small hole in the tops with a straw before baking.

INGREDIENTS | YIELDS 48 COOKIES

½ cup unsalted butter

½ cup sugar

¼ cup brown sugar

1 egg

1 tablespoon Grandma's molasses

1 teaspoon vanilla

2 cups all-purpose flour

¼ teaspoon salt

1 teaspoon baking powder

½ teaspoon freshly grated nutmeg

35 hard candies in different colors (Life Savers work well)

Cookie Decor

Stained glass cookies look especially pretty when a ribbon is threaded through the hole in the top and the cookies are hung in a window where the light shines through them. They can also be hung on the tree as special treats for the little ones to find.

1. Cream butter and sugars until light and fluffy. Add egg, molasses, and vanilla; blend well.

2. Blend in dry ingredients. Chill 1–2 hours.

3. Preheat oven to 375°F. Line a baking sheet with parchment. Break candies into a powder. Do this easily by putting all candies of one color in a zip-top bag and pounding with a meat mallet. Repeat for each color.

4. Roll out dough on a floured surface to ¼" thick. Cut into desired shapes. Using small cookie cutters, cut shapes. Place cookies on baking sheet; fill cutout areas with crushed candies.

5. Bake 8–10 minutes. Cool cookies completely in pans or candy will break off and separate from cookies.

Christmas Wreaths

To make Valentines hearts, you can substitute red food coloring for the green and shape the warm mixture into heart shapes.

INGREDIENTS | YIELDS 18 COOKIES

1 pound marshmallows
½ cup unsalted butter
1 teaspoon vanilla
1–2 teaspoons green food coloring
4½ cups cornflakes
1 package little cinnamon candies
Red shoelace candy, optional

1. In a pan over low heat, melt marshmallows, butter, vanilla, and food coloring. Stir until well blended.

2. Stir in cornflakes; blend well, coating all of cereal.

3. Drop by spoonfuls onto wax paper. Shape a hole in center with your fingers.

4. Press cinnamon candies into wreaths while still warm.

5. Tie shoelace candy into bows and press into warm wreaths. Let cool.

Chocolate-Covered Toffee Shortbread

These melt-in-your-mouth cookies are rich with brickle flavor. You can sprinkle finely chopped toasted almonds on the chocolate while it is still warm.

INGREDIENTS | YIELDS 60 COOKIES

1 cup unsalted butter
¾ cup powdered sugar
2 teaspoons vanilla
2 cups all-purpose flour
¼ teaspoon baking powder
Pinch of salt
1 cup Heath, Bits 'O Brickle, or crushed almond brickle
2 cups chocolate chips, melted

1. Beat butter until creamy. Add sugar and vanilla.

2. Combine flour, baking powder, and salt; blend into butter mixture. Stir in brickle. Roll into logs; wrap in waxed paper and chill overnight.

3. Preheat oven to 350°F. Lightly grease baking sheets.

4. Cut rolls into ⅓" thick slices. Bake 10–12 minutes. Cool.

5. When cookies are cool, pour melted chocolate over tops, spreading to smooth. Let set.

Chocolate-Mint Whoopie Pies

These sell very well at holiday bake sales. Just wrap the cookies individually in cellophane and tie a ribbon around the top.

INGREDIENTS | YIELDS 20 COOKIES

1 recipe Whoopie Pies (page 308)
¾ cup unsalted butter
1 teaspoon vanilla
½ teaspoon mint extract
2¾ cupsconfectioners' sugar
3 cups marshmallow fluff
½ cup finely crushed peppermint candy, optional
2–4 drops green food coloring

1. Mix butter, vanilla, and mint flavoring until creamy. Add confectioners' sugar a little at a time. Mix in marshmallow cream, food coloring, and crushed candy.

2. Beat until filling is light and fluffy. Chill 30 minutes.

3. Spoon filling on flat side of half the Whoopie Pies.

4. Top with rest of cookies, rounded side up.

5. These keep at room temperature about 2 days. Freeze for longer storage.

Holiday Fruit Drops

These drop cookies are similar to fruit cake, and they keep very well for a long period of time.

INGREDIENTS | YIELDS 72 COOKIES

1 cup unsalted butter
2 cups brown sugar
2 eggs
1 tablespoon rum or brandy, optional
½ cup buttermilk
3½ cups all-purpose flour
1 teaspoon baking soda
1 teaspoon salt
2 cups halved candied cherries
2 cups chopped dates
1½ cups chopped pecans
72 pecan halves

1. Cream butter and sugar until light. Add eggs, rum or brandy (if using), and buttermilk.

2. Sift dry ingredients together; stir into butter mixture. Fold in fruit and pecans. Chill one hour.

3. Preheat oven to 350°F. Line a baking sheet with parchment.

4. Drop by teaspoon onto parchment. Gently press a pecan half in center of each cookie.

5. Bake 8–10 minutes. Allow to cool completely.

Spritz Cookies

Use a cookie press to make pretty shapes with this soft cookie dough.
The dough may be colored with food coloring if you like.

INGREDIENTS | **YIELDS 36 COOKIES**

2¼ cups all-purpose flour
¼ teaspoon salt
¼ teaspoon cinnamon
1 cup unsalted butter
3 ounces cream cheese, softened
1 cup sugar
1 egg yolk
1 teaspoon vanilla
½ teaspoon almond

1. Preheat oven to 350°F. Sift dry ingredients together.

2. Blend butter and cream cheese. Beat in sugar until fluffy. Add egg, vanilla, and almond.

3. Fill a cookie press or pastry bag with dough; form cookies on an ungreased cookie sheet.

4. Bake 12–15 minutes. Cookies should be golden on the bottoms.

5. Cool completely.

Puttin' on the Spritz

Spritz cookies are delicate cookies that are beautiful when embellished. You can dip half of a cookie in chocolate, spread a layer of chocolate on the bottom of the cookie, or drizzle the cookie with chocolate stripes.

Gingerbread Houses

This dough can be used for one large gingerbread house or about six dozen gingerbread cookies.

INGREDIENTS | YIELDS 1 HOUSE

1½ cups heavy cream

1 teaspoon vanilla

2½ cups brown sugar

1⅓ cups Grandma's molasses

2 tablespoons baking soda

1 tablespoon ginger

2 teaspoons cinnamon

1 teaspoon cloves

½ teaspoon cayenne, optional

9 cups all-purpose flour

Royal Icing (page 547)

Poster board to make templates

Instructions (page 561) for assembling a gingerbread house

1. Whip cream and vanilla until it is thick and holds peaks. Beat in brown sugar and molasses.

2. Mix dry ingredients into cream mixture. Chill 30 minutes.

3. Preheat oven to 300°F. Line a baking sheet with parchment.

4. Roll dough out into large rectangles ⅛" thick. Bake 30 minutes. Place templates on cookie rectangles and cut out carefully around templates.

5. Return cookies to oven for 30 minutes. Cool completely. Assemble according to instructions on page 561.

Instant Gingerbread Houses

You can make gingerbread houses with graham crackers. Just cut the crackers in the correct shapes and use the royal icing to glue them together. It will take eight squares for one house, or two long crackers and four square ones. This is a great project to do with kids because the houses go together quickly.

Pumpkin Pie Biscotti

*If you love the flavor of ginger, ½ cup finely chopped, candied
ginger can be added to these festive biscotti.*

INGREDIENTS | YIELDS 84 COOKIES

3½ cups all-purpose flour

1½ cups brown sugar

2 teaspoons baking powder

½ teaspoon salt

2 teaspoons pumpkin pie spice

½ cup pumpkin puree, either fresh,
frozen, or canned

2 eggs

1 tablespoon vanilla

1 cup chopped pecans

2 cups white chocolate chips, melted

Quick Gift Idea

It is nice to have small gifts to give to unexpected company. Pick up a few winter-themed coffee mugs at the dollar store and fill each of them with four or five biscotti standing on end. Set the mug on a large square of holiday cellophane and bring the edges up over the mug and the biscotti. Secure the top with a twist, then tape it. Tie a ribbon around the tape and add a tag. Since biscotti keep well, you can keep them on hand for last-minute gifts.

1. Preheat oven to 350°F. Line a baking sheet with parchment.

2. Combine dry ingredients; whisk until blended. In another bowl, combine pumpkin, eggs, and vanilla; blend well. Stir dry ingredients into pumpkin mixture. Add pecans.

3. Knead dough until it holds together. Divide into 4 portions; shape each into a rectangle about 12" long and 2" wide.

4. Bake 25–30 minutes. Cool 15 minutes; cut rectangles horizontally on a slight angle to form biscotti. Cut them about ½ thick for best results.

5. Reduce oven temperature to 300°F. Return biscotti to oven; bake 15 minutes. Cool completely; drizzle with melted white chocolate.

Cranberry Cookies

Cranberry cookies are a cake type of cookie. They are traditionally made with fresh cranberries, but dried cranberries can be substituted.

INGREDIENTS | YIELDS 48 COOKIES

1 cup unsalted butter
1 cup white sugar
½ cup brown sugar
1 egg
1 teaspoon orange zest, grated
2 tablespoons orange juice
2½ cups all-purpose flour
½ teaspoon baking soda
½ teaspoon salt
2 cups chopped cranberries
¾ cups chopped walnuts
½ teaspoon orange zest, grated
2 tablespoons orange juice
1 tablespoon melted butter
1½ cups confectioners' sugar

1. Preheat oven to 375°F.

2. Cream butter and sugars until fluffy. Add egg, 1 teaspoon of orange zest, and 2 tablespoons orange juice; beat until smooth.

3. Stir together dry ingredients; add to butter mixture. Beat until well blended. Mix in cranberries and walnuts.

4. Drop by tablespoons onto baking sheet, about 2" apart. Bake 12–15 minutes, or until edges of cookies are golden. Cool.

5. Mix orange juice, butter, and confectioners' sugar until smooth; spread on cooled cookies.

Almond Crescents

You can vary the nuts in these delicate cookies for different flavors. Just omit the almond extract and add another ½ teaspoon of vanilla.

INGREDIENTS | **YIELDS 60 COOKIES**

1 cup unsalted butter
⅔ cup confectioners' sugar
1 teaspoon vanilla extract
½ teaspoon almond extract
2⅓ cups all-purpose flour
1 cup almonds, finely chopped
Confectioners' sugar

1. Preheat oven to 350°F. Line a baking sheet with parchment.

2. Cream butter and confectioners' sugar together. Add vanilla and almond extracts. Stir in flour and almonds.

3. Using about 1 tablespoon of dough for each cookie, shape dough into crescents.

4. Bake 12–15 minutes, or until done.

5. Roll gently in confectioners' sugar while warm.

Fancy Crescents

Crescent cookies can be made even more festive by dipping them in melted chocolate or white chocolate. Just dip half the cookie in the melted candy and then roll in finely chopped nuts, colored jimmies, or anything else that suits you. Allow the chocolate to set before storing with wax paper between the layers.

Corn Flake Macaroons

These chewy and crispy macaroons have been popular since the recipe came out in the 1950s. Try to make them on a dry, sunny day for best results.

INGREDIENTS | **YIELDS 36 COOKIES**

3 egg whites, room temperature
¼ teaspoon cream of tartar
1 teaspoon vanilla
1⅓ cups sugar
1 cup chopped pecans
1 cup coconut
3 cups corn flakes

1. Preheat oven to 325°F. Spray baking sheets with cooking spray.

2. Beat egg whites until foamy. Stir in cream of tartar and vanilla.

3. Gradually add sugar while beating. Beat until stiff, glossy peaks form.

4. Carefully stir in pecans, coconut, and corn flakes. Drop by rounded tablespoonfuls onto baking sheet.

5. Bake 15 minutes. Remove from baking sheet immediately. Cool

Cherry Snowballs

These are a little tricky to do. Make sure that you drain and dry the cherries very well before wrapping them in the dough or the dough won't stay on.

INGREDIENTS | **YIELDS 18 COOKIES**

1 cup unsalted butter, room temperature
½ cup confectioners' sugar
1 tablespoon water
2 teaspoons vanilla
½ teaspoon almond flavoring
½ teaspoon salt
2½ cups all-purpose flour
½ cup ground almonds
36 maraschino cherries, stemmed and drained
1 cup white chocolate, melted

1. Preheat oven to 350°F.

2. Cream butter, confectioners' sugar, water, flavorings, and salt together. Add flour and ground almonds; mix well.

3. Take dough by teaspoonfuls and put a maraschino in middle. Wrap dough around cherry; set on an ungreased baking sheet.

4. Bake 10–15 minutes, or until golden.

5. Dip cookies halfway in melted white chocolate. Let cool.

What Are Maraschino Cherries?

Maraschino cherries are cherries that have been preserved in a sugar syrup and food-color solution, generally flavored with almond. Originally, they were a delicacy reserved for royalty. In the early 1900s they were preserved with alcohol, and thus were outlawed during prohibition. More than half the maraschinos in the United States are produced in Oregon.

Chocolate-Covered Cherry Cookies

These moist, chocolaty cookies taste like chocolate-covered cherries. To give them a little more panache, melt 1 cup of white chocolate chips and drizzle over the cookies after everything else is done.

INGREDIENTS | **YIELDS 18 COOKIES**

½ cup unsalted butter
1 cup sugar
1 egg
1½ teaspoons vanilla extract
1½ cups flour
¼ teaspoon salt
¼ teaspoon baking soda
¼ teaspoon baking powder
½ cup cocoa
1 cup chocolate chips
½ cup sweetened condensed milk
1 (10-ounce) jar maraschino cherries, drained, with juice reserved

1. Preheat oven to 350°F.

2. Beat butter and sugar. Add egg and vanilla; beat until creamy.

3. Stir in dry ingredients. Roll in 1" balls; place on a cookie sheet about 2" apart. Make an indentation with your thumb in middle of cookies.

4. Melt chocolate chips with condensed milk and one tablespoon cherry juice. Cool slightly. Place 1 teaspoon of chocolate in indentation of cookies. Press 1 cherry into chocolate. Cover cherries with 1 teaspoon more chocolate.

5. Bake 10 minutes. Cool.

Eggnog Cookies

Using whole nutmegs that you grate yourself is essential to the flavor in this recipe. They are simple to grate on a small grater.

INGREDIENTS | YIELDS 36 COOKIES

¾ cup sugar

¾ cup light brown sugar

¾ cup unsalted butter, room temperature

½ cup eggnog

1½ teaspoons vanilla

1 teaspoon rum or brandy extract

2 egg yolks

1 teaspoon nutmeg

½ teaspoon cinnamon

2¼ cups all-purpose flour

1 teaspoon baking powder

½ teaspoon cinnamon

1. Preheat oven to 375°F. Line a baking sheet with parchment.

2. Beat sugars, butter, eggnog, vanilla, rum or brandy, and egg yolks together until light and fluffy.

3. Combine dry ingredients; blend in until smooth.

4. Drop by rounded teaspoonfuls onto baking sheet.

5. Bake 6–8 minutes, or until done. Cool. Glaze with Confectioners' Glaze (page 547) if you wish.

Christmas Cookie Presentation

Christmas cookies look beautiful stacked in small muffin liners. It keeps them separate and gives a very professional look to a tin of cookies. You can also wrap three cookies in colored cellophane and tie with a ribbon. Place several packages of the cookies in a cookie tin or decorative basket.

Black and White Hearts

These are not the cake-like black and whites of New York fame, although the taste is very similar. This makes a crisp, rolled sugar cookie with a delicate orange flavor.

INGREDIENTS | **YIELDS 72 COOKIES**

4½ cups all-purpose flour

2 teaspoons baking powder

1 teaspoon baking soda

1 teaspoon salt

1 cup unsalted butter

2 cups sugar

4 eggs

1 teaspoon vanilla

2 tablespoons orange juice

6 cups confectioners' sugar

⅔ cup (more or less) boiling water

2 tablespoon butter

4 tablespoons corn syrup

1 tablespoon clear vanilla

¼ cup Hershey's Special Dark cocoa

1. Sift dry ingredients. Cream together butter and sugar until light and fluffy. Add eggs, vanilla, and orange juice; beat well.

2. Add dry ingredients; blend. Chill 2 hours.

3. Preheat oven to 425°F. Grease a cookie sheet. Roll dough out on floured surface; cut with heart-shaped cutter. Bake 8–10 minutes. Cool

4. Blend confectioners' sugar, boiling water, butter, corn syrup, and vanilla until smooth; separate into 2 batches. Add cocoa to one batch.

5. Spread half of a heart with the white icing and let dry. Spread the other half with the chocolate.

Cookie Ornaments

These gingerbread cookies are sturdy and will hold up to being hung on the Christmas tree. You can add ¼ teaspoon of almond extract for a richer flavor.

INGREDIENTS | YIELDS 36 COOKIES

½ cup unsalted butter
⅔ cup brown sugar
1 egg
⅓ cup Grandma's molasses
2¾ cups all-purpose flour
1 teaspoon baking soda
2 teaspoons cinnamon
1 teaspoon ginger
½ teaspoon freshly grated nutmeg
⅛ teaspoon cloves
Royal Icing (page 547)

1. Preheat oven to 375°F. Line a baking sheet with parchment.

2. Cream butter, brown sugar, egg, and molasses.

3. Combine dry ingredients; add to butter mixture. You may need to use a dough hook to mix it; this is very stiff dough.

4. Roll dough out; cut into desired shapes. Make holes in top with straws. Bake 6–8 minutes.

5. Decorate as desired with Royal Icing; allow to dry. Thread a ribbon through hole in top and hang on Christmas tree.

Pastel Bunny Cookies

You can leave the dough plain, or separate it and knead in the food coloring by hand for an assortment of colorful spring bunnies.

INGREDIENTS | YIELDS 48 COOKIES

1 cup unsalted butter
½ cup sugar
1 egg
½ teaspoon almond extract
½ teaspoon rose water
Assorted food coloring
2½ cups all-purpose flour
Pinch of salt
Confectioners' Glaze (page 547)

1. Cream butter until light. Add sugar; beat until fluffy. Add eggs, almond extract, and rose water. If you are going to make cookies all the same color, add a few drops of food coloring.

2. Blend in flour and salt. Cover and chill overnight.

3. Preheat oven to 350°F.

4. Roll dough about an ⅛" thick on a floured surface. Cut with bunny cookie cutter. Bake 8–10 minutes.

5. Cool. Glaze with tinted confectioners' glaze, if desired.

Edible Cookie Bowl

You can make these smaller and use them for fun ice cream bowls. Just spread melted chocolate on the inside and let it set before using.

INGREDIENTS | **YIELDS 1 BOWL**

⅓ cup shortening

⅓ cup butter

¾ cup sugar

1 egg

1 teaspoon vanilla

1 tablespoon milk

2½ cups all-purpose flour

1 teaspoon baking powder

Pinch of salt

Cookie Bowl Embellishment

You can embellish the cookie bowl a number of ways if you like. Use the scrap dough to cut out small shapes and glue to the bowl with royal icing. Use icing to make scallops and other designs on the bowl. You can even make extra dough and cut it to fit the top so that you have an enclosed box. It does have to be handled with care so it doesn't break.

1. Cream shortening and butter. Add sugar; beat until light and fluffy. Beat in egg, vanilla, and milk.

2. Sift dry ingredients together; stir into dough. Cover and chill several hours.

3. Preheat oven to 350°F. Roll dough on a floured surface. Cut into round cookies.

4. Invert a stainless steel bowl on a cookie sheet. Cover with aluminum foil and spray with no-stick spray. Starting at the bottom, overlap cookies on bowl until it is entirely covered.

5. Bake 10–15 minutes. Allow to cool completely before removing stainless steel bowl.

Cranberry-Pistachio Biscotti

If you don't want to use the pistachios, you can substitute the same amount of toasted almonds in this recipe.

INGREDIENTS | **YIELDS 36 COOKIES**

¼ cup oil
¾ cup sugar
2 eggs
2 teaspoons vanilla
½ teaspoon almond extract
1¾ cups flour
¼ teaspoon salt
1 teaspoon baking powder
¾ cup dried cranberries
1 cup unsalted pistachios

1. Preheat oven to 300°F. Line a baking sheet with parchment.

2. Mix oil and sugar until blended. Add eggs, vanilla, and almond extract. Stir dry ingredients together; whisk in. Add cranberries and pistachios.

3. Divide dough in half; form each half into 12" × 2" rectangle on parchment. Bake 35 minutes.

4. Remove from oven; cool 15 minutes.

5. Reduce oven to 275°F. Cut rectangles on an angle into ½" thick slices. Lay cookies on parchment; return to oven.

6. Bake about 10 more minutes. Cool completely.

Cherry Winks

For an even more festive look for Christmas time, use red maraschino cherries in half the cookies and green maraschino cherries in the other half.

INGREDIENTS | YIELDS 30 COOKIES

¾ cup shortening
1 cup sugar
2 eggs
2 tablespoons milk
1 teaspoon vanilla
2¼ cups all-purpose flour
1 teaspoon baking powder
½ teaspoon baking soda
½ teaspoon salt
1 cup chopped pecans
1 cup chopped dates
⅓ cup maraschino cherries, chopped
2½ cups crushed cornflakes
10 maraschino cherries, quartered

1. Preheat oven to 375°F. Lightly grease baking sheets.

2. Cream shortening and sugar until light and fluffy. Blend in eggs, milk, and vanilla.

3. Sift dry ingredients together; blend into butter mixture. Stir in pecans, dates, and chopped cherries,

4. Roll teaspoons of dough into balls; roll in corn flakes. Place on baking sheet; press ¼ of maraschino cherry in top for the "wink."

5. Bake at 375°F for 10–12 minutes. Cool completely.

Variations on a Theme

When a recipe calls for the dough to be rolled in sugar or cornflakes before baking, you can vary it by rolling the dough in almost any other type of crumbs. Finely chopped coconut, graham cracker crumbs, sugar and cinnamon, finely chopped nuts, or crushed Oreos are all delicious possibilities, depending on the cookie.

Sugar Plum Drops

This is another vintage recipe. Pick out the black gumdrops and use them for something else; they don't work well in these cookies.

INGREDIENTS | YIELDS 120 COOKIES

½ cup unsalted butter
½ cup shortening
1 cup sugar
1 cup brown sugar
2 eggs
1 teaspoon vanilla
1 teaspoon soda
1 tablespoon cold water
2 cups cake flour
1 teaspoon baking powder
1 teaspoon salt
2 cups rolled oats
1 cup coconut
1 cup gumdrops, chopped
Confectioners' sugar for dusting

1. Preheat oven to 375°F. Grease baking sheets.

2. Cream butter and shortening until blended. Beat in sugars until light and fluffy. Beat in eggs and vanilla. Dissolve baking soda in water; beat in.

3. Sift dry ingredients together; beat into butter mixture. Stir in remaining ingredients.

4. Form teaspoons of dough into balls and place 2" apart on baking sheet. Bake 12 minutes.

5. Dust with confectioners' sugar.

Shortening as an Ingredient

Many times when reading vintage cookbooks, especially those printed before 1950, you will see shortening being used in almost every recipe. This is because butter was often difficult to come by before and during World War II. You can substitute butter for half the shortening, but be careful about leaving the shortening out completely. These recipes were formulated for shortening and using all butter will often change the finished product completely.

Lebkuchen

These spicy cookies are traditional German Christmas cookies that keep very well.
Store them in a closed container overnight to allow the flavors to develop.

INGREDIENTS | **YIELDS 96 COOKIES**

1 cup honey

¼ cup molasses

1 tablespoon cinnamon

¼ teaspoon freshly grated nutmeg

1½ teaspoons cloves

2 tablespoons chopped candied orange peel

2 tablespoons chopped candied citron

1 cup chopped blanched almonds

1 cup brown sugar

1½ teaspoons orange zest

1 teaspoon lemon zest

½ teaspoon baking soda

2 teaspoons hot coffee

1 egg, beaten

4½ cups all-purpose flour

Confectioners' Glaze (page 547)

1. Stir together honey, molasses, cinnamon, nutmeg, and cloves. Mix in candied orange peel, citron, almonds, brown sugar, and orange and lemon zests.

2. Stir baking soda into hot coffee; beat into honey mixture. Beat in egg. Stir in flour. The dough will be very stiff and you may need to knead in the flour with your hands. Cover and chill overnight.

3. Preheat oven to 350°F. Line a baking sheet with parchment.

4. Roll dough to ½" thickness on a floured surface. Cut into 2" × ¾" rectangles.

5. Place cookies 1 apart on baking sheets. Bake 12–15 minutes, or until just starting to brown. Cool. Glaze with Confectioners' Glaze.

Springerli

These are also spelled Springerle. However you spell them, these crispy biscotti-like cookies have been a favorite for generations.

INGREDIENTS | YIELDS 60 COOKIES

4 eggs

2 cups sugar

2 tablespoons butter, melted and cooled

2 teaspoons baking powder

¼ teaspoon salt

4 cups all-purpose flour

¼ cup anise seed

Springerle, Springerli

Springerle cookies were first made in the German-speaking areas of Europe in the 1500s. The first designs are thought to have been biblical, but over time the cookies were made with many other intricate designs, including scenes from daily life. These cookies are an art form in themselves, and the molds and rolling pins used to make them are often antique and collectible.

1. Beat eggs until very light. Add sugar and continue beating. Fold in butter. Fold in sifted dry ingredients.

2. Knead dough until smooth. Roll out ½" thick on a lightly floured surface. Roll again with a springerli rolling pin, or use a cookie stamp to stamp a design in cookies. Cut cookies at borders created by springerli rolling pin.

3. Sprinkle anise seed on a clean towel and place cookies on it.

4. Allow to stand, uncovered, overnight.

5. Preheat oven to 325°F; bake cookies on an ungreased, metal baking sheet 12–15 minutes. Store cookies for a few days to allow flavors to develop.

CHAPTER 30

Exotic Favorites (International)

Vanilla Kipferl

These cookies are originally from Austria. You can dip either one end of the crescent in chocolate or dip the two tips and leave the middle plain.

INGREDIENTS | YIELDS 36 COOKIES

Vanilla confectioners' sugar (see step 1)
⅛ teaspoon salt
2⅛ cups all-purpose flour
⅞ cup butter
½ cup confectioners' sugar
1 egg
1¼ cups ground almonds
1 teaspoon vanilla
1 cup chocolate chips, melted

What Are Kipferl?

Kipferl is a traditional cookie that fills bakeries and homes in Austria and Germany during the Christmas holidays. The unique texture and delicate flavor are created during the two resting periods in the refrigerator. You can add a length of vanilla bean to the container that you store these cookies in for more vanilla flavor. It is a great way to enhance the flavor of any vanilla-based cookie.

1. Make vanilla sugar by putting a vanilla bean in a jar with 2 cups confectioners' sugar. Cover tightly. Allow to ripen several days, shaking jar occasionally.

2. Combine salt and flour. Cut in butter until mixture resembles coarse crumbs. Add confectioners' sugar, egg, ground almonds, and vanilla. Mix well; refrigerate 30 minutes.

3. Shape dough into ropes 1" thick. Cut in 1" pieces and shape them into crescents. Place on an ungreased cookie sheet. Refrigerate 15 minutes.

4. Preheat oven to 400°F. Bake 10–15 minutes.

5. Roll warm cookies gently in vanilla confectioners' sugar; dip ends in melted chocolate.

Nanaimo Bars

This no-bake Canadian specialty is easy to make. To cut the bars without cracking the top layer of chocolate, use a serrated knife dipped in boiling water.

INGREDIENTS | **YIELDS 16 BARS**

½ cup unsalted butter, softened

¼ cup sugar

⅓ cup Hershey's Special Dark cocoa

1 egg, beaten

1¾ cups graham cracker crumbs

1 cup coconut

½ cup chopped almonds

½ cup unsalted butter, softened

3 tablespoons heavy cream

2 tablespoons instant vanilla pudding mix

2 cups confectioners' sugar

4 ounces semisweet chocolate

2 teaspoons unsalted butter

1. Combine ½ cup butter, sugar, and cocoa in a microwave-safe bowl or double boiler. Heat, stirring occasionally, until mixture is smooth.

2. Add a little of hot mixture to egg; then beat in egg. Heat mixture 2–3 minutes, stirring often.

3. Remove from heat; mix in graham cracker crumbs, coconut, and almonds. Press into bottom of ungreased 8" × 8" pan.

4. Cream together remaining ½ cup butter, cream, and pudding mix until light and fluffy. Blend in confectioners' sugar until smooth. Spread over bottom layer of pan. Chill completely.

5. Melt semisweet chocolate and 2 teaspoons of butter together in microwave. Spread in an even layer over chilled bars. Let chocolate set; carefully cut into squares. Store bars in refrigerator.

Madeleines

Use the metal Madeleine pans for best results with these. If you use the smaller size, you will get 36 rather than 24 Madeleines.

INGREDIENTS | **YIELDS 24 COOKIES**

Butter for greasing molds

¾ cup unsalted butter

4 eggs

Pinch of salt

⅔ cup sugar

Zest of 1 lemon

1 teaspoon vanilla

¾ cup all-purpose flour

Powdered sugar

Is It a Cookie or Is It a Cake?

Madeleines are actually a small sponge cake. There are numerous variations to them, but the basic method is always the same. Madeleines can be used as accompaniments to coffee or tea, or they can be used in other recipes. It is important to fold the flour gently into the eggs so as not to deflate them; all of the lightness in this recipe comes from the air which has been beaten into the eggs.

1. Preheat oven to 350°F. Grease Madeleine molds, making sure all ridges are well greased. Dust with flour. Melt butter; set aside.

2. Whip eggs and salt on high speed with a whisk attachment until tripled in volume, about 3–4 minutes. Slowly add sugar until ribbons form when you lift beaters. Fold in lemon zest and vanilla.

3. Sift flour over egg mixture; fold in carefully. Fold in butter until well mixed.

4. Spoon batter into molds, filling about ⅔ full.

5. Bake 12–14 minutes for large and 8–10 minutes for small. Unmold immediately. Cool and dust with powdered sugar.

Frosted Lebkuchen

These spicy German cookies need a few days to ripen after baking or the spices taste too strong. The dough is very sticky, but the finished product is worth it.

INGREDIENTS | YIELDS 48 COOKIES

1¼ cups sugar

¾ cup honey

2 tablespoons water

2 cups chocolate chips

1 cup almonds, chopped or slivered

½ cup candied citron or orange, chopped

2 eggs

¼ cup orange juice

2¾ cups all-purpose flour

2 teaspoons cinnamon

1 teaspoon cloves

2 teaspoons cardamom

1 teaspoon baking soda

1 teaspoon baking powder

3 tablespoons orange juice

1½ cups confectioners' sugar

1. Bring sugar, honey, and water to a rolling boil. Remove from heat; set aside to cool.

2. Stir honey mixture with chocolate chips, almonds, candied fruit, eggs, and orange juice. Sift together flour, cinnamon, cloves, cardamom, baking soda, and baking powder; add to honey mixture. Cover bowl tightly; refrigerate 3 days.

3. Preheat oven to 325°F. Line 15" × 10" pan with parchment. Spread cookie dough evenly in pan.

4. Bake 35–40 minutes. Cool.

5. Mix orange juice and confectioners' sugar to make a thin frosting. Spread over tops of cookies. Store cookies in an airtight container.

Kourabiedes

Kourabiedes means "clouds" in Greek. These melt-in-your-mouth cookies are traditional at Christmas, New Years, and many other celebrations.

INGREDIENTS | YIELDS 30 COOKIES

2 cups unsalted butter

1 cup confectioners' sugar

1 teaspoon baking powder

1½ tablespoons ouzo, brandy, or orange juice

2 egg yolks

1 teaspoon vanilla

½ cup chopped toasted almonds

6 cups all-purpose flour

Rose water

1 bag confectioners' sugar for dusting

Storing Kourabiedes

Kourabiedes will keep for several weeks in an airtight container. Dust the bottom of the container with powdered sugar and then layer the cookies with wax paper. Dust each layer of cookies with more powdered sugar. Set the container aside, uncovered, for one day before adding the airtight lid. Before serving, dust with a little more powdered sugar.

1. Cream butter and sugar until very light. Dissolve baking powder in ouzo. Stir into beaten egg yolk; slowly add to butter mixture. Add vanilla and almonds. Stir in flour gradually. Use just enough flour to get a firm dough. You may need to knead the dough by hand for the last few minutes.

2. Chill dough overnight.

3. Preheat oven to 350°F. Lightly grease baking sheet.

4. Roll dough into tablespoon-sized balls. Place on baking sheet; flatten slightly with a glass. Bake 20 minutes. Sprinkle lightly with rose water.

5. Roll cookies in confectioners' sugar while still hot. Add more confectioners' sugar when they cool.

Jan Hagels

Jan Hagels (yan HAH-ghle) are a Dutch specialty. These shortbread-like cookies are simple and fast, perfect with tea or hot chocolate on a blustery day.

INGREDIENTS | **YIELDS 48 COOKIES**

1 cup softened unsalted butter
1 cup sugar
1 teaspoon almond extract
1 egg, separated
2 cups flour
½ teaspoon cinnamon
1 tablespoon sugar
½ cup sliced almonds

1. Preheat oven to 350°F.

2. Cream butter and sugar until light and fluffy. Add almond extract and egg yolk. Add flour; blend well.

3. Press dough firmly into 10" × 15" jelly roll pan.

4. Beat egg white until foamy; brush over cookie dough. Mix cinnamon, sugar, and almonds; sprinkle over dough.

5. Bake 20–25 minutes. Cool 5 minutes. Cut into diamond shapes.

Pizzelles

Crisp and light, these Italian favorites require a Pizzelle iron to make. You can use any flavoring you like, although anise is traditional.

INGREDIENTS | **YIELDS 18 COOKIES**

6 eggs
1½ cups sugar
1 cup unsalted butter, melted
2 tablespoons anise extract
3½ cups all-purpose flour
4 teaspoons baking powder

1. Preheat Pizzelle iron.

2. Beat eggs and sugar until fluffy. Blend in butter and anise.

3. Stir in flour and baking powder.

4. Drop batter by rounded tablespoons (more or less) on Pizzelle iron.

5. Cook about 1½ minutes, until steam stops. Remove from iron; lay flat on a cooling rack and allow to cool completely.

Swedish Butternuts

These are a beautiful cookie for a holiday cookie tray. You can substitute hazelnuts for the pecans in this recipe.

INGREDIENTS | **YIELDS 60 COOKIES**

1 cup unsalted butter

½ cup sugar

1 egg yolk

1 tablespoon cream

1 teaspoon vanilla

½ teaspoon baking powder

2 cups all-purpose flour

1 cup pecans, chopped

1 egg white

60 halved candied cherries (1 for each cookie)

1. Preheat oven to 325°F. Line a baking sheet with parchment.

2. Cream butter; beat in sugar until light and fluffy. Add egg yolk, cream, and vanilla.

3. Whisk baking powder and flour together; blend into butter mixture. Stir in ½" cup of pecans.

4. Beat egg white until frothy. Form dough into walnut-sized balls; dip in egg white. Roll in remaining ½ cup pecans.

5. Place on cookie sheet; make an indentation in center with your finger. Press in a cherry half, cut side down. Bake 20 minutes.

Working with Butter

The rich taste of fresh butter is important to the Swedish Butternut recipe. Always make sure that your butter is fresh and has not taken on any flavors from the refrigerator. Keep the butter stored in an airtight container away from strong-flavored foods like onions and garlic. While many store brands of butter are fine, if you are making something that depends on the taste of the butter, consider using one of the imported European butters. They are more expensive, but worth it.

Scottish Shortbread

Classic, buttery shortbread cookies are perfect with a cup of coffee or tea. Try grinding 1 cup of oats to a powder and using that in place of 1 cup of the flour for a different taste.

INGREDIENTS | YIELDS 24 COOKIES

1 cup salted butter, room temperature
1 cup unsalted butter, room temperature
1 cup dark brown sugar
4 cups all-purpose flour
Confectioners' sugar

1. Preheat oven to 325°F. Place baking sheet in freezer to chill.

2. Cream butters and brown sugar. Stir in 3–3½ cups of flour to make a soft dough. Add a little more flour if needed. Knead a few minutes.

3. Roll out to ½ thick on a surface covered with confectioners' sugar.

4. Cut in rectangles; bake 20–25 minutes.

5. Cool completely.

French Meringues

Crispy and light, these meringues are perfect for teas, holidays, and showers. They can be tinted with food coloring if you like.

INGREDIENTS | YIELDS 36 COOKIES

4 egg whites, room temperature
¼ teaspoon cream of tartar
2¼ cups confectioners' sugar

1. Preheat oven to 200°F. Butter and flour baking sheet.

2. Beat egg whites until foamy. Add cream of tartar; beat until soft peaks start to form. Gradually beat in sugar until stiff, glossy peaks form.

3. Transfer mixture to a pastry bag. Pipe mounds on prepared baking sheet.

4. Place baking sheet in oven. Keep oven door cracked open by using a wooden spoon handle to keep it from closing all the way.

5. Bake 3 hours, or until the meringues are dry and crispy.

Bunuelos

These tender fritters are the perfect ending to any Mexican meal. Be sure to allow the dough to rest before rolling for the best texture.

INGREDIENTS | **YIELDS 24 COOKIES**

3 cups all-purpose flour
1 tablespoon baking powder
1 teaspoon salt
1 teaspoon cinnamon
2 eggs
½ cup unsalted butter, melted
1½ teaspoons vanilla
¾ cup milk
1 tablespoon sugar
1 cup sugar mixed with 1 tablespoon cinnamon
Peanut oil for frying

Bunuelos, Sopapillas, and Indian Fry Bread

These three snacks often get confused, and the truth is they are very similar. Bunuelos are softer and more like doughnuts because of the inclusion of the milk. In fact, they are often made with yeast. Fry bread is usually a simple mixture of flour and water that is fried until puffy. Sopapillas have baking powder included, but are crisper than Bunuelos. They generally have hollow centers and are served with honey.

1. Heat an electric deep fryer with clean oil in it to 375°F.

2. Wisk together dry ingredients. Beat eggs, butter, vanilla, milk, and 1 tablespoon of sugar; add to flour mixture and blend well.

3. Knead dough on a lightly floured surface until smooth. Divide into 20 pieces. Cover with a tea towel; allow to rest 45 minutes.

4. Combine 1 cup sugar and 1 tablespoon cinnamon. Roll dough out in thin circles, 5"–6" in diameter. Fry one at a time in the hot oil, turning once.

5. Drain on absorbent material; sprinkle with cinnamon and sugar.

Empire Cookies

For a dainty variation, substitute 2 teaspoons of rose water for the almond extract in this recipe. These are beautiful with candied violets or rose petals on top for a shower.

INGREDIENTS | YIELDS 12 COOKIES

½ cup unsalted butter

½ cup sugar

1 egg

1 teaspoon vanilla

2 cups all-purpose flour

1 teaspoon baking powder

½ cup raspberry jam

1 cup confectioners' sugar

¼ teaspoon almond extract

1 tablespoon hot water

The Sun Doesn't Set...

Empire cookies were named in honor of the British Empire. They are truly called Empire Biscuits, biscuit being the European term for cookie. These cookies were popular throughout Great Britain during the late 1800s and early 1900s, and became popular in Canada as time went on. They traditionally have a glacéed cherry decorating the top.

1. Preheat oven to 350°F.

2. Cream butter and sugar until light and fluffy. Beat in egg and vanilla; blend in well. Stir in flour and baking powder.

3. Roll dough to ⅛" thickness on a surface dusted with confectioners' sugar. Cut with 2" round cutter; place on ungreased baking sheets.

4. Bake 10 minutes; cool.

5. Spread half of cookies with raspberry jam. Carefully top with remaining cookies. Combine confectioners' sugar, almond extract, and enough hot water to make a thin icing. Spread over tops of cookies. Allow cookies to set for an hour before serving or storing.

Lady Fingers

Lady fingers are a wonderful cookie on their own. They are also one of the main ingredients of Tiramisu and Charlotte. You may add 1 teaspoon lemon zest if you like.

INGREDIENTS | **YIELDS 24 COOKIES**

3 eggs, separated
2 tablespoons sugar
½ cup cake flour
⅛ teaspoon cream of tartar
3 tablespoons sugar
½ teaspoon vanilla
Confectioners' sugar

1. Preheat oven to 350°F. Line a baking pan with parchment.

2. Beat the yolks and 2 tablespoons of sugar on high speed 5 minutes. Mixture will be thick and pale, and will form ribbons when beater is lifted. Blend in vanilla.

3. Sift flour over egg mixture. Do not fold in.

4. Whip egg whites until foamy. Add cream of tartar; whip to soft peaks. Gradually add 3 tablespoons of sugar. Fold egg whites and flour into yolks carefully; be sure not to deflate batter. Transfer to a pastry bag and, with bag at a 45° angle to baking sheet, pipe 3" long fingers.

5. Sift confectioners' sugar over lady fingers. Bake 8–10 minutes, or until cakes are firm. Cool 5 minutes; remove from paper while still warm.

Anzac Biscuits

These Australian cookies were designed to stay fresh for a long time. They were made to withstand shipping from Australia to battlefields all over the world during World War I.

INGREDIENTS | **YIELDS 36 COOKIES**

1 cup rolled oats
1 cup flour
1 cup brown sugar
1 cup coconut
½ cup butter
2½ tablespoons honey
1 teaspoon baking soda
3 tablespoons boiling water

1. Preheat oven to 350°F. Grease cookie sheets.

2. Combine oats, flour, brown sugar, and coconut.

3. Melt butter and honey, stirring until mixed. Dissolve baking soda in boiling water; add to honey mixture.

4. Pour liquid mixture into dry mixture; blend with your hands. Form in walnut-sized balls; place on cookie sheets. Flatten slightly.

5. Bake 12–15 minutes. Cool completely.

Not Just a Cookie...

Anzac biscuits are not just any cookie. They are the sweet part of a traditional Australian holiday that is much like Memorial Day. On Anzac Day, people all over the country take the time to remember and honor those brave men that died during the Battle at Gallipoli. It was a devastating defeat for the Australian and New Zealand Forces. ANZAC stands for Australian New Zealand Army Corps.

Rugelach

A delicious variation on these traditional Jewish holiday cookies is to substitute chocolate chips for the raisins and brush the pastry with apricot jam before adding the filling.

INGREDIENTS | **YIELDS 48 COOKIES**

2 cups flour

¼ teaspoon salt

1 cup unsalted butter

8 ounces cream cheese

⅓ cup sour cream

½ cup white sugar

1 tablespoon cinnamon

1 cup finely ground walnuts

½ cup raisins

A Bit of Rugelach Trivia

Rugelach means "little twists" in Yiddish. It is a popular cookie to eat during Shavvot and Hannukah. The cream cheese dough is not traditional, but is thought to have been developed by Philadelphia Cream Cheese in the mid 1900s. This delicious treat was generally only found in Jewish homes until Maida Heatter published her grandmother's recipe in her cookbook *Maida Heatter's Cookies*.

1. In a food processor, pulse flour, salt, butter, cream cheese, and sour cream until crumbly. Knead until it holds together; form into 4 disks. Chill overnight.

2. Pulse sugar, cinnamon, walnuts, and raisins until finely ground. Roll well-chilled disk into 9" round. Sprinkle each of rolled disks with sugar and nut mixture. Press in lightly.

3. Cut each round into 12 wedges. Roll up from base to tip. Place on ungreased baking sheet; chill 20 minutes.

4. Preheat oven to 350°F.

5. Bake 20 minutes, or until golden. Cool.

Churros

This light, fried cookie originally came from Spain, but is now linked with Mexican cuisine. Dip them in chocolate for the perfect ending to a long day.

INGREDIENTS | **YIELDS 24 COOKIES**

2½ cups water
½ teaspoon salt
3 tablespoons brown sugar
3 cups all-purpose flour
1 teaspoon baking powder
2 egg yolks
Oil for deep frying
Confectioners' sugar for dusting

1. Preheat clean oil in a deep fryer to 375°F.

2. Bring water, salt, and brown sugar to a boil, stirring until all crystals are completely dissolved. Remove from heat.

3. Add flour and baking powder; beat until mixture is smooth. Beat in egg yolks one at a time until mixture gets smooth and glossy. Cool.

4. Put cookie dough in a pastry bag fitted with a large star tip.

5. Pipe dough into fryer in 4" lengths, frying only 4–5 at a time. Use a wet knife to cut lengths of dough. Fry until golden; drain and dust with powdered sugar.

Pfeffernusse

Lard is not a very popular ingredient anymore, and it is hard to find good leaf lard. If you can't or don't wish to use it, either butter or shortening will work almost as well.

INGREDIENTS | **YIELDS 100 COOKIES**

2 cups dark corn syrup
2 cups sugar
2 cups lard, shortening, or butter
2 cups cold black coffee
1 teaspoon baking soda
1 teaspoon baking powder
1 teaspoon salt
1½ teaspoons black pepper
1½ teaspoons freshly grated nutmeg
1½ teaspoons ginger
1½ teaspoons cloves
12–13 cups flour

1. Cream all ingredients except flour together in a large bowl. Gradually add flour 2 cups at a time. Work it in until dough is smooth and a little stiffer than pastry dough.

2. Chill 1–2 days.

3. Preheat oven to 375°F. Lightly grease baking sheets.

4. Roll out dough into pencil-thin ropes. Cut each rope in 1" pieces.

5. Bake 15–20 minutes. Cool. Roll in powdered sugar.

Langues de Chat

Langues de Chat, or Cats' Tongues, is a French cookie similar to Madeleines or Lady Fingers. They are a perfect embellishment for a bowl of ice cream.

INGREDIENTS | **YIELDS 36 COOKIES**

½ cup softened unsalted butter
⅔ cup sugar
3 egg whites, room temperature
1½ teaspoons vanilla extract
1½ cups all-purpose flour
6 ounces bittersweet chocolate, melted

Egg White Magic

Beating the egg whites to the light, fluffy mounds required for many of these recipes is much easier if the egg whites are room temperature. Chill the bowl and the beaters for best results. Since the protein in egg whites reacts with acid, it is good to whip the whites in a copper bowl. This will give your egg whites a higher and lighter texture. If you don't have a copper bowl, rinse out the bowl you are using with lemon juice.

1. Preheat oven to 400°F. Lightly grease baking sheets.

2. Cream butter and sugar until light and fluffy. Beat egg whites and vanilla until stiff peaks form; fold into butter mixture. Carefully sift flour over top; fold in.

3. Put dough in a pastry bag and pipe 3" long cookies.

4. Bake 10 minutes. Cool.

5. Dip one end of cookie in melted chocolate; allow chocolate to set.

Pepparkakor

This dough is very sticky and hard to work with despite the long chilling time. The results are worth it, though. If you have trouble rolling the dough out, shape it into balls instead and flatten it with the bottom of a glass dipped in sugar.

INGREDIENTS | YIELDS 36 COOKIES

½ cup unsalted butter

1½ cups sugar

1 egg

1 tablespoon light corn syrup

¼ cup orange juice

2 teaspoons orange zest

3½ cups all-purpose flour

2 teaspoons baking soda

2 teaspoons cinnamon

2 teaspoons ground ginger

2 teaspoons ground cloves

1 teaspoon cardamom

Make a Wish

It is a Swedish custom to put one of these cookies in the palm of your hand and make a wish. Tap your index finger in the center of the cookie until it breaks. Legend has it that if the cookie breaks in three pieces, your wish will come true. Whether you get your wish or not, these spicy cookies are delicious any time of the year.

1. Cream butter, sugar, egg, corn syrup, orange juice, and orange zest.

2. Whisk dry ingredients together; stir into butter mixture until well blended.

3. Wrap tightly; allow to chill 1 day. During this time the flavors will mellow and the finished cookies will be much better.

4. Preheat oven to 400°F. Line a baking sheet with parchment.

5. Roll chilled dough out to ⅛" thickness on a floured surface. Cut into desired shapes with cookie cutters. Bake 8–10 minutes. Cool 15 minutes; remove from baking sheets. Cool completely. Flavor develops as it is stored 1–2 days.

Viennese Specials

A delicious finish for these cookies is a generous drizzle of white chocolate across the tops of the cookies. If you are feeling especially gourmet, top the white chocolate drizzle with a milk chocolate one.

INGREDIENTS | **YIELDS 48 COOKIES**

2 cups cake flour
½ teaspoon cinnamon
½ teaspoon cloves
Pinch of salt
1 cup unsalted butter
1 cup sugar
2 egg yolks
1 teaspoon lemon zest
1 cup ground walnuts
1 cup raspberry jam

1. Whisk dry ingredients together.

2. Cream butter and sugar together until light and fluffy. Add egg yolk; blend well. Gradually add dry ingredients; stir in lemon zest and walnuts. Chill 1 hour.

3. Preheat oven to 400°F. Line baking sheets with parchment.

4. Roll dough ⅛" thick between sheets of wax paper. Cut 48 circles with round cookie cutter. Place on baking sheets. Spread with a thin layer of jam.

5. Cut remaining dough into 2" × ½" strips; lay them across tops of each cookie, forming a cross. Press in gently. Bake 10–15 minutes.

Norwegian Jelly Cookies

While mint or currant jelly is traditional, you can use any type you like. If you want to try a cross-cultural experience, use jalapeño jelly. Spicy, but delicious!

INGREDIENTS | **YIELDS 24 COOKIES**

⅓ cup unsalted butter
⅓ cup brown sugar
1 egg, separated
1 cup all-purpose flour
1 cup chopped nuts
Mint jelly or currant jelly

Long Storage

If you want to store any type of thumbprint cookie for more than a couple of days, don't fill them with jelly. Freeze the cookies between layers of wax paper until you are ready to serve them. Thaw them a few minutes in a warm oven and then put the jelly into the indentation. The jelly stays fresh, the cookie stays crisp, and everyone is happy.

1. Preheat oven to 350°F. Lightly grease baking sheets.

2. Cream butter and sugar until light and fluffy. Blend in egg yolk, then flour.

3. Roll dough into 1" balls. Dip balls in egg white, then roll in nuts.

4. Place on baking sheet; press down centers with your finger to form a hollow. Bake 8 minutes.

5. Remove from oven; press down hollow again. Bake 10 more minutes. Fill centers with jelly before serving.

Homemade Fortune Cookies

If these seem to be too thick, just add water a teaspoon at a time until the batter spreads well. Do not make many at a time because you have to form them while very hot.

INGREDIENTS | **YIELDS 12 COOKIES**

1 egg white
¼ teaspoon vanilla or almond extract
Pinch salt
¼ cup all-purpose flour
¼ cup sugar

Ancient Chinese Fortune Cookies

Fortune cookies began as a military strategy in the fourteenth century in China. The story goes that when China was occupied by the Mongols, the Chinese rebels hid messages in the middle of Moon Cakes. Chu Yuan Chang disguised himself as a Taoist priest and was able to slip into guarded cities and hand the Moon Cakes to the other rebels. In this way, the uprising that formed the basis of the Ming Dynasty was successfully carried out.

1. Preheat oven to 400°F. Spray a baking sheet with no-stick spray. Write fortunes on 12 strips of paper.

2. Mix egg white and vanilla until it becomes very foamy but does not yet form stiff peaks. Mix rest of ingredients into egg white, folding carefully.

3. Place teaspoonfuls of batter 4" apart on baking sheet. Tilt sheet to make batter spread, or spread it with back of a spoon.

4. Bake 5 minutes. Quickly remove from oven; remove from cookie sheet with a spatula. Flip cookies over and lay fortune inside.

5. Fold cookies over fortunes, then fold cookie over edge of a bowl to crimp middle. Place upside down in muffin cups to hold their shape until they cool.

Baklava

Be sure to read the tips for using phyllo (also spelled filo) dough that are usually on the package. Thaw it in the refrigerator the day before you need to use it.

INGREDIENTS | **YIELDS 18 BAKLAVA**

1 pound chopped walnuts
1 teaspoon orange or lemon zest
1 teaspoon cinnamon
1 pound phyllo dough
1 cup butter, melted
1 cup white sugar
1 cup water
1 teaspoon vanilla
½ cup honey

1. Preheat oven to 350°F. Butter 13" × 9" pan thoroughly.

2. Toss chopped nuts with zest and cinnamon; set aside. Carefully unroll phyllo dough and cut stack in ½ so it fits in pan. Cover with a damp cloth.

3. Place 2 sheets of phyllo in pan; brush generously with butter. Repeat with 2 more sheets, until you have 8 sheets layered in pan, brushing each layer with butter. Sprinkle with 3 tablespoons of nut mixture. Top with 2 sheets of phyllo, brush with butter, then sprinkle with 3 more tablespoons of nuts. Continue building layers until nuts are used up. Top layer should consist of about 8 layers of phyllo brushed with butter after every 2 layers.

4. With a sharp knife, cut almost all the way through baklava in 4 long rows, then diagonally to create diamonds. Do not cut through bottom layer until serving finished baklava. This will keep it from being soggy. Bake 50 minutes.

5. Bring sugar and water to a boil, stirring until sugar is melted. Add vanilla and honey. Simmer mixture 20 minutes. When baklava comes from oven, immediately pour sauce over it. Let cool uncovered.

CHAPTER 31

Meringues

Hazelnut Meringues

These make a light, crispy meringue with the richness of nuts. You can easily substitute ground pistachios or macadamia nuts for the hazelnuts in the recipe.

INGREDIENTS | **YIELDS 96 COOKIES**

8 egg whites
¼ teaspoon cream of tartar
1 pound confectioners' sugar, sifted
2 teaspoons cinnamon
1 pound ground hazelnuts

Lose the Plastic

One of the top reasons that meringues are unsuccessful is that the egg whites are not stiff enough. The whites will not beat to stiff peaks if there is one iota of grease on the beaters, in the bowl, or even from a speck of egg yolk. Grease can hang on plastic even with the most energetic scrubbing, so always use glass or stainless steel bowls when beating meringues.

1. Preheat oven to 325°F. Line a baking sheet with parchment.

2. Beat egg whites and cream of tartar until soft peaks begin to form. Gradually add sugar and cinnamon; beat until stiff, glossy peaks form.

3. Fold in nuts.

4. Pipe onto parchment with a pastry tube, or drop by teaspoon.

5. Bake 20 minutes, or until dry. Remove from baking sheets immediately.

Pecan Dainties

These are fantastic served with coffee or coffee ice cream. For an extra special treat, dip the bottoms in melted bittersweet chocolate and let set.

INGREDIENTS | **YIELDS 36 COOKIES**

1 egg white, room temperature
Pinch of salt
1 cup brown sugar
1½ cups pecan halves

1. Preheat oven to 250°F. Line a baking sheet with parchment. Spray with nonstick spray.

2. Beat egg whites and salt until soft peaks form. Add sugar gradually; beat until stiff and glossy.

3. Gently fold in pecans.

4. Drop by teaspoonfuls on cookie sheet; bake 30 minutes.

5. Remove from baking sheet immediately.

Rice-a-Roos

*Kids love these crispy cookies. For variation, substitute the cocoa
or fruity type crisp rice cereal for the regular cereal.*

INGREDIENTS | **YIELDS 36 COOKIES**

3 egg whites
½ teaspoon salt
¼ teaspoon almond extract
1 cup sugar
2 cups crisp rice cereal
2½ cups coconut

1. Preheat oven to 300°F. Line a baking sheet with parchment.

2. Beat egg whites, salt, and almond extract until soft peaks form. Gradually beat in sugar; beat until stiff, glossy peaks form.

3. Very gently fold in rice cereal and coconut.

4. Drop by spoonfuls onto baking sheet; bake 18–20 minutes.

5. Remove from baking sheet while still hot.

Surprise Kisses

*These kisses are almost like a very light and crispy chocolate chip cookie.
Try substituting white chocolate and macadamia nuts for variety.*

INGREDIENTS | **YIELDS 36 COOKIES**

2 egg whites
⅛ teaspoon salt
⅛ teaspoon cream of tartar
½ teaspoon vanilla
¾ cup sugar
6 ounces semisweet chocolate mini chips
¼ cup chopped pecans

1. Preheat oven to 300°F. Line a baking sheet with parchment and spray with nonstick spray.

2. Combine egg whites, salt, cream of tartar, and vanilla. Beat until soft peaks form.

3. Gradually add sugar, beating constantly until stiff, glossy peaks form.

4. Fold in chocolate and nuts. Drop by teaspoonful on baking sheet.

5. Bake 25 minutes, or until meringues can be easily lifted from parchment.

Coconut Macaroons

After the cookies have baked and when they are completely cooled, drizzle them with melted milk chocolate for a wonderful variation.

INGREDIENTS | **YIELDS 36 COOKIES**

2 egg whites
1 cup sugar
1 teaspoon vanilla
½ teaspoon coconut extract
1 cup coconut
2 cups cornflakes

Just Can't Wait

Once you begin beating the egg whites, you must follow through completely. Egg whites don't wait well; they will begin to deflate within about five minutes. If the egg whites do deflate, there is really nothing to do but use them for a fluffy omelet and start over with a new batch of egg whites.

1. Preheat oven to 350°F. Line a baking sheet with parchment and spray with nonstick spray.

2. Beat egg whites until foamy. Gradually add sugar until stiff, glossy peaks form. Beat in coconut and vanilla extracts.

3. Gently fold in coconut, then cornflakes.

4. Drop by tablespoonfuls onto baking sheet.

5. Bake 12–15 minutes. Remove from baking sheet immediately.

Meringue Cases

Meringue cases are crispy bowls that are perfect for serving chocolate mousse, a scoop of ice cream, or even a simple strawberries and whipped cream dessert.

INGREDIENTS | YIELDS 12 CASES

4 egg whites
¼ teaspoon cream of tartar
Pinch of salt
1 cup sugar

Use the Right Sugar

Most people don't realize that there is more than one type of white sugar. Ultra-fine, pure cane sugar is the best to use in meringues because the crystals dissolve quickly and easily and there is less chance of deflating the meringues or overbeating the egg whites. Start adding the sugar just as the soft peaks begin to form for best volume.

1. Preheat oven to 200°F. Line a baking sheet with parchment and spray with nonstick cooking spray.

2. Beat egg whites, cream of tartar, and salt until soft peaks form.

3. Add sugar gradually, while beating egg whites to glossy, stiff peaks.

4. Drop by tablespoonfuls onto baking sheets.

5. Bake 1 hour. Leave oven door closed and let stand overnight to dry completely.

Almond Macaroons

It is imperative to the success of these cookies that the egg whites be stiff and glossy and do not deflate when the other ingredients are folded in. Be gentle!

INGREDIENTS | YIELDS 36 COOKIES

4 egg whites
⅛ teaspoon cream of tartar
¼ teaspoon salt
1 cup sugar
½ teaspoon vanilla
¼ teaspoon coconut extract
¼ cup all-purpose flour
3 cups coconut
½ cup ground almonds

1. Preheat oven to 300°F. Line a baking sheet with parchment and spray with nonstick spray.

2. Beat egg whites, cream of tartar, and salt until soft peaks form. Gradually beat in sugar until egg whites form stiff, glossy peaks that do not tip over.

3. Combine remaining ingredients; fold into egg whites in 3 parts.

4. Drop by heaping tablespoonfuls onto prepared baking sheet.

5. Bake 18–20 minutes. Cool on baking sheets.

Nut Kisses

Any nut can be used with success in this easy recipe. Add a variation to this cookie by substituting coconut for the chopped nuts.

INGREDIENTS | YIELDS 24 COOKIES

2 egg whites
Pinch of salt
½ cup sugar
½ teaspoon vanilla
½ cup chopped nuts

1. Preheat oven to 275°F. Line a baking sheet with parchment.

2. Beat egg whites and salt until soft peaks form. Gradually add sugar; beat until stiff, glossy peaks form. Beat in vanilla.

3. Fold in nuts.

4. Drop by teaspoonfuls on baking sheet.

5. Bake 40–60 minutes.

Peanut Brittle Meringue Drops

You can easily substitute crushed toffee pieces, with or without chocolate, for the peanut brittle in this recipe. Chopped sugar-glazed pecans are also delicious.

INGREDIENTS | **SERVES 24**

3 egg whites
1 cup of sugar
½ teaspoon vanilla
½ teaspoon vinegar
½ cup crushed peanut brittle

1. Preheat oven to 275°F. Line a baking sheet with parchment.

2. Beat egg whites until foamy, soft peaks form. Gradually add sugar; beat until peaks are stiff and glossy.

3. Quickly beat in vanilla and vinegar. Fold in brittle.

4. Drop from teaspoons onto baking sheet.

5. Bake 1 hour. Remove from parchment while cookies are still hot.

Condensed Milk Kisses

A variation on these is to use ½ cup peanut butter, either combined with the coconut or by substituting cornflakes for the coconut and adding with the peanut butter.

INGREDIENTS | **YIELDS 30 COOKIES**

1 can sweetened condensed milk
3 cups coconut
½ teaspoon vanilla
Pinch of salt

1. Preheat oven to 375°F. Lightly grease cookie sheet.

2. Combine all ingredients; mix well.

3. Drop by teaspoons on cookie sheet.

4. Bake 15 minutes.

5. Remove from sheet while still hot.

Graham Cracker Marguerites

This vintage recipe has many variations. Use gingersnaps instead of graham crackers, or for a S'Mores-type cookie, drizzle melted chocolate over the baked cookie.

INGREDIENTS | **YIELDS 16 COOKIES**

2 egg whites

1½ cups sugar

½ cup water

5 marshmallows, cut in fourths

½ teaspoon vanilla

2 tablespoons coconut

⅛ teaspoon salt

1 cup chopped pecans

16 graham crackers

1. Preheat oven to 350°F.

2. Beat egg whites until stiff but not dry. Boil sugar and water to the soft ball stage, about 236°F–238°F on a candy thermometer.

3. Add marshmallows; stir until dissolved.

4. Slowly pour marshmallow mixture over egg whites, beating constantly until it forms stiff peaks that hold their shape. Add vanilla, coconut, salt, and pecans.

5. Spread on graham crackers; bake 15 minutes.

Marguerites

Marguerites are a vintage recipe that became popular in the late 1920s and early 1930s when people put marshmallows in nearly everything. Marguerites always start with some sort of cracker or cookie base, and invariably have marshmallow included somewhere. The simplest Marguerites are made by spreading peanut butter on a butter cracker, topping with a marshmallow, and broiling until the marshmallow browns.

Praline Kisses

To make Maple Kisses, omit the brown sugar and add 1 cup of maple sugar. If maple sugar is not available, use ¼ cup maple syrup and ¾ cup sugar.

INGREDIENTS | **YIELDS 30 COOKIES**

1 egg white
½ teaspoon salt
1 cup brown sugar
1 cup chopped pecans

1. Preheat oven to 250°F. Line a baking sheet with parchment.

2. Beat egg white and salt until foamy, soft peaks form. Gradually add sugar, beating constantly until stiff peaks form. Fold in pecans.

3. Drop by teaspoons onto baking sheet.

4. Bake 1 hour. Cool slightly; remove from paper while still warm.

CHAPTER 32

Cookies for Special Needs

Gluten-Free Graham Crackers

Many graham cracker recipes use both honey and molasses as flavorings. To do that, just substitute 1 tablespoon of the molasses for an equal amount of the honey.

INGREDIENTS | YIELDS 36 CRACKERS

2½ cups gluten-free flour mix

½ cup brown sugar

2 teaspoons cinnamon

½ teaspoon xanthan gum

1 teaspoon gluten-free baking powder

½ teaspoon baking soda

½ teaspoon salt

⅓ cup unsalted butter, cut in chunks

3 tablespoons ice water

3 tablespoons honey

1 teaspoon vanilla

Leavening Gluten-Free Flour

Gluten-free flours sometimes need more leavening because of the lack of elasticity. If you are changing a standard recipe to a gluten free one, add about 25 percent more baking powder or soda. This will allow your baked goods to be lighter. When you are working with a yeast recipe, the yeast does not usually need to be doubled.

1. In a large bowl, mix flour mixture, brown sugar, cinnamon, xanthan gum, baking powder, baking soda, and salt until well combined.

2. Work butter into dry ingredients until mixture is crumbly. Gently stir in water, honey, and vanilla. Cover dough; chill about 1 hour.

3. Preheat oven to 325°F. Line a baking sheet with parchment.

4. Roll dough out between 2 pieces of wax paper; cut into rectangles. Remove top sheet of wax paper; lay crackers on baking sheet with remaining wax paper on top. Peel off remaining wax paper.

5. Bake 12–15 minutes.

Gluten-Free Apple Butter Drops

*Apple butter, because if its rich texture, can often substitute for butter
or oil in a recipe when you want to cut down on fat.*

INGREDIENTS | **YIELDS 36 COOKIES**

2 cups gluten-free flour mix

½ teaspoon salt

1 teaspoon baking soda

¼ teaspoon cloves

¼ teaspoon nutmeg

1 teaspoon cinnamon

½ cup unsalted butter

1 cup sugar

1 egg or equivalent in egg substitute

1 cup chopped dates

1 cup raisins

1 cup apple butter

1. Preheat oven to 375°F. Line a baking sheet with parchment. Combine baking mix and other dry ingredients and set aside.

2. Cream butter and sugar. Quickly stir in eggs, dates, and raisins.

3. Stir in dry ingredients alternately with apple butter.

4. Drop by rounded teaspoons on baking sheet.

5. Bake about 12 minutes. Let cool.

Storing Gluten-free Treats

Cookies that are baked without gluten do not have the same storage times as regular cookies. In fact, gluten-free items are at their best still warm from the oven. Plan to eat the cookies immediately, or place in the freezer for longer storage. Warm the cookies a few minutes in the oven and they will taste as fresh as if they were just baked.

Gluten-Free Chocolate Chip Cookies

You can substitute any type of baking chip for the chocolate chips in these cookies. Always read the ingredients to make sure that they are gluten free.

INGREDIENTS | **YIELDS 24 COOKIES**

¼ cup sugar
½ cup dark brown sugar
½ cup unsalted butter
1½ teaspoons vanilla
1 egg
1 cup white rice flour
¼ cup almond flour
½ teaspoon baking soda
½ teaspoon salt
1 teaspoon guar gum
1 cup chocolate chips

1. Preheat oven to 350°F. Spray a baking sheet lightly with baking spray.

2. Process all ingredients except chocolate chips until well blended.

3. Shape into small, teaspoon-sized cookies. Place on baking sheet.

4. Bake 6 minutes, or until done.

Gluten-Free Pizzelles

These are very pliable when warm, and you can roll them to make Cannoli shells, dessert bowls, or ice cream cones.

INGREDIENTS | **YIELDS 24 COOKIES**

½ cup unsalted butter
3 eggs
1 teaspoon vanilla, or a few drops of anise oil
⅔ cup sugar
2 cups gluten-free flour mix
½ teaspoon xanthan gum
1 teaspoon baking powder
Pinch of salt

1. Preheat Pizzelle iron. Melt butter; set aside.

2. Whisk eggs in a large bowl until frothy. Add vanilla and sugar; beat well. Add melted butter; blend thoroughly.

3. Beat in dry ingredients.

4. Pour batter onto Pizzelle iron; bake according to manufacturer's directions.

Gluten-Free Sugar Cookies

Be sure that your baking mix does not have xanthan gum in it before you try this recipe. If it does, leave the xanthan gum out of the recipe.

INGREDIENTS | YIELDS 36 COOKIES

½ cup shortening
½ cup unsalted butter
1 cup sugar
1 egg
2 teaspoons vanilla
½ teaspoon freshly grated nutmeg
2½ cups gluten-free flour mix
1 teaspoon baking powder
2½ teaspoons xanthan gum

1. Beat shortening, butter, and sugar on highest speed of a mixer until well blended. Blend in egg, vanilla, and nutmeg.

2. Whisk dry ingredients together; add carefully to the creamed mixture.

3. Chill dough 1 hour.

4. Preheat oven to 350°F. Roll dough out on a flat surface dusted with flour. Cut with cookie cutters.

5. Bake 12–15 minutes.

Egg-/Dairy-Free Chewy Chocolate Cookies

These cookies are dense with a rich chocolate flavor. Do not overbake them; bake them just until set for best results.

INGREDIENTS | YIELDS 36 COOKIES

1 cup hot coffee
1½ tablespoons ground flax seeds
¾ cup oil
2 cups sugar
2 teaspoons vanilla
2 cups all-purpose or gluten-free flour mix
¾ cup cocoa
½ teaspoon salt
1 cup carob chips or other nondairy chocolate chip
Sugar for rolling

1. Preheat oven to 350°F. Line a baking sheet with parchment. Add coffee to ground flax seed; set aside.

2. Cream together oil and sugar. Add coffee mixture and vanilla; beat well. Whisk together dry ingredients; stir in until well blended. Fold in chocolate chips.

3. Roll dough into 1" balls; roll in sugar.

4. Place 2" apart on a baking sheet; flatten slightly with a glass dipped in sugar.

5. Bake 10 minutes. Cool.

Egg-/Dairy-Free Chocolate Chip Cookies

To make these cookies gluten-free as well as egg/dairy free,
just substitute the flour with a gluten-free baking mix.

INGREDIENTS | **YIELDS 24 COOKIES**

1½ cups all-purpose flour

½ teaspoon salt

1 teaspoon baking soda

½ cup butter-flavored shortening

½ cup sugar

⅓ cup light brown sugar

3 tablespoons corn syrup, light or dark

2 tablespoons soymilk, rice milk, or coffee

1 tablespoon vanilla

½ cups toasted pecans, chopped (optional)

8 ounces dairy-free carob chips

1. Preheat oven to 375°F. Spray baking sheet with cooking spray.

2. Sift dry ingredients; set aside. Cream shortening and sugars until fluffy. Add corn syrup, soy milk, and vanilla; beat well.

3. Stir in flour mixture. Fold in nuts and chocolate chips.

4. Drop batter by rounded tablespoons onto prepared baking sheet.

5. Bake 10–12 minutes. Allow cookies to cool thoroughly.

Milk Substitutions

Generally, when milk is called for in any cookie recipe it is there as nothing more than a way to thin the batter. Since it is normally a small amount and does not often change anything else in the recipe, you can substitute many different liquids for the milk to make the recipe dairy free. Coffee, tea, soda, juice, soy or rice milk, almond milk, coconut milk, or even water make good stand-ins for milk in most cookie recipes.

Egg-/Dairy-Free Molasses Cookies

*If there are no nut allergies involved, up to 1 cup chopped
walnuts or pecans can be added to this recipe.*

INGREDIENTS | **YIELDS 48 COOKIES**

4 cups all-purpose flour or gluten-free
flour mix

1 teaspoon salt

1 teaspoon baking soda

1½ teaspoons ginger

½ teaspoon cloves

½ teaspoon freshly grated nutmeg

½ teaspoon cinnamon

½ cup shortening

1 cup sugar

1 cup Grandma's molasses

½ cup coffee

About 1 cup of sugar for rolling the
cookies in

1. Whisk flour, salt, baking soda, and spices together; set aside.

2. Cream shortening, sugar, molasses, and coffee together until smooth and creamy. Stir in flour mixture.

3. Cover with plastic wrap; chill dough overnight.

4. Preheat oven to 375°F. Lightly grease cookie sheets. Roll dough ¼" thick on a floured surface; cut with cookie cutters. You may also roll dough in teaspoon-sized balls. Roll in sugar; place on prepared baking sheet.

5. Bake 10–12 minutes. Cool.

Dairy-Free Substitutes for Butter

While you can use shortening for a butter substitute, there are also many other things that will work as well. Organic coconut butter adds a faint coconut flavor and chewy texture, while fruit purees and apple butter cut down on fat content. Peanut butter and other nut butters can be substituted for butter as long as there is no allergy to the nuts.

Egg-/Dairy-Free Pumpkin Cookies

Like most cookies with nontraditional ingredients, these should be eaten right away or frozen for future use. For a delicious variation, add a glaze of confectioners' sugar mixed with enough orange juice to make a spreadable glaze.

INGREDIENTS | **SERVES 36**

½ cup butter-flavored shortening
½ cup sugar
½ cup light brown sugar
½ cup grade-B maple syrup
1 teaspoon vanilla
1 cup pumpkin
2½ cups all-purpose flour
1½ teaspoons cinnamon
1 teaspoon ginger
½ teaspoon cloves
½ teaspoon freshly grated nutmeg
½ teaspoon baking soda
2 teaspoons baking powder
¼ cup chopped candied ginger

1. Preheat oven to 375°F. Spray a baking sheet with cooking spray.

2. Cream together shortening, sugars, and syrup until light and fluffy. Beat in vanilla and pumpkin.

3. Whisk dry ingredients together; add to creamed mixture. Fold in candied ginger.

4. Drop by teaspoonfuls onto prepared baking sheet.

5. Bake 8–10 minutes.

Egg-/Dairy-Free Raisin Puffs

If you are not allergic to oatmeal, you can substitute rolled oats for the quinoa flakes in this recipe.

INGREDIENTS | **YIELDS 24 COOKIES**

⅔ cup shortening
1 cup sugar
½ cup brown sugar
½ cup apple butter
2 teaspoons vanilla
2 tablespoons coconut oil, room temperature
1¾ cups gluten-free flour mix
1 teaspoon xanthan gum
½ teaspoon baking soda
1 teaspoon baking powder
1½ teaspoons cinnamon
½ teaspoon cloves
½ teaspoon salt
2 cups quinoa flakes
1 cup raisins

1. Preheat oven to 350°F. Line a baking sheet with parchment.

2. Cream shortening, sugars, apple butter, vanilla, and coconut oil on high speed until creamy.

3. Whisk dry ingredients together; blend in. Stir in quinoa and raisins.

4. Make tablespoon-sized balls of dough; place on parchment about 2" apart. Do not flatten them.

5. Bake 10–12 minutes, or until golden. Cool.

CHAPTER 33

Refrigerator Cookies

Butter Refrigerator Cookies

This basic butter cookie can be dressed up in a variety of ways. Roll the log of dough in chopped pecans or colored sprinkles to cover the sides for a beautiful finish to these cookies.

INGREDIENTS | **YIELDS 48 COOKIES**

1 cup unsalted butter

1 cup sugar

1½ teaspoons vanilla

2 egg yolks

2½ cups all-purpose flour

¼ teaspoon salt

Bring the Cookie Aisle Home

With refrigerator cookies, you can have a large variety of cookies at one time. By keeping a few rolls of a variety of doughs in your freezer, you can create cookie assortments that will make it look like you have been baking for hours. Since you only slice and bake what you need, you aren't tempted to eat the entire batch by yourself.

1. Cream butter and sugar until fluffy. Add vanilla and egg yolks; beat until creamy.

2. Whisk together dry ingredients; stir into butter mixture.

3. Shape dough into logs 2" in diameter. Roll in wax paper; place in refrigerator overnight, or freeze if desired.

4. When ready to bake, preheat oven to 350°F.

5. Slice cookies in ⅜" wide slices; place on baking sheet 2 apart. Bake 8–10 minutes.

Chocolate Swirl Cookies

This recipe will work with any two colors of dough. Just leave the chocolate out and use food color to get the tint that you want.

INGREDIENTS | **YIELDS 40 COOKIES**

½ cup unsalted butter

½ cup sugar

1 egg yolk

1 teaspoon vanilla

3 tablespoons milk

1½ cups cake flour

½ teaspoon salt

1½ ounces bittersweet chocolate, melted

Thin Icebox Cookies

This may sound very odd, but if you have a meat slicer, set the blade to a 1 or 2 and use it to slice the frozen cookie dough. If it crumbles, let it partially thaw—that should only take five minutes or so. By doing this, you get the thinnest, prettiest cookies around. Make sure the blade is both clean and sharp before starting.

1. Cream butter and sugar together until fluffy. Beat in yolk, vanilla, and milk.

2. Sift dry ingredients together; blend into dough.

3. Divide dough in ½; add melted chocolate to ½ of dough. Chill 2 hours.

4. Roll each ½ of dough out into ⅛" thick rectangle. Place one ½ on top of the other; roll up like a jelly roll. Wrap tightly in wax paper; chill overnight, or freeze.

5. When ready to bake, slice dough into ⅛" thick slices. Place on cookie sheet lined with parchment; bake at 375°F 10–15 minutes.

Date Nut Pinwheels

*If you like Fig Newtons, try making these with the fig filling
rather than the date filling. These ship very well.*

INGREDIENTS | **YIELDS 132 COOKIES**

3 cups all-purpose flour
1 teaspoon baking powder
1 teaspoon baking soda
¼ teaspoon salt
1 cup unsalted butter
1 cup brown sugar
1 cup sugar
3 eggs
1 teaspoon vanilla
1 tablespoon orange zest
Date Filling (page 550)

Another Way to Cut Icebox Cookies

Another way to cut the cookie dough cleanly is to use dental floss. Thaw the dough for about five minutes, then slide a piece of dental floss under the cookie log. Hold both ends up above the dough and then cross the ends above the log to create an X. Pull the ends in opposite directions. Slide the floss down the log the desired width (usually ⅛"). and repeat.

1. Sift together dry ingredients; set aside.

2. Cream butter and sugars until fluffy. Add eggs one at a time. Add vanilla and orange zest. Blend in flour mixture; chill 1–2 hours.

3. While dough is chilling, make date filling.

4. Divide dough into fourths; roll out each into 10" × 6" rectangle, about ⅛" thick. Spread each rectangle with ¼ of filling; roll up like a jelly roll. Wrap firmly in wax paper; chill overnight, or freeze.

5. When ready to bake, slice ⅛" thick; place on a parchment-lined baking sheet. Bake at 350°F 10–12 minutes.

Overnight Coconut Cookies

These cookies are full of coconut flavor. Make them even prettier by rolling the logs of dough in finely chopped toasted coconut before chilling.

INGREDIENTS | YIELDS 150 COOKIES

1½ cups unsalted butter

3 cups brown sugar

2 eggs

2 teaspoons vanilla

½ teaspoon salt

4 teaspoons baking powder

6 cups cake flour

⅔ cup shredded coconut

1 cup finely chopped pecans, optional

Don't Forget the Label

If you are making different types of icebox cookies, be sure to label them before you put them in the freezer. While you may think that you can tell the difference between Orange Date Pinwheels and Lemon Pistachio Swirls, after they are frozen it is much more difficult to tell. By writing on the wax paper with permanent marker or using a freezer label, it will always be a simple matter to get the dough you were looking for.

1. Cream butter and sugar until light and fluffy. Add eggs and vanilla; blend well.

2. Whisk dry ingredients together; stir into creamed mixture. Add coconut and nuts.

3. Form dough into five 2½" diameter logs; roll in wax paper. Chill overnight, or freeze.

4. When ready to bake, preheat oven to 375°F. Cover a baking sheet with parchment.

5. Slice cookies ⅛" thick; bake 10 minutes, or until just starting to brown.

Cinnamon Crisps

Any nuts can be substituted for the almonds, or you can leave them out altogether. Add more cinnamon flavor with cinnamon-flavored chips, available by the chocolate chips.

INGREDIENTS | **YIELDS 48 COOKIES**

2 cups all-purpose flour
2 teaspoons cinnamon
½ teaspoon salt
1 cup unsalted butter
1 cup sugar
1 egg
1 cup toasted almonds
1 tablespoon cinnamon
½ cup sugar

1. Whisk dry ingredients together; set aside.

2. Cream butter and sugar until light and fluffy. Beat in egg. Stir in dry ingredients; blend well. Fold in almonds.

3. Divide dough in ½; shape each ½ into log 2" in diameter. Mix 1 tablespoon cinnamon and ½ cup of sugar; spread over a piece of wax paper. Roll log of dough over sugar mixture, covering sides completely. Wrap tightly in wax paper; chill overnight, or freeze.

4. When ready to bake, preheat oven to 350°F. Lightly grease baking sheets.

5. Slice cookies ¼" thick; place 2" apart on baking sheets. Bake about 8 minutes, or until golden. Cool.

Chocolate Slice and Bakes

These cookies are perfect with a glass of cold milk. For a beautiful decoration, dip half the cookie in white chocolate and sprinkle with chocolate jimmies.

INGREDIENTS | **YIELDS 150 COOKIES**

1⅛ cups unsalted butter
1 cup sugar
1 egg
2 tablespoons milk or coffee
2 teaspoons vanilla
3¼ cups all-purpose flour
3 teaspoons baking powder
½ teaspoon salt
½ cup cocoa

1. Cream together butter and sugar until fluffy. Add egg, coffee, and vanilla; beat well.

2. Whisk dry ingredients together; blend into creamed mixture.

3. Form into logs; wrap in wax paper. Chill overnight, or freeze.

4. When ready to bake, preheat oven to 350°F. Lightly grease baking sheet.

5. Slice roll into ¼" thick slices; arrange on baking sheet. Bake 10–12 minutes.

Orange Pistachio Refrigerator Rolls

For more orange flavor, you can add 1 teaspoon of orange extract to the dough. These are especially beautiful when the baked cookies are half dipped in chocolate glaze and sprinkled with extra chopped pistachios.

INGREDIENTS | YIELDS 60 COOKIES

1 cup sugar

1 cup unsalted butter

1 egg

2 tablespoons orange juice

Grated zest of 1 orange

2¾ cups all-purpose flour

¼ teaspoons baking soda

½ cup finely chopped toasted pistachios

1. Cream together sugar and butter until fluffy. Beat in egg, orange juice, and zest.

2. Whisk dry ingredients together; blend into creamed mixture. Fold in pistachios.

3. Form into logs; wrap in wax paper; chill overnight, or freeze.

4. When ready to bake, preheat oven to 375°F. Line a baking sheet with parchment. Slice cookies ⅛" thick; place 2" apart on baking sheet.

5. Bake 10 minutes, or until done. Cool.

Peanut Butter Whirligigs

You can easily substitute your favorite jam for the chocolate in these peanut butter cookies with a beautiful swirl. Jelly does not work as well.

INGREDIENTS | YIELDS 36 COOKIES

½ cup shortening

½ cup peanut butter

½ cup brown sugar

½ cup sugar

1 egg

1¼ cups all-purpose flour

½ teaspoon baking soda

½ teaspoon salt

6 ounces of chocolate, chopped and melted

1. Cream shortening, peanut butter, and sugars until light and fluffy. Beat in egg.

2. Whisk dry ingredients together; blend into creamed mixture.

3. Roll dough into ¼" thick rectangle; spread with melted chocolate.

4. Roll up like a jelly roll; wrap in wax paper. Chill overnight, or freeze.

5. When ready to bake, preheat oven to 375°F. Slice dough ⅛" thick; place on parchment-lined baking sheet. Bake 10 minutes.

Pastel Checkerboards

These are adorable for baby showers, with the dough tinted pink and white or blue and white. They make striking sandwich cookies as well, with a tinted buttercream in the center.

INGREDIENTS | **YIELDS 60 COOKIES**

1 cup shortening

2 cups sugar

2 eggs

1½ teaspoons vanilla

½ teaspoon almond extract

3½ cups cake flour

½ teaspoon salt

2 teaspoons baking powder

Pastel food coloring (2 colors)

Keeping It Round

Often, when you take icebox cookies from the refrigerator after the chilling time is over they will be flat on the side that they were laying on. This is because the dough is soft when you put it in the refrigerator and the weight flattens the one side. You can get around that completely and have perfect, round cookies if you will set the log of dough upright in a drinking glass. Only the very bottom will be flattened; the sides will be perfectly round. Do this for the first hour when freezing cookie dough as well.

1. Cream shortening and sugar. Beat in eggs, vanilla, and almond extract. Whisk dry ingredients together; add to creamed mixture.

2. Divide dough into 2 parts. Add food coloring to 1 part until desired color is reached. Make 4 ropes, 2 of each color. Lay a rope of color A on counter with a rope of color B next to it. Lay a rope of color B on top of color A, and a rope of Color A on color B. If you look at it from the end, you should be able to see the checkerboard.

3. Press ropes gently together; wrap in wax paper. Chill overnight, or freeze for longer storage.

4. When ready to bake, preheat oven to 375°F. Lightly grease baking sheet. Slice cookies in ⅛" slices; place 2" apart on baking sheets. Cookies will be square rather than round in shape.

5. Bake 10 minutes, until just starting to color. Cool.

Almond Roll

For a tea cookie reminiscent of Victorian times, add 1 teaspoon of rose water to this dough.
Rose and almond were a favorite flavor combination among the Victorians,
and it is as delicious today as it was back then.

INGREDIENTS | YIELDS 84 COOKIES

¾ cup shortening

1 cup sugar

1 egg

½ teaspoon almond extract

2 cups all-purpose flour

¼ teaspoon salt

½ teaspoon baking soda

1 cup blanched almonds, chopped

Stripes

Another way to make icebox cookies is to lay ½" thick rectangles of dough on top of each other, varying the color with each layer. The Chocolate Slice and Bakes (page 532) and the Almond Roll are a great combination for this. Make them four to six layers high and wrap the rectangle of dough in wax paper. Chill. When you slice them, you will have rectangular, striped cookies.

1. Cream shortening and sugar together. Beat in egg and almond extract.

2. Blend flour, salt, and baking soda together; add to creamed mixture. Form into logs; roll in chopped almonds.

3. Wrap roll of dough in wax paper. Chill overnight, or freeze.

4. When ready to bake, preheat oven to 350°F. Lightly grease baking sheet. Slice cookie dough in ⅛" thick rounds; arrange 2" apart on sheet.

5. Bake 10–12 minutes. Cool.

Refrigerator Raisin Cookies

For a beautiful finish, sprinkle the tops of these with turbinado sugar just before baking. Press it into the cookie top gently. It will form a crunchy crust as the cookies bake.

INGREDIENTS | **YIELDS 60 COOKIES**

½ cup unsalted butter
¼ cup shortening
1½ cups brown sugar
2 eggs
3 cups all-purpose flour
½ teaspoon salt
½ teaspoon baking powder
½ teaspoon nutmeg
½ teaspoon soda
1 cup raisins

1. Cream together butter and shortening. Beat in sugar until fluffy. Add eggs beat well.

2. Whisk dry ingredients together; blend into butter mixture. Fold in raisins. Form into logs; wrap in wax paper. Chill or freeze.

3. When ready to bake, preheat oven to 400°F. Lightly grease baking sheet.

4. Slice cookie ⅛" thick; place 2" apart on baking sheet.

5. Bake 8–10 minutes. Cool.

Lemon and Black Pepper Cookies

You can use either finely ground or coarsely ground black pepper in these unusual cookies—it depends on your own preference. You can also use ground pink peppercorns for a subtle change.

INGREDIENTS | **YIELDS 36 COOKIES**

2 cups all-purpose flour
Grated zest of 1 lemon
1 teaspoon baking powder
½ teaspoon baking soda
¾ teaspoon black pepper
¼ teaspoon salt
½ cup unsalted butter
1 cup sugar
1 egg
3 tablespoons milk
½ teaspoon vanilla
1 tablespoon lemon juice

1. Whisk dry ingredients, including lemon zest, together in a bowl. Place in a zip-top bag; seal and allow to stand overnight so lemon flavor permeates flour.

2. Cream butter and sugar until light and fluffy. Add egg, milk, vanilla, and lemon juice; blend well. Stir in dry ingredients; blending well. Form into logs; wrap in wax paper. Chill overnight, or freeze.

3. When ready to bake, preheat oven to 350°F.

4. Slice dough ¼" thick; place on baking sheet.

5. Bake 8–10 minutes. Cool.

Cinnamon Roll Cookies

The flavor of sweet cinnamon rolls in a cookie is unusual. Add ½ cup chopped pecans with the cinnamon and sugar mixture if you like.

INGREDIENTS | **YIELDS 48 COOKIES**

1½ cups sugar

½ cup shortening

½ cup unsalted butter

2 eggs

1½ teaspoons vanilla

1 cup milk

1 tablespoon cream of tartar

2 teaspoons baking soda

1 teaspoon salt

5 cups flour

1 cup brown sugar

2 tablespoons cinnamon

Hostess Gifts

If you have never considered giving cookie dough as a gift, now is a good time to think about it. The wax paper-wrapped logs of icebox cookie dough can be wrapped in any appropriate color of tulle netting. Twist the fabric together at each end and secure with rubber bands. Now, tie pretty silk ribbons or tassels around each end. Make a label with the name of the cookie and baking directions and tie around one end with another piece of the silk ribbon. The rolls must be kept cold.

1. Cream sugar, shortening, and butter until light and fluffy.

2. Add eggs, vanilla, and milk; beat well. Whisk together cream of tartar, baking soda, salt, and flour; beat in. Cover; chill 2–3 hours. Meanwhile, mix brown sugar and cinnamon together.

3. Roll ¼ of chilled dough out on a piece of wax paper; sprinkle with ¼ of sugar mixture. Carefully roll up like a jelly roll, using wax paper to help roll. Wrap tightly in wax paper; chill overnight, or freeze. Repeat with remaining dough.

4. When ready to bake, preheat oven to 375°F. Slice cookies; arrange 2" apart on parchment-lined baking sheet.

5. Bake 8–10 minutes, or until done. Frost with confectioners icing if desired.

Chocolate Mint Checkerboards

For a Christmas cookie tray, you can divide the mint-flavored dough in half and color part of it green and the other part pink with the food coloring.

INGREDIENTS | **YIELDS 48 COOKIES**

½ cup shortening

½ cup sugar

1 egg yolk

1½ teaspoons vanilla

1½ cups flour

¼ teaspoon salt

½ teaspoon baking powder

3 tablespoons milk

1 ounce unsweetened chocolate, melted

Few drops green food coloring

½ teaspoon mint flavoring

They Have Been Framed!

For an especially nice finish to a checkerboard cookie, divide the dough into three parts. Flavor and color two parts of the dough with the darker dough color. Divide in half and set one half aside. Make the checkerboard cookies as directed. Now, roll out the reserved dough and wrap it around the checkerboard dough. Press gently to help it attach. Continue with the recipe. When you slice the cookies, they will have a frame around the outside that really sets the pattern of the cookie off and makes it extra special.

1. Cream shortening and sugar until light and fluffy. Add egg and vanilla; beat well. Sift dry ingredients together; blend alternately with milk in creamed mixture.

2. Separate dough in ½. Add chocolate to ½; mix thoroughly. Add green food color and mint flavor to other ½; mix thoroughly.

3. Roll chocolate dough into ropes about ½" in diameter. Repeat with mint dough. On a piece of wax paper, place 1 rope of chocolate next to 1 rope of mint. Top with 1 rope of mint next to 1 rope of chocolate, alternating dough to create a checkerboard. Press gently; roll in wax paper. These cookies will be square. Chill overnight, or freeze.

4. When ready to bake, preheat oven to 375°F. Lightly grease baking sheet. Slice cookies thinly; arrange 2" apart on baking sheet.

5. Bake 8–10 minutes. Cool.

Neapolitan Cookies

You will need a loaf pan to make these pretty cookies. The white dough can be flavored with coconut flavoring for a change of pace.

INGREDIENTS | **YIELDS 72 COOKIES**

½ cup unsalted butter

½ cup shortening

1½ cups sugar

1 egg

1 teaspoon vanilla

2½ cups all-purpose flour

1½ teaspoons baking powder

½ teaspoon salt

1 ounce unsweetened chocolate, melted

½ teaspoon almond extract

5 drops red food coloring

½ cup chopped pistachios, walnuts, or pecans

1. Cream together butter and shortening. Add sugar; beat until light and fluffy. Beat in egg and vanilla. Whisk dry ingredients together; blend into creamed mixture.

2. Separate dough into 3 parts. Add chocolate to 1 part, almond extract and red food coloring to 1 part, and nuts to third part.

3. Line 9" loaf pan with wax paper. Spread almond portion of dough to cover bottom of pan. Spread nut portion over that and chocolate portion on top. Cover with wax paper; press down gently. Chill overnight.

4. Preheat oven to 350°F. Line a baking sheet with parchment. Turn dough out of pan; slice lengthwise. Slice dough in ⅛" thick crosswise slices.

5. Bake 10–12 minutes. Cool.

Orange Date Pinwheels

Orange-flavored cookies with sweet date filling are an old-fashioned autumn treat. Tint the cookie dough orange for seasonal parties.

INGREDIENTS | **YIELDS 60 COOKIES**

1 cup unsalted butter
½ cup sugar
½ cup light brown sugar
1 egg
Grated rind of 1 orange
2 tablespoons orange juice
1 teaspoon vanilla
5 cups all-purpose flour
½ teaspoon salt
¼ teaspoon baking soda
1 teaspoon orange flavoring, optional
1 recipe Date Filling (page 550)

1. Cream butter and sugars until fluffy. Add egg, orange rind, juice, and vanilla; beat well. Add orange flavoring at this point if you are using it.

2. Whisk together flour, salt, and baking soda; blend in. Chill dough 2 hours.

3. Roll dough out into a rectangle; spread with date filling. Roll up like a jelly roll; roll in wax paper. Chill overnight, or freeze.

4. When ready to bake, preheat oven to 350°F; line baking sheet with parchment. Slice pinwheels ⅓ thick; place on baking sheet.

5. Bake 10 minutes.

Great for Shipping

Because of the amount of dates in these cookies they stay moist and flavorful during shipping. Arrange the cookies in layers with wax paper between layers and add a few whole cloves if you like the flavor. The cloves will lightly flavor the cookies and help keep them from molding if it takes longer than expected. Do not add any other type of cookie to this package or the flavors will mingle and the cookies will taste odd.

Lemon Pistachio Swirls

These lemony cookies are light and refreshing with the richness of pistachios. Poppy seed filling, available at baking supply houses and some grocers, can be substituted for the pistachios.

INGREDIENTS | **YIELDS 60 COOKIES**

1 cup unsalted butter
⅔ cup confectioners' sugar
2 large egg yolks
½ teaspoon vanilla
Grated zest of 2 lemons
¼ teaspoon salt
2 cups all-purpose flour
½ cup shelled pistachios
¼ cup confectioners' sugar
1 egg yolk
1 tablespoon water

1. Cream butter and sugar until light and fluffy. Add egg yolks and vanilla. Whisk lemon zest, salt, and flour together; blend into creamed mixture. Chill 2 hours.

2. Meanwhile, place pistachios and sugar in a food processor; process with on/off pulses until well ground. Add egg yolk and water; process to a smooth paste. Refrigerate until ready to use.

3. Roll dough into a rectangle on a floured surface. Spread with pistachio mixture; roll up like a jelly roll. Wrap tightly in wax paper; chill overnight, or freeze.

4. When ready to bake, preheat oven to 350°F. Line a baking sheet with parchment.

5. Slice cookies ¼" thick; arrange on baking sheet. Bake 10–12 minutes. Cool.

CHAPTER 34

Glazes, Fillings, and Frostings

Ganache

Always use pure heavy cream; try not to get the whipping cream that is made of skim milk and chemicals.

INGREDIENTS | YIELDS 2 CUPS

1 cup heavy cream
1 cup bittersweet chocolate, chopped
1 cup milk chocolate, chopped
1 cup dark chocolate, chopped
1 tablespoon Kahlua, Bailey's, or other liqueur, optional

Chocolate Truffles

If you love the rich chocolate truffles in the specialty chocolate shop, you will be happy to know that they are made of ganache. Just flavor as desired and chill overnight. In the morning, use a melon baller to create balls of ganache, which you can dip in melted chocolate or roll in cocoa.

1. Bring cream almost to a boil in microwave, about 2 minutes.

2. Remove and quickly add chocolate; stir until smooth.

3. Stir in liqueur, if desired.

4. For glaze, allow to cool slightly, then pour over cake or cookie, smoothing with a flat spatula.

5. For filling, chill Ganache, then whip until light and fluffy. Always store Ganache in refrigerator.

White Chocolate Ganache

Frangelico is a hazelnut flavored liqueur from the Piedmont region of Northern Italy. Its hints of roasted hazelnuts, cocoa, and vanilla lend a wonderful taste to this ganache.

INGREDIENTS | YIELDS 1½ CUPS

½ cup heavy cream
12 ounces white chocolate, chopped
1 tablespoon Frangelico, optional

1. Heat cream in a microwave-safe bowl until bubbles form around edge and it begins to boil, about 3 minutes.

2. Remove from microwave; stir in white chocolate until it is melted and mixture is smooth.

3. Add liqueur, if desired.

4. Cool slightly if using as a glaze; chill for use as a filling.

Lemon Curd

This tangy treat is perfect for filling Thumbprint Cookies, sandwiching Lemon and Black Pepper Cookies together, or spreading on a scone.

INGREDIENTS | **YIELDS 1½ CUPS**

3 eggs

¾ cup sugar

1 cup fresh lemon juice

2 tablespoons lemon zest

4 tablespoons butter, cut into chunks and kept cold

Great Gift Idea

Curds, whether lemon, lime, grapefruit, or orange, make wonderful gifts. Make up several batches and spoon them into small jelly jars. Place the lids on them and keep in the freezer. When you need a gift, cut a round of calico with pinking shears, place the calico between the top and the screw ring, and screw on the ring. Tie raffia around the screw ring and you have a beautiful homemade gift.

1. In a nonglass bowl over a double boiler, whisk eggs until smooth; beat in sugar and lemon juice and zest.

2. Keeping water in double boiler simmering, continue to stir curd for 7–10 minutes, or until it is thick and coats the back of a spoon.

3. Place bowl over a bowl of ice; whisk in butter, blending until smooth. Stir occasionally while allowing it to cool.

4. Place wax paper over top of curd; chill.

5. Lemon curd will keep in refrigerator about 5 days, or in freezer for 1 year.

Lime Curd

For a gourmet flavor to your lime curd, use fresh key limes if you can find them. If not, you can use the bottled key lime juice available at many grocers and on the Internet.

INGREDIENTS | YIELDS 1½ CUPS

3 eggs
¾ cup sugar
1 cup fresh lime juice
2 tablespoons lime zest
4 tablespoons butter, cut into chunks and kept cold
A few drops of green food coloring

1. In a nonglass bowl over a double boiler, whisk eggs until smooth; beat in sugar and lime juice and zest.

2. Keeping water in double boiler simmering, continue to stir curd 7–10 minutes, or until it is thick and coats the back of a spoon.

3. Place bowl over a bowl of ice; whisk in butter, blending until smooth. Add a few drops of green food coloring if desired. Stir occasionally while allowing it to cool.

4. Place wax paper over top of curd; chill.

5. Lime curd will keep in refrigerator about 5 days, or in freezer for 1 year.

Buttercream

Buttercream needs to be refrigerated, especially on very warm days. For a buttercream that will hold well out of the refrigerator, use part or all shortening.

INGREDIENTS | YIELDS 3 CUPS

3 cups confectioners' sugar
1 cup unsalted butter
1½ teaspoons vanilla extract
1 tablespoon heavy cream

1. Beat 1 cup of sugar with butter until well blended.

2. Beat in remaining sugar and vanilla.

3. Add cream to make correct consistency.

Royal Icing

Some people are concerned about salmonella in raw egg. If this is a concern for you, use the pasteurized egg whites available at the store or Eggology's organic product.

INGREDIENTS | **YIELDS 6 CUPS**

¼ cup egg whites
1 pound confectioners' sugar
1 tablespoon water
1 tablespoon lemon juice
Food coloring as desired

1. Beat egg whites until foamy. Add confectioners' sugar until mixture is smooth.

2. Mix water and lemon; add to confectioners' mixture a few drops at a time until correct consistency is reached. Add food coloring as desired.

3. Keep covered with a damp towel as you are working with it so it does not dry out.

Confectioners' Glaze

This is a light glaze that is perfect for cookies. Vary the flavor by using different extracts or using lemon, lime, or orange juice in place of the water.

INGREDIENTS | **YIELDS 1 CUP**

2½ cups confectioners' sugar
⅓ cup light corn syrup
1 teaspoon clear vanilla
3–4 teaspoons warm water

1. Beat all ingredients except water in bowl of a mixer until smooth.

2. Add water a few drops at a time, until mixture is right consistency.

Chocolate Glaze

You can use dark chocolate, bittersweet, German's Sweet chocolate, semisweet, milk chocolate, or a combination in the recipe to get exactly the flavor you want.

INGREDIENTS | YIELDS 1 CUP

¾ cup chocolate, chopped
3 tablespoons butter
1 tablespoon light corn syrup
½ teaspoon vanilla

1. Combine chocolate, butter, and corn syrup in a double boiler. DO NOT let water get above a simmer.

2. Stir until ingredients melt together and are smooth.

3. Remove from heat.

4. Add vanilla; blend well.

5. Use while warm.

Chocolate Seizing

If even a little bit of water gets into the chocolate when you are melting it, seizing will occur. The chocolate lumps up, refuses to melt, and must be thrown away. To keep this from happening, always wipe the utensils with a dry towel before using and never cover the pot of chocolate while melting. Dry your hands thoroughly before stirring so no water drips into the melting chocolate. Your chocolate will always melt just right

Peppermint Frosting

This makes a good filling for almost any kind of sandwich cookie as well as a great frosting for brownies.

INGREDIENTS | YIELDS 2½ CUPS

¾ cup shortening
4 tablespoons heavy cream
4 cups confectioners' sugar
⅛ teaspoon peppermint extract
½ cup crushed peppermint candies

1. Beat shortening and cream in a mixer until fluffy.

2. Add confectioners' sugar 1 cup at a time.

3. Beat in extract. Fold in crushed peppermints.

Egg Yolk Paint

Use clean paint brushes to paint on cookie dough before baking. This technique is great to paint folk art motifs on Christmas cookies.

INGREDIENTS | **YIELDS 2 TABLESPOONS**

1 egg yolk
¼ teaspoon water
Pastel food coloring

Stencil It

You can easily use stencils on cookies for unique and charming designs. Just lay a small stencil on the unbaked dough and dab the egg yolk paint on with a paintbrush just like you would if you were stenciling a wall. Use a clean paint brush for each different color.

1. Using a fork, beat egg yolk and water together until smooth. Separate into different dishes by teaspoonfuls. Clean foam egg cartons work great for this.

2. Add paste food coloring to each dish until desired color is reached.

3. Paint unbaked dough and then bake as directed.

4. If paint thickens as you are using it, add a little water.

Marshmallow Filling

This is great in Whoopie Pies, but there is much more that you will find yourself using it for. This is delicious as a frosting for brownies, a cake filling, or when used to sandwich Overnight Coconut Cookies (page 531) together.

INGREDIENTS | **YIELDS 2½ CUPS**

½ cup unsalted butter, room temperature
2 cups confectioners' sugar
1 teaspoon vanilla
2 cups marshmallow cream

1. Beat butter and sugar together until creamy. Add vanilla.

2. Beat on high speed until very airy and fluffy, about 5 minutes.

3. Beat in marshmallow cream, beating until well blended and light, about 2 minutes.

Cream Cheese Frosting

This is a simple but flavorful cream cheese frosting. You can add ¼ cup finely chopped candied ginger for a spicy variation.

INGREDIENTS | **YIELDS 3 CUPS**

8 ounces cream cheese, not light or nonfat

⅓ cup unsalted butter

3 teaspoons vanilla

4 cups confectioners' sugar

1 tablespoon heavy cream, if needed

1. Mix cream cheese and butter until well blended. Beat in the vanilla.

2. Slowly beat in confectioners' sugar until proper consistency is reached. If frosting is too thick when all of confectioners' sugar has been used, add cream to thin it out a little.

Filling Panache

For exceptionally pretty filled cookies, use an icing bag fitted with a large star or shell tip to pipe the frosting onto the surface of the bottom cookie. Place the other cookie on top and press gently. Rather than just a blob of frosting inside the cookie, you will have ridges and a professional finish to your sandwich cookies.

Date Filling

Date filling can be used interchangeably with the fig filling. It goes well with orange, lemon, and oatmeal cookies.

INGREDIENTS | **YIELDS 1½ CUPS**

1½ cups chopped dates

¼ cup sugar

½ cup water

1 tablespoon lemon juice

1. Cook dates, sugar, and water together, stirring often, until thickened.

2. Cool and stir in lemon juice.

Fig Filling

Fig filling is naturally sweet and delicious. Use this to sandwich oatmeal cookies together or as an unusual filling for thumbprint cookies.

INGREDIENTS | **YIELDS 1½ CUPS**

2 cups dried figs, chopped
¼ sugar
⅓ cup orange juice
½ cup pecans, chopped

1. Cook figs, sugar, and juice together until thickened. Be sure to stir often to keep from sticking.

2. Stir in pecans and cool.

Dried Fruit Fillings

Many different dried fruits can be substituted for the figs. You can also use water rather than orange juice. Try dried apples, peaches, raisins, apricots, or prunes. Vary the amount of sugar as needed with each type. In many cases, honey is a delicious substitute for the sugar. In some cases, the dried fruit will be sweet enough that the sugar need not be used at all.

Caramel Fudge Frosting

This rich caramel frosting has the texture of fudge. It is great as a topping on Baltimore Cookies (page 432).

INGREDIENTS | **YIELDS 2½ CUPS**

1½ cups packed dark brown sugar
1 cup heavy cream
2 tablespoons butter
1 teaspoon vanilla
¼ teaspoon salt

1. Bring sugar and cream to a boil, stirring constantly.

2. Once mixture comes to a boil, cover and boil 3 minutes.

3. Remove cover and boil until mixture reaches 234°F–236°F on a candy thermometer. This is the soft ball stage.

4. Remove from heat; add butter, vanilla, and salt.

5. Cool until temperature reaches 110°F; beat until mixture is thick enough to spread.

Creamy Peanut Butter Frosting

This rich frosting can be used to sandwich peanut butter cookies together, between chocolate cookies, or in thumbprint cookies. Use it with Whoopie Pies or as a frosting for brownies.

INGREDIENTS | **YIELDS 2 CUPS**

½ cup softened unsalted butter

1 cup peanut butter

2 cups confectioners' sugar

3 tablespoons heavy cream

1. Beat butter and peanut butter until smooth and well blended.

2. Mix in sugar, 1 cup at a time.

3. Use enough heavy cream to make correct consistency.

The Other Butters

Peanut butter does make a delicious frosting or filling, but it can be overpowering with some flavors. If you find you want something a little less "nutty," try almond butter, cashew butter, or even sunflower seed butter. These butters resemble peanut butter, but the taste is much lighter. They are usually available at natural food stores and some grocers.

Mocha Butter Frosting

Rich mocha frosting is delicious when used as the filling in chocolate sandwich cookies. Chill, then dip the cookies in melted chocolate for an after dinner treat.

INGREDIENTS | YIELDS 4 CUPS

½ cup heavy cream

3 tablespoons coarsely ground espresso beans

1 cup unsalted butter

6 cups confectioners' sugar

3 egg yolks

2 cups semisweet chocolate, melted

1. Heat cream; add ground espresso beans. Let steep 15 minutes; strain. Set aside to cool completely.

2. Beat butter and sugar until light and fluffy.

3. Add egg yolks; continue to beat until smooth.

4. Add cream mixture and chocolate; beat well.

Raw Egg Yolks

Egg yolks add richness to many vintage frosting recipes; however, some people are concerned about salmonella. If you are concerned about this, you can easily substitute a pasteurized egg product for the egg yolks in this recipe or leave them out completely. If you choose to leave them out, you may need to add a little more cream to get the right consistency.

Peppermint Filling

This filling is firmer than the peppermint frosting recipe given earlier in this chapter. It is best for a sturdy Oreo-type cookie.

INGREDIENTS | **YIELDS 2 CUPS**

½ cup unsalted butter
1 pound confectioners' sugar
⅓ cup half-and-half
½ teaspoon peppermint flavoring

1. Beat butter until creamy. Add confectioners' sugar gradually.

2. Add cream until mixture is thick but spreadable.

3. Beat in peppermint.

Vanilla Filling

This filling can be varied with many different flavors. Try maple, almond, coconut, banana, strawberry, or any other extract that interests you.

INGREDIENTS | **YIELDS 1½ CUPS**

2 cups confectioners' sugar
¼ cup shortening
1 egg white
½ teaspoon vanilla

1. Combine ½ cup confectioners' sugar and shortening in a bowl; beat until mixture is crumbly.

2. Beat in egg and vanilla.

3. Add rest of confectioners' sugar; beat until smooth.

4. You may need to thin this out with a little water.

Cream Filling for Whoopie Pies

This is a whipped cream-like filling that is traditionally used for Whoopie Pies. If the day is hot and humid this filling can act up. If it won't whip up, put the bowl in the freezer for a few minutes and try again.

INGREDIENTS	FILLS ABOUT 16 WHOOPIE PIES

1 cup milk
¼ cup flour
1 cup sugar
1 teaspoon vanilla
½ cup butter
½ cup shortening

Filling Variations for Whoopie Pies

Any of these Whoopie Pie fillings can be used with any of the Whoopie Pies. You can also add finely chopped nuts, crushed Oreos, chopped chocolate, crushed toffee, or any other ingredients that sound good to you to vary them. Try spreading the bottom cookie with a layer of ganache before adding the filling. By using your imagination, you can come up with unlimited delicious varieties.

1. Mix milk and flour in a microwave-safe bowl. Microwave on high, stirring in 1-minute increments until mixture becomes paste-like. Chill.

2. Beat 1 cup sugar, 1 teaspoon vanilla, butter, and shortening until mixture is fluffy.

3. Beat in cooled flour mixture; beat until mixture mounds on a spoon and is light and airy. It should double in volume.

4. Chill.

5. Place a spoonful of mixture on flat side of one cookie and top with another, flat side toward filling. Refrigerate.

Cream Cheese Filling for Pumpkin Whoopie Pies

The mellow pumpkin flavors of the cookie are brought out by the candied ginger and cream cheese combination in the filling. If candied ginger is not available, you can substitute ¼ teaspoon of powdered ginger.

INGREDIENTS | **FILLS 16 TO 18 WHOOPIE PIES**

4 tablespoons unsalted butter
4 ounces cream cheese
1 cup confectioners' sugar
½ teaspoon vanilla
2 tablespoons minced candied ginger

1. Beat butter and cream cheese together until fluffy.

2. Add rest of ingredients to butter mixture; beat until fluffy.

3. Spoon filling lightly on flat side of one cookie. Top with another cookie.

4. Serve immediately, or store in refrigerator.

Peanut Butter Filling for Whoopie Pies

For the fluffiest texture, bring all of the ingredients for Peanut Butter Filling to room temperature before mixing. If filling is too thick, you can add some cream or milk to get it to the desired consistency.

INGREDIENTS | **FILLS 16 TO 18 WHOOPIE PIES**

1 cup crunchy or creamy peanut butter, preferably homemade
½ cup unsalted butter
¼ teaspoon salt
1 cup confectioners' sugar

1. Place peanut butter and butter in bowl of a mixer. Beat at high speed until well blended and fluffy.

2. Add salt and confectioners' sugar; beat well.

3. Store in refrigerator.

CHAPTER 35

Cookie Mix in a Jar Instructions

Copy these instructions and print them out on cardstock.
Punch a hole in the cardstock to feed the raffia through and tie
to the jar. These will work for either the M&M's cookies or the
white chocolate and cranberry cookies.

1. Preheat oven to 375°F. Empty the jar of cookie mix into a large bowl.
   Blend thoroughly.

2. Add 1 stick of softened butter, 1 beaten egg, and 1 teaspoon vanilla.

3. Mix until blended.

4. Shape into walnut-sized balls and place on a parchment-lined cookie
   sheet.

5. Bake at 375°F for 10–12 minutes.

CHAPTER 36

Brownie Mix in a Jar Instructions

Copy these instructions and print them out on
cardstock. Punch a hole in the cardstock to feed the
raffia through and tie to the jar.

1. Preheat the oven to 350°F.

2. Grease and flour a 13" × 9" pan.

3. Dump the contents of the jar into a mixing bowl and blend well.

4. Mix in ¾ cup melted butter and 4 eggs. Stir until smooth.

5. Spoon into pan and bake 25–30 minutes.

CHAPTER 37

Gingerbread House Assembly

Follow these instructions to
create a beautiful gingerbread house.

1. Prepare the base for your house by covering a piece of plywood with aluminum foil.

2. Glue the front of the house and the two sides together first. Working with the front and one side, run a bead of royal icing down the edge of both pieces. Press together and hold for a minute or so. Repeat with the other side. Now, run a bead of icing down each side of the back and press onto the house. Allow to dry for an hour.

3. Using the same technique, put the roof on the house. Allow to dry completely.

4. Use royal icing to apply candies of all sorts to decorate your house.

5. When your house is finished, allow it to sit undisturbed for an hour or so to give the icing time to dry.

CHAPTER 38

Substitutions

Baking Powder: For each teaspoon, use ½ teaspoon cream of tartar and ¼ teaspoon baking soda.

Buttermilk: For each cup, place 1 tablespoon lemon juice or vinegar in the bottom of a measuring cup and fill with milk. Let stand 5 minutes.

Cardamom: Use an equal amount of ginger.

Chocolate, unsweetened: For each ounce, use 3 tablespoons unsweetened cocoa and 1 tablespoon melted butter.

Cinnamon: Use ½ the amount of nutmeg.

Cloves: Use double the amount of cinnamon and a little cayenne pepper.

Corn syrup: For each cup of corn syrup, substitute 1 cup granulated sugar and ¼ cup water to a boil and boil 1 minute. Set aside to cool.

Egg: For 1 egg, substitute 2 egg whites or 2 egg yolks or ¼ cup egg substitute.

Flour, cake: For 1 cup of cake flour, substitute ¾ cup flour plus ¼ cup cornstarch.

Ginger: Use an equal amount of cinnamon and a pinch of cayenne pepper.

Half-and-half: For each cup of half-and-half, substitute 1 tablespoon vegetable oil or melted butter and enough whole milk to make a cup.

Honey: For each cup, use 1¼ cups sugar and ¼ cup water.

Molasses: For 1 cup, substitute ½ cup honey, ½ cup brown sugar, and ¼ cup water

Nutmeg: Use ½ the amount of cinnamon and ¼ amount of ginger.

Pumpkin pie spice: For each teaspoon, mix ½ teaspoon cinnamon, ¼ teaspoon ginger, ⅛ teaspoon cloves, and ⅛ teaspoon grated nutmeg.

CHAPTER 39

Glossary

All-purpose flour
White flour which is a combination of hard and soft wheats. All-purpose flour is good for all types of baking; however, cake flour is preferred for cakes. It is available bleached or unbleached.

Baking pan
A flat pan, usually metal, that may or may not have a lip around the edge.

Beat
To make a mixture smooth by briskly stirring with a whisk, spoon, or electric beater.

Blend
To gently mix ingredients until they are completely mixed.

Boil
To bring a liquid to the temperature that causes bubbles to rise to the surface and break in a steady stream.

Cake flour
Cake flour is made from a soft wheat that creates a more delicate product than all-purpose flour. Always sift cake flour before using.

Cream
To beat butter or shortening until it has a light, fluffy consistency. Air is incorporated into the fat so the texture is lighter and fluffier.

Drizzle
To quickly pour a glaze over a baked item randomly and in a thin stream.

Dust
To lightly coat a baked good with powdered sugar.

Extract
Flavoring products that are made from the essential oil of a plant. These concentrated oils are generally suspended in alcohol. Examples are: vanilla, anise, almond, lemon, mint. Extracts are higher quality than flavorings and are preferred in these recipes.

Flavoring
Imitation extracts which are created in laboratories from chemicals. A flavoring does not have to contain any part of the item it mimics and is often completely artificial.

Fold

To gently mix ingredients. Generally, the dry ingredients are sifted over the top of the whipped or beaten ingredients and then a rubber spatula is used to cut through the mixture. The spatula is then moved across the bottom and up the other side, folding the mixture back on itself.

Food Coloring

Food-grade dyes which are used to tint various foods. Paste food colors are the best, and give the most intense color.

Glaze

A thin type of frosting that is used to add extra flavor to a cookie or cake.

Gluten

A protein present in all flour, but especially in wheat flour. It provides an elastic structure for baked goods. Many people are allergic to it and must not eat it.

Gluten-free baking mix

A baking mix can be used in place of flour that is free of gluten and nonallergenic.

Pipe

To force frosting or filling through a pastry bag.

Shortening

A solid fat made from vegetable oils. Shortening has been criticized for the high amounts of trans fatty acids it has had in the past. Manufacturers are now making it without the trans fats, or with reduced trans fats. You can also get organic shortenings that have no trans fats.

Sift

To shake flour or powdered sugar through a sifter to make it light and fluffy and to remove lumps.

Vanilla bean

Vanilla beans are the pods of a special orchid plant that vanilla is made from. It can be placed in a canister with sugar to flavor the sugar.

Whip

To beat a food, usually cream or egg whites, rapidly enough to incorporate air and cause the food to double or triple in volume.

Zest

The outer, colored portion of a citrus fruit. It is grated and added to foods to flavor them.

CHAPTER 40

Resources

All Recipes

This site has an uncountable number of recipes, and each recipe has an area for comments so you can find out if it worked for other people or not. Excellent search features and other user-friendly items make this online cookbook invaluable.
http://allrecipes.com

Bakers' Nook

Thousands of pans, decorations, and cookie cutters to help you create incredible cookies and other baked goods.
www.shopbakersnook.com

Bakespace

Bakespace is a social networking site for foodies. Socialize, have your questions answered, and find new recipes as well as new friends.
http://bakespace.com

Baking Delights

This site is where I post my own recipes on at least a daily basis and answer reader's questions.
www.bakingdelights.com

Converting Recipes

This is an excellent resource for those that do not use the same measurements as the United States. You can easily convert any recipe with these charts.
www.jsward.com/cooking/conversion.shtml

Cook's Thesaurus

Thousands of suggestions for food substitutions in one place. A great resource.
www.foodsubs.com

Daring Bakers Blog Roll

This site lists over 1,000 blogs of the members of Daring Bakers. Daring Bakers is a group of bloggers that create the same challenging recipe every month. The recipes that you will find on the various sites are top notch.
http://thedaringkitchen.com/member-blogs

Group Recipes

Another networking site for people who love to cook. Plenty of recipes to choose from.
www.grouprecipes.com

Kitchen Kraft

Kitchen Kraft is a huge site with every item imaginable to make your baking more creative, easier, and more fun.

www.kitchenkrafts.com

Nutritional Information Calculator

Enter the ingredients of any recipe and find out the calories, carbs, proteins, and other nutritional information.

http://recipes.sparkpeople.com/recipe-calculator.asp

Penzeys Spices

Wonderful, fresh spices and herbs for your cooking and baking needs.

http://penzeys.com/cgi-bin/penzeys/shophome.html

Wilton

Baking supplies of all types. A huge variety of paste food colorings, icing bags, decorator tips, and inspiration.

www.wilton.com